Pension Fund Economics and Finance

T0298570

Pension fund benefits are crucial for pensioners' welfare and pension fund savings have accumulated to huge amounts, covering a major part of worldwide institutional investments. However, the literature on pension fund economics and finance is rather limited, caused, in part, to limited data availability. This book contributes to this literature and focuses on three important areas. The first is pension fund (in)efficiency, which has a huge impact on final benefits, particularly when annual spoilage accumulates over a lifetime. Scale economies, pension plans complexity and alternative pension saving plans are important issues.

The second area is investment behaviour and risk-taking. A key question refers to the allocation of investments over high-risk/high-return and relatively safe assets. Bikker investigates whether pension funds follow the life-cycle hypothesis: more risk and return for pension funds with young participants. Many pension funds are rather limited in size, which may raise the question how financially sophisticated the pension fund decision makers are professionals or rather unskilled private persons?

The third field concerns two regulation issues. How do pension funds respond to shocks such as unexpected investment returns or changes in life expectancy? What are the welfare implications to the beneficiary for different methods of securing pension funding: solvency requirements, a pension guarantee fund or sponsor support?

This groundbreaking book will challenge the way pension fund economics is thought about and practised.

Jacob A. Bikker is professor of Banking and Financial Regulation, School of Economics, Utrecht University, Netherlands and senior researcher at the Strategy Department, Supervisory Policy Division, De Nederlandsche Bank (DNB). His research interests include financial institutions, competition, efficiency and optimal scale. He has published many papers on efficiency and optimal scale of pension funds in journals such as *Journal of Pension Economics and Finance*, *Journal of Risk and Insurance* and *Applied Economics*.

Routledge International Studies in Money and Banking

For a full list of titles in this series, please visit www.routledge.com/series/SE0403

Pension Fund Economics and Finance

Efficiency, Investments and Risk-Taking

Edited by Jacob A. Bikker

LONDON AND NEW YORK

First published 2018 by Routledge

2 Park Square, Milton Park, Abingdon, Oxfordshire OX14 4RN

52 Vanderbilt Avenue, New York, NY 10017

Routledge is an imprint of the Taylor & Francis Group, an informa business

First issued in paperback 2019

British Library Cataloguing-in-Publication Data
A catalogue record for this book is available from the British Library

Library of Congress Cataloging-in-Publication Data
A catalog record for this book has been requested

ISBN: 978-1-138-65680-2 (hbk)
ISBN: 978-0-367-87775-0 (pbk)

Typeset in Times New Roman
by Apex CoVantage, LLC

Contents

Figures

Tables

Contributors

Jacob A. Bikker is a Banking and Financial Regulation professor at the Utrecht School of Economics, Utrecht University, and senior researcher at the Supervisory Policy Division of De Nederlandsche Bank, Amsterdam. His main research interest is in competition and efficiency in banking, insurance and pensions. He has published widely on pension and other finance, including in *Review of Economics and Statistics*, *Journal of Banking and Finance*, *Journal of Risk and Insurance*, and *Journal of International Money and Finance*.

Dirk W.G.A. Broeders is professor in Pension Finance and Regulation at the School of Business and Economics of Maastricht University and a Senior Strategy Advisor at the Supervisory Policy Division of De Nederlandsche Bank. He is also a former Executive Member of the International Organization of Pension Supervisors (IOPS). He has published widely on pension finance, including in *Journal of Banking and Finance*, *Journal of Risk and Insurance*, *Journal of International Money and Finance* and *Insurance: Mathematics and Economics*.

An Chen is a professor in Insurance Economics at University of Ulm and a research fellow at Netspar. Her research interests focus on pricing of exotic derivatives and insurance contracts, occupational pension systems and optimal asset allocation for insurance companies and pension funds.

Jan de Dreu (1981) works in Debt Advisory at the Corporate & Investment Banking division of BBVA in Madrid. He advises large corporates in Europe and the US about their ratings, capital structure and liquidity. Previously, he worked in the Credit Risk Department of RBS in London, ABN AMRO in Amsterdam and at the Supervisory Policy Division of De Nederlandsche Bank. He holds a PhD in Economics from Utrecht University and has published a number of papers on topics related to the governance of financial institutions.

Janko Gorter is the head for Supervisory Strategy for De Nederlandsche Bank (DNB), central bank and prudential supervisor of the Netherlands. His academic background is in Economics. He graduated from Groningen University in 2005, and obtained his doctorate degree from this same university in 2013. He has published in, amongst others, *Applied Economics*, the *Scandinavian Journal of Economics* and the *Journal of Risk and Insurance*.

David A. Hollanders (1978) holds masters in Econometrics, Economics and History and a PhD in Economics. He lectures political economy at the department of European Studies, University of Amsterdam. His interests are the political economy of the euro-crisis and the financialization in the pension domain.

Thijs Knaap (PhD, Groningen, 2004) taught at several Dutch universities before joining the CPB Netherlands Bureau for Economic Policy Analysis. At the time of the research published in this book, he participated for CPB in the Netspar project 'The macroeconomics of pension reform'. He currently works in Hong Kong as a senior strategist for APG AM, a company that manages the investments of a number of Dutch pension funds.

Eduard H. M. Ponds (1958) holds the chair Economics of Pensions at Tilburg University. He is also employed at pension service provider APG and currently involved in research on individual pensions and choice architecture. His expertise is on pension funds, pension plan (re)design, risk management, actuarial aspects, intergenerational risk sharing, and classic and value-based ALM, valuation and behavioural economics. He introduced the so-called policy ladder as a tool to define conditional indexation by pension funds, and the value-based generational accounting method to determine generational redistribution when design and funding of collective pension plans changes.

Ward E. Romp (1976) is associate professor at the Amsterdam School of Economics of the University of Amsterdam and research fellow of Netspar. Ward holds a PhD from the University of Groningen and worked as policy consultant at a pension services provider. His current research focuses on the macroeconomic effects of pension fund policy and regulation. He has published on ageing, pensions and risk sharing in journals such as the *Journal of Public Economics*, the *European Economic Review* and the *Journal of Economic Dynamics and Control*.

Birgit Schnorrenberg is a PhD student at the University of Bonn. Her main research interests include the pricing of insurance contracts and the optimal asset allocation for insurance companies and pension funds.

Laura Spierdijk is a professor of Econometrics at the University of Groningen in the Netherlands. Her main research interests are applied econometrics in banking, insurance and finance. Her work has been published, or is forthcoming, in the *Review of Economics and Statistics*, *Journal of Econometrics*, *Journal of Banking and Finance*, *Journal of Health Economics*, and *Journal of International Money and Finance*, among others.

Onno W. Steenbeek (1967) is managing director of Strategic Portfolio Advice at APG Asset Management. This department is responsible for APG's advisory services regarding ALM and strategic asset allocation, as well as investment and pensions research. He also holds a Chair in Pension Fund Risk Management at the Erasmus School of Economics in Rotterdam, The Netherlands. Apart from lecturing on various finance subjects, he conducts academic research and publishes books and articles. Every other year, he organizes a policy-oriented pension conference at the Erasmus School of Economics.

Federico Torracchi is a macroeconomist, currently working for the World Bank. He holds a PhD in Economics from the University of Oxford (2016) with a thesis examining the impact of bank lending on the labour markets of advanced economies. His interests include New-Keynesian models of the labour market, financial intermediation models, monetary policy and macroforecasting.

Zaghum Umar is working as an Assistant Professor of Finance at Suleman Dawood School of Business, Lahore University of Management Sciences, Pakistan. As a member of the panel of the Higher Education Commission of Pakistan, he is an approved PhD supervisor. He received his PhD from the University of Groningen. He has published in the *Journal of International Money and Finance*, *Journal of Economics and Business* and *Journal of Investment Strategies*. His research interests include empirical finance, portfolio choice, alternative investments and risk management.

1   Introduction

Jacob A. Bikker

Pension fund efficiency and investment returns are crucial for pensioners' welfare. Pension funds manage huge amounts of capital, constituting a major part of worldwide institutional investments. Pension systems also have a significant impact on national economies, especially in countries where the pension funds' asset value exceeds that of the national product. However, the literature on pension fund economics and finance is rather limited, partly due to low availability of data on individual pension funds. This book contributes to the pension fund economics and finance literature with a number of relevant studies focusing on three important areas:

1.1. Pension fund efficiency

The first research field is pension fund efficiency. Inefficiency in pension fund administration and investment has a huge impact on final benefits, particularly when this accumulates over a lifetime. An increase in annual operating costs of 1% of pension fund assets may imply a cumulated reduction of 27% of final pension benefits or, equivalently, an increase of more than 37% in pension costs (see Bateman *et al.*, 2001; Bikker and de Dreu, 2009). Economies of scale have a major impact on administration and investment costs of pension funds, and they rise over time, particularly as information technology costs are to some extent constant across the individual funds, which boosts economies of scale. Economies of scale may also imply the existence of an optimal pension fund scale, which is investigated in Chapter 2. This chapter estimates different functions for administrative and investment costs, which incorporate varying assumptions about the shape of the underlying average-cost function: particularly, U-shaped versus monotonically declining. Relationships between costs and scale that are more flexible than commonly used in the literature appear to be necessary to obtain meaningful estimates of economies of scale and their differences over the various pension fund sizes. Using unique data for Dutch pension funds, this chapter finds that unused economies of scale for both administrative activities and investment are indeed extremely large and yield a concave cost function, that is, huge and positive for small pension funds, but decreasing with pension fund size. A clear optimal scale of around 40,000 participants during 1992–2000 has been observed (pointing to a U-shaped average-cost function), which increases in subsequent years to an optimal size above the largest pension fund, pointing to monotonically decreasing average costs. The shape of the unit cost functions has changed over time.

Chapter 3 investigates how complexity of the pension plans and higher service levels may also contribute to administration costs. Administrative costs per participant appear to vary widely across pension funds in different countries. Using unique data on 90 pension funds, this chapter examines the impact of scale, the complexity of pension plans and service quality on the administrative costs of pension funds, and compares these costs across Australia, Canada, the Netherlands, and the United States. With the exception of Canada, large unused economies of scale have been found to exist. Higher service quality and more complex pension plans significantly raise costs. Administrative costs also vary significantly across pension fund types, with differences of up to 100%.

A different type of efficiency relates to the administration costs of pension provisions by pension funds in comparison to those offered by life insurers. Not all employers have access to pension provisions by a pension fund, and most self-employed people have no access to pension funds at all. On the other hand, enterprises may choose the kind of institution for the pension provisions of its employees. Chapter 4 makes such comparisons of pension provision costs. First, the differences across pension plans of pension funds and life insurers are discussed. Second, operational costs and profits across the types of institutions are compared over long periods, where life insurer products are split into four categories: individuals versus groups and, for both categories, investment portfolio-linked versus guaranteed amounts in euros. This allows for more detailed insight in pension provision costs of life insurers. Finally, the impact of economies of scale on the cost comparison has been investigated.

1.2. Investment behaviour and risk-taking

The second research area is on investment behaviour and risk-taking. Obviously, investment returns are key for a favourable (*i.e.* high) level of pension benefits. But investment returns are strongly linked to investment risks. A central measure of risk-taking is the allocation of investments over (i) risky assets, such as stocks, private equity and real estate, where expected returns are higher and (ii) relatively safe assets, such as bonds, with *a priori* lower returns. This book treats various aspects of this return and risk trade-off.

Chapter 5 studies the multi-period asset allocation problem – well-known in the finance literature – for pension fund investors with an emerging-market portfolio comprising stocks, bonds and bills. Two types of investors are considered: domestic ones who invest in emerging-market assets only (with returns in local currency) and international investors, who invest in both US and emerging-market assets (with returns in US dollars). The results show that emerging-market bonds with a maturity of one year and longer can provide attractive short-run and long-run investment opportunities for domestic and internationally investing pension funds with different risk preferences.

Chapter 6 discusses the implications of mean reversion in stock prices for long-term investors such as pension funds. It starts with a general definition of a mean-reverting price process and explains how mean reversion in stock prices is related to mean reversion in stock returns. Subsequently, it shows that mean reversion makes stocks less risky for investors with long investment horizons. Next, a mean-variance efficient investor has been considered to show how mean reversion in stock prices affects such an investor's optimal portfolio allocation. Finally, the implications of the findings for the investment decisions of long-term investors are discussed.

Chapter 7 examines the impact of participants' age distribution on the asset allocation of pension funds, using a unique dataset of Dutch pension fund investment plans. Theory predicts a negative effect of age on (strategic) equity exposures. This chapter observes that a one-year increase in the average age of active participants leads to a significant and robust reduction of the strategic equity exposure by around 0.5 percentage point. Larger pension funds show a stronger age-equity exposure effect. The average age of active participants influences investment behaviour more strongly than the average age of all participants, which is plausible as retirees no longer possess any human capital.

Many pension funds are rather limited in size, which may raise the question of how financially sophisticated the pension fund decision makers are: are they professionals or closer to unskilled private persons? Using investment policy plan data of 857 pension funds with a strongly skewed size distribution, Chapter 8 develops three indicators of investor sophistication. These indicators show that pension funds' strategic portfolio choices are often based on rough and less sophisticated approaches. First, most pension funds round strategic asset allocations to the nearest multiple of 5%, similar to age heaping in demographic and historical studies. Second, many pension funds invest little or nothing in alternative, more complex asset classes, resulting in limited asset diversification. Third, many pension funds favour regional investments and as such do not fully employ the opportunities of international risk diversification. The indicators are correlated with pension fund size, in line with the expectation that smaller pension funds are generally less sophisticated than large pension funds. Using the indicators for investor sophistication, it has been shown that less sophisticated pension funds tend to opt for investment strategies with lower risk.

According to theory, institutional investors face both risk-management and risk-shifting incentives. Chapter 9 assesses the relevance of these conflicting incentives for pension funds and insurance firms. Using a unique and extended dataset, a significant positive relationship between capital and asset risk for insurers has been observed, indicating that risk-management incentives dominate the Dutch insurance industry. Risk-shifting incentives, however, also seem relevant, as stock insurers take more investment risk than their mutual peers. For Dutch pension funds, neither risk-shifting nor risk-management incentives seem to dominate in general. Interestingly, professional group pension funds take significantly less investment risk than other types of pension funds. This finding is in line with expectations, as in professional group pension funds potential incentive conflicts between pension fund participants and the employer are effectively internalized.

1.3. Risk-taking and regulation

The third main topic of this book is on risk-taking and regulation. The pension sector performs a key public task, highly important for its current and future beneficiaries but also for the current economy. Participants' savings are held for decades to invest profitably in order to meet the future promised benefits. As a consequence, this sector is strongly regulated and supervised.

Chapter 10 investigates responses to changes in solvency by occupational pension funds using a unique panel dataset containing the balance sheets of all registered pension funds in the Netherlands over a period of 13 years. A fixed-discount rate for liabilities in the supervisory framework enables the measurement of the response of pension funds to solvency shocks. Pension rights appear to be expanded, by *e.g.* indexation, or limited, by for instance setting the pension premium over its actuarially fair price, in line with the funding ratio, but the pension funds' response function exhibits two sharp and significant behavioural breaks, close to the minimum funding ratio of 105% and the target ratio of around 125%. Large funds and grey funds are relatively generous to current participants.

Adequate funding of occupational pension plans is key for security. Different methods of securing funding exist across countries: solvency requirements, a pension guarantee fund and sponsor support. The aim of Chapter 11 is to investigate the welfare implications to the beneficiary in a hybrid pension scheme. The chapter shows that the three security mechanisms can be made utility-equivalent by adjusting the pension contract specifications. The utility-equivalence approach could serve to strengthen the 'holistic balance sheet' approach, as advised by the European Insurance and Occupational Pensions Authority (EIOPA), a regulatory body of the financial sector in the European Union. It enables regulators to compare various pension systems across Europe in a single framework from a utility perspective instead of a valuation perspective.

1.4. Statements of aims

This books investigates topics which are of key importance for the following three groups: First, pension fund stakeholders, such as participants and employers. They can benefit from investigations on (i) efficiency with respect to scale, governance, organization, type of pension schemes and service level, and investment policy, where they can balance risk and returns with respect to their pension fund features and characteristics of their participants; (ii) policymakers from government and regulatory supervisors can benefit from knowledge on the most efficient structure of the pension sector, both in number of pension funds and their individual scale, as well as the legal organization, *e.g.* industry-wide funds versus company funds. Furthermore, information on investment behaviour and risk-taking are crucial for financial supervisors in developing regulation for solvency and financial stability as well as governance; (iii) all topics in this book are of great interest to academics, particularly because empirical research on these areas are generally hampered by a lack of detailed data on individual pension funds.

References

Bateman, H., G. Kingston, J. Piggott, 2001, *Forced Saving: Mandating Private Retirement Incomes*, Cambridge University Press, Cambridge.

Bikker, J. A., J. de Dreu, 2009, Operating costs of pension funds: the impact of scale, governance and plan design, *Journal of Pension Economics and Finance* 8, 63–89.

Part I
Efficiency

2 Is there an optimal pension fund size?

A scale-economy analysis of administrative and investment costs[1]

Jacob A. Bikker

2.1. Introduction

After the credit crisis, pension funds all over the world have suffered from low returns on stocks, low interest rates and, particularly funds that offer defined-benefit plans, increasing life expectancy. The operating costs of pension funds may draw less attention, although persistent inefficiencies are seriously eroding (future) benefits. Ambachtsheer (2010) stresses the role of operating efficiency in optimal pension provision and indicates that more research is needed on institutional implementation. Comparing pension funds in the Netherlands, one finds that avoidable costs may cause a 10%–20% difference between benefits paid by the smallest and by the largest pension funds, a difference that may grow even larger as returns on investment decline. Here unused economies of scale are key, so that, considering only costs, consolidation is to be recommended.

The question arises, however, whether this advice should apply to pension funds of all sizes, including the very large ones. Economic theory typically assumes either a U-shaped average-cost function or continuously decaying unit costs. Theoretical arguments and empirical evidence for the downward-sloping left leg of the U shape – and the left-hand part of the monotonically declining average-cost function – is overwhelming. Fixed costs, being inelastic to the number of participants, account for much of the unused scale economies. Particularly information and communication technology (ICT), the basis of many pension fund activities, has strong fixed-cost components. The same holds for compliance with accounting and regulatory requirements and projects. Scale economies are also reinforced by size-related bargaining power vis-à-vis external service providers with respect to investment, outsourcing and reinsurance, and contribute further to lower unit costs (Bauer *et al.*, 2010). Whereas fixed costs continue to decline as the size of the pension fund increases, the effect of bargaining power tends to taper off, for instance as the number of sizable counterparties declines. Commonly, large pension funds have difficulty finding competing counterparties for large interest-rate swaps and other derivative transactions.

The existence of an upward-sloping right leg of the U-shaped unit cost function presupposes costs that increase more than proportionally with size. The literature provides a number of examples. Key factors are inefficiencies due to managerial problems in large, complex, international firms (as often encountered in the banking industry), bureaucracy, additional layers of management and over-hiring (see Chatterton *et al.*, 2010), increasing luxury in terms of buildings and salaries, extra costs due to scarcity of qualified staff and additional costs related to over-confidence (Griffin and Tversky, 1992). Bauer *et al.* (2010) mention increasing costs of communication between the different sections of the company and the costs involved in monitoring employees, including managers. The motivation and commitment of employees may be lower in a large organization, as they contribute relatively little to the overall success of the organization, resulting in lower productivity (Canback *et al.*, 2006). Lack of a clear overview of budget and liquidity in a large firm may cause inefficient spending with respect to recruitment, equipment or offices (Canback *et al.*, 2006). Other authors point to costs due to stronger competition between units. As larger pension funds have to diversify more, they encounter more investments that lack sufficient publicly available information, leading to higher research costs (Andonov *et al.*, 2012). While promising higher investment returns, such investments also push up operational costs. The key question is whether such large firm inefficiencies outweigh the basic effect of the monotonically declining fixed costs.

Pension funds with large amounts of assets are unable to respond quickly to changes in the market, particularly when capital markets are stressed (McKenna and Kim, 1986; Bauer *et al.*, 2010; Andonov *et al.*, 2012), and therefore face market impact costs when buying or selling (Bikker *et al.*, 2007, 2008, 2010). Dyck and Pomorski (2011) also mention that increased capital inflows lead managers to pursue poorer investment ideas. These are arguments for the simultaneous existence of diseconomies of scale, but they concern investment returns rather than operating costs.

Scale-economy measures are often based on a translog cost function. This model is quadratic in nature so that it is well-suited to describe U-shaped average unit costs. However, Shaffer (1998) points out that such a cost model implies the existence of an optimal scale, as long as the cost-output size relationship is concave. He recommends the use of various cost functions with different underlying assumptions with respect to the shape of the underlying average unit cost including, in particular, models able to unrestricted Laurent cost function and the hyperbolically augmented Cobb-Douglas model.

We apply these various cost functions on a unique dataset consisting of supervisory reports by Dutch pension funds over 1992–2009, obtained from the supervisor, De Nederlandsche Bank.[2] The huge size of the dataset is of great importance, as we need ample data also on large pension funds, where possible diseconomies of scale may or may not exist. Our dataset splits operating costs into administrative and investment costs. This permits us to investigate administrative and investment activities separately. Indeed, fixed and variable costs determining economies of scale vary for these different activities, while the complexity, luxury and overconfidence arguments which may affect the possible existence of an optimal scale may also diverge across activities. Note, however, that if optimal scales do exist but vary across activities, recommendations with respect to consolidation for the sake of a cost-effective market structure are more complex, because in that case trade-offs exists between the optimal scale in terms of administration and in terms of investment.

Many drivers of scale economy and optimal scale may change over time. The increasing role of ICT is likely to enlarge scale economies, as the associated costs are likely to have a substantial fixed component. Increasing solvency regulation and accounting requirements may also add to the fixed costs. As our dataset is large, we are able to estimate scale efficiency and optimal scale on an annual basis, so that developments over time can be investigated.

Section 2.2 of this chapter gives an overview of the available literature on operating costs of pension funds and on the existence of scale economies. Section 2.3 describes the pension system of the Netherlands, while the next section analyzes the data on administrative and investment costs of Dutch pension funds and presents all other data on key characteristics of pension funds. Section 2.5 explains the cost models considered and the measurement of scale economies. Sections 2.6 and 2.7 provide the empirical results for, respectively, administrative and investment costs of pension funds. Section 2.8 summarizes the findings and concludes this chapter.

2.2. Review of the literature

Administrative costs include all expenses involved in operating a pension fund except investment costs, and as such include costs of management and staff, communication with participants, auditing and reporting and other costs charged by third parties (as in the case of outsourcing), premium collections, benefit payments, rent and depreciation. Research on pension funds' administrative costs has focused on a few countries, in particular Australia (Bateman and Valdés-Prieto, 1999; Malhotra *et al.*, 2001; Bateman and Mitchell, 2004; Sy, 2007), the US (Caswell, 1976; Mitchell and Andrews, 1981), Chile (James *et al.*, 2001), and the Netherlands (Bikker and de Dreu, 2009; Alserda *et al.*, 2017). These studies all report significant economies of scale for private pension funds. The higher cost level of small pension funds has been attributed to advantages such as higher service levels or tailor-made pension schemes (Koeleman and De Swart, 2007), but Bikker *et al.* in Chapter 3 of this book have refuted this theory. Few comparative studies have been conducted across different countries, and almost none have used a multivariate approach. Whitehouse (2000) compares defined-contribution (DC) schemes in 13 countries. For Latin American countries and Great Britain, the author finds no systematic relation between pension fund size and charges levied (consisting of costs and profit margins), and concludes that evidence on economies of scale in pension fund administrative costs is inconclusive. In a more recent study, Hernandez and Stewart (2008) compare the charge ratios in 21 countries with private DC schemes. The authors note that charge ratios tend to be lower in countries with fewer providers, thereby concluding that there is some evidence of economies of scale, assuming that those few pension providers are also relatively large. Tapia and Yermo (2008) conduct a similar analysis for countries where the pension system is based on individual retirement accounts

(IRAs): Australia, Sweden, and countries in Latin America and Central and Eastern Europe. These studies do not distinguish between investment and administrative expenses, and use charge ratios or other fee measures rather than economic costs. James *et al.* (2001) improve on this by comparing fees and administrative expenses (including investment expenses) in six Latin American countries with pension systems based on IRAs.[3] The fundamental problem with this body of research is the lack of appropriate data that would allow one to determine the relative contribution of each factor in a multivariate analysis. Instead, the authors use broad descriptive statistics on the domestic pension system to highlight bivariate relationships. Only Dobronogov and Murthi (2005) conduct a multivariate cross-country study, based on a limited number of observations, and find some evidence of economies of scale in pension funds in Croatia, Kazakhstan and Poland. In general, there are large differences in administrative costs among pension funds. Some of them reflect particular market conditions or institutional environments, while others are due to different degrees of efficiency. All in all, these studies measure scale economies, but do not focus on the existence of an optimal scale.

Investment costs include investment research as well as management and consulting fees, while transaction costs and brokerage fees are excluded, as they are normally deducted from gross returns. A few studies are known about the investment costs of pension funds, while some of the above studies are on operating expenses, which include investment costs.[4] Bauer *et al.* (2010) find for the US strong scale economies in investment costs. Costs are also higher for small cap portfolios and for portfolios which are actively managed or externally managed. Dyck and Pomorski (2011) investigate both investment costs and returns of an international sample of large pension funds. They observe significant economies of scale for both costs and returns. Broeders *et al.* (2016) also find economies of scale in investment costs for the Netherlands. Most of the superior returns come from large pension funds' increased allocation to alternative investments and realizing greater returns in this asset class. Furthermore, a large literature exists on the investment costs of mutual funds. The investment operations of pension funds are similar to those of mutual funds and many pension funds invest assets through mutual funds. Therefore, this literature can provide meaningful insights into the investment operations of pension funds as well.[5] Empirical evidence suggests the existence of substantial cost-related economies of scale in the mutual fund industry (*e.g.* Malhotra and McLeod, 1997). However, these turn out to decrease as the fund size increases and become zero as soon as the optimal size has been reached (*e.g.* Indro *et al.*, 1999 and Collins and Mack, 1997). Of course, mutual funds may incur higher costs hunting for higher returns. Ippolito (1989) compares the expenses and returns of mutual funds and index funds and found that mutual funds offset higher expenses with better results. Possibly, however, this outcome may be sensitive to the particular benchmark used, or be explained by survivorship bias (*e.g.* Malkiel, 1995). Many other studies have found that higher costs are not related to superior performance relative to the risk-adjusted rate of return (*e.g.* Jensen, 1968; Malkiel, 1995 and Malhotra and McLeod, 1997). Thus, the evidence suggests that, in general, higher costs incurred by mutual funds do not lead to higher returns. Since the investment operations of pension funds and mutual funds are similar, it seems reasonable to expect this result to hold for pension funds as well.[6] We may therefore conclude that, *ceteris paribus*, stakeholders are likely to be best served by pension funds with low investment costs. We conclude that, on the investment market, scale economies tend to exist but, according to some studies, only as long as institutions are below the optimal scale.

2.3. The pension system in the Netherlands

As in most developed countries, the institutional structure of the pension system in the Netherlands is organized as a three-pillar system. The first pillar comprises the public pension scheme and is financed on a pay-as-you-go base. It offers a basic flat-rate pension to all retirees and aims to link the benefit level to the legal minimum wage. The second pillar provides former workers an additional income from a collective, contribution-based supplementary scheme. The third pillar comprises tax-deferred personal savings, which individuals undertake at their own expense. The supplementary or occupational pension system in the Netherlands is usually organized as a funded defined-benefit (DB) plan.[7]

Supplementary schemes are usually managed on a collective basis by pension funds. There are three types of pension funds. The first type is the *industry* pension fund, which is organized for a specific industry sector (*e.g.* construction, health care, transport). Participation in an industry pension fund is mandatory for all employers operating in the sector, with a few exceptions.[8] An employer may opt out if it establishes a *corporate* pension fund that offers a better pension plan to its employees. Where a supplementary scheme is agreed by employers and employees, managed by either a corporate pension fund or an industry pension fund, participation by the workers is mandatory, governed by collective labour agreements. The third type of pension fund is the *professional group* pension fund, organized for a specific group of professionals, such as the medical profession or notaries.

2.4. Key characteristics of Dutch pension funds

The data used in this chapter were obtained from De Nederlandsche Bank (DNB), supervisor of the Dutch pension fund industry. We have annual data for the 1992–2015 period and, in addition, quarterly data on investments starting in 1999. The number of pension funds declined from around 880 during 1993–1998, via 550 in 2009 to 290 in 2013. Some 80% of the discontinued pension funds handed over their assets and liabilities to insurers; the rest have merged. Most of the dissolved funds were small, half of them numbering fewer than 250 participants. In total, we have a sample of close to 13,000 annual pension fund observations. Company funds are the largest in number, followed by compulsory industry funds, non-compulsory industry funds and professional group funds. However, Table 2.1 makes clear that in terms of participants, compulsory industry funds dominate the pension sector with, during 2010–2015, a share of 88%, followed by company funds (12%).

Table 2.1 Key data of Dutch pension funds over time (value amounts are in prices of 2004)

	1992– 1996	1997– 2001	2002– 2005	2006– 2009	2010– 2015
Administration costs per participant, in euros [a]	37.24	48.95	50.92	54.16	69.04
Investment costs per participant, in euros [a, b]	16.26	20.73	32.40	68.59	78.82
Investment costs/total assets, in % [a, b]	0.09	0.06	0.10	0.19	0.19
Number of participants, in millions (p)	9.70	13.43	16.27	17.54	17.75
Total assets, in billion euros	207.75	469.87	526.84	654.63	745.16
Liabilities, in billion euros	180.00	362.77	457.97	530.13	668.36
Real wages pension industry (thousand euros)	55.27	57.01	63.69	66.80	69.45
Compulsory industry pension fund part./p	0.81	0.82	0.82	0.84	0.88
Company pension fund participants/p	0.12	0.13	0.14	0.13	0.12
Non-compulsory industry pension fund part./p	0.02	0.02	0.03	0.01	– [e]
Professional group pension fund participants/p	0.01	0.00	0.00	0.00	0.01
Other pension fund participants/p	0.05	0.02	0.01	0.01	– [e]
Pension scheme: DC participants/p	0.03	0.02	0.05	0.07	0.07
Retirees/p	0.13	0.14	0.14	0.15	0.17
Active participants/p	0.36	0.38	0.37	0.33	0.32
Inactive participants/p	0.51	0.47	0.49	0.52	0.51
Assets per participant (thousand euros) [a]	21.41	35.00	32.37	37.33	41.93
Reporting investment costs dummy [a]	0.36	0.50	0.69	0.71	0.81
Outsourcing/administration costs [a]	0.51	0.53	0.77	0.65	0.61
Reinsurance premiums/total premiums [a]	0.10	0.04	0.01	0.03	0.02
Fixed income/total investments (ti) [a, c]	0.56	0.47	0.46	0.47	0.50
Investments in stocks/ti [a]	0.24	0.41	0.40	0.38	0.35
Real estate /ti [a]	0.12	0.10	0.10	0.10	0.10
Other assets/ti [a, d]	0.07	0.02	0.03	0.05	0.05
Private equity/ti [a]	0.00	0.01	0.02	0.03	– [e]
Commodities/ti [a]	–	0.00	0.01	– [e]	–
Hedge funds and commodities/ti [a]	–	–	–	0.04 [e]	– [e]

Note: Variable names are abbreviated within brackets: number of participants is 'p' and total investments is 'ti'.

[a] On average;
[b] to avoid the problem over underreporting, we take averages over *non-zero* investment costs (ic) only, while the variable total assets in this row refers to the sum over the pension funds where ic are non-zero;
[c] total investment is 5% smaller than total assets, the difference being one-off items;
[d] this variable is used in the regressions only for 1992–1996, as for later years it has been split into – among other things – commodities and hedge funds;
[e] change in definition. Note that the sample period for the model regressions is 1992–2009.

2.4.1. *Operating costs*

Operating costs (OC) consist of administrative costs and investment costs. Administrative costs regard the collection of contributions, record-keeping, benefit payments, communications, accounting and marketing, while investment costs refer to portfolio management, financial research, trading facilities and advice. Transaction fees and management fees of mutual funds are not included, as they are normally already deducted from the investment returns. We split OC into administrative and investment costs, because each has different characteristics and distinct determinants. Fig. 2.1 presents the administration costs per participant for the 2,000 non-zero observations over 2006–2009, expressed as averages over ten size classes with for each class the spread in average costs.[9] In this chapter, all value amounts are expressed in prices of 2004. The median costs per participant decline strongly from € 666 in the smallest class to € 39 in the largest class. The spread in costs per participant is immense, particularly in the smallest size class, ranging from € 75 to € 4,000 (respectively, the 10th and 90th percentiles), but also in the largest size class, ranging from € 14 to € 118. Of course, the largest class – containing 90% of the participants – is most important. Splitting this class into 5 or 10 subclasses would reproduce the same declining graph with reducing spread. Fig. 2.1 with the three earlier subperiods 1992–1996, 1997–2001 and 2002–2005, or for 2010–2015, looks similar.

Note that the median and the lower bounds may underestimate the costs due to possible underreporting. Some companies pay for the administration and investment activities of their own pension funds without on-charging salaries and office costs, leading to zero or lower reported costs (Bikker and de Dreu, 2009). Such underreporting is found especially for smaller pension funds.[10] In Section 2.6, where we discuss estimation results, we will prove that – due to underreporting – scale economy may be even stronger than we observe, so that our scale-economy estimates establish a lower bound.

For 2006–2009, Fig. 2.2 shows investment cost as share of total assets for the 1,650 non-zero observations, expressed as medians over ten size classes with for each class its spread.[11] Many funds report zero investment costs – as many as ca. 64% in 1992–1996, falling to 29% in 2006–2009. In many cases, investment costs

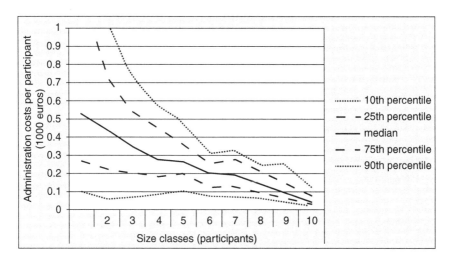

Figure 2.1 Administration costs per participant in size classes (2006–2009; 2004 prices)

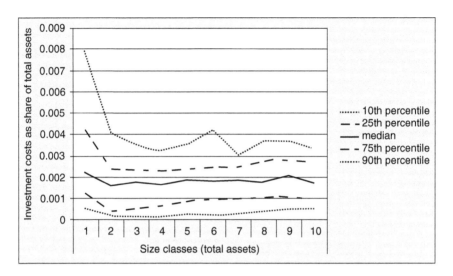

Figure 2.2 Investment costs as share of total assets (2006–2009; 2004 prices)

are hidden in the investment returns, which are (incorrectly) reported net of costs rather than gross. Underreporting of investment costs is most frequent among the smaller funds.[12] In Section 2.7, where we discuss estimation results, we will also discuss the impact of underreporting.

Scale economies seem to be absent, except possibly for the smallest size class. This is not representative for the three earlier periods, where median costs in the smallest size class were, respectively, 2.5, 2 and 1.5 times larger than in the largest size class (compared to no less than 31, 29, 15 and 12 times for administration costs). For 2010–2015, this graph would be fully flat. Also remarkable is the fact that the spread in investment costs is constant across the size classes (apart from a higher level in the first size class), without the convergence for larger classes as observed for administrative costs. Of course, the largest class – containing 85% of total assets – is of most importance. Splitting this class in 5 or 10 subclasses would show an increase in investment costs for the largest funds. We believe that two phenomena interact here: scale economies (which must exist given the presence of fixed costs) and the higher relative shares of complex assets in larger pension fund portfolios, with higher investments costs but correspondingly higher expected returns.

Fig. 2.3 shows how larger pension funds' portfolios have higher relative shares of commodities, hedge funds, private equity and real estate, which all are expected to go with higher costs, whereas the smallest pension funds tend to prefer other (simpler) assets such as money market funds. As we have the asset allocation by pension fund, regression analyses can disentangle the economies of scale effect from the size-dependent investment composition effect.

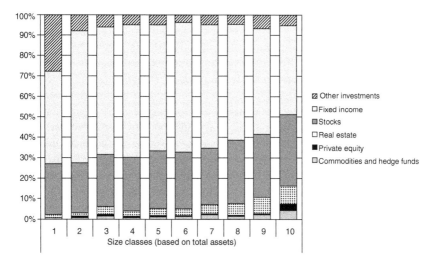

Figure 2.3 Pension fund asset allocation across size classes in 2009

2.4.2. *Other key data of Dutch pension funds*

This subsection discusses key characteristics of Dutch pension funds, which will act as control variables in the operating cost models. The first rows in Table 2.1 show that administrative costs per participant increase over the considered periods by over 85%, reflecting the rise in real wages (26%) and the costs of new activities related to new requirements as regards communication to participants, solvency and accounting regulation, et cetera. Underreporting of administrative costs, particularly salaries, has decreased over time, which contributes to higher (reported) costs. Investment costs more than quadrupled over time, and increased especially during the last years, mainly due to additional investment costs for high-risk assets, *e.g.* hedge funds, commodities and private equity. Here, the decline in underreporting over time is also a major explanation.

The total number of participants increased strongly over time from 9.7 to 17.8 million, due to increased employment (less unemployment and greater participation, in part due to an increase in part-time jobs), greater coverage, and joining in the sample of the largest pension fund in 1996 (ABP; the civil servants' pension fund). Total assets increased strongly over time as well, in real terms from € 200 to 750 billion (in prices of 2004; in running prices over 1,000 billion euro), reflecting growth in volume (participants) and in wealth (both income and building-up level). There are two basic types of pension scheme: (mainly) defined benefit (DB) and (mainly) Defined Costs (DC), where schemes of both types may have some mixed (DB and DC) characteristics. Falling from 4% in 1992 to in 1% in 1998, the share of DC increased to 7% in the later periods.

There are three categories of participants: active, inactive and retirees. Each category increased in number, while their shares remained fairly constant, with a slight increase of pensioners. The variable 'total assets per participant' reflects whether a pension fund has relatively high per capita assets and, hence, higher than average benefits.[13]

Many pension funds outsource their administration partly or fully. Especially small funds can benefit from outsourcing, as companies specializing in administrative work for many pension funds can work on a large scale and, hence, are expected to be relatively efficient. Note that where sponsor companies bear a part of their funds' administrative costs, such underreporting of costs stops as soon as outsourcing begins. Hence, outsourcing may either pick up cost reduction (negative coefficient) as well as reduced underreporting (positive coefficient). Our variable describes the percentage of costs paid to third parties. The level of outsourcing is high at more than 50% of administrative costs, increasing over time, but falling more recently. Remarkably, larger pension funds outsource relatively more than smaller ones, probably because smaller pension funds rely on administrative work by the sponsor company. Reinsurance of pension fund liabilities by an insurer is measured as the reinsurance premiums in proportion to total pension premiums. Reinsurance declined over the years from 10% to 2%, probably because many small funds have been replaced entirely by collective insurance policies.

Pension funds invest in assets such as fixed-income securities, stocks, real estate, participations or private equity, commodities, hedge funds, mortgages and money market funds. First, we have data on the first three categories (as well as 'other assets') from the annual reports of pension funds over the entire period. Table 2.1 shows an increase in stocks during the first half of the sample period, at the cost of fixed-income securities. Second, we have data on investments in private equity, commodities and hedge funds from the quarterly reports starting in 1999. Hedge fund investments have only been reported since 2007. Definitional breaks – the split in 1999 of other assets into private equity and commodities, and the split in 2007 of commodities into commodities and hedge funds – are dealt with in the empirical models. The more complex assets are expected to go with higher costs, as they are more difficult to understand and more expensive to manage. Generally, the *expected* returns of such riskier assets are higher, *ex ante* at least offsetting the extra costs. During 2006–2009 the riskier investment classes such as private equity, commodities and hedge funds became more and more popular with pension funds (Table 2.1; Bauer *et al.*, 2010). Hence a significant influence is expected on the investment costs of the pension funds that do use these risky investment classes. These assets are held by the largest funds: in 2009, the largest pension funds held 5% hedge funds and 3% private equity versus, respectively, 2% and 0.5% for other funds (see also Fig. 2.3). Using the investment shares in stocks, real estate, private equity, commodities, hedge funds and other funds, we aim – in our investment costs model – at correcting the investment costs for rewarding activities in these risky asset categories. Note that during 2010–2015, after the estimation sample period, the asset class definitions has changed again.

For almost all variables, while variation over time may be generally modest (Table 2.1), variation across pension funds is generally huge (as illustrated for costs in Figs. 2.1–2.2), so that controlling for such variation – when measuring scale economies – is crucially important.

2.5. Functional forms of operating cost models

This section discusses the functional form of various well-known cost models and the underlying assumptions with respect to the shape of the average cost per unit curve, which have a major impact on the existence and magnitude of an optimal scale. Next, we develop empirical models for administrative costs. Furthermore, this section explains the measurement of economies of scale.

2.5.1. Functional form and optimal size

The measurement and analysis of differences in pension fund cost levels is based on the assumption that an individual pension fund's production technology can be described by a production function, which links the various types of pension fund output to input factor prices, such as wages, housing rent and so on. Under proper conditions, a dual cost function can be derived, using output levels and factor prices as arguments (Coelli *et al.*, 1998, p. 43–49). In the literature, the translog cost function (TCF) to describe costs dominates other model specifications. Christensen *et al.* (1976) proposed the TCF as a second-order Taylor expansion, usually around the mean, of a generic function with all variables appearing as logarithms. This TCF is a flexible functional form that has proven to be an effective tool for the empirical assessment of efficiency, both in banking and elsewhere (Christensen *et al.*, 1976; Dietsch, 1993; Nauriyal, 1995; Edirisuriya *et al.*, 2001). It is an extension of the Cobb-Douglas function which is capable of fitting U-shaped average-cost functions.[14] A simple TCF reads as follows:

$$lnOC(o) = \alpha + \beta_1(lno) + \beta_2(lno - \overline{ln o})^2 \tag{2.1}$$

with '*OC*' for operating costs and '*o*' for output volume. Note that, in the squared term, we take the logarithm of output in deviation from its mean (denoted by the bar above the variable), in line with the Taylor expansion.[15] Here, we assume only one output measure for the expository simplification, but we consider more output measures in the empirical sections. In that case the model is extended with cross terms from both output measures. Since the Netherlands is a relatively small country, we expect little or no variation in input prices (Swank, 1996). Actually, pension funds do not report data on input prices, so that we are also unable to include pension fund-specific prices in the cost functions. We do, however, include an index of real wages in the pension sector to pick up input price effects over time.[16] Unused scale economies exist where $\beta_1 < 0$, while concavity, or a U-shaped average-cost function, requires $\beta_2 > 0$.

Shaffer (1998, page 94) proves that for a sample of monotonically declining average costs the TCF would estimate a concave function with an optimal scale, so that the existence of an optimal size and diseconomies of scale for larger firms is (incorrectly) imposed.[17] Indeed, the left leg of the TCF can be fitted to the hyperbolically declining average costs, with the optimal scale in the right-hand tail of the sample, or beyond the largest observation. Therefore, Shaffer (1998) suggests two additional cost functions to estimate scale economies which do not impose this U-shaped average-cost function.

The first alternative is the unrestricted Laurent function (ULF), which is similar to the TCF, but with two inverse terms added:

$$lnOC(o) = \alpha + \beta_1(lno) + \beta_2(lno - \overline{\ln o})^2 + \beta_3 / (lno) + \beta_4 / (lno)^2 \qquad (2.2)$$

The ULF can describe monotonically declining average cost, does not impose an optimal scale and allows different degrees of concavity for smaller and larger pension funds. For the concave properties to hold, the coefficients β_3 and β_4 should both be positive, next to β_2. According to Shaffer (1998), the improvement of the ULF over the TLF may die down for skewed size, because the squared nature of the cost-output relationship is built up by the relatively large share of observations in the smaller size region of the data sample. Therefore, he proposes a second alternative: the hyperbolically adjusted Cobb-Douglas (HACD) cost function; see also Adanu *et al.* (2009). This model reads as (again ignoring input prices):

$$lnOC(o) = \alpha + \beta_1(lno) + \beta_2 / o \qquad (2.3)$$

Thanks to the additional reciprocal term, this model can portray the U-shaped average-cost function ($\beta_1 > \beta_2$), monotonically declining average costs ($\beta_1 > 1$ and $\beta_2 > 0$) and the L-shaped average-cost function ($\beta_1 < 1$). To investigate which functional form best suits the sample data, we will apply Akaike's (1974) information criterion (AIC). In a simulation test by Shaffer (1998) on generated data, this HACD model performed best. Alserda *et al.* (2017) also introduce quadratic spline functions.

Cost elasticity (*CE*) is defined as the proportional increase in cost as a result of a proportional increase in output. In mathematical terms this results in the following expression for elasticity: $CE = \partial \ln OC / \partial \ln o$. Using Eq. (2.1–2.3), this results in, for the TCF, the ULF and the HACD respectively:

$$CE^{tcf} = \beta_1 + 2\beta_2 (lno - \overline{\ln o}) \qquad (2.4)$$

$$CE^{ulf} = \beta_1 + 2\beta_2 (lno - \overline{\ln o}) - \beta_3 / (lno)^2 - 2\beta_4 / (lno)^3 \qquad (2.5)$$

$$CE^{hacd} = \beta_1 - \beta_2 / o \qquad (2.6)$$

The second term of the *CEs* in the TCF and the ULF becomes zero when the *CEs* are evaluated around the mean of the sampled logarithms of output o_i, that is: $\overline{\ln o}$. The *CE* for the TCF is then equal to β_1, while for the ULF and the HACD, it depends on the sample observations.[18]

The scale economies (*SE*) can easily be calculated from the above by subtracting EC from unity: $SE = 1 - EC$. If the calculated *EC* has a value larger than one, this indicates diseconomies of scale; a value smaller than one indicates economies of scale and a value of exactly one indicates constant returns to scale. To calculate a possible optimal pension fund size, a value for *o* has to be found to set *CE* equal to one (or to set *SE* to zero).

2.5.2. Empirical model for administrative costs

This section specifies empirical models for administrative costs (AC), in logarithms, based on, respectively, the TCF, the ULF and the HACD functions. The TCF reads as:

$$AC_{it} = \alpha + \beta_1 \left(lnparticipants_{it} \right) + \beta_2 (lnparticipants_{it} - \overline{\ln participants})^2$$
$$+ \gamma_1 lnreal\ wage_t + \gamma_2\ governance\ dummies_{it} + \gamma_3 pension\ plan$$
$$design_{it} + \gamma_4 type\ of\ participants_{it} + \gamma_5 assets\ per\ participants_{it}$$
$$+ \gamma_6 reporting\ of\ investment\ costs_{it} + \gamma_7 outsourcing\ of$$
$$administration_{it} + \gamma_8\ reinsurance_{it} + \gamma_9 time_t + \varepsilon_{it} \qquad (2.7)$$

Subindex i refers to pension funds, while t refers to time. Output is measured as *number of participants* as many administrative activities are related to services provided to participants, mainly irrespective of the size of their pension benefits. Output is expressed in logarithms and appears linear and squared, the latter in deviation from its mean, in line with Eq. (2.1). *Real wages* is a wage index for the pension and insurance sector which acts as an input price. Its coefficient is expected to be positive. *Governance dummies* indicate, respectively, compulsory industry pension funds, company funds, professional group funds and other funds, while compulsory industry funds act as the benchmark. These dummies may pick up cost differences across pension fund types. The *pension plan design* dummy indicates pension funds with defined-benefit (DB) plans reflecting cost differences with the remaining category: defined-contribution (DC) funds. Three *types of participants* are distinguished: active participants, inactive participants and retirees, each of which may carry different costs, as administrative activities differ by type of participant. These variables are expressed as shares in the total number of participants. The share of active participants acts as benchmark. Total *assets per participant* measures whether administrative cost may increase with (future) pension benefits. The dummy variable for *reporting of investment costs* tests for incorrect reporting of investment costs under administrative costs. Costs of *outsourcing* as share of total administration costs may reflect costs differences. *Reinsurance* premiums as share of total premiums may pick up costs (other than premiums) related to reinsurance. Finally, *time* may reflect technical progress over time.

The ULF is based on Eq. (2.7) expanded with β_3 (1/ln *participants*) + β_4 (1/(ln *participants*)^2), while the HACD cost model is equal to Eq. (2.7), where the second output term is replaced by β_2 (1/*participants*). Deviations from the mean in the reciprocal terms would not make sense, *e.g.* values of zero (or close to zero) in the inverse terms would distort the equations.

2.6. Empirical results for administrative costs

This section displays the estimation results of the three different cost functions, both for the entire data sample over 1992–2009 as for each year separately. The full sample regressions combine all available information, resulting in highly significant results, while the single year regressions take into account changes over time. Table 2.2 shows the estimations of the administrative cost model for three cost functions using the full dataset of all Dutch pension funds over 1992–2009, consisting of 12,521 observations.[19] The upper panel of the table shows the estimated coefficients, the middle panel presents estimation and test statistics and the lower panel displays the first derivatives (or *CE*), the optimal scale and the cost elasticities at the mean size values of the pension funds.

Table 2.2 Estimates of the administrative cost models (1992–2009)

Variable	Translog	Unrestricted Laurent function	HACD	Simplified ULF
Participants (in logarithms)	0.717***/000	0.781***/000	0.748***/000	0.726***/000
Participants^2 (ln, mean dev.)	0.021***	0.013***	– –	0.019***
1/ participants	– –	– –	2.501***	– –
1/ (ln participants)	– –	2.495***	– –	0.217*
1/ (ln participants)^2	– –	-1.237***	– –	– –
Real wage index (ln)	[1]^f	[1]	[1]	[1]
Industry funds (NC)	0.499***	0.482***	0.308***	0.490***
Company funds	0.654***	0.648***	0.434***	0.648***
Professional group funds	0.967***	0.959***	0.734***	0.961***
Other funds	0.528***	0.521***	0.342***	0.522***
Pension plan: DC vs DB	-0.053*	-0.054*	-0.016	-0.052*
Pensioners	0.464***	0.444***	0.517***	0.465***
Inactive participants	-0.417***	-0.422***	-0.465***	-0.420***
Assets per 1000 participants	1.480***	1.424***	1.545***	1.466***
Report invest cost	-0.337***	-0.337***	-0.327***	-0.336***
Outsourcing	0.972***	0.968***	0.931***	0.97***
Reinsured	0.001**	0.001**	0.001*	0.001**
Time	0.052***	0.051***	0.050***	0.051***
Intercept	-12.517***	-13.272***	-12.445***	-12.601***
No. of observations	12,521	12,521	12,521	12,521
F-statistic	3149***	2775***	2970***	2957***
R^2, adjusted (%)	71.8	71.8	71.6	71.8
Akaike's IC	38,341	38,331	38,443	38,341
Wald test^a	1045***	532***	1006***	704***
First derivatives^c	$0.716 + 2*\underline{0.021}* (\ln p - \overline{\ln p})$	$0.781 \underline{+ 2}*0.013 (\ln p - \overline{\ln p}) - 2.495/ (\ln p)^2 + 2*1.237/(\ln p)^3$	$0.748 – 2.502/p$	$0.726 + 2*\underline{0.019} (\ln p - \overline{\ln p}) - 0.217/ (\ln p)^2$

(*Continued*)

Table 2.2 (Continued)

Variable	Translog	Unrestricted Laurent function	HACD	Simplified ULF
Optimal size (in participants)[d]	768,394	8,048,941	No optimum	1,192,868
Cost elasticity at mean[e]	0.717	0.736	0.748	0.725

Note: *, ** and *** mean significantly different from zero at, respectively, the 90%, 95% and 99% confidence level, while 000 indicates that the Wald test on constant returns to Scale (see footnote [a]) is rejected at the 99% confidence level.

[a] The Wald test regards the Constant Returns to Scale hypothesis: the coefficient of the linear term ln(number of participants) is equal to 1, and the coefficient(s) of the non-linear term(s) is (are) equal to 0;
[b] with p for 'number of participants'. See Section 2.5.1 for details;
[c] see Eq. (2.4–2.6);
[d] the optimal scale is calculated by setting the first derivative equal to one, see Section 2.5.1 for details; [e]. With 'mean' referring to the mean value of the output measure, the number of participants, see Section 2.5.1;
[f] coefficient has been set at 1 (homogeneous price relation).

2.6.1. Translog cost function

We first discuss the results of the three models with respect to the cost-output relationship and then compare them. Subsequently, we consider the coefficients of the other explanatory 936 participants, that is log (936).[20] If the number of participants increases by 1%, total administrative costs will increase by only 0.72%. This implies huge scale economies of 28%.

The cost elasticity is higher here than the 0.64 found by Bikker and de Dreu (2009) for the Netherlands over 1992–2004, which means that the extent of scale economies is lower, while the opposite is true when comparing to the 0.76 of Bikker *et al.* in Chapter 3 found in a four-country comparison over 2004–2008,[21] and the 0.82 of Alserda *et al.* (2017) using data over 2002–2013. The relationship between administrative costs and total participants is concave (coefficient of the squared term is 0.021): scale economies are almost twice as large for the very small pension funds (compared to the 28% mean), while they disappear entirely for large pension funds. The concavity is less pronounced than in Bikker and de Dreu (2009), where the coefficient of the squared term was twice as large at 0.04. Fig. 2.4 shows the plotted cost elasticity curve against pension fund size, which is a straight line in this semi-log graph. It is remarkable how small the corresponding confidence band is (not included in Fig. 2.4 for the sake of clarity), reflecting the dominant impact of scale economies. The optimal-size number of participants in a pension fund is 768,000 participants, with a 95% confidence band as wide as 368,000–1,939,000. In 2009, and later years, the Dutch pension sector had only six pension funds, which were larger than this optimal size and (hence) no longer operated under economies of scale (12 pension funds have more than 368,000 participants and two more than 1,939,000). Of course, for the assessment of optimal size and (dis)economies of scale we have to take the criticisms against the TCF into account.

2.6.2. Unrestricted Laurent cost function

The unrestricted Laurent cost function (ULF) differs from the translog function by having two additional reciprocal output terms, which are able to adjust (or generalize) the U-shaped or parabolic average costs of the TCF. Column 2 in Table 2.2 shows that both reciprocal terms are significant at the 1% level (possibly due to multicollinearity, see below). Note that the concavity term (the squared output term) is still significant, so that some support remains for the U-shaped cost curve. But the cost elasticity curve becomes flatter for pension funds with more participants (see Fig. 2.4), implying a flatter right leg of the U-shaped average-cost curve. At the same time, the cost elasticity at the mean is – at 0.736 – slightly higher than according to the TCF. The optimal scale is estimated at 8 million participants, which is much higher than the optimal scale according to the TCF (768,394 participants). This would imply that, according to the ULF, no pension fund in the Netherlands is larger than this optimal-size estimate.

2.6.3. HACD model

The third cost function considered is the HACD model, see Column 3 in Table 2.2. This model represents the monotonically decreasing (or non-increasing) average-cost function. The cost elasticity is equal to 0.75 for pension funds with 5,000 participants or more, and smaller for smaller pension funds, *e.g.* below 0.5 for ten participants (see Fig. 2.4). Hence, we find unused scale economies of 25% for larger funds and larger *SE* for smaller funds.

To compare the estimated administrative cost models, we use the Akaike IC (AIC). The ULF reaches its lowest value at 38,331, but failed the VIF test. Our

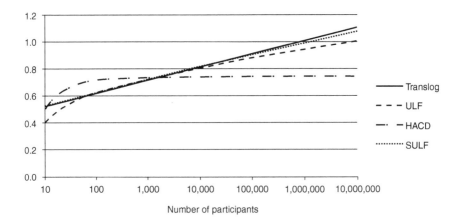

Figure 2.4 Cost elasticity and optimal scale in the administration costs model

solution is to simplify the model by deleting the second reciprocal term. This simplified ULF (SULF) and the TCF have AIC values at an equally low level (38,341), while the HACD's AIC, at 38,443, is 'significantly' higher, so that the HACD model appears to be less well-suited. Though the TCF and SULF models are highly similar in terms of goodness of fit (AIC and adjusted R^2), their corresponding optimal sizes differ: 0.8 million versus 1.2 million participants. This result supports our approach of using various cost-output models in order to reveal the underlying uncertainty about the true value of the optimal size. Moreover, it makes clear how sensitive the optimal size is for specification choices.

2.6.4. Other determinants of administrative costs

We now discuss the estimates of the other explanatory variables, stemming from the simplified ULF, which has an *ex aequo* low AIC. Note, however, that the estimated coefficients hardly vary across the four functional forms: none of the coefficients change signs and their magnitudes and significance levels hardly change. The real wage index and time are highly correlated (0.96) and do not pass the VIF test on multicollinearity, so that we cannot estimate both coefficients. In line with the standard hypothesis of price homogeneity, we set the coefficient of the wage index at 1. Four pension fund type dummies reflect type-related variation in cost efficiency, where 'compulsory industry funds' – the category with the largest number of participants – acts as reference category. Hence, the dummy variables for non-compulsory (NC) industry funds, company funds, professional group funds and other funds measure the cost-level difference with compulsory industry funds. Apparently, all four governance types are significantly more expensive in both economic and statistical terms than compulsory industry funds (after controlling for other determinants), with NC industry funds having 63% higher costs (0.63 = exp (0.490) – 1), while company funds (+91%) and professional group funds (+161%) are even more expensive. Industry funds tend to offer relatively straightforward (standard) pension plans, leading to lower costs, while many company funds and professional group funds offer more tailor-made pension schemes, which may show up in higher costs (Chapter 3). Furthermore, industry funds may face fewer transfers of accrued pension rights, because employees often stay in the same industry if they switch jobs, resulting in little additional costs for the pension fund. The cost differences are smaller than in Bikker and de Dreu (2009) for 1992–2004 and higher than in Alserda *et al.* (2017): apparently they decline over time.

On average, DC pension plans tend to have lower costs than DB schemes, but the effect is not significant at the 5% level. With respect to participants, we consider active and inactive participants and retirees. Pensioners imply 59% higher costs, compared to active participants (the reference category), possibly due to the payout of pension benefits and increased communication. Inactive participants go with 52% lower costs, which is plausible as 'sleeping' pensions are less subject to changes and need less communication, et cetera. Costs increase significantly with assets per participant, arguably because administrative costs may go up (somewhat) with total assets. An alternative explanation is that pension funds with more wealthy participants – in terms of per capita total assets – increase luxury or face higher costs due to managerial complexity; see Section 2.1.

Some pension funds report zero investment costs, which is highly unlikely to be accurate. A part of them report net investment returns instead of gross ones, coupled with investment costs. Others may include (part of) their investment costs in the administrative costs. Our dummy variable 'pension funds reporting investment costs' tests the latter suspicion. The significantly negative coefficient leads to the conclusion that some pension funds do, in fact, include investment costs in administrative costs. The positive coefficient of outsourcing of administration shows that outsourcing indicates significantly higher costs. Logically, one would expect that outsourcing reduces costs, because specialized companies exploit their larger scale, offsetting their profit margin. In practice, particularly for company pension funds, the sponsor company bears part of the administrative costs, which will thus not show up in the bookkeeping of the pension fund. Outsourcing makes such costs visible, hence the positive coefficient.

Whether a pension fund is partly or fully reinsured does not affect administrative costs significantly at the 5% level (except under the HACD model), but the economic impact is negligible. Costs increase over time, controlled for all other determinants, which may reflect an increase in accounting and supervisory requirements. The increase may also be caused by improved reporting of administrative costs over time. In any case, such effects dominate any cost-saving technical progress, *e.g.* in the area of IT and communication systems (Konings *et al.*, 2002; Chatterton *et al.*, 2010).

2.6.5. *Optimal scale estimates for individual years*

The regression results on the full dataset in Table 2.2 presents averages over 1992–2009. In order to obtain additional information about the developments over time, we re-estimate the cost models for each of the 18 years separately, and we do this for each of the three considered functional forms (Table 2.3).[22] For the same reason as above, when solving the multicollinearity problem, we simplify the ULF. Because the dummy and control variables are not especially relevant for the analysis on scale economies and optimal scale, they are neither reported in Table 2.3 nor discussed in the text.

During the years 1992–1997 the optimal pension fund size according to the translog cost function varied between 24,000 and 36,000 participants, implying that larger pension funds (representing 3% of the respective samples) faced diseconomies of scale and were less efficient than smaller pension funds. For the simplified ULF, these ranges are between 21,000 and 45,000 participants. For the HACD model Table 2.3 shows scale economies only, because this model does not indicate an optimal scale. Because the optimal scale estimate depends on the observations of the largest pension funds, we re-estimated our model with weighted least squares (where the weight is the square root of the number of participants), in order to attach more weight to the largest observations. Fig. 2.5 shows that the

Table 2.3 Scale economies and optimal scale of pension funds' administration by year

Year	Geometric mean of participant	# Observations	Costs per participant (€)	Costs per participant (euro 2000)	Translog cost function				Simplified ULM						HACD			
					Cost elasticity participants	Coeff. of squared term[a]	Optimal size (x 1,000)	Log likelihood	Cost elasticity participants	Coeff. ln participants	Coeff. of squared term[a]	Coeff. of reciprocal term[a]	Optimal size (x 1,000)	Log likelihood	Cost elasticity participants	Coeff. ln participants	Coeff. of reciprocal term	Log likelihood
1992	469	759	25.5	30.5	0.65	0.04[3]	33	−1,239	0.64	0.70	0.04[3]	−0.31	44	−1,239	0.71	0.71	3.27	−1,251
1993	478	792	26.0	30.4	0.67	0.04[3]	31	−1,288	0.67	0.66	0.04[3]	−0.13	29	−1,288	0.73	0.73	3.53	−1,298
1994	513	788	29.5	33.6	0.67	0.04[3]	36	−1,263	0.68	0.69	0.03[3]	0.32	45	−1,263	0.74	0.74	3.78	−1,272
1995	534	789	30.4	33.8	0.69	0.04[3]	24	−1,265	0.70	0.70	0.04[3]	0.23	27	−1,265	0.76	0.76	3.88	−1,275
1996	590	786	34.6	37.8	0.70	0.04[3]	29	−1,261	0.69	0.68	0.04[3]	−0.45	24	−1,260	0.75	0.75	2.62	−1,273
1997	639	776	34.8	37.2	0.76	0.03[3]	33	−1,216	0.74	0.72	0.04[3]	−0.89[1]	21	−1,214	0.79	0.79	1.32	−1,226
1998	679	784	44.3	46.4	0.73	0.03[3]	53	−1,253	0.72	0.72	0.03[3]	−0.34	43	−1,253	0.77	0.77	2.28	−1,261
1999	781	754	43.0	44.1	0.74	0.03[3]	105	−1,164	0.74	0.74	0.03[3]	0.01	106	−1,164	0.77	0.77	2.43	−1,170
2000	898	768	46.0	46.0	0.73	0.02[3]	310	−1,159	0.73	0.72	0.02[3]	−0.20	230	−1,159	0.76	0.76	2.07	−1,164
2001	1022	756	47.7	45.8	0.70	0.01[1]	>>[b]	−1,156	0.69	0.67	0.02[2]	−0.89	3,100	−1,155	0.71	0.71	0.09	−1,158
2002	1188	719	49.6	46.1	0.71	0.01[2]	>>	−1,068	0.71	0.71	0.02[1]	−0.11	>>[b]	−1,068	0.73	0.73	1.29	−1,070
2003	1339	694	51.5	46.9	0.73	0.01[1]	>>	−973	0.74	0.74	0.01	0.18	>>	−973	0.75	0.75	1.66	−974
2004	1556	647	48.0	43.2	0.71	0.01	>>	−865	0.72	0.74	0	0.62	>>	−865	0.73	0.73	1.80	−865
2005	1669	643	52.9	46.8	0.76	0.00	>>	−889	0.77	0.78	0	0.63	NO[c]	−889	0.77	0.77	1.07	−889
2006	1863	590	54.8	47.9	0.73	0.00	>>	−813	0.75	0.76		0.76	NO	−812	0.75	0.75	1.41	−813
2007	2186	542	52.9	45.5	0.68	0.00	>>	−648	0.66	0.64	0.01	−1.23	NO	−648	0.67	0.67	−0.43	−649
2008	2515	490	58.8	49.4	0.67	0.01	>>	−606	0.67	0.67	0	0.20	NO	−606	0.67	0.67	0.94	−607
2009	2981	444	62.1	51.5	0.66	0.01[1]	>>	−538	0.68	0.69	0.01	0.94	>>	−537	0.69	0.69	3.02	−538
Avgs	936				0.71				0.71						0.74			
Sum		12,521						−18,665						−18,657				−18,752

Note: 'Euro 2000' stands for: in prices of 2000. [a] Super indices 1, 2 and 3 in the column 'Coefficient of squared term' under Translog cost model indicate significance levels of, respectively, 10%, 5% and 1%; [b] '>>' means larger than 10 million participants; [c] 'NO' means: no optimum exists.

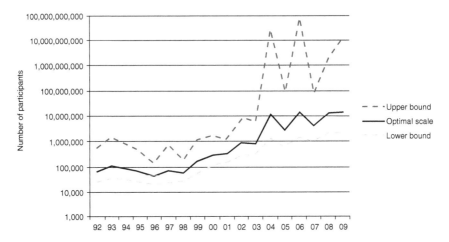

Figure 2.5 Optimal scale in the 'weighted' administrative cost model over time with confidence bands

optimal scale over 1992–1998 then is estimated at 50,000–100,000 participants, rising to 1 million in 2002–2003 and up to 5–10 million in the last years. The 95% confidence band is wide, but the upward trend is clear cut. This implies that, in 2009, each pension fund would save costs after growing or merging. The outcome reflects that over time fixed costs have increased more than proportionally. Additional supervisory and other regulation and information technology have contributed to that.

The estimated cost elasticities for the mean pension fund size show a similar pattern for all considered cost functions: fluctuation somewhat around 0.71 (TCF and ULF) or around 0.74 (HACD), rising somewhat to a higher level during 1997–2005, and sliding back in recent years. This implies that the average scale economies at the geometric mean did not fundamentally shift over time, where that mean of course shifts from almost 500 participants in 1992 to 3,000 participants in 2009. This implies that the functional forms of the TCF and the ULF in Fig. 2.4 (and the underlying unit cost function) shift over time to the right, so that the optimal scale increases. Without consolidation of the pension sector, the unused scale economies would not have remained constant, but would have increased.

2.7. Empirical results for the investment cost model

This section focuses on investment costs, which consist of portfolio management, financial research, trading facilities and advice costs. Transaction fees, brokerage fees and management fees of mutual funds are not included, as they are normally already deducted from the investment returns. As for the administrative costs investigation, a number of different costs functions will be used to estimate the scale economies. The translog function for investment costs reads as:

$$IC_{it} = \alpha + \beta_1\left(lntotal\ assets_{it}\right) + \beta_2(lntotal\ assets_{it} - \overline{\ln total\ assets})^2$$
$$+ \gamma_1 lnreal\ wage_t + \gamma_2\ governance\ dummies_{it}$$
$$+ \gamma_3 pension\ plan\ design_{it} + \gamma_4 type\ of\ participants_{it}$$
$$+ \gamma_5 assets\ per\ participants_{it} + \gamma_6 reinsurance_{it}$$
$$+ \gamma_7 asset\ allocation + \gamma_8 time_t + \varepsilon_{it} \tag{2.8}$$

The unrestricted Laurent model is based on Eq. (2.8) extended by β_3 (1/ln *total assets*) + β_4 (1/(ln *total assets*) ^{2}), while the HACD cost model is equal to Eq. (2.8) where the second term has been replaced by β_2 (1/ *total assets*). Unlike in Eq. (2.7) for administrative costs, we here use 'total assets' as output measure instead of 'number of participants'. Furthermore, we delete 'outsourcing of administration' and 'reporting of investment costs' as explanatory variables and we add 'assets allocation'. Assets allocation consists of the shares of the following asset categories: stocks, real estate, private equity, commodities, hedge funds and other assets, all as percentage of total investments. The share of bonds acts as the reference category. The coefficients of these variables represent by approximation the risk-management costs of the respective investment category, compared to that of bonds. Riskier investments cause higher investment costs due to more research, complicated transactions and extra risk management, while also having higher expected returns (Bauer *et al.*, 2010).

2.7.1. Empirical results for 1992–2009

This section displays the results of the three different cost functions for the entire data sample consisting of 7,109 annual non-zero observations of pension funds, while the next section presents results for each of the 18 years separately. The upper panel of Table 2.4 shows the regression results for the three cost functions, while the lower panel displays a possible optimal scale and the cost elasticities at the mean values for investment costs. The first derivative is used to calculate those factors.

2.7.1.1 Translog cost function

The investment cost elasticity at the (geometric) mean – of € 80 million – is 0.88. The Wald test rejects the constant returns to scale hypothesis (cost elasticity is 1, quadratic effect is 0) at the 1% significance. Hence, scale economies are important in the investment activities too (at 12%), but much less so than in administrative activities (28%) and also less than during 1992–2004 (22%); see Bikker and de Dreu (2009).[23] Apparently, fixed costs – the origin of scale economies – occur less in investment than in administration. As the squared output term coefficient is significantly different from 0, there is evidence of a concave relationship between

Table 2.4 Estimates of the investment cost model (1992–2009)

Variable	Translog	Unrestricted Laurent function	Simplified ULF	HACD
Ta (in logarithms)	0.880 ***/ooo a	1.515 ***/ooo	1.380 ***/ooo	0.938 ***/ooo
Ta^2 (in ln, mean dev.)	0.028***	−0.021	−0.015**	−
1/ta	−	−	−	655 ***
1/(ln ta)	−	87.186	57.068***	−
1/(ln ta)^2	−	−73.901	−	−
Real wage index (ln)	[1] f	[1]	[1]	[1]
Industry fund (NC)	0.095	0.091	0.093	0.088
Company fund	0.287***	0.290***	0.290***	0.242***
Prof. group fund	0.534***	0.514***	0.515***	0.481***
Other funds	0.349***	0.344***	0.345***	0.338***
Pension plan (DB/ DC)	0.024	0.006	0.006	0.018
Stocks	0.583***	0.558***	0.559***	0.555***
Real estate	1.489***	1.358***	1.362***	1.497***
Private equity	0.129	0.237	0.237	0.330
Commodities	−2.995	−3.420	−3.471*	−3.052
Hedge funds	0.954	1.020	1.023	1.284
Other funds	−0.302**	−0.274**	−0.274**	−0.255*
Pensioners	−0.050	−0.088	−0.087	−0.073
Inactive participants	0.274***	0.288***	0.289***	0.225**
Reinsured	−0.006***	−0.006***	−0.006***	−0.006***
Assets per 1000 partic.	0.090*	0.087	0.089*	0.145**
Time	0.021***	0.020***	0.020***	0.019***
Intercept	−17.420***	−31.717***	−28.103***	−17.936***
No. of obs.	7109	7109	7109	7109
F-statistic	1678 ***	1694 ***	1752 ***	1761 ***
R^2, adjusted	75.6	75.7	75.7	75.6
Akaike's IC	20,990	20,936	20,938	20,993
Wald test a	178 ***	116 ***	161 ***	110 ***
First derivative b	0.880 + 2* 0.028 (ln *t*)	1.515 + 2* 0.021 (ln *t*) − 87.186/(ln *t*)^2 + 2*73.901/(ln *t*)^3	0.84 + 2*0.026 (ln *t*) − 57.068/ (ln *t*)^2	0.938−655/*t*
Optimal scale (assets) c	690 million	565 million	690 million	No optimal point d
Cost elasticity at mean e	0.880	0.935	0.933	0.930

Note: *, ** and *** mean significantly different from zero at, respectively, the 90%, 95% and 99% confidence level, while ooo indicates that the Wald test (see footnote a below) is rejected at the 99% confidence level.

a The Wald test regards the constant returns to scale hypothesis: the coefficient of the linear term ln(total assets) is equal to 1, and the coefficients of the non-linear terms are equal to 0;
b with *t* for 'total assets'. See Section 2.5.1 for details;
c the optimal scale is calculated by setting the first derivative equal to one, see the method section for details;
d according to the HACD model, an optimal scale does not exist;
e with mean referring to the mean value of the output measure, total assets, see Section 2.5.1;
f coefficient has been set at 1 (homogeneous price relation).

investment costs and output size (total assets), implying that small pension funds face higher scale economies and large funds experience lower scale economies. Fig. 2.6 shows the plotted cost elasticity curve against pension fund size, which is a straight rising line in this semi-log graph. An optimal fund size occurs at total assets of € 690 million, with confidence interval € 567–813 million. In 2009, the Dutch pension sector numbers no fewer than 83 pension funds with total assets above € 690 million. We have observed that some pension funds underreport administrative costs, particularly smaller funds. Note that this implies that actual scale economies are likely higher than what we have found, as full reporting would have raised the cost of smaller pension funds further.

2.7.1.2. Unrestricted Laurent function

The two additional reciprocal terms of the unrestricted Laurent cost function are highly correlated (at 0.988) and do not pass the VIF test on multicollinearity. Our solution is to simplify the model by deleting the second reciprocal term (see column 'simplified ULF'). The average scale economies are only 7%. Fig. 2.6 shows that the reciprocal term of the SULF causes additional curvature, confirming the large unused scale economies of pension funds with small portfolios as found by the TCF, but rejecting diseconomies of scale for large pension funds (as does the TCF). The cost elasticity curve just crosses the constant-return-to-scale (CRS) axis (y = 1) at exactly the same point as the TCF (€ 690 million) and later bends back. This outcome suggest that all portfolio sizes above € 690 million are optimal, which makes sense from an economic view. Apparently, the average-cost curve falls gradually for smaller funds, but remains flat after the minimum average-cost level has been reached. The cost elasticity at the geometric mean (€ 80 million) is at 0.93 higher than in the TCF (0.88), but still significantly

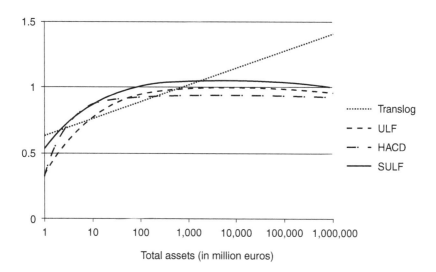

Figure 2.6 Cost elasticity and optimal scale in the investment costs model

different from CRS. Hence, the average scale economies (*SE*) according to the SULF model are 7% instead of 12% (according to the TCF). Of course, the *SE* are larger for smaller funds and virtually zero for larger funds.

2.7.1.3. HACD cost function

The third cost function considered is the HACD model; see Column 3 in Table 2.4. This model represents the monotonically decreasing average-cost function, where an optimal scale, or better, diseconomies of scale, may be absent. The cost elasticity increases to 0.93 at the geometric mean, and up to 0.94 for larger pension funds, again significantly different from CRS; see Fig. 2.6. An optimal scale is absent: unused scale economies of 6% continue to exist for pension funds of any size. Of course, the flexibility of the HACD model is limited.

To compare the estimated investment cost models, we again use the Akaike IC (AIC). Where the TCF and SULF models for administrative costs have a similar AIC value, the (S)ULF for investment cost outperforms the TCF (and HACD) fiercely. Hence, the conclusion is that for investments, scale economies do exist, but decline for larger funds with total assets up to (around) € 690 million and are absent for larger funds.

2.7.1.4. Other determinants of investment costs

We will now discuss the estimates of the other explanatory variables stemming from the SULF. Note, however, that the estimated coefficients hardly vary across the four functional forms: none of the coefficients change signs and their magnitude and significance levels hardly change. As observed above, the real wage index and time are highly correlated. In line with the standard hypothesis of price homogeneity, also here we set the coefficient of the wage index at 1. Three governance types are, in both economic and statistical terms, significantly more expensive than compulsory industry funds (after controlling for other determinants), as has been the case for administrative costs too: company funds having 34% higher investment costs, while other funds (42%) and professional group funds (67%) are even more expensive, roughly in line with Bikker and de Dreu (2009). A convincing explanation is lacking. Bauer *et al.* (2010) and Chatterton *et al.* (2010) expect lower costs for DB plans, as they make more frequent use of asset-liability matching strategies and invest more in fixed-income assets that generally entail lower costs. However, we do not find any difference between DC and DB schemes. Note that the asset allocation variables take any different investment strategies into account.

Fig. 2.3 shows that large funds hold more complex assets with correspondingly higher risk-management costs, while on the other hand, larger pension funds benefit from lower unused scale economies. Therefore we need to disentangle these two size effects. This can be done by including pension fund-specific asset allocation variables for the first size effect and output for the second size effect. The asset allocation variables do, in fact, indicate significantly higher investment research and risk-management costs for the riskier assets. This is most evident for stocks (75% more expensive than bonds) and real estate (290%). It may also hold for private equity and hedge funds, but their coefficients are not statistically significant. Other assets, including money market funds, are significantly less costly than bonds, all in line with expectations. The coefficient of commodities is not significant.

With respect to type of participants, we observe higher investment costs for inactive participants, but a clear explanation is lacking. Reinsurance, *i.e.* full or partial outsourcing of liability and investment risks, reduces investment costs significantly, as expected, but the economic impact is low. Costs increase over time, controlled for all other determinants, which may in part reflect improved reporting of investment costs over time. Of course, investment techniques, research, risk management, technical progress and reporting requirements have all significantly changed over time.

2.7.2. Optimal scale estimates for individual years

The regression results on the full dataset in Table 2.4 present averages over 1992–2009. In order to obtain additional information about the developments over time, we re-estimate each of the three considered investment cost models for each of the 18 years separately (Table 2.5).[24] For the same reason as above, when addressing the multicollinearity problem, we simplify the ULF. Because the dummy and control variables are not especially relevant for the analysis on scale economies and optimal scale, they will not be reported in Table 2.5 nor discussed in the text.

The most remarkable outcome is that the cost elasticity at the (geometric) mean increased over time by around 0.20. Comparing the first and the last five years, the cost elasticity shifted in the TCF from 0.75 to 0.95, in the SULF from 0.80 to 1 and in the HACD from 0.85 to around 1. This means that scale economies for the *average* pension fund were large in the earlier years, but declined or vanished in the later years. This contrasts with the administrative costs, where we observe elasticities and scale economies for the average fund, which are constant over time. We further observe that the coefficient of the squared output term in the TCF remains above 0.01 over the entire sample period, implying that scale economies decline with pension fund size.[25] This, too, contrasts with the administrative costs, where the coefficient of the squared output term ebbed to below 0.002, that is virtually zero, so that scale economies became equal for each size class.

Fig. 2.7 shows the ULF cost curve for three separate years, which represent the trend over time. These curves show that large unused scale economies remain present for small pension funds. For the larger funds, however, the trend indicates a change from diseconomies of scale, via constant returns to scale, towards residual or even increasing scale economies. A remarkable phenomenon shown in Fig. 2.7 is that the flexible ULF mimics the TCF for 1992 and following years, with a clear optimal scale and scale diseconomies for larger funds, while for 1999 and other years in that area, it represents the HACD model with average investment costs declining monotonically and flat cost elasticity, so that scale economies exist for all medium-sized and large pension funds and the level of scale economies is constant. For 2008 and other recent years, the curve bends further, reflecting

Table 2.5 Scale economies and optimal scale of pension fund investments by year

					Translog				Simplified ULF						HACD			
Year	Geometric mean of TA (millions)	# Observations	Cost per million euro of TA	Ditto in euro 2000	Cost elasticity	Coeff. of sqrd. term[a]	Optimal size (x million euros)	Log likelihood	Cost elasticity	Coeff. ln TA	Coeff. of sqrd. term[1]	Coeff. of reciprocal term	Optimal size (x million)	Log likelihood	Cost elasticity TA	Coeff. ln TA	Coeff. ln reciprocal term	Log likelihood
1992	41	231	940	1126	0.78	0.04[3]	649	-325	0.79	0.92	0.03	14	699	-325	0.87	0.87	661	-328
1993	36	272	893	1042	0.79	0.02[1]	2,636	-377	0.81	0.99	0.01	20	10,245	-377	0.86	0.86	584	-377
1994	34	300	713	811	0.74	0.05[3]	519	-444	0.78	1.06	0.02	31	672	-444	0.83	0.83	511	-448
1995	37	317	687	765	0.76	0.03[3]	1,757	-456	0.77	0.81	0.03	5	1,980	-456	0.84	0.84	552	-457
1996	45	337	467	510	0.76	0.03[3]	1,955	-484	0.79	1.06	0.01	31	4,009	-483	0.85	0.85	809	-485
1997	52	359	461	493	0.81	0.03[3]	1,187	-523	0.85	1.16	0.00	36	4,824	-522	0.87	0.87	297	-524
1998	66	408	433	454	0.83	0.02[1]	5,780	-571	0.91	1.50	-0.04	72	NO[b]	-567	0.89	0.90	598	-567
1999	78	410	478	491	0.88	0.01	45,703	-575	0.90	1.06	-0.01	21	NO	-575	0.90	0.90	385	-575
2000	87	447	640	640	0.88	0.02	2,529	-620	0.89	0.98	0.01	12	3,557	-620	0.91	0.91	517	-621
2001	82	477	668	641	0.89	0.01	5,983	-663	0.92	1.27	-0.02	44	NO	-662	0.93	0.93	678	-662
2002	83	462	848	788	0.89	0.01	23,925	-611	0.91	1.15	-0.01	31	NO	-610	0.92	0.92	605	-610
2003	87	482	989	900	0.92	0.02[2]	622	-674	0.94	1.14	0.00	25	572	-673	0.96	0.96	593	-674
2004	94	484	1019	917	0.91	0.03[3]	328	-736	0.93	1.11	0.02	24	275	-736	0.97	0.97	728	-739
2005	109	505	1248	1103	0.94	0.02[1]	553	-740	1.00	1.58	-0.03	78	95	-738	1.00	1.00	943	-739
2006	128	474	1140	997	0.94	0.02[1]	420	-753	1.02	1.75	-0.04	101	79	-750	1.02	1.02	1309	-750
2007	146	423	2097	1805	0.93	0.02[1]	607	-632	1.00	1.54	-0.03	76	152	-630	0.99	0.99	892	-629
2008	157	379	2550	2141	1.00	0.02[2]	171	-551	1.05	1.56	-0.03	72	42	-550	1.04	1.04	766	-550
2009	202	342	1978	1642	0.97	0.02[2]	418	-464	1.02	1.50	-0.03	71	97	-462	1.01	1.01	967	-462
Avgs	80				0.87				0.90						0.93	0.93		
Sum		7,109						-10,199						-10,181				-10,196

Note: TA stands for 'total assets' and 'euro 2000' for: in prices of 2000. [a] Super indices 1, 2 and 3 in the column 'Coefficient of squared term' under "Translog" indicate significance levels of, respectively, 10%, 5% and 1%. [b] 'NO' means: no optimum exists.

monotonically declining average costs, which describes a more complicated cost or production structure: medium-sized pension funds are unable to exploit unused scale economies (as long as they expand by small steps only), while larger pension funds are able to do so. This outcome also illustrates the shortcomings of the TCF, which can produce straight lines only (in this semi-log graph), and of the HACD model, which invariably ends in a horizontal line.

Table 2.5 shows that the optimal-size estimate fluctuates heavily over time, indicating lack of robustness. Given that the TCF may be misleading with respect to optimal scale estimates, we focus on the simplified ULF cost. For most years, the SULF elasticity curve touches the $y = 1$ or CRS axis, but Fig. 2.7 explains that the optimal scale figures may indicate the start of a (possibly ending) optimal scale range. If the curve does not touch the CRS axis, we find 'no optimum' and hence scale economies for all sizes. We conclude that in recent years an optimal scale for investment cost does not exist but that pension funds beyond a certain scale operate under conditions close to CRS.

2.8. Summary and conclusions

This chapter investigates the methodological problem of scale-economy measurement and demonstrates the sensitivity of the cost model's functional form, particularly with respect to determining optimal scale. An underlying question is whether the average costs form a U-shape, which implies existence of an optimal scale, or whether they decline monotonically, so that scale economies continue to exist at any scale. Exploring three different functional forms, we find that the often-used translog cost function has the drawback of assuming an underlying U-shaped average-cost function, as soon as the cost-output relationship becomes non-linear. The hyperbolically adjusted Cobb-Douglas model is also too limited, as it assumes a monotonically decreasing average-cost function throughout. The unrestricted Laurent function (ULF) is more general and able to describe both types of underlying average-cost functions. While the scale-economy estimates for the mean pension funds are quite similar across the three functional forms, the conclusions with respect to an optimal scale diverge widely.

Turning to the empirical results for the superior ULF, the administrative costs model shows that for the average pension fund in the Netherlands significant scale economies (SE) are about 27%. These SE are size dependent: up to 50% and more for small pension funds, but lower or even zero for larger funds. Over time, using annual estimates, the SE remain fairly constant. An optimal scale over the entire sample period is estimated at somewhat above 1 million participants, but it is much lower over 1992–1999 and increases during subsequent years to a scale above that of the largest Dutch pension fund. This suggests that average administrative costs per participant now decline without limit.

For investment costs, the picture is different. First, the SE are small at 7% for the average pension fund. The SE are larger for smaller funds and declining to zero for larger funds. The optimal scale is reached around a portfolio size of € 690 million, while larger funds remain equally cost efficient. If we focus on annual estimates, we find that the optimal scale does not shift over time, in contrast

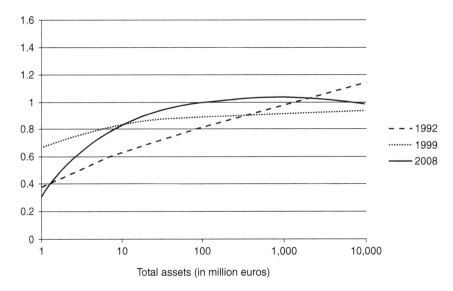

Figure 2.7 Cost elasticity and optimal scale in the simplified ULF of investment costs

to administrative cost where the optimal scale increases over time. The optimal scale estimate of investment costs fluctuates heavily over time, pointing to lack of robustness. For investment costs it is important to consider the asset allocation as well since, particularly in recent years, large pension funds invest more in risky assets which go with higher risk-management costs. Ignoring this size effect would affect the scale-economy measurement: stocks and real estate do indeed carry significant higher costs than *e.g.* bonds.

Annual operational costs have a huge impact on future pension fund benefits, because they erode pension wealth year after year. This effect is stronger the lower the returns are. Reducing such costs as much as possible should be an important policy for every pension fund. Consolidation among smaller pension funds would greatly benefit their cost efficiency. We also observe huge cost differences within each size class, with potential great possibilities to reduce costs. So, particularly for administrative activities, we find significantly higher costs for company funds and professional group funds compared to industry funds (controlled for size, et cetera), though decaying somewhat over time. Other, more idiosyncratic causes of cost difference require further investigation.

Notes

1   Update of: J.A. Bikker, 2013, *Is there an optimal pension fund size? A scale-economy analysis of administrative and investment costs*, DNB Working Paper no. 376, De Nederlandsche Bank, Amsterdam. Parts of this Working paper have been rewritten and published as J.A. Bikker, 2017, Is there an optimal pension fund size? A scale-economy analysis of administrative costs, Journal of Risk and Insurance 84 (2), 739-770. The author is grateful to Dirk Broeders and Paul Cavelaars for useful comments and Ingeborg Bikker for mathematical advice.

2 An update of these estimates with a focus on X-efficiency can be found in Alserda *et al.* (2017).

3 Note that the dataset in this study contains pure economic costs.

4 Caswell (1976), Bateman and Mitchell (2004), Dobronogov and Murthi (2005) and Mitchell and Andrews (1981) use total costs. Only James *et al.* (2001) report separate statistics on investment fees for some individual account pension schemes.

5 Mutual fund expenses and investment costs of pension funds are different. Pension funds have little if any marketing costs and administration costs are reported separately. Also, pension funds have to take the duration of their investment portfolio into account, given their liabilities. Further, mutual funds often focus on investments in one asset class (*e.g.* stocks, bonds), while pension funds generally invest in various asset classes.

6 Lakonishok *et al.* (1992) report that the pension-fund industry has consistently under-performed the market. The authors put forward that pension-fund managers may trade too much, incurring large execution and transaction costs, and may be unlucky with their timing.

7 A DB pension fund pays a defined annual amount to the participant at retirement, often a percentage of the average (or, in earlier years, final) wage. Alternatively, a DC participant pays a defined annual premium while working and the pension payout is based on premiums and investment returns.

8 Collective labour agreements do not always attain the legally compulsory industry-wide status and if attained, this status expires if the investment returns on pension assets do not meet minimum levels.

9 Borders of the size classes are, in terms of number of participants: 280, 525, 850, 1,300, 1,900, 3,000, 5,000, 11,000 and 35,000.

10 Mitchell (1998) observed the same phenomenon in Australia.

11 Borders of the size classes, in terms of total assets, are at 15, 35, 55, 85, 140, 210, 350, 650 and 1,750 million euros.

12 We expect that some of the funds that do not report (all) investment costs include them (in part) in their administrative costs. To test this assumption – and to correct for such misreporting – we define a dummy variable 'reporting of investment costs', with 1 for pension funds with positive investment costs and 0 for non-reporting funds, as an explanatory variable in the administration costs model. A negative coefficient would indicate, and roughly correct for, misreporting.

13 It may also reflect a higher level of asset accumulation, associated with a more mature fund.

14 For shortcomings of the TCF, see Shaffer (1998, p. 91).

15 White (1980) and Shaffer (1998, p. 95) explain that this specification also helps to avoid multicollinearity. Note that $\overline{\ln o}$ is the arithmetic average of the *logarithms* of output measure o_i.

16 To simplify the presentation, we do not include the price index in Eq. (2.1). Normally, a TCF would also include cross terms between output and input prices. Dropping input prices and other output measures implies that no cross terms remains.

17 Except possibly over limited ranges of scale within which marginal costs are steeply declining.

18 For the reciprocal terms in the ULF we replace ln *o* by the geometric mean of the output term. For the reciprocal term in the HACD model, arguments (to replace *o*) exist for both the geometric and arithmetic mean. This choice has no further consequences.

19 Three hundred and thirty-six pension funds are legal vehicles for directors – large share-holders and director funds for board members and supervisory board members with only one participant. They have been deleted as these pension funds are not representative and, moreover, their size would not fit into the inverse terms of the ULF (which would, respectively, be equal to 1/ln(0) and its square) and the HACD (which would be 1/0).

20 Pension funds with one participant have been excluded. The arithmetic mean is 19,991 participants. See Eq. (2.4–2.6) for the cost elasticities of the three models. The cost

elasticity in the TCF is equal to the coefficient of its linear output term. In general, this does not hold for the HACD model, except in our sample where the non-linear output coefficient is (at 2.502) small compared to the arithmetic average number of participants (19,991).
21 In their sample of large pension funds, these authors did find the same cost elasticity (0.69) for the Netherlands.
22 Note that the real wage index and 'time' need to be dropped in the annual models.
23 Broeders *et al.* (2016) estimate the impact of size on cost too, but their results cannot be expressed in (comparable) scale economies estimates, as their model is not log-linear.
24 Note that the real wage index and 'time' need to be dropped in the annual models.
25 Though not significantly different from zero during 1998–2002 and in some of the later years, see Table 2.5. For the administrative cost model, the significance ended completely after 2002; see Table 2.3.

References

Adanu, K., J. Hoehn, E. Iglesias, 2009, *Cost Function Estimation in the Water Industry – Functional Forms and Efficiency Measures*, essay 3, Department of Agricultural Economics, presented at the 2009 USDA-CSREES National Water Conference, St. Louis, MO (February), and at the First Annual Graduate Academic Conference Michigan State University, East Lansing (March).

Akaike, H., 1974, A new look at the statistical model identification, *IEEE Transactions on Automatic Control* 19, 716–723.

Alserda, G., J.A. Bikker, S.G. van der Lecq, 2017, X-efficiency and economies of scale in pension fund administration and investment, *DNB Working Paper* No. 547, De Nederlandsche Bank, Amsterdam.

Ambachtsheer, K., 2010, Future directions in measuring the financial performance of pension funds: a roundtable discussion, in: R. Hinz, R. Heinz, P. Antolin, J. Yermo (eds.), *Evaluating the Financial Performance of Pension Funds*, World Bank, Washington, DC.

Andonov, A., R. Bauer, K.J.M. Cremers, 2012, Can large pension funds beat the market? Decomposing the performance of pension funds into asset allocation, market timing and security selection components, *Netspar Discussion Papers* DP 10/2012–2062, Network for Studies on Pensions, Aging and Retirement, Tilburg.

Bateman, H., O.S. Mitchell, 2004, New evidence on pension plan design and administrative expenses: the Australian experience, *Journal of Pension Economics and Finance* 3, 63–76.

Bateman, H., S. Valdés-Prieto, 1999, *The Mandatory Private Old Age Income Schemes of Australia and Chile: A Comparison*, Mimeograph, University of New South Wales (Published as book in 2000, ISBN 13: 9780733416958).

Bauer, R., K.J.M. Cremers, R.G.P. Frehen, 2010, Pension fund performance and costs: small is beautiful, *MPRA Paper* No. 23556, Tilburg University.

Bikker, J.A., J. de Dreu, 2009, Operating costs of pension funds: the impact of scale, governance, and plan design, *Journal of Pension Economics and Finance* 8, 63–89.

Bikker, J.A., L. Spierdijk, R.P.M.M. Hoevenaars, P.J. van der Sluis, 2008, Forecasting market impact costs and identifying expensive trades, *Journal of Forecasting* 27, 21–39.

Bikker, J.A., L. Spierdijk, P.J. van der Sluis, 2007, Market impact costs of institutional equity trades, *Journal of International Money and Finance* 26, 974–1000.

Bikker, J.A., L. Spierdijk, P.J. van der Sluis, 2010, What factors increase the risk of incurring high market impact costs?, *Applied Economics* 42, 369–387.

Broeders, D., A. van Oord, D. Rijsbergen, 2016, Scale economies in pension fund investments: a dissection of investment costs across asset classes, *Journal of International Money and Finance* 67, 147–171.

Canback, S., P. Samouel, D. Price, 2006, Do diseconomies of scale impact firm size and performance?, *Journal of Managerial Economics* 4, 27–70.

Caswell, J. W., 1976, Economic efficiency in pension plan administration: a study of the construction industry, *Journal of Risk and Insurance* 4, 257–273.

Chatterton, M., E. Smyth, K. Darby, 2010, Pension scheme administrative costs, *Working Paper* No. 91, Department for Work and Pensions, London.

Christensen, L. R., W. H. Greene, 1976, Economies of scale in US electric power generation, *Journal of Political Economy* 84, 655–676.

Coelli, T. J., D. S. Prasada Rao, and G. E. Battese (1998) An Introduction to Efficiency and Productivity Analysis. Boston: Kluwer Academic Publishers.

Collins, S., P. Mack, 1997, The optimal amount of assets under management in the mutual fund industry, *Financial Analyst Journal* 53, 67–73.

Dietsch, M., 1993, Economies of scale and scope in French commercial banking industry, *The Journal of Productivity Analysis* 4, 35–50.

Dobronogov, A., M. Murthi, 2005, Administrative fees and costs of mandatory private pensions in transition economies, *Journal of Pension Economics and Finance* 4, 31–55.

Dyck, A., L. Pomorski, 2011, *Is Bigger Better? Size and Performance in Pension Plan Management*, https://www-2.rotman.utoronto.ca/facbios/file/Is_Bigger_Better_dyck_pomorski.pdf (accessed May 16, 2017).

Edirisuriya, P., G. O'Brien, 2001, Financial deregulation and economies of scale and scope: evidence from the major Australian banks, *Asia-Pacific Financial Markets* 8, 197–214.

Griffin, D., A. Tversky, 1992, The weighing of evidence and the determinants of confidence, *Cognitive Psychology* 24, 411–435.

Hernandez, D. G., F. Stewart, 2008, Comparison of costs + fees in countries with private defined contribution pension system, *Working Paper* No. 6, International Organization of Pension Supervisors (IOPS), www.iopsweb.org/Working%20Paper%206%20(Costs%20and%20fees)%20Formatte (accessed May 16, 2017).

Indro, D. C., C. X. Jiang, M. Y. Hu, W. Y. Lee, 1999, Mutual fund performance: does fund size matter?, *Financial Analysts Journal* 55, 74–87.

Ippolito, R. A., 1989, Efficiency with costly information: a study of mutual fund performance, 1965–1984, *Quarterly Journal of Economics* 54, 1–23.

James, E., J. Smalhout, D. Vittas, 2001, Administrative costs and the organization of individual retirement account systems: a comparative perspective, in: R. Holzmann, J. Stiglitz (ed.), *New Ideas About Old Age Security*, World Bank, Washington, DC; revised version published in *Private Pensions Systems: Administrative Costs and Reforms*, Paris, OECD.

Jensen, M. C., 1968, The performance of mutual funds in the period 1945–1964, *The Journal of Finance* 23, 389–416.

Koeleman, W.J.J., J.J.B. de Swart, 2007, *Kosten en baten van ondernemingspensioenfondsen* (In Dutch; Cost and benefits of company pension funds), PricewaterhouseCoopers (PWC), Amsterdam, http://docplayer.nl/6898369-Kosten-en-baten-van-ondernemingspensioenfondsen.html (accessed May 16, 2017).

Konings, J., F. Roodhooft, 2002, The effect of e-business on corporate performance: firm level evidence for Belgium, *De Economist* 150, 569–581.

Lakonishok, J., A. Schleifer, R. W. Vishny, 1992, The structure and performance of the money management industry, *Brookings Papers on Economic Activity: Microeconomics*, 339–391.

Malhotra, D. K., V. B. Marisetty, M. Ariff, 2001, Economies of scale in retail superannuation funds in Australia, *Working Paper*, Monash University.

Malhotra, D. K., R. W. Mcleod, 1997, An empirical analysis of mutual fund expenses, *The Journal of Financial Research* 20, 175–190.

Malkiel, B. G., 1995, Returns from investing in equity mutual funds 1971 to 1991, *The Journal of Finance* 50, 549–572.

McKenna, F. W., Y. H. Kim, 1986, Managerial risk preferences, real pension costs, and long-run corporate pension fund investment policy, *The Journal of Risk and Insurance* 53, 29–48.

Mitchell, O. S., 1998, *Administrative Costs in Public and Private Retirement Systems*, University of Chicago Press, Chicago.

Mitchell, O. S., E. S. Andrews, 1981, Scale economies in private multi-employer pension systems, *Industrial and Labor Relations Review* 34, 522–530.

Nauriyal, B. B., 1995, Measures of cost economies in Chilean banking: 1984–1991, *Revista de analisis economico* 10, 71–99.

Shaffer, S., 1998, Functional forms and declining average costs, *Journal of Financial Services Research* 14, 91–115.

Swank, J., 1996, How stable is the multiproduct translog cost function? Evidence from the Dutch banking industry, *Kredit und Kapital* 29, 153–172.

Sy, W., 2007, Cost, performance and portfolio composition of small APRA funds, *Working Paper*, Australian Prudential Regulation Authority, Sydney.

Tapia, W., J. Yermo, 2008, Fees in individual account pension systems: a cross-country comparison, *OECD Working Papers on Insurance and Private Pensions* No. 27.

White, H., 1980, Using least squares to approximate unknown regression functions, *International Economic Review* 21, 149–170.

Whitehouse, E., 2000, Administrative charges for funded pensions: an international comparison and assessment, pension reform primer series, *Social Protection Discussion Paper* No. 16, World Bank, Washington, DC.

3 The impact of scale, complexity and service quality on the administrative costs of pension funds[1]

A cross-country comparison

Jacob A. Bikker, Onno W. Steenbeek and Federico Torracchi

3.1. Introduction

Pension reforms, which have been at the centre of the policy debates for many years, have gained even more urgency as a result of the credit crisis. Retirement savings are one of the most important assets for the majority of people in developed countries, and a well-functioning, low-cost system is therefore crucial. Although there is no consensus on what constitutes an optimal pension system, most policymakers acknowledge the importance of cost efficiency in pension provision. Even small differences in administrative costs can have a large impact on the net rate of return on pension contributions. Costs directly affect the extent to which the intended objective of providing adequate income for retirees can be attained. Although studies on administrative costs incurred by pension funds are available, their number is limited in comparison to their topic's importance.

Administrative costs deserve greater research scrutiny, since they account for a very large portion of operational costs (Mitchell, 1998). However, difficulties in specifying the correct pension fund production function and the limited availability of data have hindered detailed empirical work on this topic. Moreover, so far all empirical studies on economies of scale in pension fund administration did not have quantitative data on service quality and the complexity of pension plans which could be included in the cost function. Koeleman and De Swart (2007) argue that smaller funds offer a more expensive albeit more personalized service. Besides, customers benefit when they can choose among more flexible, customized and varied services, even though these require a more sophisticated and costly administration. According to Koeleman and De Swart (2007), differences in administrative costs are due not only to scale economies, but also to higher service quality and the more complex underlying business model of smaller funds. Where Koeleman and De Swart had no data to support their view, our dataset enables us to test this hypothesis.

This chapter uses a unique and detailed dataset for pension funds from four countries, Australia, Canada, the Netherlands and the US, covering the period 2004–2008, to shed light on a number of important questions related to administrative costs. First, we explore whether economies of scale in pension fund administration exist. If this is the case, pension fund participants can benefit from increasing the operational scale of pension funds, thereby lowering average administrative costs. A related question is whether the cost-size relation is concave, that is, whether an optimal scale exists with economies of scale for smaller pension funds and diseconomies of scale for larger ones. Second, we analyze the impact on administrative costs of service quality and the complexity of the pension plan. Third, we assess cost differences across pension fund types and pension plan types, pointing to possible systematic inefficiencies. Fourth, we explore cross-country differences and quantify the possible effects of institutional differences on costs, while controlling for a variety of factors. Finally, we focus on each of the specific disaggregated administrative operations and assess whether economies of scale are present, to establish where scale upgrading would realize the largest benefits. The dataset we use does not contain investment cost. Investment costs contribute also to scale economies (Bikker and de Dreu, 2009; Broeders *et al.*, 2016; Alserda *et al.*, 2017), although the estimation of the scale effect is impaired by the additional cost of the complex investment products held mainly by larger pension funds. Investment costs are not affected by the service level or complexity of pension plans.

The remainder of this chapter is as follows. Section 3.2 reviews the existing literature on the administrative costs of pension funds, with particular emphasis on cross-country comparisons. Section 3.3 discusses and compares the main institutional features of the pension system in the four countries in our sample. Section 3.4 describes the dataset, reveals characteristics of pension funds and explores the relations between administrative costs, pension plan complexity and service quality on the one hand and size on the other. Section 3.5 presents the models used in the empirical analysis for two pension fund output measures, and discusses the empirical results. Finally, Section 3.6 recapitulates and draws policy recommendations.

3.2. Review of the literature

Administrative costs include all expenses to operate the pension fund except investment costs, that is, personnel costs, costs charged by third parties, rent, depreciation and so on. The administration of pension funds comprises data and contributions from employers (including record-keeping), communication with participants, policy development and compliance with reporting and supervisory requirements. Table 3.A.1 in Appendix 3.1 provides a list of administrative activities and their costs. Research on pension funds' administrative costs has focused on a few countries, in particular Australia (Bateman and Valdés-Prieto, 1999; Malhotra *et al.*, 2001; Bateman and Mitchell, 2004; Sy, 2007), the US (Caswell, 1976; Mitchell and Andrews, 1981), Chile (James *et al.*, 2001) and the Netherlands (Bikker and de Dreu, 2009; Alserda *et al.*, 2017). In all these countries, significant economies of scale were found for private pension funds whether size has been measured as number of participants or as assets under management. The main explanation is that most administrative activities from Table 3.A.1 in

Appendix 3.1 have some elements of fixed costs which, when spread among participants, reduce the cost per participant. Particularly information and communication technology, the basis of many activities, has strong fixed-cost components. This also holds for compliance with accounting and regulatory requirements and new projects. Ambachtsheer (2010) stresses the role of operational efficiency in optimal pension provision and indicates that more research is necessary on institutional implementation.

Few comparative studies have been done across different countries, and almost none have used a multivariate approach. Whitehouse (2002) compares defined-contribution (DC) schemes in 13 countries. For Latin American countries and Great Britain, the author finds no systematic relation between pension fund size and charges levied (consisting of costs and profit margins), stating that evidence on economies of scale in pension fund administrative costs is inconclusive. In a more recent study, Hernandez and Stewart (2008) compare the charge ratios in 21 countries with private DC schemes. The authors note that charge ratios tend to be lower in countries with fewer providers, thereby concluding that there is some evidence of economies of scale. Tapia and Yermo (2008) conduct a similar analysis for countries in which the pension system is based on individual retirement accounts: Australia, Sweden, and countries in Latin American and Central and Eastern Europe. However, these studies do not distinguish between investment and administrative expenses, and use charge ratios or other measures of fees rather than economic costs. James *et al.* (2001) improve on this last issue by comparing fees and administrative expenses (including investment expenses) in six Latin American countries with pension systems based on individual retirement accounts. The fundamental problem with that body of research is the lack of appropriate data that would allow one to determine the relative contribution of each factor in a multivariate analysis. Instead, the authors use broad descriptive statistics on the domestic pension system to highlight bivariate relationships. Only Dobronogov and Murthi (2005) conduct a multivariate cross-country study, based on a limited number of observations, and find some evidence of economies of scale in pension funds in Croatia, Kazakhstan and Poland.

In general, there are large differences in administrative costs among pension funds. Some of them reflect particular market conditions or institutional environments, while others are due to different degrees of efficiency. Nevertheless, Valdés-Prieto (1994) stresses that a comparison of economic efficiency both among pension funds and across countries is only meaningful if the quality of the services pension funds offer is accounted for. In his qualitative study of Chile, the US, Malaysia and Zambia, Valdés-Prieto (1994) compares the quality of the national pension systems on broad quality dimensions. The author concludes that the variation in service quality across countries might be even higher than the variation in administrative costs. Mitchell (1998) indicates that an empirical estimation of the impact of service quality on the administrative costs of pension funds is very challenging, since it is difficult to measure service quality. This is an important problem, since Chlon (2000) suggests that customers value service quality and the provision of information more highly than the charges they have to pay. This view was confirmed by Koeleman and De Swart (2007) based on a survey among participants.

There may be a difference between the costs that pension funds face and the fees they charge. Since pension funds typically do not seek profit, we would expect the two to coincide. However, privately run programs operating in imperfectly competitive markets (as, for instance, in the US) may enjoy some degree of market power and charge a price higher than production costs. Orszag and Stiglitz (2001) note that the distinction between costs and charges has been implicitly ignored by the academic literature or assumed to be of little relevance. The dataset in this chapter contains pure costs.

3.3. Institutional setting of pension provision schemes across countries

All countries' pension systems rely on a three-pillar structure, although this structure is much more institutionalized in Australia, Canada and the Netherlands than in the US. In Australia, the first pillar is a publicly run system that aims at guaranteeing a minimum income for the elderly. Benefits depend on the level of income retirees receive from other sources and are financed from the general tax revenue. The second pillar is a compulsory, privately run pension program called the superannuation guarantee. This pension program was established in Australia in 1992, when it replaced a voluntary retirement system. Since 2002, employers have been required to save at least 9% of their employees' income, though low-earning workers are excluded from contributing. Workers can invest additional income in a voluntary third pillar comprising individual retirement accounts. Since the government allows employers great freedom to invest in the pension fund of their choice, pension funds differ substantially in terms of scale, plan type, form of management and sponsor type. Plans can be acquired in the retail market or offered by the employer and are either single- or multi-employer plans, called, respectively, corporate and industry plans.

The pension system in Canada is very similar. The first pillar, created in 1952 through the Old Age Security Act, is financed through general taxation and offers a universal flat-rate pension. The second pillar is a compulsory earnings-related social insurance program. Employees earning above a minimum level must contribute 4.95% of their earnings to a centrally administered plan that functions as a partially funded system. Employee contributions are 100% matched by the employer. Benefits depend on the contributor's history, and the program aims at a 25% replacement rate based on average lifetime salary. The Canadian third pillar comprises voluntary occupational and personal pension plans, known, respectively, as occupational registered pension plans and registered retirement savings plans. These registered pension plans can be operated under a trust agreement, under an insurance company contract or under government-consolidated revenue funds for public employees. Most occupational plans are defined-benefit (DB) plans, albeit DC plans are becoming more common in the private sector (refer to Lachance *et al.*, 2003 and Milevski and Promislow, 2004, for more explanation about DB and DC). In 2004, approximately half of the Canadian labour force saved through an occupational plan (Antolin, 2008).

In the Netherlands, the Pensions Act created a first-pillar pay-as-you-go system that entitles anyone above the age of 65 to a basic pension. Since 2013, the retirement age has been moving up gradually to reach 67 and three months in 2022. The second pillar is a so-called quasi-mandatory system: the government itself does not mandate occupational schemes but, in practice, labour agreements ensure that 80% of all occupational plans are mandatory and that more than 90% of the employees are covered (Organization for Economic Co-operation and Development, hereafter OECD, 2007). Both the employer and the employee contribute to funding. Generally, the employer provides around 70% of the pension contributions. A third pillar – encouraged through special tax rules – allows people to invest in individual pension plans.

The US pension system includes a public pension, Social Security, and a means-tested Supplemental Security Income for low-income retirees. Social Security is a pay-as-you-go system financed through a 12.4% payroll tax equally shared between employee and employer. The Supplemental Security Income is financed through the general government budget. Apart from mandatory payroll contributions to Social Security, there is no compulsory occupational or individual pension scheme. The government only mandates minimum standards for pension fund operations contained in the 1974 Employee Retirement Income Security Act and subsequent amendments. Employers or groups of employers are free to set up pension plans for their employees according to their own preferences. In the past, most plans were DB in nature, but today most of them are either DC or a hybrid. One popular plan is the 401(k) scheme, under which employees can retain part of their earnings in an account often partially matched by employers. Lastly, individual accounts known as individual retirement accounts (IRAs) offer an additional vehicle to save for retirement. Voluntary plans are subject to contribution ceilings as well as special tax provisions that encourage savings. At the end of 2005, voluntary occupational pension schemes covered approximately 143 million participants, while individual plans covered 51 million participants (OECD, 2009b).

The institutional features of these four systems differ widely. First, while participation in an occupational scheme is mandatory in Australia and Canada, and, in practice, also in the Netherlands, it is not in the US. Second, average replacement rates are much higher in the Netherlands than in the other countries, although Canada has comparable rates for low-income retirees. Moreover, the replacement rate is flatter under the Dutch system than in the three other countries, where the rate declines faster for higher incomes. Antolin (2008) argues that the mandatory nature of a program and its generosity are important factors in determining participation in a voluntary pension plan. For instance, the enrollment rate in voluntary plans in the US is high, since the second pillar is not compulsory and public pensions are relatively meagre. Furthermore, the combination of a quasi-mandatory second-pillar and high-targeted replacement rates makes the Netherlands one of the few countries – with Australia – in which the total assets of second-pillar pension funds exceed 100% of the annual gross domestic product (hereafter GDP; see Table 3.1). As shown in Table 3.1, the pension contributions as a % of GDP are highest in Australia. However, the figures in Table 3.1 should be taken with caution, because costs are difficult to define uniquely across countries. Furthermore, for some countries, these figures fluctuate heavily over time.

Table 3.1 Pension fund industry overview by country (OECD global pension statistics)[a]

Country		2004	2005	2006	2007	2008	2015[f]
Assets to GDP (%)	Australia	71	80	90	110	92	122
	Canada	48	50	54	62	51	157
	Netherlands	108	122	126	138	114	178
	US	74	74	79	79	58	133
Contributions to GDP (%)[b]	Australia	7.23	7.81	8.80	15.98	9.74	
	Canada	2.30	2.24	2.57	2.56	2.15	
	Netherlands	4.64	4.97	4.44	4.26	4.02	
Operating costs to assets (%)[b,c]	Australia[d,e]	0.31	0.30	0.28	0.27	0.30	
	Canada	0.85	0.64	0.72	0.28	1.38	
	Netherlands	0.77	0.79	0.61	0.55	0.51	
Total number of pension funds[b]	Australia[d]	1,785	1,323	872	575	505	
	Canada	3,816	3,816	5,036	5,036	n.a.	8,876
	Netherlands	843	800	768	713	n.a.	279
	US						685,203

[a] The data exclude non-autonomous pension funds (book reserves).
[b] No or limited data available for the US.
[c] Operating costs include both administrative and investment expenses.
[d] Including corporate, industry, public sector and retail pension funds, but excluding small APRAs and SSFs (APRA, 2008).
[e] Operating costs include administrative expenses only.
[f] Source: OECD (2016).

All in all, we observe that the pension sector differs widely across countries, a finding that holds to a lesser degree also for the second pillar, where the pension funds operate. The US deviates from the other countries because they provide three different pension provision schemes in the first two pillars. Furthermore, the second pillar is mandatory in Australia, Canada and the Netherlands, whereas in the US it is not.

3.4. Dataset

Our dataset was provided by CEM Benchmarking (CEM) and contains 90 different second-pillar pension funds from Australia, Canada, the Netherlands and the US.[2] This dataset is based on self-reported expenses rather than charges, and thereby circumvents some of the empirical problems mentioned in Section 3.2 on the literature review. Our sample does not include costs related to asset management. The pension funds in our sample have an incentive to reveal accurate and truthful information to obtain targeted consulting and benchmarking. Our observations are from the period 2004–2008, resulting in an unbalanced panel with 254 observations. As shown in Table 3.2, the US accounts for 49 different pension funds and approximately two-thirds of the overall observations, including all first-year observations. For each pension fund, we have observations on the

Table 3.2 Sample observations of pension funds across countries and time

	Australia		Canada		Netherlands		US		All countries	
	All	*Assets*	*All*	*Assets*	*All*	*Assets*	*All*	*Assets*	*All*	*Assets*
2004	–	–	–	–	–	–	31	12	31	12
2005	9	0	8	4	9	5	28	15	54	24
2006	5	0	11	7	12	11	34	31	62	49
2007	10	9	12	10	12	12	41	41	75	72
2008	3	3	3	3	0	0	26	26	32	32
Total	*27*	*12*	*34*	*24*	*33*	*28*	*160*	*125*	*254*	*189*
Proportion to sample (%)	*11*	*6*	*13*	*13*	*13*	*15*	*63*	*61*	–	–
Number of pension funds	10	9	13	11	17	15	49	46	90	81

Note: The column labelled 'All' refers to the administration cost, number of pension funds and other explanatory variables, while the 'Assets' column refers to the number of pension funds that also provide their total assets.

following: administrative costs, split into 24 cost categories (see Appendix 3.1); the number of participants, split into three types, depending on their employment status; the number of pension plans; and information about service levels and complexity. The market value – that is, total assets – of the pension fund assets is missing for a number of pension funds, reducing the number of observations by one-quarter.

Our dataset is a non-random sample with respect to the overall population of pension funds, since CEM deals only with those pension funds that subscribe and pay for its benchmarking services. The sample contains a limited number of pension funds per country (compare Tables 3.1 and 3.2). However, the funds in the sample are large compared to the average size of pension funds in their respective countries. The average Australian fund *in our sample* is three times the size of the average Australian fund and the average Dutch fund *in our sample* is even 30 times larger than the average pension fund in the Netherlands. So the sample covers 5% (Australia) to 85% (the Netherlands) of all participants.[3] Inferences about the overall pension fund industry would be inappropriate, and we instead assume that, at most, the sample is representative of the population of large pension funds in these four countries, restricting any conclusion to this particular set. Hence, one should recognize that the sample may suffer from selection bias.

Table 3.3 provides pension fund characteristics by country. Monetary variables – namely, administrative costs and total assets – have been converted in euros at purchasing power parity (using OECD weights) to adjust for cross-country differences and changes in the relative value of a currency. Furthermore, they are expressed in 2005 prices to account for inflation. The average pension fund in the sample has approximately 400,000 members and holds 35 billion euros in assets, corresponding to over 90,000 euros per participant. Four pension funds hold assets in excess of 100 billion euros, that is, more than the annual GDP of most countries. Australian pension funds tend to be smaller in all dimensions,

Table 3.3 Weighted averages of pension fund characteristics by country

	Australia	Canada	Netherlands	US	All
Entire sample	*N=27*	*N=34*	*N=33*	*N=160*	*N=254*
Number of participants (1,000s)	128	242	818	393	400
Administrative costs per part. (euros)	97	87	69	64	71
Share of active participants (%)	54	60	37	55	53
Share of deferred participants (%)	24	7	45	18	21
Share of pensioners (%)	23	33	18	27	26
CEM complexity score[a]	0.1	−0.4	−0.4	0.2	0
Arithmetic average complexity score[a]	−0.5	−0.2	−0.7	0.3	0
Principal comp. complexity score[a]	−0.4	−0.7	−0.8	0.4	0
Subsample I	*N=23*	*N=17*	*N=33*	*N=156*	*N=229*
CEM service score[a]	−0.6	−0.1	0.0	0.1	0
Arithmetic average service score[a]	−0.4	−0.7	0.1	0.2	0
Principal complex. service score[a]	−0.1	0.3	−0.2	0.0	0
Subsample II	*N=12*	*N=24*	*N=28*	*N=125*	*N=189*
Total assets, on average (billion euros)	5	32	41	36	35
Asset per participant (1,000 euros)	61	132	72	93	93
Administrative costs per asset (%)	0.25	0.08	0.19	0.07	0.10

Note: Country averages are over observations. An alternative is to average first over observations by pension fund, obtaining pension funds characteristics, and second over pension funds. If the second step is replaced by taking weighted averages, with the number of observations as weights, we again obtain country averages over observations.

[a] All service and complexity scores reported here are standardized to allow for comparisons across the three measures. Thus, the overall sample mean is zero by construction. Note that not all 12 service measures are available for all 254 observations. For some observations the service score is an average over fewer underlying components. For this reason, the service scores are based on that smaller number of observations (see subsample I).

while the average Canadian pension fund has fewer members but more assets per member. The average Dutch pension fund is more than twice as large in terms of membership.

Pension funds in the Netherlands, as well as in the US, tend to be among the cheapest, with average yearly administrative fees of, respectively, 69 and 64 euros per participant. Canadian and Australian pension funds are, on average, the most expensive, with sample means of 87 and 97 euros per year, respectively. Administrative costs as a percentage of total assets in Canada and the US are low, whereas those in the Netherlands are higher. These figures are considerably lower than those usually found in studies of pension funds (see Section 3.2), but as our sample is biased toward the larger pension funds in each country, these funds benefit from scale economies that reduce their average administrative costs. Compared to other countries, Dutch pension funds have much more deferred or dormant participants who are no longer employed and not yet retired. This is probably due to the structure of mandatory pension schemes: employees cannot choose, so changing jobs often implies changing pension funds. Nowadays, workers can transfer their pension rights to a different pension fund, but this has not always been the case in the past.

For 75 pension funds, Fig. 3.1 presents 2007 figures of administrative costs against size in numbers of participants, both expressed in logarithms. Cost per participant ranges from 19 to 415 euro per annum, while size varies from 13,000 to 2.7 million participants. The graph suggests a negative relationship between average costs per participants and size. Pension funds from the Netherlands (indicated by N) are among the largest ones, followed by those from the US (U), as observed also from Table 3.3. Furthermore, pension funds in these countries are among the most efficient ones. At the other end, we find Australian pension finds (A) typically to be smaller and with higher cost, while those from Canada (C) take an intermediate position.

The dataset includes unique information on the service quality and the business model complexity of its pension funds. The benchmarking company defines service as 'anything a member would like, before considering costs'. Twelve variables capture several dimensions of the service quality of pension funds, such as timeliness in pension payments, amount and personalization of information, and services to employers of occupational funds. Each variable is the weighted average of finer and more precise measures (based on measures of activities of pension funds as well as satisfaction surveys among participants), and it is expressed on a 100-point scale. Table 3.4 provides an overview of the variables constituting the service quality score, as well as the weights used by the benchmarking

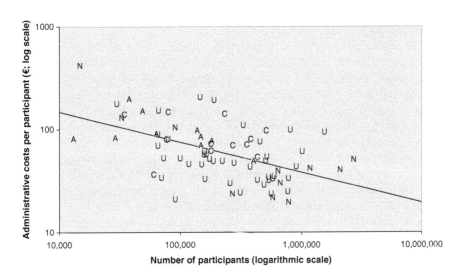

Figure 3.1 Administrative costs against size of 75 pension funds (in logarithms; 2007)

Note: A, C, N and U refer to pension funds from, respectively, Australia, Canada, the Netherlands and the US.

Table 3.4 The composite service score

	Dimension	Weight (%)
1	Annuity pension payment	18.9
2	Pension inceptions (excluding disability pension)	7.9
3	Pension benefit estimates	5.0
4	One-on-one member counselling	7.9
5	Member presentations (group information sessions)	6.7
6	Member contacts: calls, e-mails, letters	21.5
7	Mass communication	18.5
8	Service to employers	4.0
9	Outgoing pension account transfers (refunds, transfers out, payment termination)	0.3
10	Incoming pension account transfers	3.3
11	Assessment of disability pensions	5.1
12	Disaster recovery	1.0

company to construct an overall service score (see Table 3.A.2.1 in Appendix 3.2 for detailed definitions of the components of the service quality score).

Similarly, 15 different variables describe the complexity of the pension fund's business model. Complexity refers to the intricacy of the rules governing pension payments, customized services and contributions. Complexity variables are calculated as the weighted average of more specific measures of complexity, measured on a 100-point scale that increases with complexity. Table 3.5 shows the variables constituting the complexity score, as well as the weights used by the benchmarking company to construct an overall complexity score, which is the score used in our analysis (see Table 3.A.2.2 in Appendix 3.2 for detailed definitions of the components of the complexity score).

The service and complexity variables are weighted averages, with the weights being determined by CEM analysts. To aggregate the 12 service variables into a single score, seven different criteria were employed: feedback from pension fund members (obtained at on-site meetings, symposiums and peer conferences); the relative cost of each activity;[4] the relative volume of each activity; the expectations of participants based on external experience; the extent of personalized human contact; the extent of participant resource involvement; and whether or not the dimension is related to the core business of the pension fund (*i.e.* generating and administering pension payments). These criteria do not translate directly into objective and indisputable weights, but are filtered through the professional judgement of several experts who eventually elaborate the weights to be used to summarize the information. Although these values are updated every year to incorporate new feedback and past experience, some arbitrariness persists, potentially posing a threat to the validity of our analysis. We have no access to the original raw data used to compute the 12 dimensions of service quality or the 12 dimensions of complexity, but the dataset includes disaggregated data on these variables. To improve the robustness of the models, the composite score was

Table 3.5 Weights used for the composite complexity score

	Dimension	Weight (%)
1	Pension payment options	15.0
2	Customization choices	20.0
3	Multiple plan types and overlays	10.0
4	Multiple benefit formula	16.0
5	External reciprocity	3.0
6	Contractual cost-of-living-adjustment rules	4.0
7	Contribution rates	3.0
8	Variable compensation	4.0
9	Service credit rules	3.0
10	Divorce rules	3.0
11	Purchase rules	5.5
12	Refund rules	4.0
13	Disability rules	6.0
14	Translation	0.5
15	DC plan rules	3.0

calculated using two alternative operationalizations, namely, principal component analysis (PCA) and simple arithmetic averages.[5] The latter solution is straightforward and results in a 100-point variable, while the former is discussed next in more detail.

The method of PCA involves taking an orthogonal linear transformation of a set of data to reduce a large dataset into a lesser number of factors, explaining as much variation in the original variables as possible. Because each factor retains the highest variance available, the inevitable loss of information in the data reduction procedures is minimized. In this instance, the generally low cross-correlations among the original dimensions imply a data structure that is not easy to interpret in terms of a few underlying variables, so that the criteria commonly employed to determine how many factors to retain do not lead to a clear solution. During an exploratory phase, the baseline model of administrative costs in Section 3.5 was estimated with several PCA specifications, differing only in the number of service and complexity factors retained. Since increasing the number of components did not substantially change the rest of the estimation, only the first component of each variable was maintained in the final analysis presented in this chapter.[6] The CEM and arithmetic average scores for services are higher for the US and the Netherlands, whereas the PCA score is higher for Canada. Complexity is, on average, higher in the US than in the other countries, but varying with the different measures (*i.e.* CEM, equal-weighted and PCA scores).

3.4.1. Scale economies

Table 3.6 presents average administrative costs for different-sized classes. The upper panel of Table 3.6 shows costs in relation to size classes based on the number of participants. The (weighted) average of administrative costs per participant

Table 3.6 Average annual administrative costs of pension funds by size classes

Size classes based on	Number of observations	Administrative cost per participant (euros)	Total number of participants (millions)	CEM service score (1–100)	CEM complexity score (1–100)	Number of observations	Administrative cost per asset (%)	Assets per participant (1000s euros)
Number of participants (× 1,000)								
<50	23	148.5	0.7	62.7	27.3	14	0.157	159.2
50–100	37	82.2	2.7	69.6	24.7	27	0.098	88.6
100–500	125	61.6	32.7	71.6	37.1	94	0.085	87.2
500–1,000	50	44.9	35.2	66.8	36.8	38	0.133	80.3
>1,000	19	55.1	30.3	73.9	40.1	16	0.085	74.1
Total assets (billion euros)								
<10	64	81.4	8.9	71.5	27.7	64	0.115	91.6
10–20	41	52.0	10.6	71.8	34.4	41	0.085	68.5
20–50	44	74.8	19.3	70.6	36.6	44	0.077	106.4
50–100	27	51.3	21.8	73.0	38.2	27	0.052	110.1
>100	13	77.4	18.9	71.9	47.8	13	0.061	130.4

Note: The upper panel of the table is weighted by the number of pension fund members, while the lower panel is weighted by the total value of pension fund assets.

falls steadily as the class size increases. The minimum value is 45 euros for pension funds having between half a million and a million members, reflecting unused economies of scale. For bigger funds, on average, the costs are higher. Apparently, scale economies exist even for the – on average – rather large funds in our sample. The average of administrative costs per total assets (weighted by the number of participants) does not indicate this U-shaped curve (although it would if medians were used). The data also present a clearly declining trend in individual financial wealth, since the value of individual assets in small pension funds is substantially higher than in larger ones. Lastly, it is worth noting that more expensive pension funds do not seem to deliver higher service quality. Although there is no clear relation and relatively little variation in service scores, the smallest pension funds offer the lowest service quality according to this measure, while the largest pension funds provide the highest. Much stronger is the positive relation between pension fund size and the complexity score.

The lower panel of Table 3.6 shows administrative costs in relation to size classes based on total assets. The weighted average of the administrative cost per asset again reflects a U-shaped association: costs decline very rapidly when the size class increases, reaching a minimum of 0.05% of total assets for pension funds with total assets between 10 billion euros and 100 billion euros (pointing to unused economies of scale) before slightly increasing again. The (weighted) average of administrative cost per participant, however, does not show a similar shape. These patterns are similar to those for all 700 Dutch pension funds (Bikker and de Dreu, 2009; Alserda *et al.*, 2017). Again, the quality of services seems to be approximately the same across asset classes, where complexity increases with size. Appendix 3.1 shows that economies of scale are also present on a disaggregated level, where the costs of most categories of administrative activities per participant decline with size. Section 3.5 uses a multivariate model of pension fund administrative costs to further investigate economies of scale.

3.4.2. Additional number of pension plans and other services

Table 3.7 compares the administrative costs for pension funds offering multiple products and services. The two upper rows of Table 3.7 contrast pension funds offering only one type of plan and those that provide two or three plans. The weighted average of administrative costs per participant is 57 euros in the first case and 55 euros in the second. On the other hand, costs are higher in the latter instance if expressed as a percentage of pension fund assets. Nonetheless, contrary to economic theory and observations elsewhere (Mitchell and Mulvey, 2004, p. 350), the data suggest that there is little substantial difference in administrative costs for pension funds offering more than one type of plan. The complexity score decreases when several plans are offered, probably indicating that DB plans are more complicated than DC schemes. Comparing pension funds that focus on their core business of providing pension plans versus those that provide additional services (such as health cost administration,

Table 3.7 Impact of additional number of pension plans and other services

		No. of obs.	Administrative cost per participant (€)	Complexity score CEM (1–100)	Servicescore CEM (1–100)	No. of obs.	Administrative cost per asset (%)
Number of plans offered	One	166	56.4	43.1	70.1	126	0.096
	More than one	88	54.2	34.3	70.7	63	0.104
Additional services	Zero	48	55.7	32.8	65.1	29	0.095
	One or more	206	54.9	38.2	71.3	160	0.102

Note: Averages, weighted by the number of participants

tax-deferred savings plans, home mortgages, loans and asset management), we find that the weighted average of the (normal) administrative cost per participant does not rise. This is in line with expectation.

3.5. Empirical analysis

Section 3.4 describes bivariate relations between, on the one hand, average administrative costs and, on the other, pension fund size, country, service quality, pension scheme complexity and other pension fund characteristics. This section examines the marginal contribution of each variable to total cost through a multivariate panel analysis. A multivariate approach avoids misinterpretation of the coefficients, as is possible in a bivariate analysis where omitted variables may impair the relationship. We use a traditional cost function to explain administrative costs, taking into account, among other variables, all the cost determinants considered above. In theoretical frameworks, such a cost function relates the total administrative cost of a pension fund to its output volume and input prices. Pension funds provide several services, but their key functions are 'financing, recordkeeping, money management, and benefit payouts' (Mitchell, 1999, p. 3). Defining output is a well-known problem in the financial service industry. This chapter uses both a narrow and a broad definition of output. The narrow measure of output, which will be central in our analysis, is the number of participants. This definition assumes that a pension fund's services are all related to the process of providing pension benefits to the fund's members, covering 'financing, recordkeeping and benefit payouts'. This output definition is closely linked to the pension fund activities behind our topic of investigations, that is, administrative costs. In reality, however, output is multidimensional. Administrative activities (and hence, costs) may be more extensive for pension funds with larger assets per capita. Therefore, we use as an alternative measure of output the log-linear combination of both the number of participants and total assets, where the latter proxies 'money management' activities. Note that our investigations focus on administrative activities and do not regard the performance of investments as such.

We start by estimating the impact of our narrow output measure membership size (*Participants*) on pension fund total administrative costs (*AC*), while controlling for complexity and service quality scores and other determinants of administrative costs:

$$\ln AC_{ijt} = \alpha + \beta \ln \text{Participants}_{ijt} + \gamma Service_{ijt}$$

$$+ \delta Complexity_{ijt} + \Sigma_k \zeta_k Control_{ijt}{}^k$$

$$+ \sum_{j=1}^{3} \eta_j Country_j + \varepsilon_{ijt} \tag{3.1}$$

where *j* refers to countries, *i* to pension funds and *t* to time. We use logarithms to transform the administrative costs and number of participants to reduce the impact of heteroskedasticity, as well as enable the measurement of scale economies. The coefficient of the output variable, β, measures economies of scale ($\beta < 1$) or diseconomies of scale ($\beta > 1$) of the administrative activities of pension funds. Testing $\beta = 1$ is equivalent to testing the null hypothesis that administrative costs rise (exactly) proportionally with the pension fund size, that is, that economies or diseconomies of scale do not exist. To investigate whether scale economies are constant across size classes or not, we also include, as a sensitivity test, a squared term of pension fund sizes (*i.e.* numbers of participants).

The service quality and complexity scores are important control variables, since they correct for additional costs due to extra services and tailor-made qualities. These variables are missing from all other existing pension fund costs studies. We apply either CEM scores, equal-weighted scores or principal component scores, standardized to enable proper comparisons across the models.[7] We also control for the effects of pension fund types, actually their participants' occupations. Pension funds in the sample offer occupational plans for the public sector (national, local or municipal governments), teachers, other school employees (custodians, administrative clerks and other staff members), policemen, firemen and other employees of public safety agencies, workers covered by a corporate or an industry-wide collective agreement and workers in other occupational categories, such as judges.[8] These categories are not mutually exclusive, because any pension fund can offer several occupational plans (see also Table 3.A.3.1 in Appendix 3.3). A dummy variable for each type of occupation is included in the model to measure for each pension fund, whether or not it has participants working (or who have worked) in the respective type of occupation. Furthermore, the proportions of retired and deferred participants are included to take into account the impact of membership composition on the relative importance of the services performed. For instance, a pension fund with a high proportion of retirees should spend more, all else being equal, on annuity payment administration than one with a lower fraction of retirees, while sleepers are expected to be least costly, since many administrative activities have ended (*e.g.* contribution payments) or not yet started (payment of benefits). We also include the number of pension plans (one or more), where we expect a positive coefficient, since additional pension schemes could complicate the pension fund bureaucracy and internal organization.

A country dummy is included to take care of fixed effects, such as labour market conditions and institutional structures, that are peculiar to each country. The US acts as the reference group. Finally, ε_{ijt} is the idiosyncratic error term. Some of the theoretically relevant variables are not available for the individual pension funds, particularly input prices such as wages. For small countries such as the Netherlands, one might expect wages to be rather constant across the financial institutions. This case is less likely for large countries, for example, the US. We have country-wide (real) wages for the financial sector at hand, which would take wage differences across countries into account, while ignoring domestic differences across pension funds. Inclusion of the national wage levels in the model, as proxy for the input price for labour, produces insignificant coefficients.[9] We decided to not include these input price proxies in Equation (3.1) for two reasons: (i) our wage price proxy is poor and (ii) our country dummies would anyway absorb the level of such national wage prices (though not their eventual changes over time).

All models in this chapter are unbalanced panels with random effects specific to pension funds. It is common practice to test the validity of this assumption of random effect (versus fixed effects) through the Sargan-Hansen test for overidentifying conditions. However, we have a strong economic argument not to use the fixed effect model, since pension-fund-specific fixed effects would not so much eliminate the effect of disturbing omitted variables (as it should do) but rather wipe out the size of the pension fund, disturbing the estimation of economies of scale.[10] This has been tested empirically: fixed effects cause a strong downward bias of the output coefficient, thereby strongly attenuating scale economies. Ordinary least squares (OLS) estimates do not deviate significantly from the random effect estimates.

3.5.1. *Empirical results for the narrow definition of output*

Table 3.8 presents the estimation results for the multi-country and US subsamples, both based on Equation (3.1). In addition, the multi-country model is estimated with individual-country interaction effects with output to measure the national extent of economies of scale, using $\Sigma_k \, \beta_k \, (ln \; Participants \times Country_k)$ instead of $\beta \, (ln \; Participants)$. For the multi-country model, substantial unused economies of scale seem to exist (first column). The scale coefficient of the number of participants indicates that total administrative costs increase by only 76% when membership size doubles. These potential economies of scale of 24% are statistically significant at the 99% confidence level. Table 3.8 tests the significance of all coefficients (say, β) against the null hypothesis $\beta = 0$ and presents the results with asterisks (*). In addition, for the output coefficients, the more relevant tests against the null hypothesis $\beta = 1$ – that is, constant returns to scale (no scale economies) – are performed, where degrees signs (°) indicate the significance of the deviation from $\beta = 1$.

This multi-country output coefficient may hide diverging country-specific scale effects. Therefore, in the second column, we estimate a modified version

Table 3.8 Administrative costs of pension funds explained by a narrow definition of the output measure

	Multi-country sample		US[a]
	One scale parameter	Country-specific scale parameters	
Number of participants (in logs), entire sample	***/°°°0.759 (0.053)		***/°°0.809 (0.089)
Number of participants (in logs) in Australia		***/°°0.739 (0.105)	
Number of participants (in logs) in Canada		***0.945 (0.147)	
Number of participants (in logs) in NL		***/°°°0.691 (0.069)	
Number of participants (in logs) in US		***/°°°0.788 (0.089)	
Standardized CEM service quality score	***0.064 (0.018)	***0.063 (0.018)	***0.063 (0.018)
Standardized CEM complexity score	**0.044 (0.018)	**0.038 (0.017)	**0.056 (0.023)
Single pension plan offered	−0.128 (0.083)	−0.129 (0.084)	−0.068 (0.088)
Share of retired participants (%)	−0.002 (0.005)	−0.003 (0.005)	0.005 (0.008)
Share of deferred participants (%)	***−0.014 (0.003)	***−0.014 (0.003)	**−0.012 (0.004)
Public sector: national government	−0.028 (0.093)	−0.006 (0.096)	0.043 (0.175)
Public sector: state or provincial government	***0.631 (0.203)	***0.728 (0.193)	***0.808 (0.216)
Public sector: municipality	**0.106 (0.047)	**0.093 (0.048)	***0.179 (0.051)
Collective agreement (CA): teacher	*−0.126 (0.072)	−0.119 (0.073)	**−0.171 (0.085)
CA: other school employees	0.033 (0.048)	0.026 (0.049)	0.010 (0.050)
CA: police and other public safety workers	0.048 (0.038)	0.052 (0.038)	0.010 (0.037)
Collective agreement: other	***−0.213 (0.076)	***−0.212 (0.076)	***−0.249 (0.085)
Corporate pension fund	−0.071 (0.064)	−0.092 (0.073)	
Industry pension fund	0.036 (0.042)	0.011 (0.048)	
Australian pension fund	**0.349 (0.166)	0.933 (1.559)	
Canadian pension fund	*0.254 (0.136)	−1.599 (1.966)	
Dutch pension fund	***0.445 (0.133)	1.631 (1.336)	
Intercept	***7.383 (0.668)	***7.035 (1.073)	***6.540 (1.042)
Number of observations	254	254	160
χ^2 statistic[b]	345.2	354.4	151.6
R^2, overall	83.7	83.8	83.2

Note: The value terms *administrative costs* (the dependent variable) is converted into euros and expressed at the 2005 (euro) price level. The asterisks ***, ** and * denote, respectively, significance at the 99%, 95% and 90% confidence levels. For the scale variable *number of participants*, we denote values significantly different from *one* by degree signs (°) instead of asterisks; see the first rows. The Huber-White standard deviations correct for heteroskedasticity and are reported in parentheses.

[a] The US does not have pension funds in the corporate and industry pension fund categories, and these dummies variables have therefore been dropped. [b] Joint significance of coefficients.

of Equation (3.1), where the pension fund size in terms of number of participants interacts with a country dummy to allow for cross-country comparisons of scale efficiencies as in the multi-country model. This specification assumes that the impact of all variables, except membership size, on administrative costs is the same, regardless of the country in which the pension fund operates. Although it is difficult to confirm the validity of this assumption, the alternative specification is an improvement on the baseline model as it allows country-specific scale effects.[11] For three countries we observe the existence of highly significant scale economies, while for Canada the output coefficient is not statistically different from one, indicating that pension funds in this country are already operating on an efficient scale. The Netherlands is the country in which potential economies of scale remain for the relatively largest part unexploited. The scale coefficient, significantly different from one at the 99% confidence level, suggests that doubling the membership size would increase costs by only 69%, equivalent to potential economies of scale of 31%. This is in line with results found by Bikker and de Dreu (2009) for all Dutch pension funds (64%). Similarly, increasing membership by 1% in Australia and the US corresponds to an increase in total costs of 0.74% and 0.79%, both of which are also significantly different from one at, respectively, the 95% and the 99% level. Finally, the last column of Table 3.8 shows the result of analyzing the subsample of only US observations. This exercise confirms the existence of scale economies in the US at the 95% level. All three models have also been estimated with an additional squared term of the output measure *number of participants*. All squared terms have a positive sign, which is coherent with the hypothesis of a standard convex cost function, but their coefficients are statistically significant at the 90% level of confidence only, not at the 95% level, and, therefore, have been deleted in all presented model specifications. Bikker and de Dreu (2009) did observe significant squared terms using a large panel sample of the entire Dutch pension sector.

With respect to the control variable, we find, as expected, that both higher complexity and service quality increase total administrative costs, all else being equal. In all three specifications, they have significant and positive effects, respectively, at the 1% significance level (service) and the 5% significance level (complexity). This finding supports the obvious view that pension funds delivering service of a higher quality are, other things being equal, more expensive. Similarly, pension funds with a more complex business model are also more costly. The impact of service quality on administrative costs is similar across the various models in Table 3.8, but the impact of complexity on costs is somewhat higher in the US subsample. Offering only one policy plan decreases administrative costs by almost 13% in the multi-country model, and by 7% in the US sample, in line with expectations, but these effects are not statistically significant. While the percentage of retirees does not significantly reduce administrative costs, we observe a significant negative impact of the proportion of deferred participants, both multi-country and in the US, in line with expectations. This has also been found by Bikker and de Dreu (2009) for the entire Dutch pension sector.

The nature of a pension fund's occupational plans is also an important factor in determining its administrative costs. Occupational plans covering employees of a state or provincial government or of a municipality have additional administrative costs of no less than 60% to 80% and 10% to 20%, respectively. On the other hand, collective agreements covering teachers and workers in the 'other' category decrease administrative costs, on average, by roughly 20%. These relations are strongly significantly different from zero in all specifications. Hence, differences in administrative costs across pension fund types amount to around 100%. Remarkably, these coefficients in the total sample and the US subsample are similar in sign and magnitude, be it that both positive and negative effects are more pronounced for the US in all four pension fund types mentioned. Relative (in)efficiency is an obvious explanation, but complexity and service quality may also play a role, as far as they have not been picked up by the two respective indexes, which, of course, are only general approximations.

Finally, there are also significant country-specific effects on administrative costs. Pension funds in Australia, Canadian and the Netherlands are more costly than those in the US, all other determinants taken into account. These country dummies capture a large variety of effects, reflecting both the economic and institutional characteristics of the domestic pension fund markets, including (now the input prices are not incorporated in the regression) the national wage level (and other input prices at the country level), but not their eventual changes over time. However, when we include individual-country interaction effects with the output measure *number of participants*, we no longer observe statistically significant country effects. Apparently, the dummies do pick up country-specific output measurement errors in the constrained model with one multi-country scale effect. The models explain no less than around 83% of the variation in the entire sample, as well as in the US sample.

If we replace the CEM scores for complexity and service quality by equally weighted or PCA scores, all the results are rather similar in coefficient sign, size and significance. In fact, the three score measures are all mutually highly correlated,[12] implying that they can be employed as substitutes without any major change in the model estimation. Using the first component derived from PCA is the optimal choice from a statistical point of view, because it can account for most of the variance in the original set of variables. On the other hand, using the CEM composite service and complexity scores is probably a better choice, since weights are assigned on the basis of professional judgement and experience. These alternative estimates suggest that different weights for the service and complexity dimensions have a limited impact on the estimation results. Thus, we retain here and later the original CEM scores as the variables measuring service quality and business model complexity, having confidence in the judgement of experts who consider several criteria and place emphasis on the relative importance of each dimension.

3.5.2. *Empirical results for the broad definition of output*

Section 3.5.1 assumes that a pension fund's services are all related to the process of providing pension benefits to its members, where we call the number of participants the narrow measure of output. The last column in the upper panel of

Table 3.6 indicates that assets per participant decline systematically with pension fund size, when expressed as the number of participants. Apparently, participants and total assets are related. More directly, part of the administrative activities may be related to the asset portfolio. Therefore, in this subsection we use as an alternative measure the combination of the number of participants and total assets (both in logarithms), where the latter is assumed to cover administrative costs related to investment management activities:

$$\ln AC_{ijt} = \alpha + \beta_1 \ln \text{Participants}_{ijt} + \beta_2 \ln \text{Totalassets}_{ijt}$$
$$+ \gamma \, \text{Service}_{ijt} + \delta \, \text{Complexity}_{ijt} + \sum_k \zeta_k \text{Control}_{ijtk}$$
$$+ \sum_{k=1}^{3} \eta_k \text{Country}_k + \varepsilon_{ijt}$$

(3.2)

Assuming a multiplicative output model, $\beta_1 + \beta_2 < 1$ reflects economies of scale, $\beta_1 + \beta_2 > 1$ diseconomies of scale and $\beta_1 + \beta_2 = 1$ constant returns to scale. Table 3.9 provides the estimation results of these broad definition of output specifications. The inclusion of total assets may enrich our model, but it reduces the number of available observations by one-quarter. For this reason we cannot just compare these outcomes with those in Section 3.5.1. The variable *total assets* appears to be a significant determinant of administrative costs in the multi-country sample (Column 1 of Table 3.9). Apparently, administrative activities and their costs increase somewhat with the size of the investment portfolio. The inclusion of total assets reduces the size effect of the number of participants by 0.09, so that the sum of these broad definition output coefficients ($\beta_1 + \beta_2$) is at 86% somewhat higher than the narrow definition output coefficient (76%). However, this sum is also significantly lower than 1 (at the 99% level of confidence), confirming the existence of economies of scale. We draw a similar conclusion for the US (see Column 2 of Table 3.9).

The inclusion of total assets also affects the coefficients of the other control variables. The service quality score is significant, as before, with similar coefficients. The variable *single pension plan offered*, however, is now significant, while the complexity score has lost its significance. Offering of a single plan, complexity and total assets are interrelated, as also appears from their mutual correlation coefficients. A single plan is less complex, whereas complexity tends to increase with the *financial* size of the pension fund, as measured by its investment portfolio.[13] The coefficients of the variables describing the degree of retirement and inactivity of participants do not differ essentially from those in the narrow output definition model.

The pension fund type dummy coefficients hardly change: only the significance level of the teacher pension fund category is now higher, the reason being that it has, on average, a larger investment portfolio, which is now incorporated in the model by the variable *total assets* itself. The country dummy coefficients have values similar to the ones cited before, but they depend strongly on the assumed multi-country scale effect: they become insignificant when the two scale parameters are country specific.[14] The results for the US are similar to the multi-country outcomes. The goodness of fit is high, at more than 88%. The additional

Table 3.9 Administrative costs of pension funds explained by a broad definition of the output measure

	Multi-country sample	US [a]
Number of participants (in logs)	***/°°°0.671 (0.072)	***/°°°0.631 (0.090)
Total assets (in logs)	***0.188 (0.054)	***0.231 (0.062)
Standardized CEM service quality score	**0.064 (0.030)	**0.060 (0.024)
Standardized CEM complexity score	0.030 (0.031)	0.052 (0.037)
Single pension plan offered	***−0.231 (0.084)	**−0.198 (0.094)
Share of retired participants (%)	−0.000 (0.006)	0.003 (0.009)
Share of deferred participants (%)	***−0.013 (0.004)	***−0.014 (0.005)
Public sector: national government	−0.030 (0.079)	0.041 (0.157)
Public sector: state or provincial government	**0.523 (0.229)	***0.673 (0.236)
Public sector: municipality	**0.201 (0.084)	***0.286 (0.083)
Collective agreement (CA): teacher	***−0.260 (0.089)	***−0.287 (0.091)
CA: other school employees	−0.081 (0.062)	−0.077 (0.056)
CA: police and other public safety workers	0.008 (0.039)	0.001 (0.038)
Collective agreement: other	**−0.198 (0.777)	***−0.255 (0.806)
Corporate pension fund	−0.093 (0.111)	
Industry pension fund	*−0.196 (0.103)	
Australian pension fund	***0.696 (0.188)	
Canadian pension fund	**0.269 (0.132)	
Dutch pension fund	***0.629 (0.138)	
Intercept	***4.112 (0.961)	***3.474* (1.084)
Number of observations	189	125
χ^2 statistic[b]	531.5	292.8
R^2, overall	88.8	88.6

Note: Value terms (dependent variable administrative costs and explanatory variable total assets) are converted into euros and expressed at the 2005 (euro) price level. Asterisks ***, ** and * denote significance from zero at the 99%, 95% and 90% confidence levels, respectively. For the sum of the two scale variables *total assets* and *number of participants*, we denote 'significantly different from one' by degree symbols (°) instead of asterisks (see the first row). The Huber-White standard deviations correct for heteroskedasticity and are reported in parentheses.

[a] The US does not have pension funds in the corporate and industry pension fund categories, so these dummies variables have been dropped. [b] Joint significance of coefficients.

explanatory variable *total assets* increases this measure by roughly 5 percentage points (not shown here).

3.5.3. A disaggregated cost model

As mentioned, so far the models investigate total administrative costs. A similar analysis is carried out at the micro level of cost components to analyze more in detail for which cost types we observe economies of scale. The disaggregated analysis includes all 24 cost types described in Appendix 3.1, except those related to (i) disabled and other premium exceptions and (ii) compliance with the Dutch pension fund supervisor's regulations, because only the 33 Dutch observations face these costs.[15] The model being estimated is equivalent to that of Equation (3.1), but now each cost type is analyzed separately.[16] In addition, for 12 of the remaining 22 administrative activities, we possess information on the service quality of that specific activity.

The idiosyncratic errors of Equation (3.1) applied to disaggregated activity p, ε_{ijtp}, are likely to be correlated with those of the other activities: If a shock hits one activity, other activities are likely affected too. This suggests that a seemingly unrelated regression (SUR) would increase the efficiency of the estimation. However, we instead run 22 separate regressions for two reasons: first, the SUR unbalanced panel estimator developed by Biørn (2004) uses a stepwise maximum likelihood procedure that does not converge in our estimation. Second, the number of observations across types of administrative costs is not the same; thus, the sample size would be reduced if all regressions were to be estimated through SUR. In short, the separate models produce unbiased and consistent results that might, however, not be efficient.

Table 3.10 presents the results for the 22 disaggregated administrative cost components. Here the first four columns show only the country-specific output coefficient β_i from Equation (3.1) and the test results of the null hypothesis that the coefficient of the interaction term between the pension fund size and the country dummy variable is different from one, using asterisks. For most activities, there is evidence of economies of scale in at least one country, although we observe considerable variations in size. Significant economies of scale are most frequent for administrative activities in the Netherlands and the US. In addition, the average values per country, shown in the last row, clearly show that economies of scale are largest in these two countries. This finding is in line with our observations above, but the limited occurrence of economies of scale on a disaggregated level for Australia is remarkable, since we do find significant scale economies on the aggregated level. We attribute this to the relatively small sample for Australia.

The right-hand column of Table 3.10 presents the scale economies of administrative activities for the alternative model, where one output coefficient has been estimated (compared to Column 1 in Table 3.8). Here we see that activity-specific scale economies are significant at the 99% level for 12 out of 22 administrative activities, while another two activities are significant at the 95% level only: apparently, the country-specific estimates suffer from their small sample size. This right-hand column confirms that the scale economies are widespread across the administrative activities.

Most economies of scale are found for marketing and public relations and financial control with significant effects in three countries and as well as in board consulting, rules interpretation and designing new rules, with significant effects in two countries. For almost any given administrative activity, pension funds in some of the countries are already operating at their optimal size (or close to it), while in other countries they are operating inefficiently, either because they are too large or too small.

At the country level, the Netherlands and the US show the greatest extent of scale economies, while (with smaller standard deviations) Australia and Canada show less room to reduce total costs through scale effects. This finding is in line with our findings for the economies of scale of aggregated administrative costs (see Column 2 of Table 3.8). Interestingly, pension funds in the US and the Netherlands already tend to be among the cheapest and largest in the sample (see Table 3.3), yet most economies of scale can be found in these countries.

Table 3.10 Economies of scale in administrative costs in the 22 activity-specific costs

	Coefficient β (standard deviation)				One scale parameter for all countries
	Country-specific scale parameters				
	Australia	Canada	Netherlands	US	
1. Annuity pension payment	1.24* (0.14)°	0.79 (0.18)	0.77** (0.11)	0.88 (0.11)	0.87* (0.08)
2. Pension inceptions	0.97 (0.19)	0.92 (0.21)	1.19* (0.10)	0.81** (0.08)	1.00 (0.07)
3. Benefit estimates	0.61 (0.24)	1.00 (0.25)	0.48** (0.21)	0.78* (0.13)	0.62*** (0.13)
4. One-on-one counselling	0.84 (0.35)	1.43 (0.43)	0.43** (0.18)	0.89 (0.12)	0.45** (0.16)
5. Member presentations	1.05 (0.24)	0.45 (0.46)	0.35*** (0.19)	1.01 (0.18)	0.51** (0.15)
6. Member contacts	0.88 (0.15)	0.99 (0.18)	0.88 (0.10)	0.89 (0.09)	0.85** (0.07)
7. Mass communication	0.89 (0.16)	0.94 (0.24)	0.84 (0.11)	0.74** (0.10)	0.76** (0.07)
8. Data and contributions from employers	0.78 (0.19)	0.74 (0.20)	1.10 (0.11)	0.84 (0.13)	0.93 (0.08)
9. Other data	0.92 (0.53)	0.67 (0.23)	0.74* (0.14)	0.59*** (0.12)	0.66*** (0.11)
10. Billing and inspections	0.61 (0.28)	0.35 (0.56)	1.15 (0.14)	0.34*** (0.24)	0.74* (0.15)
11. Service to employers	1.17 (0.37)	1.47* (0.26)	1.11 (0.14)	0.91 (0.11)	1.06 (0.08)
12. Refunds and transfers out	1.08 (0.25)	0.81 (0.17)	0.80 (0.13)	0.71*** (0.11)	0.81*** (0.07)
13. Purchases and transfers in	2.50* (0.81)	1.14 (0.27)	0.95 (0.17)	1.11 (0.18)	1.05 (0.13)
14. Assessment of disability pensions	1.04 (0.31)	0.89 (0.70)	1.14 (0.23)	0.90 (0.17)	1.06 (0.14)
15. Board of directors	1.29 (0.24)	1.33 (0.24)	0.75 (0.16)	0.56* (0.24)	0.58** (0.16)
16. Financial control	0.95 (0.19)	0.61** (0.19)	0.62*** (0.10)	0.70* (0.14)	0.64*** (0.09)
17. Board consulting	1.19 (0.34)	0.79 (0.42)	0.14*** (0.26)	0.28** (0.30)	0.23** (0.19)
18. Marketing and public relations	0.04*** (0.34)	1.51 (0.58)	0.46** (0.18)	0.49*** (0.19)	0.37*** (0.14)
19. Rules interpretation	0.91 (0.24)	0.67* (0.19)	0.49** (0.22)	0.66*** (0.11)	0.67*** (0.09)
20. Design new rules	0.70 (0.20)	0.59** (0.20)	0.58** (0.19)	0.71* (0.18)	0.58*** (0.11)
21. Lobbying	0.43 (0.46)	0.93 (0.46)	0.52* (0.25)	0.56* (0.23)	0.34*** (0.18)
22. Major projects	0.73 (0.31)	0.36 (0.98)	0.85 (0.18)	1.09 (0.22)	0.95 (0.16)
Average values	0.95 (0.30)	0.88 (0.35)	0.74 (0.16)	0.75 (0.16)	0.71 (0.12)

Note: The significance of output coefficients different from one (not zero, as elsewhere) are indicated with ***, **, and *, denoting the 99%, 95% and 90% confidence levels, respectively.

Analyzing the 22 models for the other coefficients, we find few consistent results across cost components. Service quality and business model complexity show fewer significant relations, but all those that are significant have a positive coefficient, in line with expectations. On the other hand, there is greater heterogeneity when considering the impact of different kinds of occupational activities, membership composition and country-specific factors on administrative costs.

3.6. Conclusions

The administrative costs of pension funds are very important, for both sponsors and employees, since they may erode the wealth accrued for retirement. This chapter aims to shed light on a number of important questions related to the administrative costs of pension funds in four countries with well-developed pension systems. It explores whether economies of scale in pension fund administration exist, measures the impact on administrative costs of service quality and the complexity of the pension plan and analyzes the impact of other cost determinants.

As expected, we find strong evidence of economies of scale, similar to those found in other studies, such as James *et al.* (2001), Tapia and Yermo (2008), Bikker and de Dreu (2009) and Alserda *et al.* (2017). Overall, a 1% increase in the number of participants would increase costs by only 0.76%. In the case where total assets are included in the model as a second output measure, costs would rise by 0.86% for a size increase of 1% for both the number of participants and the amount of total assets. When we allow for country-specific scale effects, that is: different production processes across countries, we observe strong evidence of economies of scale for three out of four countries – Australia, the Netherlands and the US – while constant returns to scale cannot be rejected for Canada, possibly due to the small sample size. The scope for exploiting economies of scale is greatest for pension funds in the Netherlands and the US, even though these countries' pension funds already tend to be the largest and cheapest in the sample and their average administration costs are small relative to country-wide numbers (see, *e.g.* OECD, 2009a). Particularly for the Netherlands and the US, this outcome is confirmed when our model is applied on disaggregated administrative activities. Average costs per participants, both for our aggregated and disaggregated administrative activities, indicate a U-shape pattern, suggesting the existence of an optimal scale. However, when our model is based on the aggregated data, we do not find a statistically significant non-linear effect. The results of this chapter support actions aimed at improving the efficiency of pension funds by consolidation, but not necessarily for very large pension funds. Note that all conclusions in this chapter are under the reservation that our sample may not be fully representative of the countries' entire pension sectors.

Scale-economy estimates could be biased when smaller pension funds systematically offer a more personalized service. Our dataset allows us to test such a bias, since we have data on complexity and service quality. First, we observe that smaller funds do tend to provide fewer rather than more services, while their pension plans are also are less complex, which does not point to tailor-made pensions. Apparently, the cost inefficiencies of smaller funds are not explained by higher service quality or cut-to-size pensions. This conclusion is specific to our sample, which underrepresents the smallest pension funds. Second, we include complexity and service quality as control variables in our administrative costs model and find that both complexity and service quality significantly increase administrative costs, as expected. Furthermore, we find that offering only one policy plan substantially decreases administrative costs. Both complexity and service quality are associated with costs, but the question is what pension plan members would select if they have a choice between higher service quality and more tailor-made options on the one hand and lower costs on the other.

Administrative costs vary significantly across types of pension funds. Pension funds for, for example, employees of state or provincial governments have a remarkable 70% higher level of administrative costs, and those for municipalities 10%, other things being equal, while the costs for teacher and other (mainly non-public sector) pension funds have costs that are around 20% lower, all percentages being statistically significant. This finding points to huge potentials for efficiency improvements, on top of those stemming from consolidation. Finally, if we take all considered cost determinants into account, including country-specific scale economies, we do not observe any remaining cost difference across the four countries investigated. Hence, where the Dutch pension funds in our sample have, on average, relatively low administration costs, these are attributable to their larger scale, larger share of less costly deferred participants and lower frequency of complex pension plans.

Notes

1 Update of J.A. Bikker, O.W. Steenbeek, F. Torracchi, 2012, The impact of scale, complexity and service quality on the administrative costs of pension funds: a cross-country comparison, *Journal of Risk and Insurance* 79, 477–514.

2 CEM Benchmarking Inc. is a Toronto-based global pension benchmarking firm, focusing on the objective measurement of the investment performance, service levels and costs of pension investments and administration.

3 The smallest pension fund of our sample counts 13,000 participants.

4 Later in this chapter, we introduce alternative weighting schemes (principal component analysis and equal weighted) that do not rely on costs.

5 An alternative strategy would have employed each of the original 12 dimensions as explanatory variables in the final analysis, but the consequent reduction in the number of degrees of freedom available could have had severe implications, given the small sample at hand.

6 The first component of the PCA of the 12 service variables retains 26% of the original variance, while the first component of the PCA of the 15 complexity variables accounts for 21% of the original variance.

7 The standardization is executed any time the sample size changes, so that in every subsample analyzed the mean equals zero and the standard deviation is one.

8 Clearly, most of pension funds deal with public sector employees, but private sector employees are also present.

9 This outcome occurs also when we would delete the country dummies. Inclusion of the wage levels do not affect the other model parameters. Alternative estimation results are available on request.

10 Note that we do include fixed effects for countries (namely country dummies) as well as, in a variant, for years.

11 Fully separated country-specific equations would require fewer assumptions, but would be less reliable due to the low number of observations for all separate countries but the US.
12 If all observations are pooled, the coefficient of correlation between the original composite service score and the weighted average is 0.89, that between the original service score and the first component is 0.97 and that between the weighted average and the first component is 0.93. If these coefficients are calculated for country-specific subsamples, their values remain very high and in most cases exceed 0.90; only three out of 12 coefficients are below 0.90, and none are below 0.85.
13 Note that complexity and the number of participants are also strongly correlated at 0.4, but this is less than the complexity and total assets correlation of 0.6.
14 In that case, the country-specific effects of total assets would be insignificant, apart for the US.
15 The 22 activity-specific costs, listed in Table 3.10 and indicated by activity type number p, are investigated, except for the two pure Dutch activities ($p = 23$ and 24). Activity-specific weighted service scores are used as explanatory variables in the activity-specific costs models when available, which is the case for $p = 8, 9, 10, 16, 17, 18, 19, 20, 21$ and 22 (apart from 23 and 24), whereas aggregated averages are included otherwise.
16 But with interaction terms between the pension fund's country and its size, assuming again that the impact of all other variables on administrative cost components is the same regardless of the country wherein the pension fund operates. The results for the more simple specification with a single output variable for all countries are essentially the same. White standard deviations are calculated to adjust for heteroskedasticity.

References

Alserda, G., J. A. Bikker, S. G. van der Lecq, 2017, X-efficiency and economies of scale in pension fund administration and investment, *DNB Working Paper* No. 547, De Nederlandsche Bank, Amsterdam.
Ambachtsheer, K., 2010, Future directions in measuring the financial performance of pension funds: a roundtable discussion, in: R. Hinz, R. Heinz, P. Antolin, J. Yermo (eds.), *Evaluating the Financial Performance of Pension Funds*, World Bank, Washington, DC.
Antolin, P., 2008, Coverage of funded pension plans, *OECD Working Papers on Insurance and Private Pensions* No. 19. OECD, Paris.
APRA, 2008, *Statistics Annual Superannuation Bulletin 2008*, revised 2009, www.apra.gov.au (accessed October 15, 2009).
Bateman, H., O. S. Mitchell, 2004, New evidence on pension plan design and administrative expenses: the Australian experience, *Journal of Pension Economics and Finance* 3, 63–76.
Bateman, H., S. Valdés-Prieto, 1999, *The Mandatory Private Old Age Income Schemes of Australia and Chile: A Comparison*, Mimeograph, University of New South Wales.
Bikker, J. A., J. de Dreu, 2009, Operating costs of pension funds: the impact of scale, governance and plan design, *Journal of Pension Economics and Finance* 8, 63–89.
Biørn, E., 2004, Regression systems for unbalanced panel data: a stepwise maximum likelihood procedure, *Journal of Econometrics* 122, 281–295.
Broeders, D., A. van Oord, D. Rijsbergen, 2016, Scale economies in pension fund investments: a dissection of investment costs across asset classes, *Journal of International Money and Finance* 67, 147–171.
Caswell, J. W., 1976, Economic efficiency in pension fund administration: a study of the construction industry, *Journal of Risk and Insurance* 4, 257–273.
Chlon, A., 2000, Pension reform and public information in Poland, Pension Reform Primer series, *Social Protection Discussion Paper*, World Bank, Washington, DC.

Dobronogov, A., M. Murthi, 2005, Administrative fees and costs of mandatory private pensions in transition economies, *Journal of Pension Economics and Finance* 4, 31–55.

Hernandez, D. G., F. Stewart, 2008, Comparison of costs + fees in countries with private defined contribution pension system, *Working Paper* No. 6, International Organization of Pension Supervisions, www.iopsweb.org/Working%20Paper%206%20(Costs%20 and%20fees)%20Formatte (accessed May 16, 2017).

James, E., J. Smalhout, D. Vittas, 2001, Administrative costs and the organizations of individual account systems: a comparative perspective, in: R. Holzmann, J. Stiglitz (eds.), *New Ideas About Old Age Security*, World Bank, Washington, DC.

Koeleman, W.J.J., J.J.B. de Swart, 2007, *Kosten en baten van ondernemingspensioenfondsen* (In Dutch; Cost and benefits of company pension funds), PricewaterhouseCoopers (PWC), Amsterdam, http://docplayer.nl/6898369-Kosten-en-baten-van-ondernemingspensioenfondsen.html (accessed May 16, 2017).

Lachance, M.-E., O. S. Mitchell, K. Smetters, 2003, Guaranteeing defined contribution pensions: the options to buy back a defined benefit promise, *Journal of Risk and Insurance* 70, 1–16.

Malhotra, D. K., V. B. Marisetty, M. Ariff, 2001, Economies of scale in retail superannuation funds in Australia, *Working Paper*, Monash University.

Milevski, M. A., S. D. Promislow, 2004, Florida pension's election: from DB to DC and back, *Journal of Risk and Insurance* 71, 381–404.

Mitchell, O. S., 1998, Administrative costs in public and private retirement systems, in: M. Feldstein (ed.), *Privatizing Social Security*, University of Chicago Press, Chicago, 403–456.

Mitchell, O. S., 1999, Evaluating administrative costs in Mexico's AFORES pension system, *Pension Research Council Working Papers* No. 1. University of Pennsylvania, Philadelphia.

Mitchell, O. S, E. Andrews, 1981, Scale economies in private multi-employer pension systems, *Industrial and Labor Relations Review* 34, 522–530.

Mitchell, O. S., J. Mulvey, 2004, Potential implications of mandating choice in corporate defined benefit plans, *Journal of Pension Economics and Finance* 3, 339–354.

OECD, 2007, *Pensions at a Glance*, OECD, Paris.

OECD, 2009a, *Global Pension Statistics*, http://oecd.org/daf/pensions/gps (accessed October 20, 2009).

OECD, 2009b, *OECD Private Pensions Outlook 2008*, OECD, Paris.

OECD, 2016, *Pension Markets in Focus 2016*, OECD, Paris, www.oecd.org/finance/ private-pensions/globalpensionstatistics.htm (accessed 16 May, 2017).

Orszag, P. R., J. E. Stiglitz, 2001, Re-thinking pension reform: ten myths about social security systems, in: R. Holzmann, J. Stiglitz (eds.), *New Ideas About Old Age Security*, World Bank, Washington, DC.

Sy, W., 2007, Cost, performance and portfolio composition of small APRA funds, *Working Paper*, Australian Prudential Regulation Authority, Sydney.

Tapia, W., J. Yermo, 2008, Fees in individual account pension systems: a cross-country comparison, *OECD Working Papers on Insurance and Private Pensions* No. 27. OECD, Paris.

Valdés-Prieto, S., 1994, Administrative charges in pensions in Chile, Malaysia, Zambia, and the United States, *Policy Research Working Paper* No. 1372. The World Bank, Washington, DC.

Whitehouse, E., 2002, Administrative charges for funded pensions: an international comparison and assessment, *Social Protection Discussion Paper Series* No. 16, The World Bank, Washington, DC.

Appendix 3.1
Costs of specific administrative activities

The dataset includes information on the costs of specific administrative activities. To investigate the relation between size, service quality, complexity and administrative costs, the latter are disaggregated into 24 different sub-categories of activities, listed in Table 3.A.1 (see Table 3.A.2.3 for more extended definitions). While the sum of these types of administrative costs should equal total costs, in practice there are small discrepancies due to data collection techniques. Besides, some of the pension funds (or some countries) in the sample either do not report or do not face certain administrative costs.

Table 3.A.1 shows the average administrative costs over observations for each activity type, as well as across size classes, based on the number of participants.[1] Note that detailed data are not available for all 254 pension fund-year observations (see first column). For most categories, there is a clear U-shaped curve, with average costs first declining with size and then increasing again, pointing to, respectively, economies and diseconomies of scale. In most cases (54%), the minimum efficient scale is in the class of pension funds having between 500,000 and 1,000,000 members (see bold numbers in Table 3.A.1). This follows also from the total administrative costs, the totals shown in the last row. For three categories (13%), lowest average costs are obtained for the smaller class of 100,000–500,000 participants. In some instances (33%), average costs seem to diminish continuously, since the class size increases without any subsequent rise. In addition, in a few categories there is less regular relation between average costs and class size. Lastly, Table 3.A.1 shows the incidence of different types of costs on the total administrative costs.[2] In this respect, we observe heterogeneity across categories. Costs related to core business activities (annuity pension payment, pension inceptions and data and contribution collection), individual and mass communication with members, financial control and major projects are the main expenditure categories. At the opposite end, group presentations to members, board consulting, marketing and public relations, and rule interpretation and design have the lowest incidence.[3] These figures are important because economies of scale, to have a substantial impact on total administrative costs, should exist in activities that have a relative high incidence on total costs.

Table 3.A.1 Costs of 24 administrative activities by five pension fund size classes

Administrative activities	No. of obs.[a]	Average administrative costs per participant (in euros) by class size, based on the number of participants						Weighted average incidence on total administrative costs[b] (%)
		<50,000	50,000–100,000	100,000–500,000	500,000–1,000,000	>1,000,000	Total	
Annuity pension payment	250	9.2	4.1	4.3	3.0	**2.5**	3.3	6.0
Pension inceptions	250	10.6	6.6	**5.0**	5.0	5.1	5.1	9.6
Benefit estimates	247	4.6	3.2	2.8	1.2	**1.2**	1.8	3.3
One-on-one counselling	236	8.0	2.2	2.0	1.8	**1.3**	1.7	2.9
Member presentations	135	3.0	0.4	1.1	**0.6**	0.6	0.8	0.6
Member contacts	254	12.3	7.0	6.1	4.4	**3.9**	4.9	9.3
Mass communication	254	13.0	5.9	4.6	**2.2**	3.3	3.5	6.4
Data and contributions from employers	250	9.3	7.0	5.5	**4.1**	5.2	5.0	9.8
Data not from employers	234	6.5	2.8	**1.4**	1.6	2.0	1.7	3.5
Billing and inspections	211	1.3	1.4	**0.5**	0.9	1.4	1.0	2.0
Service to employers	230	1.7	2.9	1.9	**1.3**	2.7	1.9	3.8
Refunds and transfers out	254	10.7	4.0	3.2	**1.3**	1.8	2.2	3.9
Purchases and transfers in	241	5.7	5.1	3.2	**2.4**	2.9	2.9	4.8
Assessment of disability pensions	225	8.0	2.7	3.5	**2.4**	4.1	3.3	5.0
Board of directors	238	10.4	4.3	2.3	**0.8**	1.1	1.6	2.9
Financial control	254	23.2	9.9	4.2	**2.3**	4.5	3.9	6.8
Board consulting	216	6.7	1.5	1.3	1.3	**0.3**	1.0	1.5
Marketing and public relat.	158	2.4	1.4	0.5	0.5	**0.4**	0.5	0.6
Rule interpretation	238	5.5	2.5	1.3	1.3	**0.8**	1.2	2.2
Design new rules	218	3.7	1.4	1.0	**0.8**	1.0	1.0	1.4

(Continued)

Table 3.A.1 (Continued)

Administrative activities	No. of obs. [a]	Average administrative costs per participant (in euros) by class size, based on the number of participants						Weighted average incidence on total administrative costs [b] (%)
		<50,000	50,000– 100,000	100,000– 500,000	500,000– 1,000,000	>1,000,000	Total	
Lobbying	183	2.1	0.9	0.8	**0.3**	0.4	0.5	0.7
Major projects	203	18.8	12.9	9.1	**7.5**	11.3	9.2	13.1
Disability and other premium exceptions [c]	33	1.4	1.2	0.7	**0.4**	0.6	0.6	—
Compliance to DNB reg. [c]	33	4.0	3.1	0.7	0.6	**0.2**	0.4	—
Total [d]	168		86	62	**44**	54	55	100.0

Note: For each cost category, the lowest average-costs number is printed in bold.

[a] Excluding observations for which the cost is zero.

[b] The weighted average incidence is calculated excluding the costs of disability and premium exceptions and that of compliance with DNB regulations, because only Dutch pension funds face these types of costs. The numbers, however, are essentially the same if two costs are included.

[c] Only for Dutch pension funds (excluded in the panel analysis).

[d] The size class totals result from weighting with the respective numbers of observations divided by 250. They compare to the figures in the second column of the upper panel of Table 3.6, denoting the administrative cost per participant.

Appendix 3.2
Definitions of variables used

This appendix contains the definitions of the variables used in this chapter. Tables 3.A.2.1 and 3.A.2.2 present the variables used to determine, respectively, the service level score and the complexity score. Table 3.A.2.3 presents the definitions of administrative activities, as far as not described in Tables 3.A.2.1–3.A.2.2.

Table 3.A.2.1 Definitions of service level score components

---

1 Annuity pension payment
Annuity payments: paying incepted pensions to disability, early and normal retirees and their survivors. Deductions: processing deductions from the gross pension payment.

2 Pension inceptions (excluding disability pension)
New annuitants: calculating, finalizing and arranging annuity pensions to new payees. Changes to gross: anything that changes the gross amount of pensions (excluding disability pensions) paid to existing. Appeals about annuity pension inceptions (non-disability) to new payees.

3 Pension benefit estimates
Preparing and sending customized written estimates in response to requests from individual members.

4 One-on-one member counselling
Individual counselling on pension issues.

5 Member presentations (group information sessions)
Group counselling and presentations to plan members.

6 Member contacts
First-line communication work for active, inactive and annuitant member inquiries, *i.e.* calls, e-mails, letters.

7 Mass communication
Any benefit-related communication that is sent to all members or groups of members. The costs include design, printing and mailing activities.

8 Service to employers
Training, maintaining relationships, presentations, employer help desk, website, advice.

9 Outgoing pension account transfers
Payments that terminate a fund's relationship with a member: refunds, transfers out, payment termination.

(*Continued*)

Table 3.A.2.1 (Continued)

10 Incoming pension account transfers
Individual transfers-in/rollover of monies from external retirement systems.

11 Assessment of disability pensions
Assessment of long-term and short-term disability.

12 Disaster recovery
The speed with which service to plan members can be resumed after a major disaster takes place, if necessary from another location.

Table 3.A.2.2 Definitions of complexity score components

1 Pension payment options
The score for this element is based on the answers to 11 questions that reflect the extent to which individual plan members can choose within their plan or have additional benefits besides their individual pension benefit. This includes the option to design your own pension cash flow, spouse and/or last survivor benefits, and links with social security payments.

2 Customization choices
The score for this element reflects the extent to which associated employers are able to customize and change the pension arrangement, regarding aspects such as early retirement, part-time employees, taxation issues, contribution levels, retirement qualifications, vesting period, death benefit coverage, disability coverage.

3 Multiple plan types and overlays
The score for this element indicates the hybrid systems number of different pension plans the fund offers, *e.g.* DC, traditional DB and/or hybrid forms. In addition, it reflects whether the individual plan member is able to make choices within the plan, *e.g.* regarding the investment portfolio.

4 Multiple benefit formula
The score for this element reflects the number of different rule sets a fund applies to member groups, *e.g.* regarding different ways early retirement and survivorship benefits are calculated.

5 External reciprocity
This score reflects complexity following from arrangements with different employers for one member and possibilities to combine internal and external credit to form one joint account.

6 Contractual cost-of-living-adjustment rules
The score for this element reflects the complexity of cost-of-living-adjustment rules. These rules may be unconditional and conditional, based on wage inflation or price inflation or combinations of various possibilities.

7 Contribution rates
The score for this element reflects the complexity regarding contribution calculation and collection. Percentages may be different for different (groups of) members; contributions may be (partly) paid by employers.

8 Variable compensation
The score for this element reflects how variable compensation (such as bonuses, 'high risk' duty allowance, car allowance or overtime pay) are treated in the system.

(Continued)

Table 3.A.2.2 (Continued)

9 Service credit rules
The score for this element reflects how a year of service is determined and whether temporary workers are eligible to participate in the fund.

10 Divorce rules
This element reflects the complexity of rules regarding divorce of a plan member.

11 Purchase rules
This element reflects the different ways (groups of) plan members can purchase additional benefits, *e.g.* through rollover from other plans or via regular instalments.

12 Refund rules
This element reflects whether a fund pays a one-time death payment when a member, retiree or the retiree's beneficiary dies (apart from survivor benefits) and whether the plan employs different calculation methods.

13 Disability rules
This element reflects the complexity of rules regarding disability of a plan member.

14 Translation
This element reflects the extent to which documentation on the plan is translated into different languages.

15 DC plan rules
This element reflects the level of complexity regarding investment options for individual plan members in DC or hybrid systems.

Table 3.A.2.3 Definitions of administrative activities

		Service score[a]
1	**Annuity pension payment[b]**	1
2	**Pension inceptions[b]**	2
3	**Benefit estimates[b]**	3
4	**One-on-one counselling[b]**	4
5	**Member presentations[b]**	5
6	**Member contacts[b]**	6
7	**Mass communication[b]**	7
8	**Data and contributions from employers** Collection of data and contributions from employers	
9	**Other data** Gathering and maintaining member data that is not provided by employers	
10	**Billing and inspections** Advising employers of the required contribution rate, billing employers for contributions, collecting bad debts, employer reviews or audits, inspection and enforcement of obligation to participate in the mandatory system.	

(*Continued*)

Table 3.A.2.3 (Continued)

		Service score[a]
11	**Service to employers**[b]	8
12	**Refunds and transfers out** Payments that terminate your relationship with a member.	
13	**Purchases and transfers in** Service credit purchases for refunded past service, purchases that provide members with additional pensionable salary, individual or collective transfers-in from external retirement systems.	
14	**Assessment of disability pensions**[b]	11
15	**Board of directors** Elections, fees, expenses, CEO's office, excluding time spent on investments.	
16	**Financial control** Budgeting and forecasting, financial reporting, auditing of financial statements, actuarial work.	
17	**Board consulting** Benchmarking studies, strategic planning, fiduciary audits, but excluding portions relating to investments, half of the cost of ALM studies.	
18	**Marketing and public relations** Marketing costs to attract new employers, or new members, media relations, general communications regarding the fund, membership fees in *e.g.* councils of pension funds or international organizations.	
19	**Rules interpretation** Interpretation of existing rules sets and laws regarding the pension plan.	
20	**Design new rules** Plan contract amendments, adding new participating employers, actuarial work related to quantifying the impact of changes in the plan on behalf of unions, employers or legislators, strategic market research.	
21	**Lobbying** Maintaining relationships with government, unions and employer organizations.	
22	**Major projects** Major projects are long-lived assets that are capitalized and expensed over their useful life, which is greater than one reporting period.	

[a] These numbers indicate overlap with the definitions in the service score of Table 3.A.2.1; [b] For explanation, see Table 3.A.2.1.

Appendix 3.3

Pension fund details across countries

Table 3.A.3.1 Types of pension funds and pension plans across countries (numbers of observations)

	Australia	Canada	Netherlands	US	Total
Total numbers of observations	*27*	*34*	*33*	*160*	*254*
Type of funds					
Public sector: national government	20	22	24	102	168
Public sector: state or provincial government	0	1	0	12	13
Public sector: municipality	1	15	5	84	105
Collective agreement: teacher	5	8	3	107	123
Collective agreement: other school employees	5	15	3	106	129
Collective agreement: police and other public safety workers	5	14	3	88	110
Collective agreement: other	7	19	3	90	119
Corporate pension fund	7	8	8	0	23
Industry pension fund	14	4	25	0	43
Type of pension plans					
Defined benefits	20	34	32	137	223
Defined contribution	11	0	0	23	34
Hybrid DB/DC	13	0	4	46	63

Table 3.A.3.2 Cost of administrative activities across countries (in %)

		Australia	Canada	Netherlands	US
1	Annuity pension payment	3.45	7.68	4.97	6.25
2	Pension inceptions	2.92	7.26	11.58	9.26
3	Benefit estimates	2.41	5.44	1.83	3.28
4	1-on-1 member counselling	2.46	0.44	0.92	4.20
5	Member presentations	0.28	0.17	0.07	1.04
6	Member contacts	12.84	8.21	6.13	9.61
7	Mass communication	10.46	5.20	6.32	6.27
8	Data and contributions from employers	10.17	7.31	14.87	7.24

(Continued)

Table 3.A.3.2 (Continued)

		Australia	Canada	Netherlands	US
9	Data not from employers	1.81	2.06	6.51	2.15
10	Billing and inspections	0.28	0.33	3.93	1.20
11	Service to employers	2.02	2.92	5.61	2.88
12	Refunds and transfers-out	10.47	6.26	1.90	3.79
13	Purchases and transfers-in	0.55	9.98	3.26	5.23
14	Assessment of disability pensions	8.09	0.41	3.83	6.53
15	Board of directors	5.72	3.60	3.33	2.02
16	Financial control	12.17	6.22	4.89	7.59
17	Board consulting	1.61	3.53	1.71	1.22
18	Marketing and public relations	0.37	0.14	0.98	0.59
19	Rules interpretation	2.03	2.91	1.16	2.32
20	Design new rules	0.69	1.28	1.42	1.65
21	Lobbying	0.24	0.45	0.40	0.88
22	Major projects	8.96	18.19	12.09	14.81
	Disability and other premium exceptions	–	–	1.36	–
	Compliance to DNB regulation	–	–	0.93	–
	Total	*100.00*	*100.00*	*100.00*	*100.00*

4   Cost differences between pension funds and life insurers in providing pensions

Jacob A. Bikker

4.1. Introduction

The Dutch pension system consists of three pillars. The first pillar is the public pension scheme for all residents of the Netherlands, known as the Algemene Ouderdoms Wet (AOW; the 'general old-age law'). In addition, most employees build up a supplementary pension through their employer in the second pillar. Finally, anyone can make individual supplementary pension-saving arrangements with a bank (bank savings) or with a life insurer. These contributions or premiums may be deducted from income tax. This is the third pillar. Second-pillar pension provisions are collective insurance arrangements offered by pension funds and life insurers. Some employers have their pension scheme fully administered by a life insurer in a direct pension scheme, while some of the smaller pension funds outsource part of their insurance or investment activities to a life insurer.

In the third pillar, the self-employed (937,000 in 2015 between the ages of 15 and 65) and employees (in 2015, 9.5% of all employees) who are not eligible for a second-pillar collective arrangement can take out individual supplementary pension insurance with a life insurer. The same applies to people with a pension deficit, *e.g.* as a result of pension severance, or people who wish to further supplement their pension. Effective from 2015, pension provisions have been capped to the level of incomes up to EUR 100,000. This is expected to boost the market for individual insurance. Looking at the volume of premiums, the market share of life insurers in 2015 amounted to 34%, with just over half of this share for individual insurance.

The operating costs of pension funds (Bikker, 2017) and life insurers (PWC, 2009; Bikker, 2016) garnered much attention in recent years. In view of the above it is relevant to compare the operating costs of pension funds and life insurers with respect to pension provisions.

An initial attempt in this regard can be found in Section 4 of Bikker and de Dreu (2007). De Nederlandsche Bank (DNB), as the supervisory authority, now has more detailed data available on life insurers and life insurance market segments, which have been used in this chapter. We have provided an overview of these data in Section 4.3. Section 4.2 addresses the differences between pension funds and life insurers that have to be considered before a fair comparison can be made. Our conclusions can be found in Section 4.4.

4.2. Life insurers *vs.* pension funds

It is very complicated to draw a comparison between the operating costs for pension provisions administered by life insurers and pension funds respectively.

4.2.1. Different products

First of all, there is the question of whether life insurers are offering the same products as pension funds. This is not the case. Most pension funds offer defined-benefit (DB) schemes based on employees' last-earned or average-career salary, in some cases with guaranteed indexation against prices or wages until the moment of retirement (see Bikker and Vlaar, 2007). Life insurers are in principle not allowed to offer such schemes (*i.e.* not against fixed contributions), as they cannot spread the relevant investment, inflation and longevity risks over different generations by charging additional contributions. However, they are allowed to offer DB schemes if the employer commits to annually pay the contributions required for indexation and supplementation up to a specified percentage of employees' last-earned wages (referred to as 'backservice' in final salary pay schemes).[4]

Insurers operate on the basis of nominal pensions, with surplus profit-sharing as a means – but not a guarantee – to apply indexation.[5]

Pension funds are now increasingly offering defined-contribution (DC) schemes, in which the benefits depend on investment results. These can be compared to the unit-linked insurance policies offered by life insurers.

4.2.2. Mandatory membership

It is important to note that in terms of costs, pension funds and life insurers are incomparable in a number of aspects. First of all, the fact that membership in a pension fund is mandatory for employees significantly reduces the costs for pension funds, while life insurers must attract customers and therefore in recent years have had to spend over 20% of their operating costs on marketing and acquisition. It must be noted that these costs also cover the advice on pension accumulation for customers, so customers will not regard them as a waste of resources. Mandatory membership in pension schemes delivers significant societal savings on education and orientation costs. It should be noted that direct pension schemes administered by life insurers also benefit from mandatory membership, which means they do not have to incur acquisition costs for these schemes.

4.2.3. Adverse selection

As membership in life insurers' individual policies is not mandatory, this will also give rise to costs related to adverse selection: people with poorer health and correspondingly a greater chance to die will be more inclined to take out life insurance with death benefits. Conversely, people with good health will be more inclined to take out a lifetime annuity policy. To counter these adverse selection effects, applications for life insurance usually involve significant medical examination and selection expenses. These expenses do not play a role in pension funds' mandatory membership schemes.[6]

4.2.4. *Different organizational structures*

Differences in organizational structure also lead to differences in costs. Most insurers are for-profit companies, while pension funds are not-for-profit organizations. For the sake of comparison, corporate taxes on profit and surplus profit (after profit-sharing) must be added as costs for the policy holder. The question is whether return on equity should also be added, as pension funds need part of the contributions to build up or repair their buffer capital. In a sense, pension fund stakeholders must also contribute some sort of share capital. In the long term, however, these funds will ultimately benefit the stakeholders again, *e.g.* because the profits are used for indexation (see Bikker and Vlaar, 2007). The buffer itself will pass on to the next generation, however.

4.2.5. *Different supervisory regimes*

Finally, insurers must hold capital to cover insurance contract risk, which means that capital costs (or profits before taxes) must also be included in the costs. Pension funds must cover their nominal obligations at a rate of approximately 105% and in addition hold a solvency buffer to cover investment and longevity risk. The buffer for average funds amounts to approximately 25%. More generally, pension funds in the Netherlands must comply with the Financial Assessment Framework (*Financieel Toetsingskader – FTK*), while insurers in the European Union must comply with the Solvency II framework. Differences between these supervisory regimes may disrupt the level playing field for pension provisions between pension funds and life insurers.

4.2.6. *Economies of scale*

Recent research (Bikker, 2016, 2017) has shown that life insurers and pension funds can benefit from significant economies of scale; see also Section 4.3. This can also affect the comparison between life insurers and pension funds, as the latter tend to be much larger than the former, as can be seen from Tables 4.A.1 and 4.A.2 in Appendix 4.1. On the other hand, large insurers are usually much larger than small pension funds, which means that the transfer of pension schemes and outsourcing of activities by pension funds to life insurers can also be the result of economies of scale.

The differences between the products and cost structures of pension funds and life insurers must be considered in examining the differences in costs described below.

4.3. Cost differences: life insurers *vs.* pension funds

Table 4.1 shows a selection of core data over 1995–2015 for pension funds and life insurers: operating costs, profits, contributions and technical provisions.[7] The figures show averages of five-year (or four-year) periods in order to reduce fluctuations, which is particularly important with respect to profits – which are very volatile. The products offered by life insurers are broken down into individual and collective products, and consequently into endowment insurance and unit-linked insurance, *i.e.* four sub-categories in total. This breakdown is also applied to the core data in Table 4.1.

Table 4.1 Core data for life insurers and pension funds

	Life insurers				Pension funds
	Individual		*Collective*		
	Endowment insurance	*Unit-linked insurance*	*Endowment insurance*	*Unit-linked insurance*	
Operating costs in % of contributions					
1997–2000	15.7	16.0	9.6	4.3	6.3
2001–2005	13.0	18.3	11.7	5.8	4.3
2006–2010	13.4	17.2	12.3	7.6	3.8
2011–2015	*17.2*	*13.9*	*11.2*	*9.9*	*3.5*
Average	12.6	13.9	9.4	5.7	3.9
Profits in % of contributions					
1997–2000	8.7	−0.2	19.1	3.3	–
2001–2005	9.1	0.9	21.9	0.1	–
2006–2010	3.9	1.1	−3.0	0.9	–
2011–2015	*16.1*	*4.1*	*−13.9*	*−4.5*	–
Average	8.0	1.2	5.8	0.1	–
Operating costs and profits in % of contributions					
1997–2000	24.4	15.8	28.7	7.6	6.3
2001–2005	22.1	19.2	33.6	5.9	4.3
2006–2010	17.3	18.3	9.3	8.5	3.8
2011–2015	*33.3*	*18.0*	*−2.7*	*5.4*	*3.5*
Average	20.6	15.1	15.2	5.9	3.9
Contributions (in EUR million)					
1997–2000	8,627	5,299	3,431	2,806	8,694
2001–2005	10,092	6,579	3,581	4,478	19,599
2006–2010	10,272	5,736	4,050	4,475	26,912
2011–2015	6,545	3,374	4,330	3,835	31,517
Technical provisions (in EUR million)					
1997–2000	58,406	8,598	45,037	25,345	319,147
2001–2005	77,350	25,557	51,233	38,380	449,259
2006–2010	92,500	46,781	57,041	46,448	592,637
2011–2015	85,208	52,051	83,181	57,202	968,932

Source: DNB.

Endowment insurance policies guarantee payment at a specified moment or specified moments related to death or life. A risk insurance policy guarantees a specified amount upon death, and a mixed policy guarantees a specified amount during life after *e.g.* 30 years, or earlier in the event of death before this time. This latter type of insurance can also be used to repay an endowment mortgage or savings-based mortgage. An endowment insurance policy that pays out at *e.g.* the age of 65 may be used for a pension, for example in the form of annual or monthly payments. With unit-linked insurance policies, the contributions are invested at the members' risk, but any results are also mostly for the members' benefit. These products can be used for pension savings, but also to repay a mortgage loan.

It should be noted that the data are not broken down into pension provisions on the one hand and other life insurance provisions on the other, and that no separate detailed and comparable data are available on collective provisions and direct pension schemes. Survey data on the technical reserves of direct pension schemes are available for a number of years, however, and these vary from EUR 22.4 billion in 1997 to EUR 31.3 billion in 2008 to EUR 47.9 billion in 2015. These amounts are smaller than the figures for each of the two collective products' sub-categories. I think you have to start a new page here, as in the proof, the Table title was disconnected from the table

Table 4.1 starts with operating or administration costs expressed as a percentage of gross contributions.[8] The cost margins of pension funds have declined steeply over the last couple of decades, from 6.3% in 1997–2000 to 3.5% in 2011–2015.[9] Important reasons for this decline include the strongly increased size of pension funds (resulting in increased economies of scale), the significant rise in contributions (causing the cost margin to decline, assuming at least part of the costs are constant) and advanced automation (curbing the rise of costs).

Life insurers' operating costs as a percentage of contributions vary strongly by sub-category. Collective life insurance policies have lower cost margins than individual policies, but they are still well above those of pension funds after the year 2000. Despite consolidation and automation, this sub-category does not show a declining trend. The decrease in contributions for all four sub-categories is striking, in particular for the 2011–2015 period. This has caused the cost margin to increase, assuming at least part of the costs are constant, while at the same time the contributions at pension funds have seen a sharp increase.

For life insurers, the profits (after profit-sharing) are deducted from the contributions before the assets are allocated to the technical provisions to be paid out at a later stage.[10] The profit and loss margins are largest for endowment insurance policies for which the life insurers bear the investment risk, and smallest for unit-linked insurance policies for which the members bear this risk. The profit margins for the two collective sub-categories have declined sharply over time, and have even been negative in the last five-year period. Apparently this segment of the market, with actuarial knowledge on both sides of the table, is very competitive. There is a strong contrast with the sub-categories related to individual insurance policies, where profit margins have been relatively high over the last five-year period.

For the comparison of life insurers and pension funds it is best to look at the sum of cost and profit margins. Over the 2011–2015 period, for unit-linked insurance policies this sum is more than 50% higher than for pension funds, at 5.4% and 3.5% respectively – which can be said to be modest in view of the differences described in Section 4.2, and is in line with earlier five-year periods. The situation is rather different for endowment insurance policies, however. First, the loss margin exceeded the cost margin in the period 2011–2015, which means in effect that life insurers are 'subsidizing' these policies. This is not a sustainable situation, of course, and it shows the life insurers are operating in a difficult market, also as a result of low interest rates. For endowment insurance policies, the latest five-year period differs significantly from earlier periods, in which the sum for cost and profit margins was rather high compared to those for unit-linked insurance policies and pension funds. I think you have to start a new page here, as in the proof, the Table title was disconnected from the table

Table 4.2 summarizes the results by taking the average of endowment and unit-linked insurance policies for insurers: the cost and profit margins for collective insurance policies over the 2011–2015 period are extremely low, also compared to those of pension funds, which strongly contrasts with earlier periods and the margins for insurance policies.

In their approximation-based comparison for 2004, Bikker and de Dreu (2007) found a seven-fold cost and profit margin for individual life insurance policies compared with pension funds. Based on the disaggregated data that are now available, the factor for that year would be 6.2 (3.5% against 21.8%). At present, this relation is even more out of balance as a result of declining costs for pension funds; see Table 4.2. This stresses the importance of introducing collective arrangements for the self-employed, since individual arrangements are not cost-effective. Capping mandatory pension savings (to the level of incomes up to EUR 100,000) means that individuals must take recourse to less cost-effective options if they want to supplement their pension over the part of their income exceeding this cap.

Table 4.2 Operating costs and profits in % of contributions for life insurers and pension funds

	Life insurers			Pension funds
	Individual	*Collective*	*Total*	
1997–2000	21.1	19.2	20.5	6.3
2001–2005	20.9	18.2	20.1	4.3
2006–2010	17.7	8.9	14.6	3.8
2011–2015	*28.1*	*1.1*	*15.9*	*3.5*
Average	*22.0*	*11.5*	*17.6*	*3.9*

Source: DNB.

4.3.1. Effect of economies of scale

Cost margins not only vary by organizational structure, but also by the size of financial institutions. This may be important for the sectors' structure policy as well as for the options for deciding where to hold pension savings. Table 4.3 shows the cost and profit margins of pension funds over the 2011–2015 period for four size categories based on total assets, with the following limits in EUR million: 100, 1,000 and 10,000. The spread in cost margins varies enormously, ranging from 15.2% for the smallest funds to 2.7% for the largest institutions. It should be noted that the largest pension funds serve two-thirds of the members, which means that unutilized economies of scale only affect one-third of the members. I think you have to start a new page here, as in the proof, the Table title was disconnected from the table

Table 4.4 shows that the operating costs for life insurers range from 20%–22% for organizations with less than EUR 1 billion worth of total assets to around

Table 4.3 Operating costs for pension funds according to size categories (2011–2015)

Size categories based on	Operating costs/gross contributions (%	No. of pension funds[a]	No. of active members (x 1,000)
0–100	15.2	92	46
100–1,000	6.4	173	301
1,000–10,000	5.0	66	1,463
> 10,000	2.7	15	3,624
Average/[total]	3.5	[346]	[5,434]

Source: DNB [a] All data concern averages over the 2011–2015 period. Averages of numbers of pension funds have been rounded off.

Table 4.4 Operating costs for life insurers according to size categories (2011–2015)

Size categories based on total assets (EUR million)	Operating costs/gross contributions (%)							No. of life insurers[a]
	Individual			Collective			Total	
	Endowment insurance	Unit-linked insurance	Sub-total	Endowment insurance	Unit-linked insurance	Sub-total	Total	
0–100	35.1	7.4	20.6	44.2	17.9	20.4	20.6	7
100–1,000	23.2	11.8	21.6	54.2	–	54.2	22.0	13
1,000–10,000	19.6	9.0	15.3	10.9	4.5	8.7	14.4	14
> 10,000	15.7	15.7	15.7	11.1	10.1	10.6	13.1	6
Average/[total]	17.2	13.9	16.1	11.2	9.9	10.6	13.6	[40]

Source: DNB [a] All data concern averages over the 2011–2015 period. Averages of numbers of life insurers have been rounded off.

15% for individual insurance and 9–11% for collective insurance at the larger institutions. The economies of scale are clear, but less pronounced than pension funds, and less systematic for the sub-categories. This is partly due to the fact that every insurer administers many different individual and collective contracts, with relatively high levels of variable costs. In terms of contributions, the fourth size category comprises 72% of all individual insurance policies and 96% of all collective insurance policies.

Profits as a percentage of contributions can be broken down into size categories, like in Table 4.4. Except for individual endowment insurances policies (in which profits increase with size) there is no correlation whatsoever between profit margins and size categories.

PWC (2009) gives an interesting comparison based on a sample of 7,000 collective pension contracts concluded between employers and life insurers in 2006 and 2007, based on non-publicly available data of life insurers. The data were provided by the six largest life insurers, *i.e.* those listed in the bottom row of Table 4.4 (above 'average'). In three size categories between 100 and 100,000 members, life insurers turn out to charge less operating costs than pension funds.[11] This may be explained by the fact that life insurers can combine contracts and are able to achieve economies of scale. This does not provide a complete picture, however, because the most expensive contracts (*i.e.* those with less than 100 members) could only be found with life insurers in the sample and the cheapest (with more than 100,000 members) only with pension funds. Moreover, the less cost-effective, smaller life insurers were not included in the sample.

4.4. Conclusion

This chapter compares the operating costs of pension provisions administered by pension funds and life insurers. With their insurance products, life insurers play an important part in serving the public interest. Their policies can mean a significant wealth increase for individuals as a result of tailor-made provisions. The costs for products of life insurers differ from those of pension funds with respect to the (i) individual approach, (ii) the need for acquisition (promotion, distribution and advice), (iii) the costs caused by adverse selection and (iv) the profit objective. On average, the operating costs for life insurers are four times higher than those for pension funds in administering individual pension schemes, and six times higher if the profit margin is included.[12] This particularly affects the self-employed and employees wishing to supplement their pension in the third pillar. Capping pension build-up up to an annual maximum is not therefore cost-effective.

Pension funds can offer collective pension provisions based on mandatory participation at low operating costs, while life insurers can offer collective pension provisions at lower costs than individual provisions. On average, their costs exceed those of pension funds times three. PWC's study (2009) of direct pension schemes even points to lower costs for large collective contracts offered by larger insurers. Over the last five years, life insurers have offered collective pension provisions against significantly lower costs compared with pension funds, if the average profit margin (or rather loss margin) is included: together this comprises 1.1% of contributions against 3.5% for pension funds. Life insurers have become very competitive in this market segment, although a sustainable business model cannot be built on losses.

Notes

1 The weighted average costs of administrative activities are defined as $\Sigma_n w_n C_{in}$, with C_{in} the administrative costs of activity i for pension fund n. The weight of pension fund n, w_n, is defined as $p_n / \Sigma_n p_n$, with p_n the number of participants of pension fund n.
2 Weighted average incidence of different activities on total administrative costs is defined as $\Sigma_n w_n C_{in} / AC_n$, with AC_n the total administrative costs of pension fund n.
3 Note that marketing costs are very modest. Pension funds are not profit seekers (such as life insurers), which keeps marketing costs low. In most cases, they do not compete for the custom of participants as it is typically employers that choose a pension fund. In the Netherlands, membership of industry funds is generally mandatory.
4 In addition to direct pension schemes and collective contracts comparable to the schemes offered by pension funds, life insurers also offer reinsurance contracts and individual policies for individual customers including pension provisions and other insurances. Pension funds do not offer such products.
5 In some cases, partial indexation is guaranteed.
6 In addition, most people opting for annuity policies tend to be better educated, have higher incomes, better health and a higher average life expectancy, which is reflected in pricing. This affects the contributions rather than the operating costs of life insurers, however.
7 Life insurers do not separately report their investment management costs, as these are not part of operating costs but are included under the income from investments item. Pension funds do separately report their investment management costs; these are not included in the operating costs in Table 4.1.
8 As pensions have very long durations (in 2012: on average 17.5 years for pension funds against 13.5 for insurers), pension funds relatively hold more assets, causing their cost margins expressed in total assets to be smaller than those expressed in contributions.
9 This figure could be slightly higher for previous periods as a result of partial under-reporting of costs by smaller pension funds in particular.
10 Note that this concerns the profits on the existing portfolio, *i.e.* on past production.
11 Significant economies of scale can be seen within these three categories (PWC, 2009, p. 8).
12 The annual recurring costs per policy amount to EUR 50–100 (all figures in this footnote concern 2006). The non-recurring costs per risk insurance policy, including the medical examination, amount to EUR 300–500, while for endowment insurance policies (*e.g.* mortgages) and annuities (direct annuities and endowment insurance policies with an annuity clause) they can amount up to EUR 1,500–2,000. In the latter case this also includes advice.

References

Bikker, J. A., 2016, Performance of the life insurance industry under pressure: efficiency, competition and consolidation, *Risk Management & Insurance Review* 19, 73–104.
Bikker, J. A., 2017, Is there an optimal pension fund size? A scale-economy analysis of administrative costs, *Journal of Risk and Insurance* 84, 739–769.
Bikker, J. A., J. de Dreu, 2007, Operating costs of pension schemes, in: O. Steenbeek, S. G. van der Lecq (eds.), *Costs and Benefits of Collective Pension Systems*, Springer, Berlin, Heidelberg, New York, 51–74.

Bikker, J. A., P.J.G. Vlaar, 2007, Conditional indexation in defined benefit pension plans in the Netherlands, *Geneva Papers on Risk and Insurance – Issues and Practice* 32, 494–515.

PWC, 2009, *Uitvoeringskosten van pensioenregelingen: Een onderzoek naar de kosten van verzekeraars en pensioenfondsen voor de uitvoering van collectieve pensioenregelingen* (In Dutch; Operating costs for pension provisions: an investigation to costs of insurers and pension funds for the performnce of pension provisions) April 23, 2009, PricewaterhouseCoopers, commissioned by the Dutch Association of Insurers, 68.

Appendix 4.1

Table 4.A.1 Core data for pension funds over time

Period	No. of pension funds	Industry-wide pension funds	Company pension funds	Assets in EUR billion	Average assets in EUR billion *	Members x million	Members per pens. fund x 1,000	Costs per member
1997–2000	1027	88	919	428	1.8	13.5	14.2	41.9
2001–2005	881	102	758	521	1.9	16.2	21.0	54.5
2006–2010	646	93	534	708	2.4	17.6	32.7	64.2
2011–2015	387	72	298	1020	3.2	17.8	51.3	63.1

Source: DNB * 2014 prices in EUR.

Table 4.A.2 Core data for life insurers over time

Period	No. of life insurers	With collective insurance	Assets in EUR billion	Average assets in EUR billion *	Contributions in EUR billion
1997–2000	106	46	220	2.819	21
2001–2005	88	38	264	3.664	25
2006–2010	66	26	317	5.529	25
2011–2015	41	20	395	9.840	18

Source: DNB * 2014 prices in EUR.

Part II

Investment behaviour and risk-taking

5 The eligibility of emerging-market bonds for pension fund portfolios

Zaghum Umar and Laura Spierdijk

5.1. Introduction

The last decade has witnessed a renewed interest of researchers in portfolio choice theory, with a particular emphasis on the portfolio choice problem of a multi-period investor (*e.g.* Kim and Omberg, 1996; Campbell and Viceira, 1999; Balduzzi and Lynch, 1999; Barberis, 2000; Lynch, 2001; Bekaert and Ang, 2002; Chapados, 2011; Campbell and Viceira, 2002; Campbell *et al.*, 2003). The variability of expected asset returns over time is one of the main distinctions that sets apart the multi-period portfolio choice problem from its single-period counterpart. The distinctive characteristics of the multi-period portfolio choice have been known at least since Samuelson (1969) and Merton (1969, 1971, 1973). However, the recent empirical evidence that asset returns contain a predictable component has motivated researchers to revisit the multi-period portfolio choice problem (*e.g.* Keim and Stambaugh, 1986; Campbell, 1987, 1991; Brennan *et al.*, 1997; Fama and French, 1988, 1989; Harvey, 1994; Barberis, 2000; Lynch, 2001; Ang and Bekaert, 2007).

A multi-period investor's asset demand can be decomposed into the myopic demand and the intertemporal hedging demand. The myopic demand for an asset is the demand in a single-period context, when the investment opportunity set is assumed to be constant. The myopic demand is static in nature and similar to the demand derived in the classical mean-variance framework. Intertemporal hedging demand arises when an investor seeks to hedge against adverse changes in future investment opportunities.

Campbell and Viceira (1999) analyze the influence of the hedging motive on the total demand for stocks in a multi-period setting. They propose an approximate analytical solution to the Merton model for an infinitely lived investor with one risky asset and a single state variable. Campbell *et al.* (2003) go one step further and extend the Campbell and Viceira (1999) model to include more assets and state variables, by applying a simple numerical procedure in conjunction with an approximate analytical solution. They consider the multi-period asset allocation problem of an infinitely lived investor with the Epstein-Zin utility and derive this investor's myopic and intertemporal hedging demand for stocks, bonds and T-bills. They use a vector autoregressive (VAR) model to specify the behaviour of asset returns and state variables. The authors show that there is a sizable demand for US stocks and bonds. In particular, the hedging motive explains a substantial part of a conservative investor's demand for stocks. In Campbell *et al.* (2003), the intertemporal hedging demand for US stocks stems from the predictability of stock returns from the dividend yield, due to which negative stock returns in the present are associated with positive expected returns in the future. In this way, stocks can be used to hedge the variation in their own future returns.

Rapach and Wohar (2009) apply the approach of Campbell *et al.* (2003) to the US and six other developed countries (Australia, Canada, France, Germany, Italy and the UK). They find that in all countries the myopic demand for bonds is the main component of the total demand for fixed-income securities. In addition to the point estimates of the mean optimal demand for assets, Rapach and Wohar (2009) provide confidence intervals quantifying the amount of parameter uncertainty associated with the estimates. These confidence intervals turn out to be wide, reflecting a considerable amount of parameter uncertainty.

The goal of this chapter is to shed more light on the short-run and long-run risk-return properties of emerging-market bonds. Historically, international investors used to invest in emerging-market bonds denominated in US dollars. Recently, local-currency fixed-income securities in emerging markets have become more widely available (Miyajima *et al.*, 2012). Due to limited data availability, bond markets have received relatively little attention in the emerging-markets literature (Bekaert and Harvey, 2003). Some basic stylized facts derived from one-period returns are reported by Burger and Warnock (2007), but little remains now about the risk-return profile of particularly local-currency bonds in emerging markets. Because bond returns are negatively correlated with short-term interest-rate levels, they may hedge against fluctuations in investment opportunities over the business cycle. On the other hand, bonds are exposed to inflation risk, which is particularly relevant for long-term investors. Inflation-hedging is important for all long-term investors, but especially for those investing in high-inflation countries.

Our study extends the analyses of De Vries *et al.* (2011) and Spierdijk and Umar (2014) by considering more countries and by adding bonds to the emerging-market investor's asset menu. We first consider domestic investors in seven emerging market economies (Brazil, India, Malaysia, Mexico, Poland, South Africa, Thailand) and the US, with returns in the local currency. The domestic investor's asset menu consists of domestic stocks and bonds, as well as a domestic short-term money market instrument (the benchmark asset). We analyze this investor's demand for assets during the period February 2002–July 2012. Subsequently, we move on to an international investor with returns in US dollars, who can invest in local stocks and bonds in Argentina, Brazil, Chile, China, Colombia, Malaysia, Mexico, Peru, Philippines, Poland, Russia, South Africa or Turkey. The other options on the international investor's asset menu are US stocks, bonds and T-bills (where the latter is referred to as the benchmark asset). We study the international investor's optimal demand for assets during the period June 1999–July 2012. We calculate the optimal demand for assets for international and domestic investors, assuming different levels of risk aversion. Furthermore, we decompose the total demand for stocks and bonds in the myopic and intertemporal hedging demand using the approach of Campbell *et al.* (2003). An asset with a relatively high intertemporal hedging demand is attractive for an investor in the long run due to its ability to perform well in the event of adverse future circumstances, whereas an asset with a high myopic demand is attractive due to favourable immediate single-period expected returns. In addition to the point estimates of the mean demand for assets, we provide confidence intervals to quantify the amount of parameter uncertainty. Accounting for estimation uncertainty is particularly relevant in emerging markets, where data availability is often limited. We also analyze the demand for assets over time.

The present chapter makes use of different bond indices for international and domestic investors. The data for US dollar bond prices are available over a longer period and for more countries. Data availability constraints explain why our sample of emerging markets is geographically diverse, covering countries in Asia, the Far-East, Latin America and Eastern Europe.

We find that emerging-market bonds can be attractive for both domestic and international investors with different degrees of risk aversion. Some countries have bond markets that are particularly attractive for short-term investors, whereas the bond markets in other countries are interesting for long-term investors only (or for both long-term and short-term investors). In the former group of countries, bonds provide favourable immediate single-period expected returns. In the latter group of countries, bond returns perform well in the event of adverse future circumstances. For both domestic and international investors, emerging-market stocks can also provide attractive long-term and short-run investment opportunities. Also US bonds can be a favourable short-run investment option for international investors, but it is hardly ever optimal to invest in US stocks.

Whenever we establish a substantial and significant hedging demand for bonds or stocks, two conditions are met. First, their excess returns are predictable (from the term-spread and the book-price ratio, respectively), due to which these assets can be used to hedge the variation in their own future returns. Second, parameter uncertainty is sufficiently limited to make the hedging demand significant. We generally establish relatively wide confidence intervals for the estimated myopic and hedging demands, which indicates that there tends to be a high degree of parameter uncertainty involved with the approach.

The remainder of this chapter is organized as follows. The approach of Campbell *et al.* (2003) is outlined in Section 5.2. Section 5.3 is devoted to the data choices and the data's sample properties. We discuss and interpret the domestic and international investor's demand for assets in Section 5.4. Section 5.5 concludes. An online appendix with supplementary material provides some additional output.

5.2. Methodology

This section outlines the approach of Campbell *et al.* (2003). Let $R_{p,t+1}$ be the real return of a portfolio of n assets, for an infinitely long-lived investor with Epstein-Zin preferences defined over a fixed stream of consumption. Let $R_{1,t+1}$ be the simple real return on the benchmark asset (a short-term money instrument) and $R_{i,t+1}$ $R_{i,t+1}$ $(i=2.3, \ldots, n)$ $(i = 2,3,\ldots,n)$ the simple real return on the remaining n-1 assets. The portfolio return writes as

$$R_{p,t+1} = \sum_{i=2}^{n} \alpha_{i,t}(R_{i,t+1} - R_{1,t+1}) + R_{1,t+1}, \qquad (5.1)$$

where $\alpha_{i,t}$ is the portfolio weight for asset i. The log real return is denoted as $r_{i,t+1}$ $=\log(R_{i,t+1}+1)$, for all i. Let x_{t+1} be the vector of excess returns such that

$$x_{t+1} = [r_{2,t+1} - r_{1,t+1}, \ldots, r_{n,t+1} - r_{1,t+1}]'. \qquad (5.2)$$

Let s_{t+1} be the vector of the other state variables (also referred to as instruments), such as the dividend yield and the short rate. We stack $r_{1,t+1}$, x_{t+1} and s_{t+1} in a $m \times 1$ vector, z_{t+1}, resulting in the state vector

$$z_{t+1} = [r_{1,t+1}, x_{t+1}, s_{t+1}]'. \qquad (5.3)$$

The system of state variables is assumed to follow a first-order vector autoregression for z_{t+1}:

$$z_{t+1} = \varphi_0 + \varphi_1 z_t + v_{t+1}, \qquad (5.4)$$

where φ_0 is the $m \times 1$ vector of intercepts, and φ_1 is the $m \times m$ matrix of slope coefficients, and v_{t+1} is an m-dimensional vector of shocks that is iid normally distributed with mean 0 and covariance matrix Σ_v, such that

$$\Sigma_v = Var_t(V_{t+1}) = \begin{pmatrix} \sigma_1^2 & \sigma_{1x}' & \sigma_{1s}' \\ \sigma_{1x} & \Sigma_{xx} & \Sigma_{xs}' \\ \sigma_{1s} & \Sigma_{xs} & \Sigma_{ss} \end{pmatrix}. \qquad (5.5)$$

The innovations v_t are assumed to be homoscedastic and independently distributed over time, but cross-sectional correlation is allowed. σ_1^2 denotes the variance of the innovations to the return on the benchmark asset; σ_{1x} is the vector of covariances between the innovations to the benchmark asset returns and the other asset returns (with (N-1)elements); σ_{1s} is the vector of covariances between the innovations to the benchmark asset returns and the instruments (with $(m-n)$elements); Σ_{xx} is the covariance matrix of the innovations to the excess returns (with $(n-1) \times (n-1)$ elements); Σ_{xs} is the covariance matrix of the innovations to the excess returns and the instruments (with $(m-n) \times (n-1)$ elements); Σ_{ss} is the covariance matrix of the innovations to the instruments (with $(m-n) \times (m-n)$ elements).

Following Epstein and Zin (1989, 1991), Campbell *et al.* (2003) define the recursive preferences of an investor over an infinite investment horizon as

$$U(C_t, E_t(U_{t+1})) = ((1-\delta)C_t^{(1-\gamma)/\theta} + \delta(E_t(U_{t+1}^{1-\gamma}))^{1/\theta})^{\theta/(1-\gamma)}, \qquad (5.6)$$

where C_t is the consumption at time t, $E_t(\cdot)$ is the conditional expectation given all information at time t, $0<\delta<1$ is the time-discount factor, $\gamma > 0$ is the coefficient of relative risk aversion, $\theta \equiv (1-\gamma)/(1-\psi^{-1})$ and >0 is the elasticity of intertemporal substitution. A higher value of δ reflects a more patient investor and a higher value of γ corresponds with a more risk-averse investor.

The budget constraint for an investor with wealth W_t is

$$W_{t+1} = (W_t - C_t)R_{p,t+1}. \tag{5.7}$$

Given the budget constraint defined in Equation (5.7), Epstein and Zin (1989, 1991) derive the Euler equation for consumption of asset i in portfolio p as

$$E_t((\delta(\frac{C_{t+1}}{C_t})^{-1/\psi})^\theta R_{p,t+1}^{-(1-\theta)} R_{i,t+1}) = 1 \tag{5.8}$$

For the power utility case (with $\gamma=\psi^{-1}$ and $\theta=1$), the first-order condition in Equation (5.8) reduces to the standard one. Campbell *et al.* (2003) combine the approximate analytical solution of Campbell and Viceira (1999, 2001) with a simple numerical procedure to calculate the optimal portfolio and consumption choices for any values of γ and ψ. Campbell *et al.* (2003) approximate the log real return on the portfolio in a way that is exact in continuous time and highly accurate for short-time intervals. Furthermore, log-linear approximations of the budget constraint (first order) and the Euler equation (second order) are used.[1] The optimal portfolio (α_t) and consumption (c_t-w_t) rules are given by

$$\alpha_t = A_0 + A_1 z_t \tag{5.9}$$

and

$$c_t - w_t = b_0 + B_1' z_t + z_t' B_2 z_t, \tag{5.10}$$

where c_t and w_t are the log levels of C_t and W_t, respectively. A_0 (dimension $(n-1) \times 1$), $A_1((n-1\times m)$, $b_0(1\times1)$, $B_1(m\times1)$ and B_2 $(m\times m)$ are constant coefficient matrices that are functions of γ, ψ, δ, $\times$, $\check{n}_0$, ϕ_1 and Σ_v, with $\rho = 1 - exp[E(c_t - w_t)]$.

With the focus on an investor's optimal portfolio, we are mainly interested in the parameters of Equation (5.9). Following Merton (1969, 1971), Campbell *et al.* (2003) derive expressions for A_0 and A_1 in Equation (5.9) that divide the total demand into myopic and intertemporal hedging components:

$$A_0 = (1/\gamma)\Sigma_{xx}^{-1}(H_x\varphi_0 + 0.5\sigma_x^2 + (1-\gamma)\sigma_{1x})$$
$$+(1-(1/\gamma))\Sigma_{xx}^{-1}(-\Lambda_0/(1-\psi)) \tag{5.11}$$

and

$$A_1 = (1/\gamma)\Sigma_{xx}^{-1}H_x\varphi_1 + (1-(1/\gamma))\Sigma_{xx}^{-1}(-\Lambda_1/(1-\psi)), \tag{5.12}$$

where H_x denotes the selection matrix that selects the vector of excess returns (x_t) from z_t. σ_x^2 denotes the vector of diagonal elements of Σ_{xx}; $\wedge_0$ and $\wedge_1$ denote matrices whose values depend on B_0, B_1, B_2 γ, ψ, δ, ρ, ϕ_0, ϕ_1 and Σ_v. For full details we refer to Campbell *et al.* (2003). The first term in Equation (5.11) and the first term in Equation (5.12) sum to the total myopic demand for an asset. The myopic demand refers to the demand for an asset in a single-period context, similar to the demand derived in a static mean-variance framework, with a constant investment opportunity set. The second term in Equation (5.11) and the second term in Equation (5.12) sum to the total intertemporal hedging demand. The latter demand arises in a multi-period portfolio choice problem, when an investor accounts for changes in the investment opportunity set and tries to hedge against adverse future shocks. It is readily seen that an investor with logarithmic utility (i.e. $\gamma=1$ and $\theta=0$) will have a zero hedging demand. The hedging demand will also be zero when investment opportunities are constant over time.

The more risk averse the investor, the more eager she is to hold assets that deliver wealth when investment opportunities are poor. Consequently, the hedging demand is usually positive for sufficiently risk-averse investors. By contrast, a less risk-averse investor prefers to hold assets when investment opportunities are favourable. For such an investor the hedging demand tends to be negative.

5.3. The data

We follow the approach of Campbell *et al.* (2003) to estimate the myopic and hedging demands for assets, as outlined in Section 5.2. The present section describes the data choices we have to make in order to apply this approach to emerging markets.

We consider investors in several emerging market economies and the US, with returns denominated in either the local currency (domestic investors) or in US dollars (international investors). The domestic investor's asset menu contains a short-term money market instrument (called the benchmark asset), a stock market index and a government bond index, all in the local currency. Specifically, we focus on domestic investors in Brazil, India, Malaysia, Mexico, Poland, South Africa, Thailand and the US during the February 2002–July 2012 period (resulting in 126 monthly observations). The international investor can invest in the US, as well as in Argentina, Brazil, Chile, China, Colombia, Malaysia, Mexico, Peru, Philippines, Poland, Russia, South Africa or Turkey. The international investor's investment options are US and emerging-market stocks and bonds, as well as a 3-month US T-bill (the benchmark asset). All her asset returns are denominated in US dollars. The international investor's sample period is June 1999–July 2012 (yielding 158 monthly observations).

Throughout, we use monthly data series obtained from Thomson Reuters Datastream. We work with log returns and log inflation rates everywhere. Real returns on the benchmark asset are calculated by subtracting the monthly inflation rate from the monthly nominal return. We obtain excess returns by subtracting the nominal return on the relevant short-term money market instrument (the benchmark asset) from the nominal asset return. For the domestic investor, we use the inflation rate of the relevant domestic market to calculate real returns on the benchmark asset. For the international investor we use the US inflation rate. The book-price ratio corresponding to a stock index – used as a predictor of stock excess returns – is calculated as the ratio of the index's total book value divided by its total market value.[2]

5.3.1. Data choices

Table 5.1 displays the data series used by the domestic investor. The benchmark asset for each country is listed in the table's first panel. The choice of the benchmark asset is mainly driven by data availability considerations. The mnemonics for the equity indices are listed in the table's second panel. Bond returns are calculated from the JP Morgan Government Bond Index-Emerging Markets (GBI-EM) total return indices. These indices are emerging-market debt benchmarks that track local-currency bonds issued by emerging-market governments, with maturities of one year and longer. Their mnemonics are in the third panel of Table 5.1. The mnemonics for the inflation rate series used for each country are shown in the fourth panel. We use the nominal return on the short-term money market instrument, the book-price ratio and the term spread as the predictor variables in our VAR specification; these variables are listed in the first, fifth and sixth panels of Table 5.1. The domestic investor's term spread is calculated as the difference in nominal yield between the relevant GBI-EM bond index and the benchmark asset.

The first panel in Table 5.2 shows the Datastream mnemonics for the international investor's equity total return indices. For Colombia, Peru and Russia, Datastream's equity indices are available in the domestic currency only. We therefore convert the local-currency returns to US dollars using the corresponding exchange rate, which is also taken from Datastream. The exchange rate mnemonics are listed in the first panel of Table 5.2. We use the total returns on the JP Morgan Emerging Markets Bond Index (EMBI) to calculate the international investor's emerging-market bond excess returns. The latter index is commonly used as a benchmark to track the (US dollar) total returns of tradable external debt instruments in emerging markets, with maturities of one year and longer. The bond mnemonics are listed in the second panel of Table 5.2. The international investor's predictor variables are the nominal return on the 3-month US T-bill, the book-price ratio of the corresponding stock market index (third panel) and the term spread (fourth panel). The term spread will be used as a predictor of bond excess returns and is calculated as the difference in nominal yields between the JP Morgan EMBI Total Return Index and the 3-month US T-bill.

Campbell *et al.* (2003) and Rapach and Wohar (2009) use the dividend yield as the main predictor of stock excess returns. Similar to Spierdijk and Umar (2014), we establish strong explanatory power for the book-price ratio throughout. We therefore replace the dividend yield by the book-price ratio. We will come back to this issue in Section 5.4.[3]

Table 5.1 Sample statistics (domestic investor)

Country	Real returns benchmark asset			Stock excess return				Bond excess return				Inflation rate			Book-price ratio		Term spread	
	Mnemonic	mean	std.dev.	mnemonic	mean	std.dev.	SR	mnemonic	mean	std.dev.	SR	mnemonic	mean	std.dev.	mean	std.dev.	mean	std.dev.
Brazil	BRSELIC	0.70	0.46	TOTMKBR	0.19	6.13	0.03	JGEMBBR	−0.10	2.01	−0.05	BRCONPRCF	0.52	0.41	0.09	0.02	0.07	0.27
India	INTB91D	−0.09	0.80	TOTMKIN	0.98	8.30	0.12	JGEMBIN	0.07	1.93	0.04	INCONPRCF	0.59	0.79	2.59	1.03	0.12	0.10
Malaysia	MYTBB04	0.04	0.44	TOTMKMY	0.70	4.08	0.17	JGEMBMY	0.13	0.93	0.14	MYCONPRCF	0.19	0.44	0.58	0.09	0.10	0.06
Mexico	MXCTM91	0.25	0.36	TOTMKMX	0.91	4.71	0.19	JGEMBMX	0.26	1.64	0.16	MXCONPRCF	0.35	0.34	0.50	0.14	0.06	0.09
Poland	POIBKON	0.19	0.42	TOTMKPO	0.18	6.56	0.03	JGEMBPO	0.19	1.07	0.17	POCONPRCF	0.23	0.36	0.63	0.14	0.07	0.12
South Africa	SATBL3M	0.21	0.45	TOTMKSA	0.61	5.01	0.12	JGEMBSA	0.24	1.88	0.13	SACONPRCF	0.47	0.45	0.45	0.07	0.04	0.14
Thailand	THBTIBN	−0.05	0.61	TOTMKTH	1.10	7.22	0.15	JGEMBTH	0.21	1.86	0.11	THCONPRCF	0.25	0.59	0.49	0.14	0.14	0.09
US	FRTBS3M	−0.06	0.44	TOTMKUS	0.22	4.65	0.05	JGGIAU$	0.49	2.06	0.24	USCPANNL	0.20	0.43	0.42	0.08	0.11	0.12

Note: This table displays monthly sample statistics for the domestic investor. The sample period ranges from February 2002 until July 2012. The mean and standard deviations are in percentages. 'SR' stands for the (sample) Sharpe ratio. Because of unavailability of the book-price ratio, we report the dividend yield for Brazil.

Table 5.2 Sample statistics (international investor)

	Stock excess returns					Bond excess returns				Book-price ratio		Term spread	
	Mnemonic	Exchange rate	Mean	Std.dev.	SR	Mnemonic	Mean	Std.dev.	SR	Mean	Std.dev.	Mean	Std.dev.
Argentina	TOTMAR$		−0.38	9.17	−0.04	JPMGARG	−0.29	9.70	−0.03	0.73	0.27	1.43	1.20
Brazil	TOTMBR$		1.13	10.36	0.11	JPMGBRA	1.00	4.98	0.20	3.91	0.95	0.57	0.33
Chile	TOTMCL$		0.87	6.10	0.14	JPMGCHI	0.49	1.81	0.27	0.61	0.16	0.26	0.11
China	TOTMCA$		0.22	8.34	0.03	JPMGCHN	0.41	1.78	0.23	0.39	0.12	0.21	0.10
Colombia	TOTMKCB	COLUPE$	1.39	7.80	0.18	JPMGCOL	0.87	3.23	0.27	1.30	0.92	0.46	0.19
Malaysia	TOTMMY$		0.75	5.58	0.13	JPMGMAL	0.54	2.09	0.26	0.58	0.09	0.27	0.12
Mexico	TOTMMX$		0.93	6.98	0.13	JPMGMEX	0.71	2.24	0.32	0.53	0.15	0.37	0.14
Peru	TOTMKPE	PERUSO$	1.14	6.29	0.18	JPMGPER	0.87	3.84	0.23	0.67	0.40	0.45	0.18
Philippines	TOTMPH$		0.44	6.97	0.06	JPMGPHL	0.78	2.52	0.31	0.66	0.21	0.45	0.15
Poland	TOTMPO$		0.38	9.86	0.04	JPMGPLD	0.47	1.96	0.24	0.61	0.14	0.26	0.12
Russia	TOTMKRS	CISRUB$	1.34	11.07	0.12	JPMGRUS	1.50	4.75	0.32	1.00	0.36	0.59	0.55
South Africa	TOTMSA$		0.95	8.13	0.12	JPMGSAF	0.64	2.44	0.26	0.46	0.07	0.32	0.13
Turkey	TOTMTK$		0.53	14.97	0.04	JPMGTUR	0.82	4.09	0.20	0.63	0.20	0.50	0.21
US	TOTMKUS		0.02	4.82	0.00	JGUSAU$	0.31	1.43	0.22	0.38	0.10	0.15	0.10

Note: This table shows monthly sample statistics for the international investor. The sample period ranges from June 1999 until July 2012. The mean and standard deviations are in percentages. 'SR' stands for the (sample) Sharpe ratio. Because of unavailability of the book-price ratio, we report the dividend yield for Brazil.

5.3.2. Sample statistics

The domestic investor's sample statistics are reported in Table 5.1. Most of the emerging-market assets have higher sample Sharpe ratios than their counterparts in the US (where the sample Sharpe ratio is defined as the mean excess return divided by the sample standard deviation). Bonds are the only exception; the highest monthly sample Sharpe ratio of 0.24 is found for the US, while the lowest is established for Brazil (-0.05). India is the country whose money market instrument has the highest Sharpe ratio (0.8). The emerging market with the highest equity Sharpe ratio is Mexico (0.19). The lowest equity Sharpe ratios are found for Brazil and Poland (which both have a value of 0.03).

We move on to the sample statistics for the international investor as reported in Table 5.2. The equity indices of Peru and Colombia exhibit the highest sample Sharpe ratios, which are both equal to 0.18. The lowest Sharpe ratio is found for Argentina (-0.04). Also the Sharpe ratio of US stocks is relatively low (0.00). Emerging-market bonds tend to have higher sample Sharpe ratios than US bonds. Bonds in Mexico and Russia have the highest sample Sharpe ratios (of 0.32), whereas Argentina's Sharpe of -0.03 is lowest across all emerging markets. The US bond Sharpe ratio equals 0.22.

5.4. Empirical results

In line with Rapach and Wohar (2009) and Spierdijk and Umar (2014), we keep the approach tractable by imposing that investors can only invest in one emerging-market country at the time. We use a first-order VAR model to capture the time-varying nature of expected asset returns. We use the book-price ratio as the main predictor of stock excess returns. The nominal return on the benchmark asset and the term spread are used as the main predictors of bond excess returns (Campbell *et al.*, 2003).

For each domestic investor in a specific emerging-market country, the resulting VAR model is 6-dimensional and contains the domestic real return on the benchmark asset, the real stock and bond excess returns, the nominal return on the benchmark asset, the book-price ratio associated with the stock index and the term spread. For the international investor the VAR model is 10-dimensional and consists of the real and nominal returns on the benchmark asset, the real stock and bond excess returns for the US and the emerging market, the nominal return on the 3-month US T-bill and the domestic and US book-price ratios and term spreads.[4] Throughout, the VAR models contain the natural logarithm of the book-price ratios on the stock index. The estimated coefficients of the VAR model, based on OLS, are shown in the online appendix with supplementary material; see Tables I–II (domestic investor) and Tables III–VIII (international investor).

5.4.1. The domestic investor's demand for assets

The domestic investor's asset menu comprises domestic stocks, bonds and a short-term money market instrument, where the latter acts as the benchmark asset. As explained in Section 5.2, the demand for assets depends on several variables. Besides the estimated model parameters, we need relevant values for ψ (intertemporal elasticity of substitution), γ (degree of risk aversion) and δ (annual time-discount factor) in order to estimate Equations (5.11) and (5.12). We follow Spierdijk and Umar (2014) and use the values $\psi=1$ (intertemporal elasticity of substitution), $\gamma=2, 5, 7, 10$ (coefficient of relative risk aversion) and $\delta =0.92$ (annual time-discount factor) to cater for investors' different time preferences.

The mean optimal asset demand is derived from Equation (5.9) by replacing A_0 and A_1 by their estimated counterparts and z_t by its time average. The demand for each asset is decomposed into total, myopic and hedging demand. Both the total and the myopic demand over all assets sum to 100%, whereas the hedging demand over all assets in the investment set sums to 0%. The total, myopic and hedging demands are expressed as a percentage of the real initial wealth that is invested in a particular asset. A negative demand for an asset indicates a short position.[5] The point estimates of the mean optimal asset demand are subject to parameter uncertainty, because they boil down to functions of the estimated VAR-model parameters. To quantify this uncertainty, we follow Rapach and Wohar (2009) and estimate confidence intervals in addition to the point estimates using the Delta method.

The demand for local bonds is significant in Malaysia (where both the myopic and hedging demand are significant), Poland (myopic and hedging), South Africa (myopic), Thailand (myopic) and the US (myopic and hedging). Furthermore, the demand for domestic stocks is significant and substantial in India (myopic and hedging), Malaysia (myopic and hedging), Mexico (myopic) and South Africa (myopic and hedging).

The significant myopic demand for domestic assets in the above countries follows from these assets' relatively favourable Sharpe ratios. The significant hedging demand for stocks and bonds in the aforementioned countries stem from the predictability of these assets' returns from some of the predictor variables. For example, the VAR model for Malaysia shows that the lagged nominal return on the short-term money market instrument and the lagged term spread have the usual positive effect on the expected bond excess return, while the associated residual correlations are negative (particularly the correlation between the residuals of the bond excess return and term-spread equations). Together, these two effects make bonds able to hedge against the variation in their own future returns. That is, investors are generally long in assets that have high Sharpe ratios (such as bonds). A negative shock to bond excess returns implies a deterioration of investment opportunities for such investors. A strongly negative correlation between the innovations of the bond excess return and term-spread equations means that a negative shock to bond excess returns is generally accompanied by a positive shock to the term spread. The positive coefficient of the lagged term spread in the bond excess-return equation implies that the positive term spread will have a positive impact on expected bond excess returns in the next period. Therefore, low bond returns in the present tend to be followed by higher expected excess returns in the future, thus providing a hedge in the long run. The lagged book-price ratio in Malaysia's stock return equation has a significantly positive coefficient and the associated residual correlation is strongly negative. In a similar way as described for bonds, this gives stocks the ability to hedge against the variation in their own future returns. Hence, we generally find the term spread to be the most influential predictor variable in terms of the hedging demand for bonds. The positive impact of the lagged term spread on the expected bond excess return is usually explained by interpreting the term spread as an embedded maturity risk premium (Fama and French, 1989). Similar to Spierdijk and Umar (2014), we find that the book-price ratio rather than the dividend yield accounts for the hedging demand for stocks. More specifically, we find that a VAR model with the dividend yield instead of the book-price ratio underestimates the hedging demand for stocks. Chan and Chen (1991) argue that the book-price ratio acts as a proxy for a firm's relative level of distress. According to Fama and French (1992), the book-price equity premium stems from the higher risk premiums assigned to high book-price firms due to their increased risk of distress. Our results suggest that it is crucial to account for distress risk during the sample period 2002–2012. This seems intuitive, given that the sample spans a very turbulent period in both developed and emerging economies.[6]

Of course, parameter uncertainty should be sufficiently small for the hedging demand to turn out significant. Tables 5.3–5.4 show that the hedging demand for stocks and bonds turns out significant in a few countries (see above). Although the hedging demand for domestic bonds and stocks tends to be positive for most countries under consideration, parameter uncertainty is too large for the hedging demand to turn out significant. In particular, for Brazil the demand for none of the assets is significant. Of course, this does not necessarily have to imply that there are no attractive investment opportunities for short-run and long-run investors in this country. It is more likely that the 6-dimensional VAR model that describes the investment opportunities involves too much parameter uncertainty. A more parsimonious model could provide more significant results. In general, the confidence intervals for the mean asset demand are relatively wide, which is in line with Rapach and Wohar (2009) and Spierdijk and Umar (2014). The relatively wide confidence intervals emphasize that the outcomes of the intertemporal portfolio choice model should be interpreted with some caution.

Finally, we analyze the domestic investor's demand for stocks and bonds over time. Instead of using the time average of Z_t in Equation (5.9), we use Z_t itself and depict the time-varying demand for stocks as a function of time; see Figures I–III in the online appendix with supplementary material (for $\gamma=7$, $\psi=1$ and $\delta=0.92$). The demand for bonds tends to be higher in magnitude and more volatile than the demand for stocks. Bonds can have substantial myopic and hedging demand.

5.4.2. The international investor's demand for assets

We follow the same approach to estimate the international investor's total, myopic and hedging demand. The international investor's asset menu consists of emerging-market stocks and bonds in one of the countries under consideration, together with US stocks, bonds and 3-month T-bills. Again we consider parameter values $\psi=1$ and $\gamma=2, 5, 7, 10$ and use the annual time-discount factor $\delta=0.92$. The international investor's mean total, myopic and hedging demand for stocks are reported in Tables 5.5–5.9.

Table 5.3 Total, myopic and intertemporal hedging demand for domestic investors

Brazil

CRRA	Stocks Total	Stocks Myopic	Stocks Hedge	Bonds Total	Bonds Myopic	Bonds Hedge	Bills Total	Bills Myopic	Bills Hedge
2	**75.9**	**73.7**	**2.2**	**−140.2**	**−190.0**	**49.7**	**164.3**	**216.2**	**−51.9**
L	−130.4	−133.1	−72.0	−1131.6	−1262.2	−101.3	−739.5	−710.0	−221.0
U	282.3	280.5	76.5	851.1	882.3	200.8	1068.1	1142.5	117.1
5	**35.1**	**29.8**	**5.3**	**−43.1**	**−76.9**	**33.7**	**108.0**	**147.1**	**−39.1**
L	−56.4	−53.0	−44.4	−442.4	−505.9	−49.1	−273.9	−223.5	−145.5
U	126.6	112.5	55.0	356.2	352.1	116.6	490.0	517.7	67.3
7	**27.1**	**21.4**	**5.7**	**−26.2**	**−55.3**	**29.2**	**99.0**	**133.9**	**−34.9**
L	−40.4	−37.7	−33.3	−312.6	−361.8	−34.3	−178.1	−130.8	−118.5
U	94.7	80.5	44.8	260.3	251.1	92.6	376.2	398.6	48.8
10	**21.1**	**15.1**	**5.9**	**−13.7**	**−39.2**	**25.5**	**92.6**	**124.0**	**−31.4**
L	−27.7	−26.2	−23.6	−215.1	−253.7	−22.1	−104.1	−61.3	−95.2
U	69.9	56.5	35.5	187.7	175.4	73.1	289.3	309.4	32.4

India

CRRA	Stocks Total	Stocks Myopic	Stocks Hedge	Bonds Total	Bonds Myopic	Bonds Hedge	Bills Total	Bills Myopic	Bills Hedge
2	**165.4**	**102.7**	**62.8**	**4.0**	**75.7**	**−71.7**	**−69.5**	**−78.4**	**8.9**
L	39.3	24.6	9.7	−438.1	−132.5	−332.8	−468.8	−275.9	−230.2
U	291.5	180.8	115.8	446.1	284.0	189.5	329.9	119.1	248.0
5	**92.1**	**40.7**	**51.4**	**−71.1**	**24.0**	**−95.1**	**79.0**	**35.3**	**43.7**
L	15.5	9.5	1.2	−491.1	−59.4	−447.3	−310.7	−43.7	−289.7
U	168.7	71.8	101.7	348.9	107.4	257.1	468.7	114.3	377.1
7	**68.9**	**28.9**	**40.0**	**−71.3**	**14.2**	**−85.5**	**102.4**	**57.0**	**45.4**
L	8.0	6.6	−2.9	−464.3	−45.5	−430.4	−266.8	0.5	−284.2
U	129.8	51.1	82.9	321.7	73.8	259.5	471.6	113.5	375.1
10	**48.4**	**20.0**	**28.4**	**−63.5**	**6.8**	**−70.3**	**115.1**	**73.2**	**41.9**
L	1.5	4.5	−6.5	−422.2	−35.2	−395.6	−225.7	33.5	−271.6
U	95.3	35.5	63.3	295.2	48.7	255.0	455.9	112.9	355.4

Malaysia

CRRA	Stocks Total	Stocks Myopic	Stocks Hedge	Bonds Total	Bonds Myopic	Bonds Hedge	Bills Total	Bills Myopic	Bills Hedge
2	**474.5**	**255.3**	**219.2**	**1608.5**	**843.5**	**765.0**	**−1983.0**	**−998.8**	**−984.2**
L	204.7	105.2	82.1	551.6	312.4	168.2	−3137.6	−1583.3	−1633.5
U	744.3	405.5	356.2	2665.3	1374.5	1361.8	−828.3	−414.3	−334.9
5	**363.6**	**101.4**	**262.2**	**1404.6**	**326.1**	**1078.5**	**−1668.2**	**−327.5**	**−1340.6**
L	165.2	41.3	108.9	380.1	113.8	207.0	−2763.9	−561.2	−2268.3

Mexico

CRRA	Stocks Total	Stocks Myopic	Stocks Hedge	Bonds Total	Bonds Myopic	Bonds Hedge	Bills Total	Bills Myopic	Bills Hedge
2	**299.5**	**212.6**	**86.9**	**346.3**	**283.6**	**62.7**	**−545.9**	**−396.5**	**−149.6**
L	34.4	20.8	−15.6	−323.0	−132.3	−278.2	−1193.7	−780.5	−502.7
U	564.6	404.5	189.4	1015.7	699.5	403.7	102.0	−11.9	203.4
5	**153.2**	**85.6**	**67.5**	**200.0**	**112.5**	**87.5**	**−253.2**	**−98.2**	**−155.0**
L	8.3	8.9	−23.8	−259.7	−53.8	−263.6	−725.9	−251.9	−528.3

(Continued)

Table 5.3 (Continued)

	Brazil									India								
	Stocks			Bonds			Bills			Stocks			Bonds			Bills		
CRAA	Total	Myopic	Hedge	Total	Myopic	Hedge	Total	Myopic	Hedge	Total	Myopic	Hedge	Total	Myopic	Hedge	Total	Myopic	Hedge
U	561.9	161.5	415.5	2429.1	538.4	1949.9	-572.4	-93.8	-413.0	298.0	162.4	158.9	659.8	278.8	438.6	219.6	55.5	218.2
7	315.2	72.1	243.1	1297.4	227.6	1069.9	-1512.7	-199.7	-1313.0	116.5	61.5	55.1	166.4	79.9	86.4	-182.9	-41.4	-141.5
L	146.9	29.1	105.0	310.9	76.0	185.3	-2560.1	-366.5	-2248.8	3.3	6.6	-22.3	-218.8	-38.8	-225.7	-584.2	-151.2	-475.1
U	483.6	115.0	381.3	2283.9	379.2	1954.4	-465.2	-32.8	-377.2	229.7	116.3	132.5	551.5	198.7	398.5	218.4	68.4	192.1
10	264.4	50.1	214.3	1160.5	153.7	1006.9	-1324.9	-103.8	-1221.2	86.7	43.3	43.4	138.8	55.5	83.3	-125.5	1.2	-126.7
L	126.2	20.0	95.7	231.7	47.5	144.0	-2304.7	-220.6	-2128.9	0.5	4.9	-19.2	-173.2	-27.6	-180.6	-453.9	-75.7	-409.9
U	402.6	80.1	332.9	2089.3	259.8	1869.7	-345.2	13.0	-313.4	172.8	81.7	105.9	450.9	138.7	347.2	202.9	78.1	156.5

Notes: This table reports the domestic investor's mean asset demand for each emerging-market country, together with the corresponding confidence intervals, for risk aversion coefficients γ=2, 5, 7, 10. Here 'L' denotes the lower limit and 'U' the upper limit of confidence interval. The demand for assets is based on ψ =1 (elasticity of intertemporal substitution) and δ=0.92 (annual time-discount factor).

Table 5.4 Total, myopic and intertemporal hedging demand for domestic investors (continued)

Poland / South Africa

	Poland									South Africa								
	Stocks			Bonds			Bills			Stocks			Bonds			Bills		
CRAA	Total	Myopic	Hedge	Total	Myopic	Hedge	Total	Myopic	Hedge	Total	Myopic	Hedge	Total	Myopic	Hedge	Total	Myopic	Hedge
2	31.6	-10.1	41.7	1747.6	1014.3	733.3	-1679.2	-904.2	-775.1	277.7	135.7	142.0	436.1	323.7	112.4	-613.8	-359.4	-254.4
L	-138.5	-110.8	-37.4	835.0	515.6	271.0	-2545.4	-1371.0	-1221.2	72.4	19.5	43.4	-7.4	86.5	-134.9	-1096.4	-624.1	-510.6
U	201.7	90.6	120.9	2660.2	1512.9	1195.7	-813.1	-437.4	-328.9	483.0	251.9	240.7	879.7	561.0	359.7	-131.2	-94.7	1.8
5	55.9	-4.2	60.1	1231.4	402.8	828.6	-1187.2	-298.6	-888.7	202.9	54.3	148.6	214.3	127.0	87.3	-317.2	-81.3	-235.9
L	-62.1	-44.5	-27.5	460.7	203.6	202.9	-1935.5	-485.1	-1501.8	62.3	7.9	46.4	-171.6	32.1	-236.2	-722.5	-187.1	-570.5
U	173.8	36.0	147.7	2002.0	602.0	1454.2	-439.0	-112.0	-275.6	343.5	100.8	250.7	600.1	221.9	410.8	88.2	24.5	98.8
7	54.1	-3.1	57.2	1040.7	286.3	754.4	-994.8	-183.2	-811.6	168.4	38.8	129.5	162.0	89.5	72.4	-230.3	-28.3	-202.0
L	-45.2	-31.8	-22.1	332.2	144.2	139.6	-1688.3	-316.4	-1417.7	52.4	5.6	40.0	-189.9	21.8	-238.0	-598.3	-103.9	-523.7
U	153.5	25.6	136.5	1749.2	428.5	1369.2	-301.4	-50.0	-205.6	284.3	72.0	219.1	513.8	157.3	382.8	137.7	47.2	119.7
10	48.3	-2.3	50.6	853.0	199.0	654.1	-801.4	-96.7	-704.7	134.0	27.2	106.8	121.3	61.4	59.8	-155.2	11.4	-166.6
L	-32.8	-22.4	-17.7	218.1	99.5	77.8	-1427.5	-189.9	-1276.1	41.9	4.0	32.3	-188.8	14.0	-223.1	-478.9	-41.5	-460.6
U	129.5	17.8	118.9	1487.9	298.4	1230.4	-175.2	-3.5	-133.3	226.0	50.4	181.2	431.3	108.9	342.8	168.4	64.2	127.3

Thailand / USA

	Thailand									USA								
	Stocks			Bonds			Bills			Stocks			Bonds			Bills		
CRAA	Total	Myopic	Hedge	Total	Myopic	Hedge	Total	Myopic	Hedge	Total	Myopic	Hedge	Total	Myopic	Hedge	Total	Myopic	Hedge
2	182.0	144.3	37.7	312.0	396.7	-84.8	-393.9	-441.0	47.1	-14.0	46.4	-60.4	1097.2	687.9	409.3	-983.2	-634.3	-348.9
L	-11.9	-10.5	-12.4	-189.2	161.9	-508.0	-855.2	-765.6	-351.2	-320.8	-104.0	-248.1	152.5	75.4	30.8	-1841.7	-1220.8	-701.7
U	375.8	299.0	87.8	813.2	631.5	338.4	67.3	-116.4	445.3	292.9	196.9	127.2	2041.8	1300.5	787.7	-124.7	-47.8	4.0
5	80.1	57.9	22.3	206.3	154.6	51.7	-186.5	-112.5	-74.0	-11.4	18.5	-29.9	603.3	275.2	328.1	-491.9	-193.6	-298.3
L	-6.0	-4.0	-10.1	-255.8	60.6	-382.8	-615.3	-242.3	-495.2	-237.7	-41.8	-211.1	71.5	30.2	9.9	-980.3	-428.2	-608.9
U	166.3	119.7	54.7	668.4	248.7	486.2	242.3	17.4	347.2	214.9	78.7	151.4	1135.1	520.2	646.4	-3.5	40.9	12.3
7	58.7	41.4	17.3	200.7	108.5	92.2	-159.4	-49.9	-109.6	-9.0	13.1	-22.1	463.8	196.6	267.3	-354.9	-109.7	-245.2
L	-4.0	-2.8	-8.0	-227.8	41.2	-315.8	-564.3	-142.7	-508.3	-197.0	-29.9	-178.3	53.5	21.6	7.1	-734.9	-277.2	-503.0
U	121.4	85.6	42.6	629.3	175.8	500.3	245.4	42.9	289.2	179.0	56.2	134.1	874.2	371.6	527.4	25.2	57.8	12.7
10	42.3	29.1	13.3	194.5	73.9	120.6	-136.9	-3.0	-133.9	-8.6	9.1	-17.7	347.5	137.5	209.8	-238.9	-46.8	-192.2
L	-2.3	-1.9	-5.9	-198.6	26.7	-257.5	-514.3	-68.0	-506.0	-158.2	-21.0	-145.2	41.8	15.2	7.9	-524.6	-164.0	-395.4
U	87.0	60.0	32.5	587.6	121.1	498.8	240.5	62.1	238.1	141.0	39.3	109.8	653.1	260.1	411.8	46.8	70.5	11.1

Table 5.5 Total, myopic and intertemporal hedging demand for international investors

CRAA	Argentina Stocks			Argentina Bonds			US Stocks			US Bonds			US Bills		
	Total	Myopic	Hedge	Total	Myopic	Hedge	Total	Myopic	Hedge	Total	Myopic	Hedge	Total	Myopic	Hedge
2	**12.6**	**-9.4**	**22.0**	**-16.5**	**-16.8**	**0.3**	**280.3**	**134.8**	**145.5**	**1346.5**	**1013.1**	**333.4**	**-1523.0**	**-1021.8**	**-501.3**
L	-154.1	-162.5	-29.1	-153.6	-139.6	-34.9	-86.1	-105.7	-34.9	65.0	219.4	-321.8	-2928.0	-1880.5	-1205.1
U	179.3	143.7	73.1	120.7	106.0	35.5	646.8	375.4	325.9	2628.0	1806.9	988.7	-118.0	-163.0	202.5
5	**9.7**	**-3.6**	**13.3**	**-2.2**	**-6.3**	**4.1**	**233.6**	**53.3**	**180.3**	**879.6**	**402.2**	**477.4**	**-1020.6**	**-345.5**	**-675.2**
L	-71.2	-64.9	-34.4	-63.2	-55.5	-23.8	-31.9	-42.9	-20.2	-173.6	84.7	-352.7	-2163.4	-688.9	-1562.9
U	90.5	57.6	61.1	58.7	42.8	32.0	499.2	149.5	380.9	1932.8	719.6	1307.5	122.2	-2.1	212.6
7	**7.5**	**-2.6**	**10.1**	**-0.2**	**-4.3**	**4.2**	**201.3**	**37.8**	**163.6**	**739.8**	**285.8**	**454.0**	**-848.5**	**-216.7**	**-631.9**
L	-55.5	-46.3	-32.1	-45.7	-39.5	-19.7	-26.2	-30.9	-19.4	-217.6	59.0	-350.4	-1880.5	-462.0	-1488.6
U	70.6	41.2	52.3	45.4	30.8	28.1	428.9	106.4	346.6	1697.3	512.5	1258.5	183.4	28.6	224.9
10	**5.7**	**-1.7**	**7.4**	**1.0**	**-2.8**	**3.9**	**165.0**	**26.1**	**138.8**	**607.4**	**198.5**	**408.9**	**-679.1**	**-120.1**	**-559.0**
L	-43.0	-32.3	-28.4	-32.5	-27.4	-15.9	-23.3	-21.9	-19.6	-239.0	39.8	-335.1	-1584.9	-291.7	-1347.6
U	54.3	28.9	43.2	34.6	21.7	23.6	353.3	74.2	297.2	1453.8	357.2	1152.8	226.8	51.6	229.6

CRAA	Brazil Stocks			Brazil Bonds			US Stocks			US Bonds			US Bills		
	Total	Myopic	Hedge	Total	Myopic	Hedge	Total	Myopic	Hedge	Total	Myopic	Hedge	Total	Myopic	Hedge
2	**118.6**	**96.8**	**21.8**	**350.8**	**156.2**	**194.5**	**-111.5**	**-125.1**	**13.7**	**1541.9**	**909.4**	**632.5**	**-1799.8**	**-937.3**	**-862.5**
L	-290.3	-271.2	-32.8	-308.5	-280.5	-61.9	-671.8	-578.1	-191.4	690.6	430.9	87.9	-3040.5	-1782.6	-1467.9
U	527.5	464.8	76.3	1010.0	593.0	451.0	448.9	327.8	218.8	2393.3	1387.9	1177.1	-559.2	-92.1	-257.1
5	**62.3**	**39.3**	**23.1**	**336.4**	**62.0**	**274.4**	**-7.8**	**-50.9**	**43.1**	**1034.1**	**361.4**	**672.7**	**-1325.0**	**-311.7**	**-1013.3**
L	-111.5	-107.9	-18.6	-74.8	-112.7	3.4	-347.0	-232.0	-178.0	251.2	170.1	-11.4	-2319.7	-649.7	-1793.2
U	236.2	186.5	64.7	747.5	236.6	545.4	331.4	130.3	264.2	1817.0	552.7	1356.8	-330.3	26.2	-233.4
7	**49.3**	**28.3**	**21.0**	**311.5**	**44.0**	**267.5**	**11.9**	**-36.7**	**48.6**	**853.8**	**257.0**	**596.8**	**-1126.5**	**-192.6**	**-933.9**
L	-77.0	-76.8	-14.5	-37.4	-80.7	12.4	-269.1	-166.1	-153.4	104.9	120.4	-87.7	-2049.0	-433.9	-1713.4
U	175.7	133.4	56.5	660.4	168.7	522.6	293.0	92.7	250.7	1602.7	393.6	1281.3	-204.1	48.7	-154.5
10	**38.5**	**20.1**	**18.4**	**276.2**	**30.5**	**245.6**	**24.0**	**-26.1**	**50.1**	**681.9**	**178.7**	**503.2**	**-920.5**	**-103.2**	**-817.3**
L	-51.6	-53.5	-11.1	-17.2	-56.8	13.3	-204.1	-116.7	-126.4	-19.2	83.1	-157.3	-1762.5	-272.0	-1567.0
U	128.6	93.7	48.0	569.5	117.8	477.9	252.0	64.5	226.5	1383.0	274.3	1163.7	-78.6	65.6	-67.7

CRAA	Chile Stocks			Chile Bonds			US Stocks			US Bonds			US Bills		
	Total	Myopic	Hedge	Total	Myopic	Hedge	Total	Myopic	Hedge	Total	Myopic	Hedge	Total	Myopic	Hedge
2	**242.4**	**215.2**	**27.3**	**1227.3**	**416.0**	**811.2**	**41.0**	**-100.8**	**141.7**	**401.9**	**641.9**	**-240.0**	**-1812.6**	**-1072.4**	**-740.2**
L	4.9	17.6	-42.4	24.7	-235.1	165.6	-334.8	-342.4	-44.9	-1320.5	-282.2	-1186.6	-3244.2	-1835.5	-1493.1
U	480.0	412.8	96.9	2429.9	1067.2	1456.9	416.7	140.8	328.4	2124.4	1566.1	706.5	-380.9	-309.2	12.7
5	**118.3**	**86.3**	**32.0**	**1033.8**	**167.7**	**866.0**	**154.8**	**-41.1**	**195.9**	**-17.7**	**252.6**	**-270.2**	**-1189.2**	**-365.5**	**-823.7**
L	1.5	7.3	-31.5	128.6	-92.6	151.1	-105.9	-137.7	-3.4	-1367.4	-117.2	-1352.4	-2389.9	-670.9	-1782.8
U	235.2	165.3	95.6	1939.0	428.1	1581.0	415.4	55.5	395.1	1332.1	622.3	811.9	11.4	-60.2	135.4
7	**91.6**	**61.8**	**29.9**	**904.1**	**120.5**	**783.7**	**154.7**	**-29.7**	**184.4**	**-72.9**	**178.4**	**-251.3**	**-977.6**	**-230.9**	**-746.7**
L	1.0	5.3	-26.3	116.6	-65.4	121.9	-68.1	-98.8	2.2	-1266.7	-85.8	-1266.4	-2074.8	-449.1	-1680.5
U	182.3	118.2	86.0	1691.6	306.3	1445.5	377.5	39.3	366.7	1121.0	442.6	763.8	119.6	-12.7	187.1
10	**69.8**	**43.4**	**26.5**	**759.8**	**85.0**	**674.8**	**141.6**	**-21.2**	**162.8**	**-95.8**	**122.8**	**-218.6**	**-775.4**	**-129.9**	**-645.4**
L	0.2	3.8	-21.5	90.5	-45.1	85.7	-44.5	-69.5	2.9	-1128.0	-62.2	-1135.0	-1756.2	-282.7	-1518.9
U	139.5	82.9	74.5	1429.0	215.1	1263.9	327.6	27.1	322.7	936.4	307.8	697.7	205.5	22.9	228.0

Note: This table reports the mean asset demand for each emerging-market country and the US, together with the corresponding confidence intervals, for risk aversion coefficients $\gamma=2, 5, 7, 10$. Here 'L' denotes the lower limit and 'U' the upper limit of confidence interval. The demand for assets is based on $\psi=1$ (elasticity of intertemporal substitution) and $\delta=0.92$ (annual time-discount factor).

Table 5.6 Total, myopic and intertemporal hedging demand for international investors (continued)

	China Stocks			China Bonds			US Stocks			US Bonds			US Bills		
CRAA	Total	Myopic	Hedge	Total	Myopic	Hedge	Total	Myopic	Hedge	Total	Myopic	Hedge	Total	Myopic	Hedge
2	10.7	39.0	-28.3	759.8	522.2	237.6	238.2	58.3	180.0	1494.6	620.8	873.8	-2403.4	-1140.3	-1263.0
L	-149.5	-51.2	-107.6	5.9	2.7	-48.5	-56.8	-97.2	15.0	263.4	-53.7	200.0	-3681.5	-1795.4	-1951.5
U	171.0	129.3	50.9	1513.6	1041.8	523.6	533.2	213.7	345.0	2725.8	1295.3	1547.7	-1125.3	-485.2	-574.5
5	-18.1	15.8	-33.9	479.3	211.0	268.3	236.6	22.8	213.8	1213.4	244.2	969.2	-1811.2	-393.8	-1417.4
L	-132.6	-20.3	-120.7	34.9	3.1	-19.8	4.0	-39.4	25.3	224.7	-25.8	165.9	-2868.7	-655.9	-2265.0
U	96.3	51.9	52.8	923.7	418.9	556.8	469.2	85.0	402.3	2202.0	514.1	1772.5	-753.8	-131.7	-569.8
7	-17.1	11.3	-28.5	392.4	151.8	240.7	210.0	16.1	194.0	1047.1	172.4	874.6	-1532.4	-251.6	-1280.8
L	-114.4	-14.4	-107.3	31.9	3.2	-17.3	7.4	-28.4	20.9	159.3	-20.5	110.2	-2481.8	-438.8	-2088.0
U	80.2	37.1	50.4	752.9	300.3	498.6	412.7	60.5	367.1	1934.8	365.3	1639.1	-583.1	-64.4	-473.7
10	-13.3	8.0	-21.3	311.6	107.3	204.3	176.2	11.0	165.2	867.4	118.6	748.8	-1242.0	-145.0	-1097.0
L	-93.5	-10.0	-89.5	24.8	3.2	-17.2	5.8	-20.1	14.1	88.2	-16.5	49.3	-2071.5	-276.1	-1833.1
U	67.0	26.1	47.0	598.4	211.4	425.7	346.7	42.1	316.3	1646.7	253.8	1448.3	-412.5	-13.8	-361.0

	Colombia Stocks			Colombia Bonds			US Stocks			US Bonds			US Bills		
CRAA	Total	Myopic	Hedge	Total	Myopic	Hedge	Total	Myopic	Hedge	Total	Myopic	Hedge	Total	Myopic	Hedge
2	129.3	109.1	20.2	781.0	411.8	369.2	-46.3	-110.8	64.5	270.5	555.4	-284.8	-1034.6	-865.5	-169.1
L	-134.1	-107.7	-48.9	105.5	26.6	10.3	-480.6	-324.3	-200.7	-1287.6	-263.6	-1160.7	-2788.0	-1772.0	-1141.0
U	392.7	326.0	89.4	1456.6	797.0	728.2	388.0	102.7	329.7	1828.7	1374.3	591.0	718.7	41.0	802.7
5	53.5	43.7	9.9	704.5	165.2	539.3	42.0	-44.7	86.7	-172.8	219.2	-391.9	-527.3	-283.3	-244.0
L	-71.9	-43.1	-49.2	158.4	11.1	92.2	-279.1	-130.1	-176.6	-1486.4	-108.6	-1473.4	-2010.1	-646.1	-1451.1
U	178.9	130.4	68.9	1250.6	319.2	986.4	363.2	40.7	350.0	1140.9	546.9	689.6	955.5	79.5	963.1
7	36.4	31.2	5.2	671.5	118.2	553.3	52.6	-32.1	84.8	-260.6	155.1	-415.7	-399.9	-172.4	-227.5
L	-58.5	-30.7	-45.8	170.5	8.2	115.9	-220.7	-93.1	-150.0	-1457.5	-79.1	-1458.3	-1752.6	-431.7	-1393.8

	Total	Myopic	Hedge	Total	Myopic	Hedge	Total	Myopic	Hedge	Total	Myopic	Hedge	Total	Myopic	Hedge
U	131.3	93.1	56.2	1172.5	228.2	990.7	326.0	28.9	319.5	936.3	389.3	626.9	952.7	86.8	938.7
10	**23.1**	**21.9**	**1.2**	**629.7**	**83.0**	**546.7**	**56.8**	**−22.7**	**79.4**	**−317.6**	**107.1**	**−424.7**	**−291.8**	**−89.2**	**−202.6**
L	−47.8	−21.5	−41.7	175.3	6.0	132.1	−169.6	−65.4	−122.1	−1382.8	−57.0	−1390.6	−1496.5	−270.8	−1285.0
U	93.9	65.2	44.1	1084.0	160.0	961.3	283.1	20.0	280.9	747.5	271.1	541.1	912.9	92.4	879.8

	Malaysia Stocks			Malaysia Bonds			US Stocks			US Bonds			US Bills		
CRAA	Total	Myopic	Hedge	Total	Myopic	Hedge	Total	Myopic	Hedge	Total	Myopic	Hedge	Total	Myopic	Hedge
2	**222.6**	**172.5**	**50.1**	**1321.0**	**422.7**	**898.3**	**9.6**	**−50.5**	**60.1**	**213.1**	**635.8**	**−422.7**	**−1666.4**	**−1080.6**	**−585.9**
L	−13.8	18.9	−70.2	392.3	−6.8	317.4	−349.3	−268.9	−116.8	−1485.0	−367.4	−1358.4	−3518.5	−2151.6	−1489.7
U	459.0	326.1	170.4	2249.7	852.2	1479.1	368.6	167.9	237.0	1911.3	1639.0	513.1	185.6	−9.5	318.0
5	**161.4**	**68.9**	**92.4**	**1401.3**	**171.8**	**1229.5**	**83.1**	**−20.8**	**103.9**	**−268.4**	**248.7**	**−517.1**	**−1277.3**	**−368.6**	**−908.7**
L	1.9	7.5	−35.6	476.3	0.1	419.9	−187.4	−108.2	−108.2	−1718.1	−152.6	−1746.3	−2834.4	−797.0	−2137.2
U	320.9	130.4	220.5	2326.3	343.5	2039.1	353.6	66.6	316.0	1181.3	650.0	712.2	279.7	59.8	319.7
7	**143.8**	**49.2**	**94.5**	**1351.3**	**124.0**	**1227.4**	**92.5**	**−15.2**	**107.7**	**−329.4**	**175.0**	**−504.4**	**−1158.2**	**−233.0**	**−925.2**
L	7.0	5.3	−23.5	464.1	1.4	417.0	−148.0	−77.6	−94.6	−1664.3	−111.7	−1699.9	−2593.0	−538.9	−2138.2
U	280.6	93.1	212.6	2238.6	246.6	2037.7	333.0	47.3	309.9	1005.4	461.6	691.1	276.6	73.0	287.8
10	**125.8**	**34.4**	**91.4**	**1261.9**	**88.1**	**1173.8**	**94.3**	**−10.9**	**105.2**	**−349.2**	**119.7**	**−468.9**	**−1032.8**	**−131.3**	**−901.5**
L	9.8	3.7	−13.9	429.4	2.3	391.1	−116.2	−54.7	−80.9	−1544.2	−81.0	−1578.8	−2325.2	−345.4	−2048.2
U	241.8	65.2	196.7	2094.4	173.9	1956.5	304.7	32.8	291.3	845.8	320.3	641.1	259.7	82.9	245.2

Table5.7 Total,myopicandintertemporalhedgingdemandforinternationalinvestors(continued)

CRAA	Mexico Stocks			Mexico Bonds			US Stocks			US Bonds			US Bills		
	Total	Myopic	Hedge	Total	Myopic	Hedge	Total	Myopic	Hedge	Total	Myopic	Hedge	Total	Myopic	Hedge
2	238.4	167.4	71.0	1227.8	742.6	485.2	-342.8	-292.1	-50.7	24.0	158.9	-134.9	-1047.4	-676.8	-370.6
L	-300.5	-289.4	-46.9	-397.9	-250.6	-206.3	-962.4	-763.9	-281.4	-1443.8	-554.0	-1070.4	-2412.8	-1518.5	-1128.9
U	777.3	624.2	188.9	2853.4	1735.8	1176.7	276.8	179.8	179.9	1491.8	871.8	800.6	318.0	164.9	387.8
5	146.8	67.9	79.0	786.7	297.6	489.1	-109.7	-118.3	8.6	-3.8	60.2	-64.0	-720.0	-207.3	-512.7
L	-99.1	-114.9	-23.9	-227.6	-99.7	-182.6	-481.7	-307.0	-231.1	-1148.9	-225.1	-1044.4	-1869.9	-544.1	-1462.2
U	392.8	250.6	181.9	1801.0	694.9	1160.8	262.2	70.4	248.2	1141.4	345.5	916.4	429.9	129.4	436.9
7	120.1	48.9	71.2	644.8	212.8	432.0	-59.9	-85.2	25.3	5.1	41.4	-36.3	-610.1	-117.9	-492.2
L	-63.5	-81.7	-18.0	-184.1	-71.0	-161.9	-364.5	-219.9	-189.9	-1012.4	-162.4	-950.3	-1666.0	-358.5	-1415.0
U	303.6	179.4	160.4	1473.8	496.6	1025.9	244.8	49.6	240.6	1022.5	245.3	877.6	445.7	122.7	430.5
10	95.6	34.7	60.9	513.0	149.2	363.8	-25.7	-60.4	34.7	15.7	27.3	-11.6	-498.6	-50.8	-447.8
L	-39.1	-56.7	-13.6	-147.3	-49.5	-139.4	-269.4	-154.7	-149.9	-871.6	-115.5	-836.6	-1443.3	-219.3	-1306.4
U	230.3	126.1	135.5	1173.3	347.9	866.9	218.0	33.9	219.2	903.0	170.1	813.4	446.1	117.7	410.9

CRAA	Peru Stocks			Peru Bonds			US Stocks			US Bonds			US Bills		
	Total	Myopic	Hedge	Total	Myopic	Hedge	Total	Myopic	Hedge	Total	Myopic	Hedge	Total	Myopic	Hedge
2	144.3	135.0	9.3	531.9	211.5	320.3	135.4	-23.3	158.7	1019.0	771.3	247.7	-1730.5	-994.5	-736.1
L	-100.7	-49.3	-71.6	125.1	-13.5	106.5	-183.8	-187.4	-33.5	16.4	225.1	-337.9	-2964.4	-1658.2	-1409.3
U	389.2	319.2	90.3	938.6	436.6	534.1	454.7	140.9	350.9	2021.5	1317.5	833.3	-496.7	-330.7	-62.8
5	66.6	55.1	11.6	456.3	83.9	372.4	203.8	-9.8	213.6	516.6	306.4	210.2	-1143.4	-335.6	-807.8
L	-63.8	-18.6	-64.7	121.7	-6.1	99.7	-48.2	-75.5	4.4	-367.7	88.0	-544.2	-2201.1	-601.1	-1675.6
U	197.0	128.8	87.8	790.9	173.9	645.2	455.8	55.9	422.8	1400.9	524.8	964.6	-85.6	-70.1	59.9
7	51.1	39.9	11.3	406.6	59.5	347.0	192.6	-7.2	199.8	381.6	217.9	163.7	-931.8	-210.1	-721.8
L	-51.6	-12.8	-56.2	100.6	-4.7	81.1	-26.4	-54.2	9.6	-435.6	61.9	-569.4	-1902.1	-399.7	-1566.0
U	153.8	92.5	78.7	712.6	123.8	613.0	411.5	39.7	390.0	1198.8	373.9	896.8	38.4	-20.4	122.5

CRAA	Philippines Stocks			Philippines Bonds			US Stocks			US Bonds			US Bills		
	Total	Myopic	Hedge	Total	Myopic	Hedge	Total	Myopic	Hedge	Total	Myopic	Hedge	Total	Myopic	Hedge
10	39.3	28.4	10.8	348.5	41.3	307.2	170.2	−5.3	175.5	270.6	151.5	119.1	−728.6	−115.9	−612.6
L	−40.5	−8.4	−46.7	74.5	−3.7	58.4	−13.8	−38.2	10.2	−464.4	42.3	−563.1	−1596.8	−248.7	−1400.0
U	119.0	65.3	68.3	622.6	86.3	556.1	354.2	27.6	340.7	1005.5	260.7	801.3	139.7	16.8	174.8

CRAA	Philippines Stocks			Philippines Bonds			US Stocks			US Bonds			US Bills		
	Total	Myopic	Hedge	Total	Myopic	Hedge	Total	Myopic	Hedge	Total	Myopic	Hedge	Total	Myopic	Hedge
2	−50.3	−34.6	−15.8	1447.6	759.3	688.4	40.9	−23.3	64.2	136.8	600.3	−463.5	−1474.9	−1201.6	−273.3
L	−400.9	−271.4	−156.3	498.6	278.6	182.6	−291.4	−201.4	−153.4	−1373.2	−174.3	−1347.6	−3254.2	−2150.8	−1236.0
U	300.2	202.2	124.8	2396.7	1239.9	1194.1	373.1	154.7	281.8	1646.8	1374.9	420.6	304.3	−252.5	689.5
5	−36.1	−14.0	−22.1	1205.5	303.8	901.8	102.9	−9.4	112.4	−361.0	237.9	−598.9	−811.3	−418.2	−393.1
L	−248.5	−108.8	−163.2	370.5	111.4	221.8	−170.2	−80.6	−127.2	−1726.1	−72.0	−1757.2	−2395.5	−797.8	−1702.4
U	176.3	80.7	119.0	2040.5	496.1	1581.7	376.1	61.8	352.0	1004.0	547.8	559.4	772.9	−38.6	916.2
7	−32.7	−10.1	−22.6	1113.1	217.0	896.1	104.3	−6.8	111.0	−445.4	168.9	−614.2	−639.3	−269.0	−370.3
L	−206.4	−77.8	−148.9	331.7	79.6	218.4	−137.5	−57.6	−109.4	−1718.8	−52.5	−1751.0	−2120.5	−540.1	−1669.5
U	141.1	57.6	103.7	1894.4	354.4	1573.7	346.1	44.1	331.5	828.0	390.3	522.5	842.0	2.1	928.9
10	−29.6	−7.2	−22.4	1013.3	151.9	861.4	98.2	−4.8	102.9	−496.2	117.1	−613.3	−485.7	−157.1	−328.6
L	−169.1	−54.6	−131.3	296.1	55.7	211.6	−109.5	−40.4	−91.6	−1653.7	−37.9	−1682.9	−1835.7	−346.9	−1561.5
U	109.9	40.3	86.5	1730.5	248.2	1511.2	305.8	30.8	297.5	661.2	272.1	456.2	864.4	32.7	904.3

Table 5.8 Total, myopic and intertemporal hedging demand for international investors (continued)

CRAA	Poland Stocks			Poland Bonds			US Stocks			US Bonds			US Bills		
	Total	Myopic	Hedge	Total	Myopic	Hedge	Total	Myopic	Hedge	Total	Myopic	Hedge	Total	Myopic	Hedge
2	78.9	41.1	37.7	959.9	506.0	453.8	-8.9	-15.3	6.4	539.0	537.1	1.9	-1468.8	-969.0	-499.8
L	-139.0	-113.9	-35.5	-129.6	-23.2	-163.2	-541.9	-354.8	-223.4	-736.6	-223.0	-752.6	-3187.7	-1986.5	-1323.1
U	296.7	196.2	110.9	2049.4	1035.2	1070.9	524.1	324.3	236.1	1814.7	1297.3	756.3	250.1	48.5	323.5
5	62.8	16.9	46.0	672.3	205.1	467.2	21.3	-7.4	28.6	326.1	209.9	116.2	-982.4	-324.4	-658.0
L	-55.3	-45.2	-23.1	-159.7	-6.6	-194.2	-332.8	-143.2	-221.6	-813.6	-94.3	-858.8	-2393.9	-731.5	-1758.9
U	181.0	78.9	115.0	1504.2	416.7	1128.6	375.3	128.4	278.9	1465.7	514.0	1091.2	429.0	82.7	442.9
7	54.4	12.2	42.1	560.9	147.7	413.1	26.3	-5.9	32.2	282.5	147.5	135.0	-824.1	-201.6	-622.5
L	-38.4	-32.1	-18.7	-148.5	-3.4	-179.5	-271.5	-102.9	-196.1	-786.7	-69.8	-823.4	-2115.3	-492.5	-1703.4
U	147.1	56.6	102.9	1270.2	298.9	1005.8	324.2	91.2	260.6	1351.8	364.8	1093.3	467.0	89.2	458.5
10	45.3	8.8	36.5	452.1	104.8	347.3	27.2	-4.8	32.0	243.7	100.8	142.9	-668.3	-109.6	-558.7
L	-26.3	-22.2	-15.0	-130.4	-1.0	-157.4	-217.0	-72.7	-166.9	-734.5	-51.4	-761.9	-1821.8	-313.2	-1573.3
U	116.8	39.8	88.0	1034.6	210.5	852.0	271.4	63.2	230.9	1221.9	252.9	1047.7	485.3	94.1	455.9

CRAA	Russia Stocks			Russia Bonds			US Stocks			US Bonds			US Bills		
	Total	Myopic	Hedge	Total	Myopic	Hedge	Total	Myopic	Hedge	Total	Myopic	Hedge	Total	Myopic	Hedge
2	170.1	31.0	139.1	740.5	591.5	149.1	-456.8	-233.7	-223.1	589.8	427.3	162.5	-943.7	-716.1	-227.5
L	-9.3	-116.6	56.6	136.8	161.5	-94.2	-926.7	-514.6	-476.3	-522.5	-131.3	-647.2	-2313.7	-1470.7	-1104.5
U	349.5	178.6	221.6	1344.3	1021.4	392.4	13.1	47.2	30.1	1702.1	986.0	972.1	426.4	38.5	649.4
5	131.5	12.8	118.7	323.8	237.4	86.4	-191.2	-94.7	-96.5	676.4	167.7	508.7	-840.5	-223.2	-617.2
L	35.9	-46.2	48.4	-2.0	65.4	-119.6	-509.1	-207.0	-341.0	-375.2	-55.7	-448.4	-2064.5	-524.9	-1671.5
U	227.1	71.8	189.0	649.6	409.3	292.4	126.7	17.6	148.0	1727.9	391.1	1465.8	383.6	78.5	437.0
7	107.6	9.4	98.3	235.9	169.9	66.0	-124.4	-68.2	-56.1	634.0	118.2	515.8	-753.2	-129.3	-623.9
L	32.5	-32.8	38.7	-17.9	47.1	-107.5	-391.3	-148.4	-273.4	-350.4	-41.3	-405.6	-1881.0	-344.7	-1636.3
U	182.8	51.5	157.9	489.7	292.8	239.5	142.5	12.0	161.1	1618.4	277.8	1437.1	374.6	86.1	388.5
10	84.3	6.8	77.5	168.5	119.3	49.2	-75.5	-48.4	-27.1	564.5	81.1	483.3	-641.8	-58.9	-582.9
L	26.4	-22.7	29.0	-24.2	33.4	-91.0	-293.3	-104.5	-212.0	-329.2	-30.6	-369.2	-1649.9	-209.6	-1514.7
U	142.2	36.3	126.1	361.3	205.3	189.3	142.4	7.8	157.8	1458.1	192.9	1335.8	366.3	91.8	348.9

Table 5.9 Total, myopic and intertemporal hedging demand for international investors (continued)

CRAA	South Africa Stocks			South Africa Bonds			US Stocks			US Bonds			US Bills		
	Total	Myopic	Hedge	Total	Myopic	Hedge	Total	Myopic	Hedge	Total	Myopic	Hedge	Total	Myopic	Hedge
2	**87.7**	**77.1**	**10.6**	**1160.6**	**453.3**	**707.3**	**-57.6**	**-77.7**	**20.1**	**219.9**	**548.6**	**-328.7**	**-1310.6**	**-901.4**	**-409.3**
L	-110.6	-94.1	-34.0	225.8	-41.5	234.8	-476.2	-329.1	-190.2	-984.8	-107.9	-1026.7	-2895.0	-1816.2	-1178.0
U	285.9	248.2	55.2	2095.5	948.1	1179.9	361.1	173.8	230.4	1424.6	1205.1	369.2	273.7	13.4	359.5
5	**29.8**	**31.0**	**-1.2**	**1061.5**	**183.4**	**878.1**	**60.4**	**-31.9**	**92.3**	**-153.4**	**215.2**	**-368.6**	**-898.4**	**-297.8**	**-600.5**
L	-68.5	-37.5	-47.3	294.4	-14.5	281.5	-253.8	-132.5	-150.1	-1224.4	-47.5	-1271.0	-2214.3	-663.8	-1622.4
U	128.1	99.5	44.8	1828.7	381.3	1474.8	374.6	68.8	334.6	917.7	478.0	533.8	417.6	68.2	421.3
7	**18.6**	**22.3**	**-3.7**	**980.2**	**132.0**	**848.3**	**75.5**	**-23.1**	**98.6**	**-217.1**	**151.7**	**-368.8**	**-757.2**	**-182.8**	**-574.4**
L	-58.3	-26.7	-45.8	291.8	-9.4	276.5	-196.8	-95.1	-125.0	-1210.1	-36.0	-1249.9	-1956.0	-444.3	-1572.8
U	95.4	71.2	38.5	1668.7	273.4	1420.0	347.8	48.8	322.2	776.0	339.5	512.2	441.6	78.7	424.1
10	**10.7**	**15.7**	**-5.0**	**881.3**	**93.4**	**787.9**	**79.5**	**-16.6**	**96.1**	**-254.6**	**104.1**	**-358.7**	**-616.9**	**-96.6**	**-520.3**
L	-48.9	-18.6	-42.2	278.9	-5.6	262.9	-149.8	-67.0	-101.0	-1150.9	-27.4	-1182.9	-1681.5	-279.7	-1452.3
U	70.3	50.0	32.3	1483.8	192.4	1312.9	308.7	33.8	293.1	641.8	235.6	465.5	447.6	86.5	411.7

CRAA	Turkey Stocks			Turkey Bonds			US Stocks			US Bonds			US Bills		
	Total	Myopic	Hedge	Total	Myopic	Hedge	Total	Myopic	Hedge	Total	Myopic	Hedge	Total	Myopic	Hedge
2	**-9.4**	**7.1**	**-16.5**	**707.1**	**309.8**	**397.4**	**-33.5**	**-56.2**	**22.7**	**917.6**	**787.1**	**130.6**	**-1481.9**	**-947.7**	**-534.1**
L	-121.3	-73.7	-53.1	44.3	-68.2	89.3	-472.6	-306.2	-188.4	-189.8	151.2	-442.0	-2715.1	-1640.0	-1160.3
U	102.4	87.8	20.1	1370.0	687.8	705.4	405.6	193.7	233.8	2025.0	1422.9	703.2	-248.6	-255.4	92.0
5	**-16.3**	**2.7**	**-19.0**	**630.7**	**124.2**	**506.5**	**44.4**	**-22.6**	**66.9**	**420.4**	**312.0**	**108.4**	**-979.2**	**-316.3**	**-662.8**
L	-77.2	-29.6	-54.3	132.6	-27.0	136.9	-258.5	-122.5	-155.0	-490.0	57.6	-629.4	-2009.1	-593.3	-1489.6
U	44.6	35.0	16.3	1128.8	275.4	876.2	347.2	77.4	288.9	1330.8	566.4	846.2	50.8	-39.3	163.9
7	**-17.0**	**1.9**	**-18.8**	**587.0**	**88.9**	**498.1**	**54.8**	**-16.2**	**71.0**	**297.4**	**221.5**	**75.9**	**-822.2**	**-196.1**	**-626.2**
L	-65.4	-21.2	-50.5	148.3	-19.2	147.1	-198.4	-87.6	-127.7	-530.2	39.7	-639.1	-1763.6	-393.9	-1433.5
U	31.5	25.0	12.9	1025.6	196.9	849.1	308.0	55.2	269.6	1125.0	403.3	791.0	119.1	1.8	181.1
10	**-16.9**	**1.2**	**-18.1**	**534.4**	**62.4**	**472.1**	**58.4**	**-11.4**	**69.7**	**197.2**	**153.6**	**43.5**	**-673.1**	**-105.9**	**-567.2**
L	-55.1	-14.9	-45.7	156.0	-13.3	151.8	-147.6	-61.3	-100.5	-536.5	26.4	-619.0	-1511.0	-244.4	-1319.2
U	21.3	17.4	9.5	912.9	138.0	792.3	264.3	38.6	240.0	930.9	280.9	706.1	164.8	32.7	184.8

The demand for emerging-market bonds is significant for Brazil (where only the hedging demand is significant, for more conservative investors), Chile (hedging), China (myopic), Colombia (myopic), Malaysia (myopic), Peru (hedging), Philippines (myopic and hedging), Russia (myopic), South Africa (hedging) and Turkey (hedging). The demand for US bonds is significant and substantial for Argentina (myopic), Brazil (myopic), China (hedging), Peru (myopic) and Turkey (myopic). Whenever bonds have favourable Sharpe ratios, the myopic demand for these assets tends to be substantial and significant (provided that the amount of parameter uncertainty is small enough). Again the VAR estimates and the residual correlations show that particularly the term spread accounts for the hedging demand for bonds, but not in all countries parameter uncertainty is sufficiently limited to make the hedging demand significant.

The international investor's demand for emerging-market stocks is significant for Chile (myopic and hedging), Malaysia (myopic), Russia (hedging). The hedging demand for US stocks is only significant for international investors who consider China or Peru as their foreign target market. The myopic demand for US stocks is often negative, but never significant. The negative myopic demand for US stocks in countries other than China and Argentina can be explained from the relatively low Sharpe ratios for this asset class. The VAR models' estimated coefficient and residual correlation matrices show that it is the book-price ratio that causes the hedging demand for stocks. However, also here it holds that parameter uncertainty is not always small enough to ensure significance of the hedging demand.

Again we investigate the change in demand for stocks and bonds over the sample period (for $\gamma=7$, $\gamma = 7$, $\psi=1$ and $\delta=0.92$). Figures IV–VIII in the online appendix show the total and hedging demand for US and emerging-market bonds in the online appendix with supplementary material. For both asset classes the hedging motive tends to be a major component of the total demand for bonds, but also the myopic demand can be substantial. A striking pattern for most countries is the opposite movements in the demand for US and emerging-market bonds, which suggests that bonds do not only act as a hedge against unfavourable changes in their own returns, but also against adverse movements in another country's bond index returns.

In a similar way we analyze the dynamics of the demand for US and emerging-market stocks; see Figures IX–XIII in the online appendix. Because it is difficult to establish a common pattern across different countries, we focus on the last years of the sample period. After the stock market collapse at the end of 2008, we observe a sharp rise in the demand for particularly US stocks, followed by a gradual decline. During the years after the 2008 stock market crash the demand for US stocks tends to be higher than the demand for emerging-market stocks and the hedging motive seems responsible for the major part of this demand.

5.5. Conclusions

The potential of higher risk-adjusted returns coupled with diversification benefits has attracted investors toward emerging-market assets. This chapter quantifies the myopic and intertemporal hedging demand for bonds in emerging markets. We calculate a domestic investor's demand for local-currency bonds and an international investor's demand for US-dollar emerging-market bonds.

In developed markets, long-term government bonds are often considered attractive investment options for risk-averse investors. Our results show that also emerging-market bonds with a maturity of one year and longer can be attractive for domestic and international investors with different risk preferences, in both the short run and the long run. Some emerging economies have bond markets that are particularly attractive for short-term investors, whereas the bond markets in other emerging countries are interesting for long-term investors only (or for both short-term and long-term investors). In the former group of countries, bonds provide favourable immediate single-period expected returns. In the latter group of countries, bond returns perform well in the event of adverse future circumstances.

For both domestic and international investors, emerging-market stocks can also provide attractive long-term and short-run investment opportunities. For international investors it is hardly ever optimal to invest in US stocks. By contrast, US bonds can be a favourable short-run investment opportunity.

Whenever we establish a substantial and significant hedging demand for bonds or stocks, two conditions are met. First, their excess returns are predictable (from the term spread and the book-price ratio, respectively), due to which the assets can be used to hedge the variation in their own future returns. Second, parameter uncertainty is sufficiently limited to make the hedging demand significant.

The relatively wide confidence intervals for the estimated demand for assets indicate that there is often a high degree of parameter uncertainty involved. Longer data samples and more parsimonious models to describe the time-varying nature of expected asset returns could contribute to reducing the amount of estimation uncertainty. We leave this as a topic for future research.

Notes

1 These approximations are exact for $\psi=1$.
2 The book-price ratio is alternatively referred in the literature as the book-to-market ratio.
3 Due to unavailability of the book-price ratio, we use the dividend yield as the stock return predictor variable for Brazil.
4 Similar to Rapach and Wohar (2009), we assume that the exchange rates used to convert local-currency asset prices into US dollars are exogenous. Furthermore, they play no role in the international investor's VAR models.
5 We notice that many markets do not allow short selling. However, we do not impose any borrowing or short-selling constraints because we want to isolate the pure intertemporal effects of return predictability.
6 Because the VAR models including both the dividend yield and the book-price ratio give similar outcomes as the model containing the book-price ratio only, we opt for the most parsimonious model and leave out the dividend yield throughout.

References

Ang, A., G. Bekaert, 2007, Stock return predictability: is it there? *Review of Financial Studies* 20, 651–707.

Balduzzi, P., A. Lynch, 1999, Transaction cost and predictability: some utility cost calculations, *Journal of Financial Economics* 52, 47–78.

Barberis, N., 2000, Investing for the long run when returns are predictable, *Journal of Finance* 55, 225–264.

Bekaert, G., A. Ang, 2002, International asset allocation with regime shifts, *Review of Financial Studies* 15, 1137–1187.

Bekaert, G., C. Harvey, 2003, Emerging markets finance, *Journal of Empirical Finance* 10, 3–55.

Brennan, M., E. Schwartz, R. Lagnado, 1997, Strategic asset allocation, *Journal of Economic Dynamics and Control* 21, 1377–1403.

Burger, J., F. Warnock, 2007, Foreign participation in local currency bond markets, *Review of Financial Economics* 16, 291–304.

Campbell, J., 1987, Stock returns and the term structure, *Journal of Financial Economics* 18, 373–400.

Campbell, J., 1991, A variance decomposition for stock returns, *Economic Journal* 101, 157–179.

Campbell, J., Y. Chan, L. Viceira, 2003, A multivariate model of strategic asset allocation, *American Economic Review* 67, 41–80.

Campbell, J., L. Viceira, 1999, Consumption and portfolio decisions when expected returns are time varying, *Quarterly Journal of Economics* 114, 433–495.

Campbell, J., L. Viceira, 2001, Who should buy long-term bonds? *American Economic Review* 91, 99–127.

Campbell, J., L. Viceira, 2002, *Strategic Asset Allocation: Portfolio Choice for Long-Term Investors*, Oxford University Press, Oxford.

Chan, K., N. Chen, 1991, Structural and return characteristics of large and small firms, *Journal of Finance* 46, 1467–1484.

Chapados, M., 2011, *Portfolio Choice Problems: An Introductory Survey of Single and Multiperiod Models*, Springer, Heidelberg.

De Vries, E. W., R. Eyden, R. Gupta, 2011, Intertemporal portfolio allocation and hedging demand: an application to South Africa, *Working Paper* No. 2011–26, University of Pretoria, Department of Economics.

Epstein, L., S. Zin, 1989, Substitution, risk aversion, and the temporal behavior of consumption and asset returns: a theoretical framework, *Econometrica* 57, 937–969.

Epstein, L., S. Zin, 1991, Substitution, risk aversion, and the temporal behavior of consumption and asset returns: an empirical investigation, *Journal of Political Economy* 99, 263–286.

Fama, E., K. French, 1988, Dividend yields and expected stock returns, *Journal of Financial Economics* 22, 3–25.

Fama, E., K. French, 1989, Business conditions and expected returns on stocks and bonds, *Journal of Financial Economics* 25, 23–49.

Fama, E., K. French, 1992, The cross-section of expected stock returns, *Journal of Finance* 47, 427–465.

Harvey, C., 1994, Predictable risk and returns in emerging markets, *Review of Financial Studies* 8, 773–816.

Keim, D., R. Stambaugh, 1986, Predicting returns in the stock and bond markets, *Journal of Financial Economics* 17, 357–390.

Kim, T. S., E. Omberg, 1996, Dynamic nonmyopic portfolio behavior, *Review of Financial Studies* 9, 141–161.

Lynch, A., 2001, Portfolio choice and equity characteristics: characterizing the hedging demands induced by return predictability, *Journal of Financial Economics* 62, 67–130.

Merton, R., 1969, Lifetime portfolio selection under uncertainty: the continuous-time case, *Review of Economics and Statistics* 51, 247–257.

Merton, R., 1971, Optimum consumption and portfolio rules in a continuous-time model, *Journal of Economic Theory* 3, 373–413.

Merton, R., 1973, An intertemporal capital asset pricing model, *Econometrica* 41, 867–887.

Miyajima, K., M. Mohanty, T. Chan, 2012, Emerging market local currency bonds: diversification and stability, *Working Paper* No. 391, Bank of International Settlements, Basle.

Rapach, D., M. Wohar, 2009, Return predictability and the implied intertemporal hedging demands for stocks and bonds: international evidence, *Journal of International Money and Finance* 28, 427–453.

Samuelson, P., 1969, Lifetime portfolio selection by dynamic stochastic programming, *Review of Economics and Statistics* 51, 239–246.

Spierdijk, L., Z. Umar, 2014, Stocks for the long run? Evidence from emerging markets, *Journal of International Money and Finance* 47, 217–238.

6 Mean reversion in stock prices

Implications for long-term investors[1]

Laura Spierdijk and Jacob A. Bikker

6.1. Introduction

A widely held belief in economics is that what goes up, must come down – eventually (De Bondt, 1991). In terms of stock prices this belief translates into the concept of (long-run) mean reversion, which states that a decline in stock prices is most likely to be followed by an upward price movement, and vice versa.

The presence or absence of mean reversion has important economic implications. Because mean reversion in stock prices induces negative autocorrelation in stock returns (a result that will be derived in Section 6.4), the variance of stock returns is less than proportional to the investment horizon. The relatively low long-term volatility increases the attractiveness of stocks as a long-term investment (which we will illustrate in Section 6.5). Furthermore, if stock prices are mean reverting in the long run, low stock prices are followed by relatively high expected future returns, which could encourage long-term investors such as pension funds to invest in equity after a stock market downturn (Vlaar, 2005). Indeed, some studies propose trading strategies based on mean reversion in stock prices to generate excess returns (Balvers *et al.*, 2000, Gropp, 2004).

Several theories have been put forward to explain mean reversion in stock prices. These explanations hinge on the tenet of market efficiency. The efficient market hypothesis states that all available information is reflected in the value of a stock (Fama, 1991). Mean reversion in stock prices may reflect market inefficiency. According to Poterba and Summers (1988), mean reversion may be caused by the irrational behaviour of noise traders, resulting in stock prices that take wide swings away from their fundamental value. Irrational pricing behaviour, in turn, can be caused by fads (McQueen, 1992; Summers, 1986), overreaction to financial news (De Bondt and Thaler, 1985, 1987) or investor's opportunism (Poterba and Summers, 1988). However, stock-price mean reversion does not necessarily contradict market efficiency (Fama and French, 1988a). Assuming that all available information is incorporated into stock prices, the value of a stock is determined by the expected returns per share. Consequently, mean reversion is observed when expected returns are mean reverting (Summers, 1986). In an empirical study, Conrad and Kaul (1988) find that the time-varying process of a stock's expected return reverts back to its mean over time. Fluctuations in expected returns may be explained from uncertainty about the survival of the economy, caused by *e.g.* a world war or a depression (Kim *et al.*, 1991). Alternatively, they can be caused by rational speculative bubbles or uncertain business prospects (McQueen, 1992). Alternative explanations for mean reversion in stock prices have been provided by, among others, Chan (1988), Ball and Kothari (1980), Zarowin (1990), Conrad and Kaul (1993) and Ball *et al.* (1995).

After the seminal studies by Summers (1986), Poterba and Summers (1988) and Fama and French (1988a), an ongoing debate has emerged in the literature as to whether stock prices and stock returns are mean reverting or not. The substantial amount of recent publications in this field (Ang and Bekaert, 2007; Goyal and Welch, 2008; Boudoukh *et al.*, 2008; Pastor and Stambaugh, 2009, 2011; Spierdijk *et al.*, 2012) illustrates that the mean-reverting behaviour of stocks is still an important issue. The cause of the debate lies in the fact that testing for mean reversion is inherently difficult due to a lack of historical data on stock prices. Accurate estimation of the degree of long-run mean reversion requires very long stock price series, which are not available. For example, if stock prices were to revert back to their fundamental value every 20 years, one would need at least 1,000 to 2,000 yearly observations to obtain reliable estimations. Moreover, the likely structural breaks during long sample periods further complicate statistical analysis of mean reversion (Spierdijk *et al.*, 2012). These methodological difficulties explain why mean reversion is a controversial issue in the economic literature.

The goal of this chapter is not to provide a final answer to the question whether stock prices and returns are mean reverting or not. Instead, we aim at making investors aware of the economic consequences of mean-reverting behaviour of stocks. The remainder of this chapter therefore focuses on describing relevant properties of mean-reverting stock prices and the resulting implications for long-term investors such as pension funds.

The setup of this chapter is as follows. Section 6.2 provides a formal definition of mean reversion in stock prices, based on the seminal work of Summers (1986). A detailed overview of the mean-reversion literature appears in Section 6.3. Section 6.4 calculates the volatility and autocovariances function of single-period and multi-period returns in the presence of mean reversion. Because the variance of stock returns is related to the associated investment risk, single-period and multi-period variances and autocovariances contain crucial information for investors. This section also explains how mean reversion in stock prices is related to mean reversion in stock returns. Furthermore, we show how the concept of mean reversion is related to the concept of covariance-stationary. In Section 6.5 we consider a mean-variance efficient investor with an investment horizon of up to 20 years and investigate the implications of mean reversion in stock prices for optimal asset allocation and the profitability of trading strategies. Finally, we conclude in Section 6.6.

6.2. Definition of mean-reversion stock prices

This section describes the stock price model of Summers (1986), which allows for mean reversion in stock prices; see also Poterba and Summers (1988) and Fama and French (1988a). This model provides a convenient and descriptive framework for the mean-reverting behaviour of stock prices, as we will explain in detail later in this section.

6.2.1. Permanent and transitory price components

Summers (1986) defines a mean-reverting log price process p_t as the sum of a permanent and a transitory component:

$$p_t = p_t^* + z_t .$$ (6.1)

The permanent component p_t^* models the intrinsic value of a stock, whereas z_t represents a slowly decaying covariance-stationary price component.[2] It is assumed that p_s^* and z_t are uncorrelated for all s and t. As an example, Summers (1986) models z_t according to a first-order autoregressive model:[3]

$$z_t = \mu + \varphi z_{t-1} + \eta_t$$ (6.2)

with μ the intercept, $0 < \varnothing < 1$ the autoregressive (persistence) parameter and η_t white noise with variance σ^2. A shock to the permanent component p_t^* at time t is immediately incorporated into the future stock price. In contrast, a price shock through the transitory component z_t will slowly decay towards zero over time. Fama and French (1988a) specify the underlying intrinsic value process p_t^*, satisfying:

$$p_t^* = p_{t-1}^* + \delta_t$$ (6.3)

where δ_t is white noise with variance τ^2. It is assumed that η_s and δ_t are independent for all s and t. The transitory price component induces mean reversion in the (log) stock price. To make the stock price's mean-reverting behaviour more directly observable, one may rewrite Equation (6.1) as

$$p_t = \tilde{\mu} + \tilde{p}_t^* + \varphi(z_{t-1} - (\tilde{\mu} + \tilde{p}_t^*)) + \eta_t$$ (6.4)

which tells us that the price process p_t is mean reverting around the value $\tilde{\mu} + \tilde{p}_t^*$ where $\tilde{\mu} = \mu/(1 - \varphi)$ equals the long-run mean of the transitory price component and where $\tilde{p}_t^* = p_t^* /(1 - \varphi)$.

A convenient way to characterize the speed of mean reversion is the *half-life*. The half-life associated with the price process in Equation (6.1) is defined as the number of periods it takes z_t to absorb half of a unit shock. The first-order autoregressive structure of z_t ensures that the half-life has a closed-form solution; it equals $h = \log(0.5)/\log(\varphi)$ (Kim *et al.*, 2007), which is properly defined for $0 < \varphi < 1$. For example, with $\varphi = 0.8$ the half-life equals 3.1 periods.

The parameter φ plays an important role as it determines the speed of mean reversion, but the variances τ^2 (corresponding to the permanent price component) and σ^2 (transitory price component) are crucial as well. If the variance of the permanent price component is much larger (smaller) than the variance of the transitory component, the latter plays a less (more) important role, resulting in weak (strong) mean reversion. We will make these relations more precise in Section 6.4.

6.2.2. Generalization

Although the mean-reverting price process defined by Equations (6.1), (6.2) and (6.3) may seem restrictive, it is more general than is apparent at first sight. This generality explains the model's suitability as a tool for describing the mean-reverting behaviour of stock prices.

To allow the price process to be consistent with the efficient market hypothesis, the random walk should be nested in the specification for the stock price. This explains why the permanent price component in Equation (6.1) is chosen to be a random walk. The price process in Equation (6.1) follows a random walk for $\wp = 1$, but deviates from the efficient market hypothesis for $0 < \varphi < 1$. Hence, only the choice for a first-order autoregressive (AR) process could possibly be restrictive. A seemingly more general specification defines z_t in Equation (6.1) as a covariance-stationary, mean-reverting process with mean 0. But every covariance-stationary series can be written as a moving average (MA) process of infinite order – a result known as Wold's decomposition theorem. If the MA process is invertible, it can be written as an AR process of infinite order, which brings us one step closer to our AR(1) process. The only restrictive aspect of the first-order AR process is its order.

We may therefore want to consider a generalization of the previously considered mean-reverting price process by relaxing the assumption of a first-order AR process for the transitory price component. Instead of an AR(1) process we could assume an AR(p) process as approximation of an AR process of infinite order, for any $p = 1, 2, \ldots$.

With z_t equal to a higher-order autoregressive model, the half-life is more difficult to calculate. It can be obtained from the impulse response function corresponding to a unit shock in z_t. If α_i represents the impulse response of z_{t+1} to a unit shock in z_t at time t ($i = 1, 2, \ldots$), then the half-life h is calculated as the largest value j which satisfies $\alpha_{j-1} \geq 0.5$ and $\alpha_j < 0.5$. When j lies between two consecutive integer values, linear interpolation is used to determine the value of h. Notice that the impulse responses coincide with the coefficients of the infinite-order MA representation of the AR model.

The ability of the stock-price model of Summers (1986) to allow for mean reversion in stock prices, in combination with the simplicity of the specification based on a first-order autoregressive transitory price component (particularly the straightforward expression for the half-life), explains why most studies confine the analysis of the transitory price process to a first-order autoregressive model. We will elucidate the statistical properties of the mean-reversion model in Section 6.4, but first we will review the literature.

6.3. Literature

Since the seminal studies by Summers (1986), Poterba and Summers (1988) and Fama and French (1988a), an ongoing debate has emerged in the literature as to whether stock prices are mean reverting or not. Testing for mean reversion is inherently difficult because of the limited supply of historical data on stock prices. Accurate estimation of the degree of long-run mean reversion requires very long data series, which are not available. It is possible to make use of monthly overlapping returns to increase the number of observations, but this leads to serious statistical problems (as we will explain in Section 6.3.1). Moreover, structural breaks in the behaviour of stock prices are likely to occur during long sample periods, complicating the statistical analysis of mean reversion (Spierdijk *et al.*, 2012). These issues explain why, even after 20 years of mean-reversion research, it is still difficult to quantify the degree of mean reversion in stock prices.

Two different methods have been used in the literature to test for mean reversion. The first approach tests for mean reversion in a way that does not require estimation of the fundamental value process p_t^* in Equation (6.1). This method is known as the approach of *absolute* mean reversion. The second method proceeds in a different way and starts with the estimation of the fundamental value process p_t^*. This method is referred to as *relative* mean reversion, because it has stock prices reverting relative to a specified mean value. We will explain both methods in more detail in this section. We will also review some recent studies analyzing mean reversion in stock returns.

6.3.1. Absolute mean reversion

Fama and French (1988a) derive a regression model to test whether the autocorrelation pattern in stock returns is consistent with the model defined by Equations (6.1)–(6.3). For values of $\varnothing$ close to unity, the negative autocorrelation in stock returns is stronger for long-horizon than for short-horizon returns. Fama and French (1988a) therefore examine several investment horizons between one and ten years. This approach establishes significant mean reversion, explaining 25%–40% of the variation in the three–five-year stock returns.

Poterba and Summers (1988) use a specific property of the random walk to test for mean reversion. Mean reversion of stock prices implies that the variance of stock returns grows less than proportionally with time. Poterba and Summers (1988) apply the variance-ratio test of Cochrane (1988) to detect this implication of mean reversion. The m-year variance ratio is defined as the ratio of the m-year return variance to the one-year return variance, divided by m. When this ratio is equal to one, the random walk hypothesis cannot be rejected. Poterba and Summers (1988) find mean reversion over long investment horizons in the United States. Similar results have been established for several developed countries. The lack of significance in their results is attributed to the absence of more powerful tests to reject the null hypothesis.

Both Fama and French (1988a) and Poterba and Summers (1988) analyze the period from 1926 to 1985 and work with yearly overlapping stock returns to increase the number of observations. The issue of dependence, which is inherent in the use of overlapping observations, is resolved by applying the method of Hansen and Hodrick (1980). Richardson and Smith (1991) criticize this approach and address the problem of small-sample bias. They show that the evidence supporting long-term mean reversion disappears if they remove the small-sample bias. Moreover, Richardson and Stock (1990) argue that the use of a larger overlapping interval at longer investment horizons increases the power of the statistical tests used to test the random walk hypothesis. Their more powerful statistical test does not result in a rejection of the random walk hypothesis. Jegadeesh (1991) raises the issue of seasonality caused by the use of monthly overlapping stock returns.

Apart from these latter issues, the approach of Fama and French (1988a) has come in for other types of criticism as well. McQueen (1992) addresses the issue of heteroskedasticity in the sample period. The highly volatile years tend to have a larger influence on the results because of their relatively heavy weights. McQueen (1992) finds that the highly volatile periods exhibit stronger mean-reverting tendencies and that the overall evidence for mean reversion is therefore overstated. Kim and Nelson (1998) and Kim *et al.* (1998) criticize Fama and French (1988a) and Poterba and Summers (1988) on similar grounds. The issue of heteroskedasticity is directly linked to another point of criticism. Past periods of high volatility may not be representative of current stock-price behaviour. Poterba and Summers (1988) note that the Great Depression exerted substantial influence on the estimates of the mean-reversion parameters. Excluding this period considerably weakens the evidence for mean reversion. Kim *et al.* (1991) divide the total sample period into a period before and a period after World War II and conclude that mean reversion is a pre-World War II phenomenon only. Furthermore, the post-war period reveals mean aversion, indicating a structural break in stock-price behaviour.[4]

6.3.2. Relative mean reversion

The lack of evidence for mean reversion is often attributed to small sample sizes in combination with statistical tests for mean reversion that lack power. A substantial improvement in estimation accuracy may be achieved by explicitly specifying the fundamental value process (called the benchmark) around which the mean reversion occurs. The important question here is how to proxy the fundamental value process, which is inherently unobserved. According to the Gordon growth model, the value of a stock equals the discounted future cash flows generated by the stock (Gordon, 1959). In practice, these cash flows are the dividends to be paid out to the owners. Instead of estimating future dividends, one may use earnings as a proxy of future cash flows towards investors. Other possible proxies are valuation ratios, such as dividend yield or price-earnings ratios.

Campbell and Shiller (2001) examine the mean-reverting behaviour of dividend yields and price-earnings ratios over time. Theoretically, these variables are expected to be mean reverting, since fundamentals are determinants of stock prices. If stock prices are high in comparison to company fundamentals, an adjustment to either stock prices or fundamentals may be expected. Campbell and Shiller (2001) find that adjustment of the ratios towards an equilibrium level is driven more by stock prices than by company fundamentals. Coakley and Fuertes (2006) consider the mean-reverting behaviour of valuation ratios and attribute it to differences in investor sentiment. The authors conclude that financial ratios revert to their long-term average value. In earlier work, Fama and French (1988b) link the dividend yield to the expected returns on a stock and find that the latter have a mean-reverting tendency.

A second specification of fundamental value is based on asset pricing models. Ho and Sears (2004) link the mean-reverting behaviour of stocks to the Fama-French three-factor model and conclude that such models cannot capture the mean-reverting behaviour of stock prices. Similar conclusions emerge from Gangopadhyay and Reinganum (1996). However, they argue that mean reversion can be explained by the CAPM if the market risk premium is allowed to vary over time. Note that this fluctuation is in accordance with the theoretical explanation of mean reversion in efficient markets; expected returns fluctuate in a mean-reverting manner (Summers, 1986). Gropp (2004) argues that valuation ratios are inherently flawed, because information on company fundamentals cannot be compared to stock prices due to the delay in adjustment. Expected future dividends and earnings influence a stock's fundamental value, which cannot be captured by the current dividend yield or the price-earnings ratio. Moreover, the loss of information due to the use of proxies may contribute to the failure to recognize mean-reverting behaviour.

According to Balvers *et al.* (2000), the stationary relation between the fundamental value of a stock and a benchmark index permits direct assessment of the speed of mean reversion. Moreover, they use annual rather than monthly data to avoid the problem of seasonality. To estimate the mean-reversion process more accurately, Balvers *et al.* (2000) adopt a panel data approach. Comparing the real stock-price indices of 18 countries to a world index benchmark during the 1970–1996 period, they establish significant mean reversion, with a half-life of approximately 3.5 years. The half-life measures the period it takes stock prices to absorb half of a shock. Balvers *et al.* (2000) find a 90% confidence interval for the half-life equal to [2.4, 5.9] years.

In a related study, Spierdijk *et al.* (2012) analyze mean reversion in the stock markets of 18 OECD countries during the years 1900–2009. In this period it takes stock prices about 18.5 years, on average, to absorb half of a shock. However, using a rolling-window approach they establish large fluctuations in the speed of mean reversion over time. Their analysis suggests that the speed at which stocks revert to their fundamental value is faster in periods of high economic uncertainty, caused by major economic and/or political events. The highest mean-reversion speed is found for the period including the Great Depression and the start of World War II. Furthermore, the early years of the Cold War and the period containing the Oil Crisis of 1973, the Energy Crisis of 1979 and Black Monday in 1987 are also characterized by relatively fast mean reversion. During periods with relatively low economic uncertainty, mean reversion is virtually absent; *i.e.* the speed of mean reversion is very slow and subject to high estimation uncertainty. Overall, they document half-lives ranging between 2.0 and 22.6 years.

6.3.3. *Mean reversion in stock returns*

Many recent studies investigate predictability of stock returns (Ang and Bekaert, 2007; Goyal and Welch, 2008; Boudoukh *et al.*, 2008; Pastor and Stambaugh, 2009, 2011). Predictability of stock returns from dividends or other fundamental factors may give rise to negative autocorrelation in stock returns. Negative autocorrelation in stock returns is generally referred to in the literature as *mean reversion in stock returns*. The empirical evidence for mean reversion in stock returns is also thin. In Section 6.4.4 we will show that mean reversion in stock price implies mean reversion in stock returns, but that generally, the reverse is not true: mean reversion in stock returns does not necessarily imply mean reversion in stock prices. In this chapter we will mainly focus on mean reversion in stock prices because the latter type of mean reversion implies the former.

6.3.4. *Where do we stand?*

The literature has found little evidence for long-run mean reversion in stock prices while the evidence for mean reversion in stock returns is also thin. The substantial number of recent publications in this field illustrates the ongoing debate among economists about the mean-reverting behaviour of stocks. As explained in the introduction of this chapter, it is not our goal to provide a final answer to the question whether stock prices or returns are mean reverting or not. Instead, we want to make investors aware of the implications of mean-reverting behaviour in stocks. The remainder of this chapter therefore focuses on the implications of mean reversion for long-term investors such as pension funds.

6.4. Properties of multi-period returns

This section calculates variances and autocovariances of single-period and multi-period stock returns in the presence of mean reversion in stock prices. Because the variance of stock returns is associated with the investment risk associated with this asset class, single-period and multi-period variances contain crucial information for investors.

6.4.1. *One-period returns*

In the framework of Section 6.2, the restriction $0 < \varphi < 1$ induces negative autocorrelation in one-period log stock returns $r_t = p_t - p_{t-1}$, because for $k = 1, 2, \ldots$.

$$
\begin{aligned}
\gamma_k(r_t) &= Cov(r_t, r_{t+k}) \\
&= Cov(\Delta p_t^* + \Delta z_t, \Delta p_{t+k}^* + \Delta z_{t+k}) \\
&= Cov(\Delta p_t^*, \Delta p_{t+k}^*) + Cov(\Delta z_t, \Delta z_{t+k}) \\
&= [-\sigma^2 \varphi^{k-1}(1-\varphi)] / [1+\varphi] < 0
\end{aligned}
\tag{6.5}
$$

The function $\gamma_k(r_t)$ is called the autocovariance function of r_t. The one-period return variance equals

$$\gamma_0(r_t) = \tau^2 + \sigma^2 / [\varphi(2-\varphi)]. \tag{6.6}$$

Throughout, z_t represents a covariance-stationary process for $0 < \varphi < 1$ with autocovariance function

$$\gamma_k(z_k) = \sigma^2 \varphi^k / (1-\varphi^2) \ [k = 0, 1, 2, \ldots]. \tag{6.7}$$

We see that, for k tending to infinity, $\gamma_k(r_t)$ decays geometrically to 0 for $0 < \varphi < 1$. This means that the negative correlation between r_t and r_{t-k} diminishes with k. Hence, two returns are virtually uncorrelated if they are sufficiently apart in time. Also, if φ approaches unity (reflecting a very slow speed of mean reversion), $\gamma_k(r_t)$ tends to zero. The same holds for φ close to 0, in which case the transitory price process approaches white noise, with no mean reversion. Furthermore, the higher the variance of the transitory price process σ^2, the more dominant the transitory price component relative to the permanent component and the more negative $\gamma_k(r_t)$. These relations illustrate that both φ and σ^2 (and particularly σ^2 relative to τ^2) determine the mean-reverting behaviour of stock prices.

6.4.2. Multi-period returns

From the perspective of a long-term investor, we may also be interested in multi-period returns. For the (non-overlapping) m-period returns $r_t(m) = \Sigma_{j=1}^{m} r_{t+j}$, we calculate the first-order autocovariance, yielding

$$\gamma_1(r_t(m)) = Cov(r_t(m), r_{t+m}(m)) \tag{6.8}$$

$$\begin{aligned}
&= Cov(\Sigma_{i=1}^{m} r_{t+i}, \Sigma_{j=m+1}^{2m} r_{t+j}) \\
&= \Sigma_{i=1}^{m} \Sigma_{j=m+1}^{2m} Cov(r_{t+i}, r_{t+j}) \\
&= \Sigma_{i=1}^{m} \Sigma_{j=m+1}^{2m} \gamma_{j-i}(r_t) < 0
\end{aligned} \tag{6.9}$$

because $\gamma_{j-i}(r_t) < 0$. Similarly, also the higher-order autocovariances turn out negative. Also of interest to a long-term investor is the variance of the m-period returns. For $m = 2, 3, \ldots$ we find:

$$\begin{aligned}
\gamma_0(r_t(m)) &= Var(r_t(m)) \\
&= m\gamma_0(r_t) + \Sigma_{j=1}^{m} \Sigma_{i=1}^{j-1} \gamma_{j-i}(r_t)
\end{aligned} \tag{6.10}$$

For $\sigma^2 > 0$ and $0 < \varphi < 1$, we find $\gamma_0(r_t(m)) < m\gamma_0(r_t)$. With mean reversion in stock prices, the variance of the m-period returns is smaller than m times the one-period variance; the variance increases less than proportionally with the investment horizon. Hence, for long investment horizons stocks are relatively less risky than for short horizons.

6.4.3. Higher-order AR model

For an AR(p) process, introduced in Section 6.2.2, the derivations in Sections 6.4.1 and 6.4.2 remain the same. The only aspect we have to adjust is the autocovariance function. An AR(p) process of the form:

$$z_t = \varphi_1 z_{t-1} + \varphi_2 z_{t-2} + \varphi_3 z_{t-3} + \ldots + \varphi_k z_{t-k} + \eta_t \qquad (6.11)$$

is characterized by the recursive autocovariance function

$$\gamma_k(z_t) = \Sigma_{j=1}^p \varphi_j \gamma_{|k-j|}(z_t) \qquad (6.12)$$

and variance

$$\gamma_0(z_t) = \Sigma_{j=1}^p \varphi_j \gamma_j(z_t) + \sigma^2. \qquad (6.13)$$

We see that the sign of the autocovariances depends crucially on the AR coefficients $\varphi_1, \ldots, \varphi_p$. If the autocovariance function remains positive at all lags, the main conclusions of the analysis in Sections 6.4.1 and 6.4.2 will remain unaffected.

6.4.4. Mean reversion in prices vs. mean reversion in returns

In the model of Equations (6.1)–(6.3), the negative autocorrelation in stock returns (cf. Equations (6.5) and (6.10)) is a direct consequence of the mean-reverting behaviour of the underlying stock price. The converse is not true: negative autocorrelation in stock returns generally does not imply the presence of mean reversion in stock prices. We illustrate this property with the following example. The fundamental value process p_t^* is taken to be a series of iid random variables with a Cauchy distribution, whereas the transitory price component follows an arbitrary covariance-stationary AR(1) model, independent from the fundamental value process.[5] Because the mean of the Cauchy does not exist (it is not finite), the price process is not mean reverting. Admittedly, the example is empirically not very relevant, but it illustrates our main point. The return process (*i.e.* log price *differences*) generally does not uniquely determine the price process (*i.e.* log price *levels*).

6.4.5. The relation between mean reversion and covariance-stationary

A property related to mean reversion is covariance-stationary. The properties of mean reversion (in the sense of Summers [1986]) and covariance-stationary are equivalent in an AR(k) model. To prove this equivalence, we assume that the process pt follows a covariance-stationary AR(1) model of the form

$$p_t = \mu + \varphi p_{t-1} + \eta_t \qquad (6.14)$$

Alternatively, we can write p_t as the sum of a permanent price component and a transitory price component:

$$p_t = \tilde{\mu} + z_t \tag{6.15}$$

where $\tilde{\mu} = 1/(1 - \varphi)$ and $z_t = \varphi_r z_{t-1} + \eta_t$. Notice that the assumed covariance-stationary of p_t ensures the existence of the long-run mean $\tilde{\mu}$. From Equation (6.15) we see that p_t is mean reverting in the sense of Summers (1986), with the fundamental value process equal to $\tilde{\mu}$. Conversely, if the AR(1) process is mean reverting in the sense of Summers (1986), the fundamental value process has to be equal to 0 $< \tilde{\mu} < \infty$, which requires $0 < \varphi < 1$; *i.e.* covariance-stationary.

In models outside the class of AR(k) models the concepts of mean reversion and covariance-stationary are not necessarily equivalent. We illustrate this with the (stylized) fundamental value process depicted in Fig. 6.1, which increases linearly over time. The (stylized) price process moves around the fundamental value. Evidently, the stock price is not mean stationary (and thereby not covariance-stationary), yet it is mean reverting around the fundamental value process in the sense of Summers (1986) and Fama and French (1988a). Conversely, it is easy to find a covariance-stationary process that is not mean reverting. The simplest example is a series of iid normally distributed variables.

The dashed line is a stylized representation of the fundamental value process, which increases over time. The oscillating curve represents the stylized mean-reverting price process, which mean-reverts around the non-stationary fundamental value process.

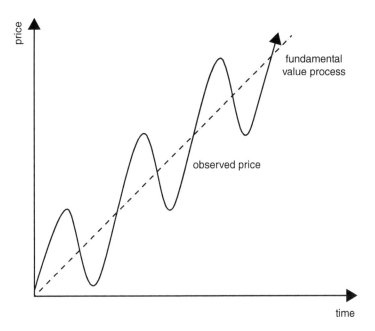

Figure 6.1 Example of a non-stationary mean-reverting process

6.5. Mean reversion and mean-variance efficient portfolios

This section assesses the economic implications of mean reversion in stock prices for long-term investors. The starting point is a mean-variance efficient investor that determines its optimal portfolio weights solely on the basis of the mean and covariance structure of the asset returns in its investment set. A mean-variance efficient investor will hold the portfolio with the lowest volatility for a given level of the expected portfolio return, or the portfolio with the highest expected return for a given level of the portfolio volatility.

6.5.1. Outline

We consider a long-term investor that wants to divide his wealth between stocks and bonds in mean-variance optimal proportions. We consider investment hori-zons ranging between 1, 5, 10 and 20 years. To construct an empirically relevant example, we base the parameter values on historical data.

6.5.1.1. Expected returns and volatilities of stocks and bonds

We assume the following values, corresponding to monthly stock returns (in the notation of Section 6.2): $\mu = 0.9\%$ (expected return of stocks), $\varphi = 0.975$ (reflect-ing a speed of mean reversion of 2.3 years), $\sigma = 3.2\%$ (volatility of the error term in the transitory price component) and $\tau = 3.2\%$ (volatility of the error term of the permanent price component). These parameters correspond to a monthly standard deviation of 4.5%, a figure that is based on the Datastream US Aggregate Stock Market Index during the period from January 1982 until August 2010. For the bond index we assume a monthly expected return of 0.7% and a volatility of 1.4%, which has been based on the historic performance of the Citigroup US Overall Bond Investment Grade Total Return Index during the same period. The latter index is investable through various Exchange Traded Funds and Exchange Traded Notes. To isolate the effect of mean reversion in stock prices on the opti-mal portfolio weights, we exclude *a priori* the presence of mean reversion in the bond returns.

6.5.1.2. Correlation between stock and bond returns

The monthly contemporaneous correlation between the stock and bond indices is assumed to be 0.2, which equals the historical correlation between the aforemen-tioned stock and bond indices during the sample period. The contemporaneous multi-period correlations are assumed to be 0.18 (one year), 0.17 (five years), 0.17 (ten years) and 0.17 (20 years).[6]

6.5.1.3. Risk-free yield curve

The risk-free rate is based on the nominal interest-rate term structure as compiled by the Dutch Central Bank (De Nederlandsche Bank).[7]

6.5.1.4. Variance ratio of permanent and transitory returns

We assume that the variance of the permanent and transitory price components contribute equally to the total stock return variance – a choice that has been motivated by the results documented in Poterba and Summers (1988). In the subsequent analysis we define the *variance ratio* as the return variance of the permanent price component divided by the return variance of the transitory component.[8] Later we will address the influence of the variance ratio by means of a sensitivity analysis.[9]

6.5.2. Optimal portfolio weights

The right-hand side panel in the upper half of Table 6.1 (captioned 'variance ratio = 1:1') displays optimal stock and bond allocations for investment horizons between one and ten years. The optimal portfolios that we consider explicitly are the global minimum variance portfolio (GMVP) and the tangency portfolio (TP). The GMVP is the mean-variance efficient portfolio with the lowest portfolio volatility, whereas the TP is the mean-variance efficient portfolio with highest possible risk-adjusted excess return. Fig. 6.2 displays the TP and GMVP in the mean-variance space. According to the Capital Asset Pricing Model, investors invest their wealth in a combination of the risk-free rate and the tangency portfolio.

The coloured area in this figure represents, in a stylized way, the set of all possible portfolios. The horizontal axis gives the portfolio volatility, whereas the vertical axis provides the expected portfolio return. The solid curve that starts in the global minimum variance portfolio (GMVP) and that marks the upper side of the

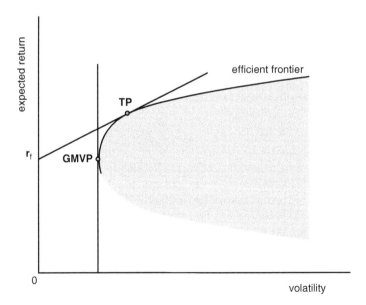

Figure 6.2 Mean-variance efficient portfolios

Table 6.1 Optimal portfolio weights (in percentage) with and without mean reversion in stock prices

	variance ratio = 1:1				variance ratio = 1:2				variance ratio = 1:3			
	w_s	w_b	μ_p	σ_p	w_s	w_b	μ_p	σ_p	w_s	w_b	μ_p	σ_p
	with mean reversion				with mean reversion				with mean reversion			
GMV												
1 year	4.36	95.64	8.50	4.80	4.44	95.56	8.51	4.80	4.48	95.52	8.51	4.80
5 years	5.37	94.63	42.64	10.70	5.73	94.27	42.69	10.69	5.93	94.07	42.71	10.68
10 years	5.86	94.14	85.41	15.11	6.45	93.55	15.08	14.90	6.79	93.21	85.63	15.06
20 years	6.26	93.74	171.00	21.34	7.07	92.93	171.39	21.27	7.54	92.46	171.62	21.24
TP												
1 year	7.20	92.80	8.57	4.82	7.30	92.70	8.58	4.82	7.36	92.64	8.58	4.82
5 years	8.40	91.60	43.01	10.75	8.88	91.12	43.07	10.74	9.14	90.86	43.10	10.73
10 years	9.05	90.95	86.17	15.18	9.83	90.17	86.36	15.15	10.27	89.73	86.46	15.13
20 years	9.57	90.43	172.59	21.44	10.64	89.36	173.11	21.38	11.26	88.74	173.40	21.35
	without mean reversion				without mean reversion				without mean reversion			
GMVP												
1 year	4.14	95.86	8.50	4.81	4.14	95.86	8.50	4.81	4.14	95.86	8.50	4.81
5 years	4.43	95.57	42.53	10.73	4.43	95.57	42.53	10.73	4.43	95.57	42.53	10.73
10 years	4.43	95.57	85.06	15.18	4.43	95.57	85.06	15.18	4.43	95.57	85.06	15.18
20 years	4.43	95.57	170.13	21.47	4.43	95.57	170.13	21.47	4.43	95.57	170.13	21.47
TP												
1 year	6.90	93.10	8.57	4.83	6.90	93.10	8.57	4.83	6.90	93.10	8.57	4.83
5 years	7.14	92.86	42.86	10.78	7.14	92.86	42.86	10.78	7.14	92.86	42.86	10.78
10 years	7.14	92.86	85.71	15.24	7.14	92.86	85.71	15.24	7.14	92.86	85.71	15.24
20 years	7.13	92.87	171.42	21.55	7.13	92.87	171.42	21.55	7.13	92.87	171.42	21.55

Note: This table reports the optimal portfolio weights for the global minimum variance portfolio (GMVP) and the tangency portfolio (TP). The investment categories are stocks (Datastream US Aggregate Stock Market Index) and bonds (Citigroup US Overall Bond Investment Grade Total Return Index) for different values of the variance ratio. The variance ratio is defined as the return variance of the permanent price component divided by the return variance of the transitory component. The risk-free rate is based on the nominal interest-rate term structure as compiled by the Dutch Central Bank. The last two columns in each panel display the expected portfolio return (μ_p) and the portfolio volatility (σ_p).

coloured area is the mean-variance efficient set which comprises all mean-variance efficient portfolios. A portfolio is mean-variance efficient if it has the highest expected return, given a certain volatility level or if it has minimum volatility for a given level of the expected return. Two mean-variance efficient portfolios are explicitly highlighted: the global minimum variance portfolio (GMVP) and the tangency portfolio (TP). The former is the mean-variance efficient portfolio with the lowest volatility, whereas the latter is the mean-variance efficient portfolio with highest possible risk-adjusted excess return. The risk-adjusted excess return is the expected excess return divided by the volatility, also known as the Sharpe ratio. The tangency portfolio is obtained by drawing a straight line from the risk-free rate (denoted r_f on the vertical axis) tangent to the mean-variance efficient frontier.

Without mean reversion in stock returns (see the lower half of Table 6.1), the optimal portfolio weights are nearly independent from the investment horizon. This is because the mean and variance of both stock and bond returns increase proportionally with the investment horizon. A negligible horizon effect is induced by the risk-free rate that increases non-proportionally with the investment horizon and by the correlation between stock and returns that varies slightly over the investment horizon. With mean reversion in stock prices (see the upper half of Table 6.1), the variance of stock returns increases less than proportionally, making stocks more attractive for longer investment horizons. This explains why we observe a small increase in the optimal portfolio weights assigned to stocks for longer investment horizons. For the GMVP the maximum difference in stock allocations with and without mean reversion is less than 2.5 percentage points, while for the TP the maximum difference is less than 2 percentage points. All in all, the results in Table 6.1 make clear that the optimal portfolio allocations are not very sensitive to the presence of stock-price mean reversion.

6.5.3. Realistic portfolio weights for pension funds

For Dutch pension funds the optimal portfolio weights obtained in Section 6.5.2 are not very realistic. Therefore we also consider a pension fund that invests 50% of his wealth in stocks and 50% in bonds. The equal division between stocks and bonds corresponds to the so-called standard asset allocation in the Dutch Financial Assessment Framework (FTK) for pension funds. The left-hand panel of Table 6.2 (captioned 'variance ratio = 1:1') displays the resulting expected portfolio returns and volatilities with and without mean reversion in stock prices (otherwise using the same assumptions as in Section 6.5.2), again for investment horizons equal to 1, 5, 10 and 20 years. With mean reversion in stock prices, the portfolio volatility is lower than without mean reversion, as expected. Yet the differences in portfolio volatility are small; the maximum difference (attained with a 20-year investment horizon) is less than 4 percentage points.

6.5.4. Sensitivity analysis

The assumption of mean reversion in stock prices does not substantially affect the optimal portfolio allocations and perceived portfolio risk in Sections 6.5.2 and 6.5.3, but this may be due to the choice of parameters in the mean-reversion model. We attempted to make these values as realistic as possible by calibrating them from historical data. In this section we perform a sensitivity analysis by altering the parameter choices made in Sections 6.5.2 and 6.5.3.

6.5.4.1. Persistence parameter

One of the parameters responsible for mean reversion in our model is ϕ, which is directly related to the speed of mean reversion (see Section 6.2.1). The choice $\phi = 0.975$ has been taken from Fama and French (1988a) who make the same assumption in their simulations. This value of the persistence parameter boils down to a half-life of 27.4 months, or 2.3 years. Poterba and Summers (1988) differ only marginally from this and use $\varphi = 0.98$. Balvers *et al.* (2000) establish a half-life of 3.5 years, which corresponds to $\varphi = 0.9836$. Spierdijk *et al.* (2012) establish time-varying annual values of φ between and 0.704 and 0.97 (corresponding to monthly values of 0.9712 and 0.9975, respectively), resulting in half-lives of, respectively, 2 and 23 years.

6.5.4.2.   *Variance ratio*

The other influential parameter in our mean-reversion model is the return variance of the transitory price process, in particular in relation to the return variance of the permanent price process. We assumed equal variances in Section 6.5.2. This assumption was based on Poterba and Summers (1988), who state that 'The point estimates imply that transitory components account for more than half of the monthly return variance, a finding confirmed by international evidence'. However, in their simulations they put the return variance of the transitory price component at three times the return variance of the permanent price process (*i.e.* a ratio of 1:3), whereas Fama and French (1988a) use a 1:2 ratio.

6.5.4.3.   *Optimal portfolio weights under different assumptions*

We use aforementioned alternative values for φ and the variance ratio as input for a sensitivity analysis. Throughout, we calibrate the other parameter values in such a way as to keep the variance of stock returns at 4.5% on a monthly basis.

It turns out that the value of φ in the alternative range, as indicated above, leads to much the same output as before. By contrast, the variance ratio has a more substantial influence on the optimal portfolio weights; see the middle and right-hand panel in the upper half of Table 6.1 (captioned 'variance ratio 1:2' and 'variance ratio 1:3'). The larger the transitory component of stock prices, the stronger their mean reversion. This translates into higher optimal weights for stocks and lower portfolio volatility. The maximum difference in the portfolio weights with and without mean reversion is between 2 and 5 percentage points. Similarly, if an investor divides his wealth equally between stocks and bonds, the risk exposure of his portfolio decreases with the variance ratio if we assume that stock prices are mean reverting; see the middle and right-hand side panel in the upper half of Table 6.2 (captioned 'variance ratio 1:2' and 'variance ratio 1:3'). The maximum difference in portfolio volatility with and without mean reversion equals 5.3 percentage points. Obviously, the variance ratio has no influence on the optimal portfolio weights if there is no mean reversion in stock prices (see the lower half of Table 6.1).

6.5.5.   *The role of the variance ratio*

Our sensitivity analysis shows that the choice of the variance ratio may have substantial impact on investment decisions. If the variance ratio is high – meaning that stock prices are strongly mean reverting – stocks become relatively less risky

Table 6.2 Expected portfolio return and portfolio risk (in percentage) with and without mean reversion in stock prices

	variance ratio = 1:1		variance ratio = 1:2		variance ratio = 1:3	
	μ_p	σ_p	μ_p	σ_p	μ_p	σ_p
	with mean reversion		with mean reversion		with mean reversion	
1 year	9.60	11.30	9.60	11.22	9.60	11.17
5 years	48.00	22.18	48.00	21.78	48.00	21.58
10 years	96.00	30.74	96.00	29.97	96.00	29.56
20 years	192.00	34.60	192.00	33.41	192.00	32.79
	without mean reversion		without mean reversion		without mean reversion	
1 year	9.60	11.55	9.60	11.55	9.60	11.55
5 years	48.00	23.33	48.00	23.33	48.00	23.33
10 years	96.00	32.99	96.00	32.99	96.00	32.99
20 years	192.00	38.08	192.00	38.08	192.00	38.08

Note: This table reports the expected portfolio return (μ_p) and the portfolio risk (σ_p) for an equally weighted portfolio, for different values of the variance ratio. The variance ratio is defined as the return variance of the permanent price component divided by the return variance of the transitory component. The two investment categories are stocks (Datastream US Aggregate Stock Market Index) and bonds (Citigroup US Overall Bond Investment Grade Total Return Index). The risk-free rate is based on the nominal interest-rate term structure as compiled by the Dutch Central Bank.

in the long run, making it optimal to invest a relatively large share of wealth in stocks. However, if the true variance ratio is lower than the assumed value, the perceived risk exposure is lower than the actual risk exposure. Hence, too much wealth is allocated to stocks, resulting in a non-optimal overexposure to risk.

As noted by Fama and French (1988a), estimation of the variance ratio is subject to various difficulties. Estimation is only possible in an indirect way and requires very long sample periods owing to the slowly moving nature of the transitory price component. Available stock return series are relatively short, yielding estimates that suffer from large parameter uncertainty. Accurate assessment of the parameter uncertainty is complicated by the use of overlapping returns – an issue discussed in Section 6.3.1. Consequently, the true value of the variance ratio remains highly uncertain. If the true variance ratio is 1:n, with n larger than 3, the effects on portfolio allocation will even be larger than established in Section 6.5.4.3.

6.5.6. Dealing with uncertainty about the variance ratio

Given the uncertainty involved with the variance ratio, it is prudent for a risk-averse investor to use a conservative estimate of this ratio.[10] To see this, suppose that an investor is uncertain about the degree of mean reversion in stock prices. If it overestimates the mean reversion in stock prices, this will result in an overexposure to risk. In an adverse scenario with falling stock-prices, this would result in negative investment returns. Conversely, if the investor underestimates stock price mean reversion, it will cause underexposure of risk. Amid rising stock prices, this would result in too low investment returns. Because the investor is risk averse, it will always prefer the risk of earning too low profits over the risk of incurring too high losses. The strength of the investor's preference depends on its degree of risk averseness. For a very risk-averse investor it is optimal to base the portfolio weights on an assumption of no or little stock-price mean reversion. For an investor that is only little risk averse, by contrast, it is optimal to assume a higher degree of mean reversion. In sum, it is optimal policy for any risk-averse investor to make conservative assumptions about the degree of stock-price mean reversion.[11]

6.5.7. *Trading strategies*

Several studies propose trading strategies based on mean reversion in stock prices and show that these strategies yield excess returns; see *e.g.* Balvers *et al.* (2000). The latter study establishes a half-life of 3.5 years in a model of relative mean reversion. The authors consider a *contrarian* trading strategy (which consists, loosely speaking, of buying past losers and selling past winners; cf. De Bondt and Thaler [1985]), based on rolling-window estimates of the underlying mean-reversion model. They show that such a strategy is able to generate (risk-adjusted) excess returns.[12] Clearly, if stock-prices were to follow a random walk, it would not be possible to earn excess returns. Hence not only does the optimal asset allocation affect the degree of stock price mean reversion, but the profitability of trading strategies crucially depends on it as well.

6.6. Conclusions

There has been an ongoing debate as to whether stock prices and stock returns are mean reverting in the long run. This chapter has discussed the implications of mean-reverting behaviour in stock-prices for long-term investors. We showed that the variance of stock returns increases less than proportionally with the investment horizon if stock prices are mean reverting. Subsequently, we assessed the consequences of stock price mean reversion for mean-variance efficient portfolios. If stock prices are mean reverting, stocks are relatively less risky for longer investment horizons, so that a larger share of wealth may be allocated to stocks. The same is true if stock returns show negative autocorrelation, which is often referred to in the literature as mean reversion in stock returns (in which case stock prices are not necessarily mean reverting).

   Given the impact of mean-reverting behaviour of stocks on asset allocation decisions and the profitability of trading strategies, it is important for investors to know whether or not stock prices and stock returns exhibit mean reversion. Until now, the literature has not yet found strong evidence in favour of mean-reverting behaviour, but this may also be due to the difficulties involved in the empirical assessment of mean reversion. Hence, it is unclear whether stock prices and stock returns are mean reverting or not. Bearing in mind that the investor will underestimate the risk exposure of stocks if he or she overestimates the degree of mean reversion, it seems prudent for a risk-averse investor to base investment decisions on conservative assumptions regarding the mean-reverting behaviour of stocks.

Notes

1 An extension of: L. Spierdijk, J.A. Bikker, 2012, Mean reversion in stock prices: implications for long-term investors, *Journal of Investment Strategies* 2, 1–12.
2 A time-series z_t is covariance-stationary if its mean, variance and autocovariance function are finite and constant over time; *i.e.* if $E(z_t) = \mu < \infty$, $\text{var}(z_t) = \sigma^2 < \infty$ and cov $(r_t; r_{t+k}) = \gamma_k$.
3 An autoregressive (AR(1)) process is covariance-stationary if and only if $|\varphi| < 1$.
4 Mean aversion is movement of stock prices away from their mean value over time.
5 The (standard) Cauchy distribution has probability density function
$$f(x) = 1/[\pi(1+x^2)].$$
6 These figures have been obtained by applying the Vector Autoregression methodology of Hodrick (1992) to the aforementioned stock and bond indices. The approach proposed by Hodrick (1992) provides a robust alternative to methods based on overlapping stock returns.
7 URL: www.statistics.dnb.nl/popup.cgi?/usr/statistics/excel/t1.3nm.xls.
8 More formally, the variance ratio is equal to $\tau^2 / [\sigma^2 / \varphi(2 - \varphi)]$; cf. Equation (6.6).
9 We do not use our own stock-price series to estimate the variance ratio, because reliable estimation of the variance ratio requires very long data series. Our own series spans less than 30 years, which is much too short. We therefore base our choice of the variance ratio on the literature.
10 We mention here that the Dutch Financial Assessment Framework for pension funds requires pension funds to hold capital buffers as to keep the probability of a funding deficit below 2.5%. Dutch pension funds are not allowed to base their buffer calculations on the assumption of mean reversion, unless they use the internal model approach and prove that mean reversion is very likely to be present in stock-prices or returns. However, Dutch pension funds have not yet pursued this approach. Neither for the continuity test, nor for the cost of covering pension premia, pension funds are allowed to assume that stocks become less risky in the long run. Nevertheless, some Dutch pension funds may take mean reversion into account in their investment strategy.
11 Our argument that it is prudent for a risk-averse investor to be conservative about the degree of mean reversion in stock prices can be formalized by means of a Bayesian analysis. This is clearly beyond the scope of this panel chapter. We therefore leave this as a topic for future research.
12 We notice that Balvers *et al.* (2000) do not claim that their contrarian investment strategy is profitable in practice. An explanation for this reservation is that their analysis ignores the issue of transaction costs.

References

Ang, A., G. Bekaert, 2007, Stock return predictability: is it there? *Review of Financial Studies* 20, 651–707.
Ball, R., S.P. Kothari, 1980, Nonstationary expected returns: implications for tests of market efficiency and serial correlations in returns, *Journal of Financial Economics* 25, 51–74.
Ball, R., S.P. Kothari, J. Shanken, 1995, Problems in measuring performance: an application to contrarian investment strategies, *Journal of Financial Economics* 38, 79–107.

Balvers, R., Y. Wu, E. Gilliland, 2000, Mean reversion across national stock markets and parametric contrarian investment strategies, *Journal of Finance* 55, 745–772.

Boudoukh, J., M. Richardson, R. F. Whitelaw, 2008, The myth of long-horizon predictability, *Review of Financial Studies* 21, 1577–1605.

Campbell, J. Y., R. J. Shiller, 2001, Valuation ratios and the long-run stock market outlook: an update, *NBER Working Papers*, National Bureau of Economic Research, Cambridge Massachusetts.

Chan, L.K.C., 1988, On the contrarian investment strategy, *Journal of Business* 61, 147–163.

Coakley, J., A.-M. Fuertes, 2006, Valuation ratios and price deviations from fundamentals, *Journal of Banking and Finance* 30, 2325–2346.

Cochrane, J. H., 1988, How big is the random walk in GNP? *Journal of Political Economy* 96, 893–920.

Conrad, J., G. Kaul, 1988, Time-variation in expected returns, *Journal of Business* 61, 409–425.

Conrad, J., G. Kaul, 1993, Long-term market overreaction or biases in computed returns? *Journal of Finance* 48, 39–64.

De Bondt, W.F.M., 1991, What do economists know about the stock market? *Journal of Portfolio Management* (Winter Issue), 84–91.

De Bondt, W.F.M., R. H. Thaler, 1985, Does the stock market overreact? *Journal of Finance* 40, 793–805.

De Bondt, W.F.M., R. H. Thaler, 1987, Further evidence on investor overreaction and stock market seasonality, *Journal of Finance* 42, 557–581.

Fama, E. F., 1991, Efficient capital markets: II, *Journal of Finance* 46, 1575–1617.

Fama, E. F., K. R. French, 1988a, Dividend yields and expected stock returns, *Journal of Financial Economics* 22, 3–25.

Fama, E. F., K. R. French, 1988b, Permanent and temporary components of stock prices, *Journal of Political Economy* 96, 246–273.

Gangopadhyay, P., M. R. Reinganum, 1996, Interpreting mean reversion in stock returns, *The Quarterly Review of Economics and Finance* 36, 377–394.

Gordon, M. J., 1959, Dividends, earnings and stock prices, *Review of Economics and Statistics* 41, 99–105.

Goyal, A., I. Welch, 2008, A comprehensive look at the empirical performance of equity premium prediction, *Review of Financial Studies* 21, 1455–1508.

Gropp, J., 2004, Mean reversion of industry stock returns in the US, 1926–1998, *Journal of Empirical Finance* 11, 537–551.

Hansen, L.P., R. J. Hodrick, 1980, Forward exchange rates as optimal predictors of future spot rates: an econometric analysis, *Journal of Political Economy* 88, 829–853.

Ho, C.-C., R. S. Sears, 2004, Dividend yields and expected stock returns, *Quarterly Journal of Business and Economics* 45, 91–112.

Hodrick, R. J. 1992, Dividend yields and expected stock returns: alternative procedures for inference and measurement, *Review of Financial Studies* 5, 357–286.

Jegadeesh, N., 1991, Seasonality in stock price mean reversion: evidence from the US and the U.K, *Journal of Finance* 46, 1427–1444.

Kim, C.-J., C. R. Nelson, 1998, Testing for mean reversion in heteroskedastic data II: autoregression tests based on Gibbs-sampling-augmented randomization, *Journal of Empirical Finance* 5, 385–396.

Kim, C.-J., C. R. Nelson, R. Startz, 1998, Testing for mean reversion in heteroskedastic data based on Gibbs-sampling-augmented randomization, *Journal of Empirical Finance* 5, 131–154.

Kim, J.H., P. Silvapulle, R.J. Hyndman, 2007, Half-life estimation based on the bias-corrected bootstrap: a highest density region approach, *Computational Statistics and Data Analysis* 51, 3418–3432.

Kim, M.J., C.R. Nelson, R. Startz, 1991, Mean reversion in stock prices? A reappraisal of the empirical evidence, *Review of Economic Studies* 58, 515–528.

McQueen, G., 1992, Long-horizon mean-reverting stock prices revisited, *Journal of Financial and Quantitative Analysis* 27, 1–18.

Pastor, L., R.F. Stambaugh, 2009, Predictive systems: living with imperfect predictors, *Journal of Finance* 64, 1583–1628.

Pastor, L., R.F. Stambaugh, 2011, Are stocks really less volatile in the long run? *Journal of Finance* 67, 431–478.

Poterba, J.M., L.H. Summers, 1988, Mean reversion in stock prices: evidence and implications, *Journal of Financial Economics* 22, 27–59.

Richardson, M., T. Smith, 1991, Tests of financial models in the presence of overlapping observations, *Review of Financial Studies* 4, 227–254.

Richardson, M., J.H. Stock, 1990, Drawing inferences from statistics based on multiyear asset returns, *NBER Working Papers*, National Bureau of Economic Research, Cambridge Massachusetts.

Spierdijk, L., Bikker, J.A., P. Van den Hoek, 2012, Mean reversion in international stock markets: an empirical analysis of the 20th century, *Journal of International Money and Finance* 31, 228–249.

Summers, L.H., 1986, Does the stock market rationality reflect fundamental values? *Journal of Finance* 41, 591–601.

Vlaar, P., 2005, Defined benefit pension plans and regulation, *DNB Working Papers* No. 63, De Nederlandsche Bank, Amsterdam.

Zarowin, P., 1990, Size, seasonality, and stock market overreaction, *Journal of Financial and Quantitative Analysis* 25, 113–125.

7 Pension fund investment policy, risk-taking, ageing and the life-cycle hypothesis[1]

Jacob A. Bikker, Dirk W.G.A. Broeders, David A. Hollanders and Eduard H. M. Ponds

7.1. Introduction

The main aim of this chapter is to assess whether Dutch pension funds' strategic investment policies depend on the age of their participants. A pension fund's strategic investment policy reflects its objectives, presumed to be optimizing return, given the risk aversion of its participants, while the actual asset allocation may depart from the objective as a result of asset price shocks, since pension funds do not continuously rebalance their portfolios (Bikker *et al.*, 2010). In this chapter, we focus particularly on the strategic allocation of assets to equities and bonds as representing, respectively, risky and safe assets. The argument for age-dependent equity allocation stems from optimal life-cycle saving and investing models (*e.g.* Bodie *et al.*, 1992; Campbell and Viceira, 2002; Cocco *et al.*, 2005; Ibbotson *et al.*, 2007). An important outcome of these models is that the proportion of financial assets invested in equity should decrease over the life cycle, thereby increasing the proportion of the relatively safer bonds. The key argument is that young workers have more human capital than older workers. As long as the correlation between labour income and stock market returns is low, a young worker may better diversify away equity risk with their large holding of human capital.

Dutch pension funds effectively are collective savings arrangements, covering almost the entire population of employees. This chapter verifies whether pension funds take the characteristics of their participants on board in their decision-making on strategic investment allocation, and to what extent. We investigate whether – in line with the life-cycle saving and investing model – more mature pension funds pursue a more conservative investment policy, that is, whether they hold less equity in favour of bonds.

For pension funds' strategic asset allocation in 2007, we find that a rise in participants' average age reduces equity holdings significantly, as the theory predicts. A cross-sectional increase of active participants' average age by one year appears to lead to a significant and robust drop in strategic equity exposure by around 0.5 percentage point. As a pension fund's asset allocation is determined by many other factors, this awareness of the optimal age-equity relationship and its incorporation in their strategic equity allocation is remarkable. We also find that the equity-age relationship is stronger for active participants than for retired and deferred participants.[2] This is in line with the basic version of the life-cycle model where retirees should hold a constant fraction of their wealth in equities, as they no longer possess any human capital. We also observe that other factors, *viz.* pension fund size, funding ratio and participants' average pension wealth, influence equity exposure positively and significantly, in line with expectations. Pension plan type and pension fund type, however, do not have significant impact.

The negative equity-age relationship has been found in other studies as well. For pension funds in Finland, Alestalo and Puttonen (2006) report that a one-year average age age increase reduced equity exposure in 2000 by as much as 1.7 percentage points. Likewise, for Switzerland in 2000 and 2002, Gerber and Weber (2007) report a negative relation between equity exposure and both short-term liabilities and age. The effect they find is smaller yet significant, as equity decreases by 0.18 percentage point if the average active participant's age increases by one year. For the US, Lucas and Zeldes (2009) did not observe a significant relationship between the equity share in pension assets and the relative share of active participants.

The setup of this chapter is as follows. Section 7.2 highlights the theoretical relationship between the participant's age and equity investments, stemming from the life-cycle saving and investing model. Section 7.3 describes important characteristics of pension funds in the Netherlands. Section 7.4 investigates the age dependency of asset allocation empirically using a unique dataset of 472 Dutch pension funds at end-2007. The next section presents a number of variants of our model, which act as robustness tests. Section 7.6 concludes.

7.2. Life-cycle saving and investing

In the late 1960s economists developed models which put forward that individuals should optimally maintain constant portfolio weights throughout their lives (Samuelson, 1969; Merton, 1969). A restrictive assumption of these models is that investors have no labour income (or human capital). However, as most investors do in fact have labour income, this assumption is unrealistic. If labour income is included in the portfolio choice model, the optimal allocation of financial wealth of individuals changes over their life cycle (for an overview, see Bovenberg *et al.*, 2007).

The basic version of the life-cycle model with risk-free human capital (see Campbell and Viceira, 2002) can be summarized by the following equation for the optimal fraction of stock investment, denoted by w:

$$w = \frac{H + F}{F} \frac{\mu - R^f}{\gamma \sigma^2}. \tag{7.1}$$

Here H is the human capital, that is, the total of current and discounted future wages, of an individual, and F is the person's current financial capital. The risk premium of the stock market is given by $\mu - R^f$, while γ and σ^2 denote, respectively, the individual's constant relative risk aversion and the variance of stock market returns. The preferred allocation to risky assets should be based on total wealth, being the sum of financial wealth and human capital. As can be seen from

(7.1), more human capital leads to a higher optimal investment in stocks. Furthermore, it follows that retirees should invest a constant fraction of their financial wealth in equities, as their human capital is depleted.[3]

Not only do young workers have more human capital, they also have more flexibility to vary their labour supply – that is, to adjust the number of working hours or their retirement date – in the face of adverse financial shocks. Flexible labour supply acts as a form of self-insurance for low investment returns. Bodie *et al.* (1992) show that this reinforces the optimality result, *i.e.* that younger workers should have more equity exposure. Teulings and De Vries (2006) calculate that young workers should even go short in bonds equal to no less than 5.5 times their annual salary in order to invest in stock.[4] The negative age dependency of asset holdings corresponds to the rule of thumb that an individual should invest (100 – age) % in stocks (see Malkiel, 2007).

The negative relationship between age and equity exposure in the portfolio is usually derived under the assumption that human capital is close to risk free, or at least is not correlated with capital return. Benzoni *et al.* (2007) put forward that the short-run correlation is low indeed, while in the longer run, labour income and capital income are co-integrated, since the shares of wages and profits in national income are fairly constant. This finding implies that the risk profile of young workers' labour income is equity-like and that they should therefore hold their financial wealth in the form of safe bonds to offset the high-risk exposure in their human capital. For that reason, Benzoni *et al.* (2007) suggest that the optimal equity share in financial assets is hump-shaped over the life cycle: co-integration between human capital and stock returns dominates in the first part of working life, whereas the decline in human capital accounts for the negative age dependency of optimal equity holdings later in life.

This chapter focuses on the investment behaviour of pension funds. One may ask whether the pension fund should be responsible for optimal age-dependent equity allocation, as participants may adjust their privately held investments so that their total assets, including those managed by the pension fund, reflect their optimal allocation. There are four arguments in favour of optimal investment behaviour by the pension fund on behalf of its participants. First, not all participants have privately held assets permitting the required adjustment where the pension fund is suboptimal. Second, and probably more important, most participants of course have neither sufficient financial literacy nor the willingness to carry out such an adjustment (Lusardi and Mitchell, 2007; Van Rooij, 2008). For these reasons, most pension plans take care of investment decisions, often by default. Third, insurance companies are a very cost-inefficient alternative for private offsetting of pension funds' suboptimal investment behaviour (Bikker and de Dreu, 2007; Chapter 4). And fourth, pension funds are able to broaden the risk-bearing basis by distributing risk across generations. This option is not available to individuals.

7.3. Characteristics of Dutch pension funds

As in most developed countries, the institutional structure of the pension system in the Netherlands is organized as a three-pillar system. The first pillar comprises the public pension scheme financed on a pay-as-you-go base. It offers a basic flat-rate pension to all retirees. The benefit level is linked to the statutory minimum wage. The second pillar is that of fully funded 'supplementary' pension schemes managed by pension funds. The third pillar comprises tax-deferred personal savings, which individuals undertake on their own initiative. The Dutch pension system is unique in that it combines a state-run pay-as-you-go scheme in the first pillar with funded occupational plans in the second pillar. The first pillar implies that young individuals cede part of their human capital to older generations in exchange for a claim on part of the human capital of future generations. Given the life-cycle hypothesis, this type of intergenerational risk sharing reinforces the preference of younger people to invest in equity (Heeringa, 2008).

The supplementary or occupational pension system in the Netherlands is organized mainly in the form of funded defined-benefit (DB) plans. The benefit entitlement is determined by years of service and a reference wage, which may be final pay or the average wage over the years of service. Most Dutch pension plans are based on average wage. Because corporate sponsors have no legal obligation to cover any shortfall in the pension funds, the residual risk is borne by the participants themselves.[5] This type of plan may also be labelled as hybrid, having characteristics of both defined-benefit and defined-contribution plans. It is partly DB by nature in that the yearly accrual of pension rights is specified in the same way as in a traditional DB plan, and partly DC because the yearly indexation is linked to the financial position of the fund and therefore related to the investment returns (Ponds and Van Riel, 2009).[6]

The defined-benefit formula takes the public scheme into account. The DB pension funds explicitly base their funding and benefits on intergenerational risk sharing (Ponds and Van Riel, 2009). Shock-induced peaks and troughs in the funding ratio are smoothed over time, thanks to the long-term nature of pension funds. Pension funds typically adjust contributions and indexation of accrued benefits as instruments to restore the funding ratio. Whereas higher contributions weigh on active participants, lower indexation hurts older participants most.[7] The less flexible these instruments are, the longer it takes to adjust the funding level, and the more strongly shocks will be shared with future (active) participants. Effectively, intergenerational risk sharing extends the risk-bearing basis in terms of human capital. The literature on optimal intergenerational risk-sharing rules in pension funding concludes that intergenerational risk sharing within pension funds should generally lead to more risk-taking by pension funds compared to individual pension plans (*e.g.* Gollier, 2008; Cui *et al.*, 2011). Thus Dutch pension funds, with their strong reliance on intergenerational risk sharing, may be expected to invest relatively heavily in risky assets.

There are three types of pension funds in the Netherlands. The first is the *industry-wide* pension fund, organized for a specific sector of industry (*e.g.* construction, health care, transport). Participation in an industry-wide pension fund is mandatory for all firms operating in the sector. A corporate can opt out only if it establishes a *corporate* pension fund that offers a better pension plan to its employees than the industry-wide fund. Where a supplementary scheme exists, either as a corporate pension fund or as an industry-wide pension fund, participation by workers is mandatory and governed by collective labour agreements. The third type of pension fund is the *professional group* pension fund, organized for a specific group of professionals such as physicians or notaries.

The Dutch pension fund system is massive, covering 94% of the active labour force. But whereas all employees are covered, the self-employed need to arrange their own retirement plans. As reported by Table 7.1, the value of assets under management at the end of 2007 amounted to € 690 billion, or 120% of Dutch gross domestic product (GDP), increasing to € 1,176 billion (173% of GDP) at end 2015. In 2007, more than 85% of all pension funds were of the corporate pension fund type, falling to 74% in 2015. Of the remaining pension funds, most are industry-wide funds, besides a small number of professional group funds. The industry-wide pension funds are the dominant players, both in terms of their relative share in total active participants (> 85%) and in terms of assets under management (> 70%). The corporate pension funds encompass over a quarter of the remaining assets, serving 10-12% of plan participants. Professional group pension funds are mostly very small.

In the post-WW II period, pension plans in the Netherlands were typically structured as final-pay defined-benefit plans with (de facto) unconditional indexation. After the turn of the century, pension funds in the Netherlands, the US and the UK suffered a fall in funding ratios. In order to improve their solvency risk management, many pension funds switched from the final-pay plan structure to average-pay plans with conditional indexation. In many cases, indexation is ruled by a so-called policy ladder, with indexation and contribution tied one-to-one to the funding ratio (Ponds and Van Riel, 2009). Under an average-pay plan, a pension fund is able to control its solvency position by changing the indexation rate.

Fig. 7.1 documents that Dutch pension funds increased their exposure to equities over time. Between 1995 and 2007 the median equity exposure tripled from 10.8% to 31.8%. This increase over time is a combined effect of more pension funds choosing a positive equity exposure (see P_{10} and P_{25} indicating, respectively, the 10th and 25th percentile), and pension funds increasing their exposure.

Table 7.1 Pension funds in the Netherlands (end-2007)

	Number of funds	Assets	Active participants	DB	DC
	In %				
Corporate pension funds	85	27	12	90[a]	10[a]
Industry-wide pension funds	13	71	87	96[a]	4[a]
Professional group pension funds	2	3	1	83[a]	17[a]
	In absolute numbers				
Total	713	*€ 690 bln*	5,559,677		

Source: DNB. [a] Figures as per the beginning of 2006.

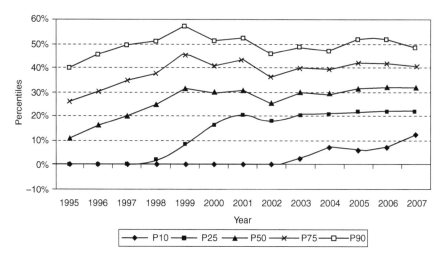

Figure 7.1 Development of strategic equity exposure

7.4. Empirical results

Our dataset provides information on pension fund investments and other characteristics for the year 2007. The figures are taken from supervisory reports to De Nederlandsche Bank, the pension funds' prudential supervisor. Pension funds in the process of liquidation – that is, about to merge with another pension fund or to reinsure their liabilities with an insurer – are exempt from reporting to DNB. The original dataset covers 569 (reporting) pension funds, of which 472 (or 83%) invest on behalf of the pension fund beneficiaries, while the remainder are fully reinsured and do not control the investments themselves. Nineteen pension funds do not report the average age of their participants and 54 do not report their strategic asset allocation. Three pension funds with funding ratios above 250% were disregarded. These are special vehicles designed to shelter savings from taxes and therefore not representative of the pension fund population we are interested in. Another three pension funds with assets worth over one million euros per participant were excluded for the same reason, as these are typically special funds serving a small number of company board members. These funds, as well as 15 others for which one or more explanatory model variables were unavailable, were omitted from the regressions, so that our analysis is based on the remaining 378 pension funds, including all of the largest pension funds.

Table 7.2 presents descriptive statistics of our dataset, with age and strategic equity allocation as key variables. One possible age measure, the average age of all participants in a pension fund, including active and deferred participants and retirees, equals 50, ranging widely across pension funds between 35 and 79. An alternative definition of age is the average age of *active* participants, which equals 45, varying across pension funds from 35 to 63. The proportion between retired and deferred participants also varies strongly across pension funds, reflecting the

Table 7.2 Descriptive statistics of our dataset including 378 pension funds (2007)[a]

	Mean	*Median*	*Other percentiles*	
Variable:			*10%*	*90%*
Average age of active participants	45.2	44.6	39.9	50.1
Average age of all participants	50.2	49.7	41.7	59.6
Strategic equity exposure (in % of total investments)	32.9	33.0	16.4	46.4
Actual equity allocation (in %)	33.2	33.6	17.6	46.9
Average assets of participants (in € 1,000s)	81.2	58.4	11.7	155.4
Share of retired (in %)	20.9	17.4	4.0	41.5
Share of deferred participants (in %)	42.3	40.8	23.3	65.7
Share of active participants (in %)	36.8	36.5	15.3	59.8
Funding ratio (in %)	139.4	135.4	120.2	163.9
Total assets (in million €)	1,791	150	20.3	2,153
Total number of participants (in thousands)	42.3	2.5	0.4	43.3
Defined-benefit schemes (in %)	0.97	1	1	1
Defined-contribution schemes (in %)	0.03	0	0	0
Industry-wide pension funds (in %)	0.20	0	0	1
Corporate pension funds (in %)	0.78	1	0	1
Professional group pension funds (in %)	0.02	0	0	0

Source: DNB calculations.

[a] That is, the minimum number of pension funds included in the various regression analyses.

various positions these pension funds occupy in the life cycle or the dynamic development of their industry sector or sponsor firm. The share of equity in fund's strategic asset allocation averages 32.9%, but ranges from 0% to 91%. Actual equity allocation differs from the strategic asset allocation due to free-floating (meaning that asset allocation is not constantly rebalanced after stock-price changes), and appears to average 33.2%. Furthermore, Table 7.2 presents statistics on other pension fund characteristics, many of which act as control variables in the regression (see below). The 10% and 90% percentiles reveal that these characteristics tend to vary strongly. In our analysis we distinguish between the age of active and the age of total participants.

7.4.1 Average age of active participants

Most life-cycle theories suggest that the relationship between average age and equity allocation is negative (Equation (7.1); see also Malkiel, 2007), while others postulate a hump-shaped relationship (Benzoni *et al.*, 2007). Lucas and Zeldes (2009) investigate a relationship between the share of active participants and the equity allocation, also assuming a non-linear age pattern: a (constant) effect during the active years and zero during the retirement years. Gerber and Weber (2007) regarded two definitions of average age: age of all participants and age of active participants, where the latter implies a non-linear functional form of average age, due to the truncation at retirement age.[8] Instead of choosing one of the various specifications found in the literature, we follow the theoretical life-cycle model expressed in Equation (7.1): equity investment declining with the age of participants during their active years and remaining constant after retirement. In Dutch regulation deferred participants are treated equal to retirees. As such it is fair to assume a constant equity exposure. Hence, our key age-dependent model for pension funds' strategic equity allocation of reads as:

$$Strategic\ equity\ allocation_i = \alpha + \beta_1\ age\ active_i + \beta_2\ share$$
$$retired_i + \beta_3\ share\ deferred_i + \gamma\ log\ (size)_i + \delta\ funding\ ratio_i$$
$$+ \varepsilon\ DB_i + \zeta\ PGPF_i + \eta\ IPF_i + u_i \qquad (7.2)$$

where i represents the pension fund and *age active* stands for the average age of each pension fund's active participants.[9] In theory, the full age distribution of all participants matters for the asset allocation, but that dataset is not available. Therefore, as a first step, we take average age as a summary statistic. Percentages of both retired and deferred participants (denoted by, respectively, *share retired* and *share deferred*) incorporate the (different) constant effect of each group on the equity allocation.

A control variable *size* is included as larger pension funds tend to invest more in equity (Bikker and de Dreu, 2009; Chapter 8). One argument may be that the size of a pension fund will go hand in hand with its degree of professionalism, investment expertise and willingness to exploit return-risk optimization. The pension fund's size is defined as its total number of participants, where we take logarithms of size to reduce possible heteroskedasticity. The *funding ratio* is a determinant of equity allocation as a higher funding ratio provides a larger buffer against equity risk and thus may encourage risk-taking. A higher risk margin for equity is required under the Dutch supervisory regime (Bikker and Vlaar, 2007). Note that – unlike the actual equity allocation – strategic equity allocation is not affected directly by price shocks, although gradually, over time, it may be influenced somewhat by trends in the stock market (Bikker *et al.*, 2010). A set of dummy variables may reflect different behaviour patterns related to different types of pension plan (DB versus DC) or pension fund (professional group pension funds [*PGPF*] and industry-wide pension funds [*IPF*] versus corporate pension funds).[10] Finally, u_i denotes the error term.

The left-hand panel of Table 7.3 presents the estimation results of Equation (7.2), based on the average age of *active* participants. A one-year increase in the average age of *active* participants is associated with a drop in equity exposure of around 0.4 percentage point (first column in Table 7.3).[11] Unweighted estimation attaches equal informational value to each observation of a pension fund, irrespective of whether it has ten participants or 2.5 million. By contrast, a regression weighting each pension fund proportionally according to its size (measured by numbers of participants), assigns equal importance to each participant. Such a weighting regression would yield results which are more closely in line with economic reality.[12] The negative coefficient of age increases to 0.5 in the weighted regression case, while its statistical significance rises sharply. This result confirms the negative relationship between age and risky assets as the life-cycle hypothesis

Table 7.3 Impact of the average age of *active* participants on the strategic equity allocation of pension funds (2007)

	Equation (7.2)				Idem, including 'personal wealth'			
	Unweighted		Weighted		Unweighted		Weighted	
	coef.	*t-value*	*coef.*	*t-value*	*coef.*	*t-value*	*coeff.*	*t-value*
Average age of active participants	−0.39	−2.50	−0.51	−5.54	−0.44	−2.88	−0.56	−6.20
Share of retired participants	0.09	1.91	−0.06	−1.33	0.04	0.89	−0.12	−2.60
Share of deferred participants	0.03	0.71	−0.25	−9.68	0.09	2.09	−0.17	−4.73
Total number of participants (in logs)	1.07	2.74	0.94	3.57	1.07	2.79	0.78	2.98
Funding ratio	0.20	6.86	0.28	9.51	0.20	6.89	0.27	9.46
Personal pension wealth (in logs)	–	–	–	–	4.03	5.21	2.23	3.74
Dummy defined-benefit plans	1.62	0.45	6.51	1.35	0.37	0.10	6.00	1.27
Dummy professional group funds	1.68	0.41	−1.17	−0.22	0.56	0.14	−0.95	−0.18
Dummy industry-wide funds	−4.14	−2.09	−0.74	−0.51	0.37	0.18	0.89	0.60
Constant	9.30	0.96	15.71	1.89	−5.02	−0.51	9.48	1.13
R^2, adjusted	0.16	–	0.50	–	0.21	–	0.52	–
Number of observations	380	–	380	–	378	–	378	–

supposes, while it rejects the '100 – age' rule of thumb, as our estimate is at -0.5 significantly lower (in absolute terms) than -1. Our results are similar in direction but not in size to the findings of Gerber and Weber (2007, for Switzerland) and Alestalo and Puttonen (2006, for Finland), who find 'active-age' coefficients of, respectively, -0.18% and -1.73%.

In Equation (7.2), the coefficient of retirees is not significant. Only in the weighted regression case do we find a small but statistically significant reduction of the equity share for pension funds having relatively many deferred participants. One percentage point more retirees implies a 0.25 percentage point reduction in equity allocation. The absence of this effect in the unweighted regression implies that only the larger pension funds take the optimal equity allocation associated with deferred participants into account.[13] This is confirmed when we drop, as a robustness test, the two largest pension funds (30% of all participants): the two dependency ratios drop to near or total insignificance (results not shown here).[14] Remarkably, in that case, the absolute value of the age effect increases further to 0.66.

Note that it is difficult to compare the coefficients of the average age of active participants on the one hand and those of retirees and deferred participants ratios on the other, as their units are different. From a time-series perspective, the age impact of active participants on equity allocation is stronger than that of deferred participants: 0.51 versus 0.25 (for the weighted regression). Moreover, the average age impact accumulates (as age increases each year), where the ratio effects are one-off: one joins the groups of deferred or retired participants only once. The cross-section perspective also uses the variation in the explanatory variables across pension funds. Here the outcomes are inconclusive. Therefore, we will not draw definite conclusions on the treatment of active versus inactive participants until we obtain results based on the average age of *all* participants in Section 7.4.2, which are easier to interpret.[15]

Turning to the other determinants of the equity allocation in Table 7.3, we observe that the effect of (the logarithm of) size appears to be positive and sizeable (with values around 1) which tallies with the stylized fact that large pension funds invest more in equity. The marginal effect of size – number of participants – on equity exposure is itself dependent on size, due to its logarithmic specification. An increase in the number of participants from 10,000 to 100,000 is associated with an increase of equity allocation by 2.5 percentage points. One reason may be that because larger funds are in a better position to invest in a more elaborate risk-management functions, they can accept riskier investments. Another may be that the largest pension funds are 'too big to fail' (major problems cannot be ignored by the government) which engenders a moral hazard. We measure size as the total number of participants.[16] The variable total assets would be an alternative size measure but a drawback of total assets might be that this measure cannot safely be regarded as exogenous, because high equity returns would – for pension funds with a high equity allocation – enlarge both their size and their equity exposure. This is the more important given that pension funds do not continuously rebalance their asset portfolios; see Bikker *et al.* (2010). As a robustness check, we replace the number of participants by total assets as size measure and estimate the model using instrumental variables. The size coefficient does not change much, and remains significant (see Table 7.A.1 in Appendix 7.1).

Pension funds with higher funding ratios invest more in equity, because their buffers are able to absorb mismatch risk. This is supported by regulation, which requires that the probability of underfunding be less than 2.5% on a one-year horizon; see Broeders and Pröpper (2010). This permits better funded pension funds to take more risks. The coefficient of around 0.25 implies that an increase of the funding ratio by 1% translates into an increase of the equity allocation by one-quarter percentage point. Note that the funding ratio does not suffer from endogeneity problems, as the dependent variable is strategic – not actual – equity allocation. Indeed, the actual equity exposure would be affected, as high stock returns simultaneously increase both the funding ratio and the equity allocation (at least under 'free-floating'). Because the strategic equity allocation may nevertheless have been adjusted to stock market developments, albeit gradually, we alternatively lag the funding ratio (that is, take 2006 figures) in our robustness analyses; see Section 7.5. As expected, the results hardly change. The dummy variables for pension plan type or pension fund category do not have significant coefficients, except the dummy indicating industry-wide pension funds, which points to fewer equity holdings. Over time, the borderline between DB and DC pension plans is increasingly blurring, as DB plans often show also some characteristics of DC plans (see Section 7.3). Furthermore, the number of DC plans is at 10% quite low while strong *a priori* assumptions about equity allocation across plan types are absent.

The goodness of fit of basic equation (7.2), measured by the adjusted R^2, rises from 0.16 for the unweighted model to 0.50 for the weighted specification, confirming that the weighted model explanation is superior.

In order to take the possible impact of changes in risk aversion into account, we add the average *pension wealth* of the participants in a pension fund to our equity-allocation model as an extra explanatory variable. This variable is defined as total pension fund wealth per participant and reflects the average (intended) level of the pension benefits[17] and the pension plan's maturity. We assume a similar average duration of a participant's relationship with their pension fund across all pension funds, the duration being the sum of the endured employment contract and the endured retirement period, so that wealth reflects the (intended) level of a participant's pension benefits. We take logarithms of this variable to reduce possible heteroskedasticity.[18]

The results are presented in the right-hand panel of Table 7.3. The coefficient of (the logarithm of) personal pension wealth is statistically significant and varies from 4 (unweighted) to 2.2 (weighted). The marginal effect of an increase in personal wealth depends on its level, due to the logarithmic specification. Starting from the average value of 81,000, an increase by one standard deviation of 78,000 is associated with an increase of equity allocation by 1.5 percentage points. These results indicate that pension funds with higher wealth per participant invest relatively more in equity, thereby accepting more risk. The active participants' age effect is slightly stronger in this specification than in the model without the wealth variable. Notably, the share of retirees now also has a significant impact on the equity allocation. For retirees, pension funds invest relatively less in equity, just as has been observed for deferred participants. The coefficients of size and funding ratio do not change after inclusion of the wealth variable. None of the dummy variables for pension plan type or pension fund category carry statistically significant coefficients. Apparently, no systematic differences remain across types of pension plan or pension fund after the incorporated model variables have been taken into account. In fact, the alternative model including the wealth variable has a slightly better goodness of fit than basic equation (7.2).

7.4.2. Average age of all participants

So far, we have assumed that the average age of active participants is the key variable in explaining the equity-allocation ratio and that, as retirees who no longer possess any human capital anymore, they hold a constant fraction of their financial wealth in equities. An alternative specification of our model involves equal treatment of all participant categories, where the impact of age on equity allocation is concerned. This model has been used by Malkiel (2007) and

Gerber and Weber (2007). Therefore, we replace the three age-related variables in Equation (7.2) by one average age of all participants ('age total'), resulting in:

$$\text{Strategic equity allocation}_i = \alpha + \beta \text{ age total}_i + \gamma \text{ log (size)}_i$$
$$+ \delta \text{ funding ratio}_i + \varepsilon \text{ } DB_i + \zeta \text{ } PGPF_i + \eta \text{ } IPF_i + u_i. \tag{7.3}$$

Table 7.4 reports the estimation results of Equation (7.3). The age coefficient of the average age of all participants is now insignificant for both the unweighted and the weighted regressions (left-hand panel). If personal wealth is added to Equation (7.3), the age coefficient becomes significant at -0.17 and -0.38 for, respectively, the unweighted and the weighted regression (right-hand panel). The all participants' average age plays a role but with smaller (negative) magnitudes and lower levels of significance than the active participants' average age in Table 7.3. All these outcomes point to a limited role for the all participants' average age compared to the active participants' average age. The results confirm that in reality, the age of active participants has been taken into account, while retirees contribute to the equity allocation with a constant, age-independent share of equities, each of which is in line with the life-cycle hypothesis.

Other model coefficients are roughly in line with what we have observed before. We consider the results of Table 7.3 as the most convincing estimates, for three reasons. First, from an economic point of view, Equation (7.2) reflects a richer

Table 7.4 Impact of the average age of *all* participants on pension funds' strategic equity allocation (2007)

	Equation (7.3)				Idem, including 'personal wealth'			
	Unweighted		Weighted		Unweighted		Weighted	
	coeff.	t-value	coeff.	t-value	coeff.	t-value	coeff.	t-value
Average age of all participants	−0.04	−0.48	0.07	0.92	−0.17	−2.00	−0.38	−4.65
Total number of participants (in logs)	1.51	4.05	2.45	9.37	1.59	4.33	1.22	4.45
Funding ratio	0.21	7.10	0.33	9.89	0.20	6.83	0.29	9.55
Personal pension wealth (in logs)	–	–	–	–	3.67	5.02	3.79	8.93
Dummy defined-benefit plans	0.76	0.21	3.69	0.66	−0.60	−0.17	3.97	0.78
Dummy professional group funds	0.59	0.14	1.62	0.26	−1.81	−0.46	−0.57	−0.10
Dummy industry-wide funds	−5.22	−2.79	−7.11	−4.79	−0.12	−0.06	0.46	0.29
Constant	−6.63	−0.92	−41.67	−5.00	−13.21	−1.86	−18.50	−2.31
R^2, adjusted	0.15	–	0.33	–	0.20	–	0.45	–
Number of observations	385	–	385	–	383	–	383	–

specification of the age-equity relationship, in line with the life-cycle hypothesis. Second, if the average ages both of all participants and of active participants are included in our models of Tables 7.3 and 7.4, the coefficient of active age is larger than that of total age in all eight cases (in absolute terms), the coefficient of active age is significantly negative in all eight cases (as expected) and the coefficient of total age is never significantly negative. Third, formal testing of Tables 7.3 and 7.4 against a general model encompassing both Equations (7.2) and (7.3) provides evidence in favour of Table 7.3 (that is, Equation (7.2)); see Appendix 7.2.[19] Therefore, we take Equation (7.2) as our basic model specification and Table 7.3 as the most relevant estimates.

7.5. Robustness checks

The specification in the previous section rests on several assumptions regarding relevant covariates, variable definition and functional form. This section considers various departures from the assumptions underlying Equation (7.2), using weighted regression.

As a first approximation, we have so far assumed the effect of the average age of (active) participants on the equity allocation to be linear. However, Benzoni *et al.* (2007) suggest that the relation between age and equity exposure may be hump-shaped rather than linear. They suggest that the age effect is positive in the younger age cohorts, due to the positive long-term correlation between capital returns and return on human capital (that is, the wage rate). Benzoni's age-equity relation reaches a maximum around a certain point (seven years before retirement), after which it is downward-sloping, as the long-term correlation of wages and dividends loses relevance. A simple but effective way to allow for a non-linear relationship is the inclusion of a quadratic age term in the regression, known as a second-order Taylor-series expansion, approximating an unknown, more complex relationship. The respective weighted regression model results show that the age coefficients are not in line with the assumption of Benzoni *et al.* (2007) about the investment behaviour of pension funds (Table 7.5, first column), as the squared term coefficient is not significant and economically has the 'wrong' sign. Hence, we find no support for Benzoni et al.'s theory.

With regard to the dependent variable 'strategic equity allocation', several robustness checks may be considered. First, shocks in equity prices affect the funding ratio, but as observed in Section 7.4 they may also have a certain impact on a fund's strategic equity allocation, which could create an endogeneity problem. For this reason we here lag the funding ratio; see Table 7.5, second column. Although the sample is somewhat smaller, the results hardly change, especially in terms of significance. The magnitude of the (lagged) funding ratio coefficient is slightly smaller here than in the unlagged specification.

Second, four pension funds have zero equity exposure. This runs counter to the OLS assumption that the dependent variable is of a continuous nature. In practice, equity exposure is censored at 0% and 100%. One may further argue that moving from zero equity allocation to a positive fraction requires an intrinsically different decision than raising an already positive equity exposure. One way to address this

Table 7.5 Alternative specifications of the weighted regression model as robustness tests (2007)

	Strategic equity allocation				Tobit regression: (censored at 0)[a]		Actual equity allocation	
	Incl. squared age		Funding ratio lagged					
	coeff.	t-value	coeff.	t-value	coeff.	t-value	coeff.	t-value
Average age of active participants	−0.51	−5.56	−0.39	−2.95	−0.50	−5.54	−0.44	−3.69
Ditto, squared [b]	0.01	0.59	−	−	−	−	−	−
Share of retired participants	−0.05	−1.29	−0.13	−2.71	−0.06	−1.34	−0.14	−3.13
Share of deferred participants	−0.26	−9.39	−0.31	−10.19	−0.25	−9.71	−0.33	−12.02
Total number of participants (in logs)	0.95	3.59	1.30	4.44	0.95	3.62	1.05	3.97
Funding ratio	0.28	9.37	−	−	0.28	9.54	−	−
Funding ratio, lagged (2006)	−	−	0.19	5.65	−	−	0.16	5.15
Dummy defined-benefit plans	6.47	1.34	4.05	0.71	6.46	1.35	7.31	1.55
Dummy professional group funds	−1.40	−0.26	−15.76	0.004	−1.12	−0.21	−14.01	−2.83
Dummy industry-wide funds	−0.77	−0.53	−2.13	0.183	−0.72	−0.50	−1.95	−1.36
Constant	16.46	1.95	26.61	0.013	15.57	1.88	34.24	3.61
R^2, adjusted	0.50	−	0.41	−	0.07[c]	−	0.46	−
Number of observations	380	−	363	−	380	−	368	−

[a] There are four censored observations, that is, four observations with zero equity exposure; [b] expressed as the deviation from the average age of participants (as in the Taylor-series expansion), allowing for easier interpretation of the coefficients; [c] this is the so-called pseudo R^2.

is to omit zero observations for equity, restricting attention to funds with positive equity allocations. This does not alter the essence of the results (not shown here). A more elegant alternative approach is the Tobit model which takes some degree of censoring into account. Table 7.5, third column, reports the Tobit outcomes. The effect of age and the other OLS results from Table 7.3 do not change substantially.

Third, where pension funds do not constantly rebalance their portfolio after stock-price changes, the actual equity exposure of pension funds may differ from their strategic equity allocation. Bikker *et al.* (2010) document that pension funds' assets are indeed partially free-floating. As strategic asset allocation reflects a fund's actual decision, it is better suited for determining the decision-making and conscious behaviour of pension funds. On the downside, however, this may affect comparability with other studies, such as Alestalo and Puttonen (2006) and Gerber and Weber (2007). Also, while the strategic asset allocation reflects a fund's intention, it does not give its actual behaviour. Table 7.5, right-hand columns, documents regression results for the actual stock allocation. To avoid endogeneity, we lag the funding ratio by one year. Sign and size of the coefficients hardly change, though the magnitude of the (lagged) funding ratio coefficient is slightly smaller than it is in the other regressions. Table 7.A.2 in Appendix 7.1 repeats the Table 7.5 results but with personal wealth as an extra explanatory variable. The results are quite similar, confirming the robust nature of the investigation.

Finally, we also applied our model to strategic *bond* allocation instead of strategic *equity* allocation, where we expect a positive rather than a negative sign for age dependency. The results (not shown here) deviate slightly, as bonds are not the exact complement of equity, due to other investment categories. These estimates confirm the age-bond relationship: the strategic bond exposure is significantly higher when the average age of active participants is higher.

7.6. Conclusion

This chapter addresses the effect of the average age of pension funds' participants on their strategic equity allocation. Our *first* and key finding is that Dutch pension funds with higher average participant age have significantly lower equity exposures than pension funds having younger participants. This negative age-dependent equity allocation may be interpreted as an (implicit) application of the optimal life-cycle saving and investing theory. The basic version of this theory assumes a low correlation between wage growth and stock returns. It predicts that the vast amount of human capital of the young has a strong impact on asset allocation because of risk diversification considerations, as human capital has a different risk profile than financial capital. This awareness of the optimal age-equity relationship for pension funds, and its incorporation in the strategic equity allocation, is notable.

A second finding is that the average age of *active* participants has a much stronger impact on investments than the average age of *all* participants. This is in line with the standard version of life-cycle theory which suggests that retirees with depleted human capital should invest a constant fraction of their financial wealth in equities.

A third result is that the age effect is much stronger in larger pension funds than in smaller ones. Apparently, larger funds' investment behaviour is more closely aligned with the age dependency from the life-cycle hypothesis. A non-linear age effect allowing a hump-shaped pattern, as suggested by Benzoni *et al.* (2007), could not be confirmed. However, other factors significantly influencing the strategic equity allocation are the pension fund's size, funding ratio and average personal pension wealth of participants, which all have positive coefficients. If we include personal wealth in our model, we do not observe any effect of pension fund type or pension scheme type on funds' equity exposure.

This research provides valuable insights for contemporary policy issues to do with the ageing of society. As society grows older, pension funds will adapt their investment strategies to the needs of the average active participant who will get older over time. This may result in a safer investment strategy. According to the life-cycle saving and investing theory, this is less than optimal for younger participants with low-risk human capital, who will not be able to fully utilize the diversification between human and financial capital. At the same time, this policy may be too aggressive for retirees, whose interests are not weighted that heavily by the pension fund boards. This leads to the recommendation that it might be optimal policy for pension funds to replace the average age-based policy by a cohort-specific investment policy as has been suggested by Teulings and De Vries (2006), Ponds (2008) and Molenaar and Ponds (2012/2013).

Notes

1 An update of Bikker, J.A., D. Broeders, D. Hollanders, E. Ponds, 2012, Pension funds' asset allocation and participant age: a test of the life-cycle model, *Journal of Risk and Insurance* 79, 595–618.
2 Deferred participants are former members who are entitled to future benefits, but who are no longer in the service of the employer.
3 After retirement human wealth is depleted ($H = 0$), so that the optimal equity allocation equals $w = \left(\mu - R^f\right) / \gamma\sigma^2$. This reveals that the retiree still has equity exposure based on his risk aversion parameter γ.
4 A variant of this approach is to buy a house financed by a mortgage loan, as happens much more frequently. However, this does not reflect a well-diversified portfolio.
5 Although there is no legal obligation, a corporation might experience a moral obligation to participate in sharing losses of its pension fund. Also note that the Netherlands has no pension guarantee fund as opposed to, *e.g.* the US, the UK and Germany. Instead Dutch pension funds are exposed to solvency regulation, see, *e.g.* Broeders and Pröpper (2010).
6 In recent years a few corporate pension plans where designed as Collective DC plans in which the pension promise is still based on average wage but where the contribution rate is fixed for an extended, typically a five-year, period. Although employers can treat such schemes as DC for accounting purposes, from a legal and therefore regulatory point of view they are treated as DB schemes. Our data do not allow the distinction between DB and CDC plans.
7 In an average wage defined-benefit scheme, the accrued pension rights of the active members are often also subject to conditional indexation.
8 Alestalo and Puttonen (2006) had data available on active participants only.
9 Concerning the impact of age on asset allocation, we cannot distinguish between the life-cycle effect on the one hand and age-dependent risk aversion on the other. However, as the equity allocation is determined by the pension-fund board, the life-cycle effect is more likely to dominate than the risk aversion of the elderly who are not represented in the board.
10 Willingness of the sponsor company to compensate investment losses could be a relevant explanatory variable also. In practice however, we hardly observe this willingness, except for a few corporate pension funds. Industry-wide pension funds service multiple corporations and it is unlikely that losses can be fairly distributed amongst those corporations.
11 The Goldfeld-Quandt test indicates that the model's heteroskedasticity does not increase with pension fund size.
12 For instance, dropping the largest two pension funds from the unweighted sample would not noticeably affect the regression results (representing less than 1% of the number of observations; result not shown here), whereas they include no less than 30% of participants.
13 To some extent, as the age impacts of active and deferred participants in Equation (7.2) diverge. Equation (7.3) in Section 7.4.2 is an alternative with equal treatment of both categories.

14 All results in this article marked 'not shown here' are available by request from the authors.

15 Note that when we include both average age of active participants and average age of all participants in Equation (7.2) and (7.3), we only obtain significant negative coefficients for the former explanatory variable. The coefficient of the former variable is also always larger (in absolute terms) than that of the latter variable. This indicates that the effect of active participants is larger than that of inactive participants.

16 The question may arise whether the number of participants is truly exogenous. If pension funds with higher equity allocation earned higher returns (or, better, a higher risk-return trade off), employees might be persuaded to join the firms related to these pension funds. Over the last decade, however, Dutch pension funds' equity portfolios did not perform better than their bond portfolios. Note that where participants are linked to a certain industry, they cannot change pension funds, due to the mandatory industry-wide pension regime. And even in a wider context, pension plans turn out to have only limited impact on job choice.

17 The average intended level of the pension benefits is proportional to the product of the participant's average salary level and its replacement rate.

18 Note that privately held assets may also affect the overall optimal asset allocation of participants. However, due to lack of available data, pension funds cannot take privately held assets of participants into account.

19 The logarithms of model likelihood in Table 7.3 are substantially higher than those in Table 7.4. Likelihood ratio tests reject the Equation (7.3) models (Table 7.4) in favour of the Equation (7.2) models (Table 7.3). We take the difference in degrees of freedom into account as Equation (7.3) has two additional explanatory variables compared to Equation (7.2). The test is not a pure test on restrictions, as one explanatory variable is different: average age of all participants versus average age of active participants. For this test we exclude the additional five observations in Table 7.3 (concerning pension funds without active participants), so that we use the same sample for both models.

References

Alestalo, N., V. Puttonen, 2006, Asset allocation in Finnish pension funds, *Journal of Pension Economics and Finance* 5, 27–44.

Benzoni, L., P. Collin-Dufresne, R. S. Goldstein, 2007, Portfolio choice over the life-cycle when the stock and labour markets are cointegrated, *Journal of Finance* 62, 2123–2167.

Bikker, J. A., D.W.G.A. Broeders, J. de Dreu, 2010, Stock market performance and pension fund investment policy: rebalancing, free float, or market timing? *International Journal of Central Banking* 6, 53–79.

Bikker, J. A., J. de Dreu, 2007, Operating costs of pension schemes, in: O. W. Steenbeek, S. G. van der Lecq (eds.), *Costs and Benefits of Collective Pension Systems*, Springer, Berlin, Heidelberg, New York, 51–74.

Bikker, J. A., J. de Dreu, 2009, Operating costs of pension funds: the impact of scale, governance and plan design, *Journal of Pension Economics and Finance* 8, 63–89.

Bikker, J. A., P.J.G. Vlaar, 2007, Conditional indexation in defined benefit pension plans in the Netherlands, *Geneva Papers on Risk and Insurance – Issues and Practice* 32, 494–515.

Bodie, Z, R. C. Merton, W. F. Samuelson, 1992, Labour supply flexibility and portfolio choice in a life cycle model, *Journal of Economic Dynamics and Control* 16, 427–449.

Bovenberg, L., R. Koijen, T. Nijman, C. Teulings, 2007, Savings and investing over the life cycle and the role of collective pension funds, *De Economist* 155, 347–415.

Broeders, D.W.G.A., M. Pröpper, 2010, Risk-based supervision of pension funds in the Netherlands, in: M. Micocci, G. N. Gregoriou, G. Batista Masala (eds.), *Pension Fund*

Risk Management: Financial and Actuarial Modelling, Chapman and Hall, Boca Raton, 474–507.

Campbell, J. Y., L. M. Viceira, 2002, *Strategic Asset Allocation: Portfolio Choice for Long-Term Investors*, Oxford University Press, Oxford.

Cocco, J. F., F. J. Gomes, P. J. Maenhout, 2005, Consumption and portfolio choice over the life cycle, *The Review of Financial Studies* 18, 491–533.

Cui, J., F. De Jong, E.H.M. Ponds, 2011, Intergenerational risk sharing within funded pension schemes, *Journal of Pension Economics and Finance* 10, 1–29.

Gerber, D. S., R. Weber, 2007, Demography and investment behaviour of pension funds: evidence for Switzerland, *Journal of Pension Economics and Finance* 6, 313–337.

Gollier, C., 2008, Intergenerational risk sharing and risk taking of a pension fund, *Journal of Public Economics* 92, 1463–1485.

Heeringa, W., 2008, Optimal life cycle investment with pay-as-you-go pension schemes: a portfolio approach, *DNB Working Paper* No. 168, De Nederlandsche Bank, Amsterdam.

Ibbotson, R. G., M. A. Milevsky, P. Chen, K. X. Zhu, 2007, *Lifetime Financial Advice: Human Capital, Asset Allocation, and Insurance*, CFA Institute, Research Foundation Publications, April, 1–95.

Lucas, D. J., S. P. Zeldes, 2009, How should public pension plans invest? *American Economic Review: Papers and Proceedings* 99, 527–532.

Lusardi, A., O. S. Mitchell, 2007, Financial literacy and retirement preparedness: evidence and implications for financial education, *Business Economics* 42, 35–44.

Malkiel, B. G., 2007, *A Random Walk Down Wall Street: The Time-Tested Strategy for Successful Investing*, W.W. Norton and Company, New York.

Merton, R. C., 1969, Lifetime portfolio selection under uncertainty: the continuous-time case, *The Review of Economics and Statistics* 51, 247–257.

Molenaar, R. M., E.H.M. Ponds, 2012/2013, Risk sharing and individual lifecycle investing in funded collective pensions, *Journal of Risk* 15, 103–124.

Ponds, E.H.M., 2008, Naar meer jong en oud in collectieve pensioenen (In Dutch: 'Towards more young and old in collective pensions'), *Inaugural Speech*, April 11, 2008, Tilburg University.

Ponds, E.H.M., B. Van Riel, 2009, Sharing risk: the Netherlands' new approach to pensions, *Journal of Pension Economics and Finance* 8, 91–105.

Rooij, M.C.J. van, 2008, *Financial Literacy, Retirement Provisions, and Household Portfolio Behavior*, Dissertation, Utrecht University, The Netherlands, www.dnb.nl/en/binaries/PhDThesis%20Maarten%20van%20Rooij_tcm47-211413.pdf (accessed May 17, 2017).

Samuelson, P. A., 1969, Lifetime portfolio selection by dynamic stochastic programming, *Review of Economic and Statistics* 51, 247–257.

Teulings, C., C. de Vries, 2006, Generational accounting, solidarity and pension losses, *De Economist* 146, 63–83.

Appendix 7.1

Alternative estimations

This appendix tests an alternative specification of Equations (7.2) and (7.3). The left-hand panel of Table 7.A.1 reports the impact of the average age of *active* participants on strategic equity allocation where the log of total assets has been added as an explanatory variable. This variable replaces the number of participants as a measure of size. Note that the coefficient of total assets is highly significant, implying that large pension funds have higher equity exposures. The fact that we use strategic equity allocation as the dependent variable reduces possible endogeneity effects.[1] Similarly, the right-hand panel of Table 7.A.1 shows the results for the model with the age of *all* participants and total assets as size measure.

Table 7.A.2 repeats the robustness tests of Table 7.5, but based on a model including personal wealth. The conclusion remains that our analyses are robust for these kinds of changes in the specification.

Table 7.A.1 Impact of the average age on the strategic equity allocation of pension funds with total assets as a measure of size (2007)

| | Equation (7.2) | | | | Equation (7.3) | | | |
| | Unweighted | | Weighted | | Unweighted | | Weighted | |
	coeff.	t-value	coeff.	t-value	coeff.	t-value	coeff.	t-value
Average age of active participants	−0.35	−2.39	−0.52	−5.84	–	–	–	–
Share of retired participants	0.06	1.17	−0.08	−1.97	–	–	–	–
Share of deferred participants	0.05	1.22	−0.20	−6.60	–	–	–	–
Average age of all participants	–	–	–	–	−0.02	−0.28	−0.18	−2.72
Total assets (in logs)	1.62	4.68	1.07	4.75	1.62	4.89	2.14	12.74
Funding ratio	0.20	6.84	0.27	9.56	0.20	6.57	0.31	9.90
Dummy defined-benefit plans	1.03	0.29	6.05	1.27	−0.11	−0.03	3.54	0.69
Dummy professional group funds	0.75	0.19	−0.73	−0.14	−0.71	−0.17	0.74	0.13
Dummy industry-wide pension funds	−3.92	−2.27	−0.73	−0.58	−3.11	−1.95	−4.18	−3.60
Constant	−2.09	−0.21	9.84	1.17	−12.46	−1.70	−31.76	−4.25
R^2, adjusted	0.19	–	0.51	–	0.16	–	0.42	–
Number of observations	381	–	381	–	389	–	389	–

Table 7.A.2 Alternative specifications of the weighted regression model as robustness tests (2007)

	Strategic equity allocation				Tobit regression: (censored at 0)[a]		Actual equity allocation	
	Incl. squared age		Funding ratio lagged					
	coeff.	t-value	coeff.	t-value	coeff.	t-value	coeff.	t-value
Average age of active participants	−0.58	−6.34	−0.38	−2.91	−0.56	−6.22	−0.42	−3.61
Ditto, squared [b]	0.01	1.28	–	–	–	–	–	–
Share of retired participants	−0.12	−2.61	−0.19	−3.53	−0.12	−2.62	−0.21	−4.38
Share of deferred participants	−0.17	−4.85	−0.23	−5.17	−0.17	−4.75	−0.23	−5.79
Total number of participants (in logs)	0.78	3.00	1.18	4.03	0.79	3.03	0.88	3.37
Funding ratio	0.27	9.23	–	–	0.27	9.5	–	–
Funding ratio, lagged (2006)	–	–	0.19	5.72	–	–	0.16	5.31
Personal pension wealth (in logs)	2.35	3.91	1.86	2.64	2.22	3.76	2.37	3.84
Dummy defined-benefit plans	5.88	1.24	3.41	0.60	5.95	1.26	5.10	1.09
Dummy professional group funds	−1.44	−0.27	−0.95	−0.18	−0.91	−0.17	−14.23	−2.93
Dummy industry-wide funds	0.91	0.62	0.89	0.60	0.9	0.62	−0.11	−0.07
Constant	10.72	1.28	9.48	1.13	9.35	1.13	24.16	2.49
R^2, adjusted	0.52	–	0.43	–	0.08[c]	–	0.48	–
Number of observations	378	–	362	–	378	–	367	–

[a] There are four censored observations, that is, four observations with zero equity exposure; [b] expressed as the deviation from the average age of participants (as in the Taylor-series expansion), allowing for easier interpretation of the coefficients; [c] this is the pseudo R^2.

Appendix 7.2

Testing alternative model specifications for the impact of demographic variables

Table 7.A.3 presents estimation results for a more general model of the impact of demographic variables on pension funds' strategic equity allocation, which encompasses both Equations (7.2) and (7.3). This specification allows testing of the models of these equations. Equation (7.2) results when the coefficients of the average ages of retired and deferred participants and the three interaction terms are jointly set to zero, while Equation (7.3) is obtained when the coefficients of the three average ages and the shares of retired and deferred participants are all set to zero while at the same time, the coefficients of the three interaction terms are assumed identical. Note that Equations (7.2) and (7.3) are not nested, so that we cannot test the two alternatives against each other.

Using an F-test for restrictions, only one model, Equation (7.2) with personal wealth (unweighted), is not rejected at the 5% significance level, while a second model, Equation (7.2) without personal wealth (unweighted), is not rejected at the 1% significance level. All four Equation (7.3) models considered, with and without personal wealth and weighted as well as unweighted, are rejected, even at the 1% significance level. For all four models, the F-test statistic is higher for Equation (7.3) than for Equation (7.2), reflecting that Equation (7.3) is rejected more strongly (in three cases) or rejected instead of not rejected (one case). This confirms our empirical evidence and theoretical arguments in favour of Equation (7.2). Apart from the restrictions, the coefficients in Table 7.A.3 are informative as well: the consistent and significant coefficient of the average age of active participants, and the non-significance of the other demographic coefficients is noteworthy and adds to the evidence favouring Equation (7.2) over Equation (7.3).

Table 7.A.3 A general model for the impact of demographic variables on pension funds' strategic equity allocation (2007)

	General model				Idem, including 'personal wealth'			
	Unweighted		Weighted		Unweighted		Weighted	
	coeff.	t-value	coeff.	t-value	coeff.	t-value	coeff.	t-value
Average age of active participants	−0.50	−1.92	−0.50	−2.70	−0.60	−2.38	−0.79	−4.02
Average age of retired participants	0.02	0.09	−0.20	−1.00	−0.10	−0.57	−0.61	−2.71
Average age of deferred participants	0.12	0.28	1.04	2.32	0.05	0.12	1.00	2.28
Share retired participants	1.96	3.21	0.72	0.87	0.78	1.21	−0.46	−0.53
Share deferred participants	0.00	0.01	−0.31	−0.76	0.05	0.11	0.13	0.30
Interaction age and share active	0.00	0.20	−0.01	−0.87	0.00	0.40	0.00	0.19
Interaction age and share retired	−0.02	−2.56	−0.02	−1.29	−0.01	−0.81	0.00	0.34
Interaction age and share deferred	0.00	0.27	−0.01	−0.73	0.00	0.58	−0.01	−0.74
Total number of participants (in logs)	0.96	2.43	1.21	4.51	1.00	2.60	1.11	0.27
Funding ratio	0.21	7.00	0.29	9.92	0.19	6.55	0.27	9.41
Personal pension wealth (in logs)	–	–	–	–	4.01	4.68	2.66	3.83
Dummy defined-benefit plans	1.82	0.49	5.51	1.12	1.77	0.49	7.08	1.47
Dummy professional group funds	−1.23	−0.28	−4.53	−0.78	−2.07	−0.49	−4.20	−0.74
Dummy industry-wide funds	−3.15	−1.56	−2.44	−1.66	0.68	0.32	−0.27	−0.17
Constant	−1.44	−0.05	7.61	0.26	−8.63	−0.31	4.63	0.16
R^2, adjusted	0.17	–	0.53	–	0.22	–	0.55	–
Number of observations	377	–	377	–	377	–	377	–

8   Investor sophistication and risk-taking[1]

Jan de Dreu and Jacob A. Bikker

8.1. Introduction

During the recent credit and sovereign debt crises, pension funds sustained huge investment losses. The crash in equity prices, coupled with a dramatic decline of long-term interest rates used to discount liabilities, slashed pension funds' funding ratios (defined as total assets divided by discounted pension liabilities), with only limited relief from increased bond prices. In 2008 alone the market value of total pension assets in the Netherlands dropped by more than 17%. Together with the impact of lower discount rates, the crisis caused the funding ratio to fall in that year by no less than 49 percentage points. Strikingly, however, sustained losses varied considerably across pension funds, illustrating considerable differences among pension fund's investment policies. These losses have severe consequences since in many countries pension funds play a central role in investing pension savings and providing old-age benefits. This is particularly evident in the Netherlands where the assets of pension funds exceed GDP. Most Dutch pension funds now face significant funding gaps and are forced to increase premiums, cut wage or price indexation and, in a number of cases, even to cut pension rights. Evidently, these investment losses have profound implications and have raised questions as to risk-taking by pension funds and the quality and sophistication of their investment policies.

For pension funds, determining the asset allocation strategy is the most important decision in the investment process. Setting the optimal asset allocation strategy involves two decisions. First, the level of risk preference must be determined in line with the funding ratio and preferences of pension scheme participants and sponsor companies. Second, the allocation of investments to different asset classes should be chosen to maximize expected returns, given a pension fund's liabilities and its risk preference. Both tasks are highly complex and it is to be expected that the expertise and abilities of different investors in performing them will vary. We examine pension fund investors' sophistication in setting an optimal asset allocation (task 2) and how this relates to their risk preferences, expressed in terms of risky investments (task 1).

A major contribution in the finance literature on optimal asset allocation is the two-fund separation theorem, which prescribes investors to hold an optimal portfolio of risky assets in combination with the risk-free asset (Tobin, 1958). This optimal portfolio should be mean-variance efficient, implying that for a given expected return, no additional diversification can lower the portfolio's overall risk (Markowitz, 1952). These theorems are building blocks of CAPM, which states that there is only one optimal risk portfolio, that is, the market portfolio (Sharpe, 1964). If this is the correct model, asset allocations for investors with different risk preferences should be simply different linear combinations of the riskless asset and the market portfolio. This implies that investors, including pension funds, should keep the ratio of bonds to equities and other asset classes unchanged across all portfolios and vary allocations to the risk-free asset, reflecting varying risk preferences. The finding that investors hold different proportions of risky assets – including the ratio of bonds to equities – conflicts with the two-fund separation theorem and is called the Asset Allocation Puzzle (see also Canner *et al.*, 1997).

While we concern ourselves with institutional investors, the literature on the sophistication of asset allocation decisions has mostly focused on private investors (individuals or households). Empirical research has shown that private investors invest in ways that are hard to reconcile with standard theory and that have been labelled investment mistakes (Campbell, 2006; Calvet *et al.*, 2007, 2009a, b). Private investors often use simple rules of thumb in allocating their wealth across asset classes, resulting in suboptimal investment portfolios. The behavioural finance literature classifies such suboptimal investment decisions as behavioural biases or cognitive errors. Individuals use heuristics, or rules of thumb, because they have limited attention, memory, education and processing capabilities. A number of papers have shown that individual investors often rely on simple asset allocation rules. Examples of such rules are asset allocations that tend to be either zero or 100% in equities (Agnew, Balduzzi and Sundén, 2003) and investor's use of the $1/n$ rule to allocate their money among the n funds they invest in (Huberman and Jiang, 2006). Benartzi and Thaler (2001) show that some private investors use the $1/n$ rule to allocate investments equally among eligible investment funds offered in pension plans and, consequently, that the equity allocation of investors is influenced by the proportion of stock funds offered. The natural conclusion is that the use of heuristics can lead to suboptimal asset allocation by private investors.[3] Other recorded investor mistakes are (i) insufficient diversification (Calvet *et al.*, 2007; Goetzmann and Kumar, 2008), (ii) inertia (Agnew *et al.*, 2003; Campbell, 2006; Calvet *et al.*, 2009a) and (iii) holding of losing stocks and selling winning stocks (Dhar and Zhu, 2006; Calvet *et al.*, 2009a).

The tendency to round figures coarsely or to choose attractive numbers is also documented in a number of demographic and historical studies. For instance, self-reported age data in countries or periods characterized by low average levels of education often show high frequencies at attractive, 'round' numbers. This phenomenon is called age heaping. Individuals with limited knowledge about their age are found to have a higher propensity to choose a 'plausible' number. These individuals do not choose random numbers, but instead have a systematic tendency to choose attractive numbers, particularly those ending in 5 or 0. Age heaping is reported for a number of data sources, including census returns, tombstones and tax data. Demographic studies have shown that age heaping is correlated to education (*e.g.* Bachi, 1951), income (*e.g.* Myers, 1976), illiteracy (Budd and Guinnane, 1991) and, more generally, human capital (A'Hearn, Baten and Crayen, 2009).

While there is a growing literature documenting behavioural biases of private investors, much less is known about professional parties. Institutional investors are generally considered to be more sophisticated than private investors and are therefore assumed to invest more optimally. A number of theoretical papers argue that more sophisticated investors suffer less from cognitive biases or irrational behaviour (*e.g.* Banerjee, 1992, DeLong et al., 1990, Hirshleifer *et al.*, 1994 and Shleifer and Summers, 1990). However, there is little empirical evidence documenting (i) the investment behaviour of institutional investors or (ii) how this behaviour is influenced by their level of sophistication.

To fill this gap in the literature, we study the investment behaviour of institutional investors with varying degrees of sophistication. Scale advantages should enable large pension funds to hire competent experts and consultants and spend more time and resources on optimizing their investment policies. Consequently, large pension funds should have a lower propensity to use heuristics in determining their asset allocation, but should instead use more advanced rules to guide investment policy. The more sophisticated investors are also expected to be more knowledgeable about the range of investment options available to them, and consequently to have a larger proportion of investments in other assets than bonds and equities. These factors should enable more sophisticated pension fund investors to apply better asset class allocation strategies than those of less sophisticated pension funds.

The influence of sophistication on risk-taking is not self-evident. Less sophisticated investors may underestimate risks and consequently take more risk by investing in high risk, high (expected) return assets. Alternatively, less sophisticated investors may be more risk averse, thus compensating for weaker risk-management skills, *e.g.* the ability to measure and control risk and implement diversification strategies. The latter conjecture is confirmed by previous research, showing that risk tolerance in individuals is negatively correlated with financial knowledge and education (Grable, 2000). We hypothesize that, by analogy, the sophistication of institutional investors correlates also positively to risk-taking.

We investigate the investment policies of 857 Dutch pension funds during the 1999–2006 period and a smaller number of pension funds during the 2007–2010 period. At the end of 2010, total pension fund assets in the Netherlands amounted to € 775 billion, or 132% of GDP (OECD, 2011). In 2015, these numbers are € 1,210 billion and 178% of GDP (OECD, 2016), ranking the Dutch pension system in terms of the asset-to-GDP ratio as the largest in the world, after Denmark.

We find that pension funds' asset allocation policies often seem to be relatively simple and that they vary widely, in line with the asset allocation puzzle. This raises the question whether all pension funds implement optimal asset allocation strategies, given their specific profiles and preferences.

To investigate this, we develop three measures of sophistication. The first measure assumes that less sophisticated pension funds are less knowledgeable about their (unpublished) optimal asset allocation, or use human judgement more, and are therefore more likely to choose plausible figures rather than the outcomes of detailed calculations. For example, they may use multiples of 5% to set their strategic asset allocation. The strategic investment allocation reflects pension funds' (unpublished) investment objectives, which they report to their prudential supervisor, De Nederlandsche Bank (DNB). The strategic asset allocation must meet supervisory requirements. The actual asset allocation may depart from the objective as a result of asset price shocks, since pension funds do not continuously rebalance their portfolios (Bikker *et al.*, 2010). We find that most pension funds do, in fact, apply such a coarse approach in allocating wealth to investment classes. This finding is similar to age heaping found in sociological and historical studies, where it is considered an indication of limited education.

Our second measure records how much pension funds invest in alternative, more complex asset classes such as commodities and real estate (versus more simple classes such as money market and mixed asset funds), thereby improving asset diversification.[4] We find that pension funds that apply rounding to multiples of 5% tend to diversify less to such more complex asset classes. Third, we examine 'home bias' and find that many pension funds favour regional investments, thereby limiting international diversification. We also find that all three indicators are correlated to pension fund 'size', indicating that smaller pension funds are generally less sophisticated than large funds, which is in line with our expectation.

In accordance with the asset allocation puzzle, we observe for Dutch pension funds that there are large differences in asset allocation strategies across pension funds. Specifically, relative holdings of bonds and equities, investments in more complex asset classes and international diversification all vary significantly. Whereas specific conditions such as size (reflecting scale economies with respect to *e.g.* asset management and risk management), funding ratio, age distribution of participants, type of pension plans or type of pension fund contribute to this spread (Chapter 7), the variation remains largely unexplained. An important question is whether pension fund investors' sophistication influences risk-taking. It would be a rational risk-management strategy for pension fund investors with less financial expertise to reduce exposure to risks that are not well understood. We investigate the impact of sophistication on risk-taking by estimating a model for the strategic bond allocation, where our measures of sophistication are added as explanatory variables. The empirical results indicate that less sophisticated pension funds have a significantly lower risk profile, investing more in bonds and less in equities.

There are at least two reasons why the pension sector in the Netherlands provides an ideal setting to study the impact of investor sophistication on risk-taking. First, total assets under administration, our measure of the size of pension funds, which may be related to sophistication, varies widely. Pension funds range in size from small institutions – with assets below one hundred million euro (almost two-thirds of the funds) – to very large institutions with assets of more than one hundred billion euro. The variation in terms of participants is also wide, from less than 100 participants (5% of institutions) to more than a million participants. Large institutions include industry-wide pension funds such as ABP, the public servants pension fund, and PFZW, the health care fund, which are among the biggest in the world. Small institutions are mostly company funds that provide pensions for the employees of a single company. Second, DNB collects comprehensive data on the investment policies of all these institutions, which allows us to study their asset allocation strategies.

This chapter is organized as follows. Section 8.2 describes our dataset, while Section 8.3 develops three measures of sophistication in pension funds' investment behaviour and examines their mutual connection and relationship to size and other characteristics of pension funds. Section 8.4 investigates the influence of investment sophistication on risk-taking. Section 8.5 provides an update of our approach for 2007–2010 as a robustness test, while the last section concludes.

8.2. Data on pension funds

We use a detailed dataset on the investments of 857 Dutch pension funds, consisting of quarterly figures for 1999:Q1–2006:Q4. The data is from DNB, responsible for the prudential supervision of pension funds and their regulatory compliance. For each pension fund, data is or should be available on its strategic asset allocation, asset sales and purchases and on the market value of investments in various asset classes. Pension funds generally do not fully and continuously rebalance their actual asset allocation to match their strategic allocation policies (Bikker *et al.*, 2010). As a result, actual asset allocations reflect both active policy decisions by pension funds and (recent) returns on the portfolio holdings. We investigate strategic asset allocations, since these fully reflect active choices of pension funds, in contrast to actual asset allocations, which are also influenced by market price shocks. The sample is an unbalanced panel, as not all pension funds are included throughout the sample period, due to new entrants, mergers, dissolutions and reporting failures.[5] Pension funds with evident reporting errors have been excluded.[6] Over 2001–2006, the sample represents around 95% to 99% of pension funds' participants in the Netherlands. Our sample includes 664 company pension funds, 97 industry-wide pension funds and 11 professional group pension funds; the status of 85 funds is unknown.[7]

Table 8.1 presents summary statistics after cleaning up the data. The size of pension funds in the sample ranges from small pension funds with total investments worth less than € 1 million, to large pension funds such as ABP, the public servants pension fund, with total investments of over € 200 billion. (End of 2016 ABP controls 420 billion euro [ABP, 2017].) The average size of pension fund assets is € 785 million. The number of pension funds varies over the quarters between 510 and 657. Given the total number of pension funds, 857 (after data selection), this implies that each quarter a substantial number of pension funds are – in that quarter – not present in our dataset, due in part to the data clean up. To compare pension funds with different levels of sophistication, we define three size classes: small (investments of up to € 100 million), medium (€ 100–1,000 million) and large (> € 1 billion). Although large in number (63% of the institutions), the small pension funds administer only 2% of total pension fund assets. Conversely, whilst large pension funds represent only 8% of institutions, they administer 86% of total pension fund assets.

Table 8.1 Summary statistics for various pension fund sizes[a] (1999:Q1–2006:Q4)

	Mean value	Standard deviation	Maximum	Minimum	Number of observations
Number of pension funds	614	38	657	510	19,174
Small funds	388	49	438	252	12,165
Medium-sized funds	171	13	188	135	5,429
Large funds	50	6	61	38	1,580
Number of participants	25,135	148,440	2,710,422	1	18,739
Small funds	2,030	11,668	299,195	1	11,801
Medium-sized funds	15,640	46,541	659,342	9	5,392
Large funds	234,613	458,625	2,710,422	3,425	1,546
Total investments, € mln	785.2	6,740.0	204,000.0	0.1	19,174
Small funds, € mln	28.4	26.8	99.9	0.1	12,165
Medium-sized funds, € mln	319.6	206.9	998.6	100.0	5,429
Large funds, € mln	8,211.4	22,200.0	204,000.0	1,006.0	1,580

[a] Small pension funds have investments of € 0–100 million, medium-sized funds € 100–1,000 million and large funds over € 1 billion.

All investment figures are split into the respective currencies. We define home bias as more than proportional investments in the euro area. Other characteristics of pension funds, such as number of participants, funding ratio and percentage of pensioners, are available on an annual basis. Where desirable, we interpolate and extrapolate these variables to obtain quarterly values.

8.3. Investor sophistication

In order to assess the sophistication of pension funds' investment policies, we develop three measures of sophistication, based on the data discussed above: (i) the use of gross rounding, (ii) investments in alternative, more complex asset classes minus investment in alternative simple assets and (iii) home bias.

8.3.1. *Gross rounding of asset allocations*

We first examine the use of rounded numbers in pension funds' strategic asset allocation. The histograms in Fig. 8.1 show the strategic equity and bond allocations of Dutch pension funds.[8] Two patterns stand out. First, and most remarkably, strategic allocations cluster around multiples of 5%. Table 8.2 shows that the frequencies of 5% multiples used for strategic allocations to both equities and bonds far outstrip those of other numbers. Apparently, pension funds strongly favour round percentages for strategic equity and bond allocations to the nearest 5%. The graphs further suggest that coarse rounding to the nearest 10% is more frequent than rounding to 5%. Apparently, sets of ten are even more attractive than sets of five. Just as Agnew *et al.* (2003) observes for private investors, we also notice that some pension funds take extreme positions of 0% and 100% in equities or bonds.[9] Second, the dispersion of strategic equity and bond allocation across pension funds is large. The graphs show little or no convergence around a certain strategic

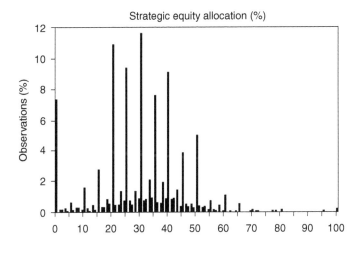

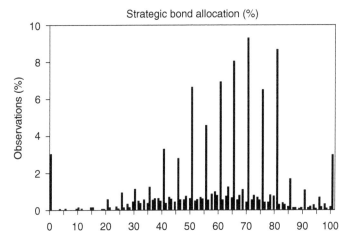

Figure 8.1 Frequency distribution of strategic equity and bond allocations of 857 pension funds (1999:Q1–2006:Q4)

asset allocation indicating that (beliefs about) optimal asset allocation levels vary widely across pension funds, perhaps (partly) due to diverging conditions such as risk aversion and ageing.

Attractive numbers for rounding should be simple to remember and easy to use for calculations. Multiples of 10%, 5% and also 2% fit the bill. We classify pension funds that use these multiples for their strategic equity and bond allocations as 'using attractive numbers'. Coarse rounding may point to less sophistication in line with findings for demographic studies. Alternatively, the preference of pension funds to use attractive numbers for their strategic asset allocation may be

Table 8.2 Attractive numbers used for strategic allocation to both equities and bonds (in %; 1999:Q1–2006:Q4)

Attractive numbers	Small funds[a]	Medium-sized funds	Large funds	All funds	Uniform distribution
Multiples of 10%	37	28	11	33	1
Multiples of 5%	66	57	29	61	4
Multiples of 2%	41	33	19	37	25

[a] Size classes are defined in Table 8.1.

due to the absence of compelling arguments for more 'precise' allocation figures. The latter explanation would be in line with DeMiguel *et al.* (2007), who find that simple heuristics such as the $1/n$ rule generate returns similar to those of more complicated portfolio choice models in the presence of estimation errors. If this alternative explanation were true, we would expect no significant impact of coarse rounding on risk-taking. However, our empirical results presented later in this chapter point elsewhere.

Table 8.2 shows the percentages of pension funds that use attractive numbers for their strategic allocation to both equities and bonds. The number 66% for multiples of 5% by small pension funds (first column, second row) indicates that two-thirds of these pension funds use 5% multiples for their strategic allocation to both equities and bonds, leaving only 34% of funds allocating other percentages, which may include 5% multiples to either bonds or equity. We compare this to the incidence of attractive numbers for both equity and bond allocations under a uniform distribution. As already suggested by Fig. 8.1, multiples of 5% (including tens) occur most frequently. On average, 61% of pension funds use multiples of 5% for their strategic allocation to both equities and bonds, far above the 4% expected in a uniform distribution of integers between 0% and 100%. Multiples of 10% are reported at slightly more than half the frequency for multiples of 5% indicating that, on average, pension funds slightly prefer even over odd multiples of 5%. The difference between multiples of 10% and multiples of 2% is only marginal indicating low preference for percentages ending in 2, 4, 6 and 8. We only consider integers to calculate the uniform distribution, while in the dataset we only consider multiples of 10.0%, 5.0% and/or 2.0% to be attractive numbers. In fact, however, almost one-fifth of the pension funds report their asset allocations in decimals. So in reality, the expected use of attractive numbers under the uniform distribution would be even lower than assumed here.

We test whether multiples of, respectively, 10%, 5% and 2% for investments in equities and bonds occur more frequently (H_1) than under a uniform distribution of integers between 0% and 100% (H_0), using Pearson's chi-squared test on observed versus expected percentages under a uniform distribution (A'Hearn, Baten and Crayen, 2009). The uniform distribution is rejected at the 1% significance level for all three multiples, across all three size classes of pension funds,[10] except the use of even numbers for large pension funds.

Table 8.2 also shows that small pension funds use attractive numbers significantly more frequently than medium-sized pension funds, while large pension funds use attractive numbers least frequently. We test whether the frequencies of certain multiples are equal (H_0) or different (H_1), using the t-test on the equality of means, respectively, between small and medium-sized funds, and between medium-sized and large funds.[11] We find that the different frequencies between small, medium and large pension funds, across all types of multiples, are significant at the 1% level.[12]

Table 8.3 shows the frequency distribution of combinations of strategic equity and bond allocations when they are both rounded to 5%. Each non-zero cell presents the frequency of a combination linked to (i) a bond allocation with a percentage as in the upper row and (ii) an equity allocation with a percentage as in the left-hand column. The bottom row gives aggregations for the frequencies corresponding to the respective bond allocations, and the right-hand column gives summations for the frequencies related to the respective equity allocations.

In line with Fig. 8.1, the table confirms that there is a wide variety of investment policies with little convergence to a certain average or median strategy. The most common strategic allocations are between 20% and 50% for equities and between 50% and 80% for bonds (see shaded cells). The diagonal reflects the frequencies of pension funds where the allocations to equities and bonds add up to 100%, hence without investments in other assets (see *e.g.* shaded cells). These diagonal cells add up to 36.8%.

The hypothetical optimal asset allocation of pension funds depends on risk preferences of participants and sponsors (determined by *e.g.* the age structure of participants), expected risks and returns of the different asset classes, the funding ratios and macroeconomic variables such as wage growth, inflation and real interest rates. Typically, Asset-Liability Management (ALM) studies take these factors into account. Such studies could be used to obtain supposed optimal asset allocation estimates, using Monte Carlo simulations based on preferences (such as the risk-return trade off) and on market return and volatility assumptions. However, in practice, ALM studies are not used directly to optimize portfolio investments across asset classes. Rather, they are used as input for a human appraisal process. The widespread use of multiples of 5% indicates that the determination of strategic asset allocations is often based on rough estimates rather than precise measures.

Table 8.4 presents the use of attractive strategic asset allocation numbers by small, medium-sized and large pension funds over time. The statistics confirm that small funds are more likely than large funds to choose multiples of 5% for their investment strategies. On average, 66% of small pension funds choose a multiple of 5% for their strategic equity and bond allocations compared to only 56% of medium-sized funds and 29% of large funds. There is some variation over time: the use of 5% multiples increases until 2002 (for large funds: 2003) and decreases afterwards. This may be an indication that the use of ALM models in determining the strategic allocation has increased since 2002/2003. However, the finding that the use of 5% multiples is inversely related to size is consistent over the years. Based on a t-test, we find that differences in the use of 5% multiples between small, medium-sized and large pension funds are significant at the 1% level for each year. These findings suggest that small pension funds use less sophisticated asset allocation rules more often than large funds.

Table 8.3 Frequency distribution of 5% multiples in strategic equity and bond allocations (in % of observations; 1999:Q1–2006:Q4)

(%)	Bonds																					
Equities	0	5	10	15	20	25	30	35	40	45	50	55	60	65	70	75	80	85	90	95	100	Sum
0	1.8										0.1				0.1	0.1	0.1		0.2	0.3	2.9	5.9
5							0.1												0.1	0.2		0.5
10						0.1									0.1	0.1		0.4	0.7			1.5
15											0.1				0.1	0.1	0.9	1.0				2.1
20	0.1								0.2		0.1			0.4	0.6	0.8	7.2					9.3
25	0.1									0.1		0.4	0.2	1.2	1.5	5.1						8.3
30	0.1								0.2			0.8	1.0	1.7	6.3							10.0
35								0.1	0.1	0.4	0.4	0.8	1.1	3.7								6.4
40							0.1		0.5	0.6		1.8	3.3									6.9
45			0.1						0.1	0.4	1.8											3.0
50	0.1			0.1	0.1	0.1			0.9	0.3	2.8											4.4
55						0.1	0.1	0.1	0.1													0.6
60						0.1	0.1	0.2	0.5													1.0
65						0.1	0.1	0.1														0.3
70							0.1															0.1
75																						0.0
80					0.2																	0.2
85																						0.0
90																						0.0
95	0.1																					0.1
100	0.3																					0.3
Sum	2.6	0.0	0.1	0.1	0.4	0.6	0.8	0.6	2.5	2.3	5.7	3.8	6.0	7.1	8.7	6.2	8.2	1.4	1.0	0.6	2.9	60.8

Note: Cells in the upper triangular with values below 0.05% are shown as blanks.

Table 8.4 Multiples of 5% used for strategic asset allocation over time and across size classes (1999–2006; in %)

Year	Small [a]	Medium-sized	Large	Total
1999	60	48	22	54
2000	64	51	25	57
2001	66	57	26	61
2002	70	64	29	65
2003	70	60	32	64
2004	70	61	30	64
2005	66	57	31	59
2006	65	52	32	56
Unweighted average	*66*	*56*	*29*	*60*

[a] Size classes are defined in Table 8.1.

8.3.2. Allocation to alternative asset classes

We investigate how pension funds allocate investments across different asset classes. Our dataset distinguishes the following asset classes: equities, bonds, real estate, mortgages and loans, commodities, mixed mutual funds and money market instruments.[13] More than 50% of pension funds base their strategic asset allocation on bonds and equities only and do not consider alternative asset classes such as real estate or commodities. This suggests that these pension funds limit their scope for higher expected returns and/or further risk diversification.

Table 8.5 presents the allocation of pension funds' wealth across asset classes for pension funds of various size categories. It shows that larger pension funds allocate higher proportions of their investments to equities and lower proportions to bonds, compared to smaller pension funds. Medium-sized funds take an intermediate position. Larger pension funds, seeking better risk diversification

Table 8.5 Average strategic asset allocation by size class (1999:Q1–2006:Q4)

	Equities	Bonds	Alternative simple investments [b]	Alternative complex investments [c]	Average investments (mln euro)
Size classes pension funds[a]	*In %*				
0–100 (small)	27	64	4	5	28
100–1,000 (medium-sized)	36	56	1	7	320
>1,000 (large)	41	45	1	13	8,211

Note: All allocation numbers are simple averages in percentages.

[a] Based on total investments (in € millions). [b] Simple alternative investments include money market funds and mixed mutual funds. [c] Complex alternative investments include real estate, commodities and loans.

and/or higher returns, also invest more in alternative investments than small and medium-sized funds. We split alternative investments into two categories: relatively simple assets (money market funds and mixed mutual funds) and more complex assets (real estate, commodities and loans). This split shows that larger pension funds invest significantly more in alternative complex assets, but less in alternative simple assets, compared to small funds. This behaviour is probably driven in part by supervisory regulations, which require a more sophisticated risk management for institutions that invest in more complex alternative investments. Differences between small, medium-sized and large pension funds for all asset categories distinguished are significant at the 1% level (based on a *t*-test on the equality of means as used in Table 8.2), except for simple alternative investments between medium-sized and large pension funds. Over time, diversification to alternative investments has been quite stable, on average, with a slight downward trend for all size classes.

Table 8.6 provides further insight in the relationship between investments in complex alternative assets and pension fund sizes. The upper panel of this table shows that 83% of small pension funds invest less than 10% of their assets in alternative, complex assets *vs.* 69% for medium-sized funds and 34% for large funds. Only 18% of small funds invest more than 10% in sophisticated assets whereas 66% of the large funds do so. The lower panel of Table 8.6 shows that pension funds that round to 5% multiples invest significantly less in alternative complex assets. The outcomes of this table confirm the finding that large funds diversify their investments more. Furthermore, this behaviour turns out to be inversely correlated with heaping.

For a pension fund whose risk management is not sophisticated, it may make sense to invest more in simple alternative investments, as opposed to complex alternative investments that are not fully understood. However, this approach implies less diversification: *a priori* lower investment returns (at given risk levels) so that sophistication remains 'better'. Nonetheless, it may be relatively costly for

Table 8.6 Pension funds that invest in alternative complex assets[a] (in % of all pension funds; 1999:Q1–2006:Q4)

Size classes pension funds[b]		Investments in alternative complex assets			
		0%	*0–10%*	*10–20%*	*>20%*
0–100	(small)	62	21	11	7
100–1,000	(medium-sized)	44	25	22	10
>1,000	(large)	10	24	44	22
Use of 'attractive numbers' for strategic asset allocation					
Pension funds that round to 5%		67	14	14	5
Funds that do not round to 5%		31	35	20	14

Note: All statistics are simple averages in %.

[a] Alternative complex asset classes include real estate, commodities and loans. [b] Based on total investments (in € millions).

small funds to invest in complex alternative investments. It is difficult to distinguish between unsophisticated or 'suboptimal' investment policies and the most appropriate (but less rewarding) investments for small funds. Nevertheless, we can do this by controlling for the size effect, which reflects the scale of the risk-management unit, so that we observe pension fund investment behaviour in deviation from its fund size. This is what happens indirectly when, in Section 8.4, we use the sophistication measures together with size as explanatory variables in the risk aversion or bond allocation model of Equation (8.3).

8.3.3. Home bias

We investigate to what degree pension funds diversify their investments geographically. International diversification can provide significant benefits by reducing risk for a given level of expected returns. However, not all investors exploit these diversification benefits to the full, as evidenced by their limited ownership of foreign shares. This phenomenon has been documented using macroeconomic data (*e.g.* French and Poterba, 1991), firm-specific data (*e.g.* Kang and Stulz, 1997), as well as investor-specific data (*e.g.* Karlsson and Norden, 2007). The main explanations point to explicit and implicit barriers to international investments. Other explanations include the use of domestic assets to hedge against unexpected changes in inflation and cognitive biases. However, these explanations have not been able to fully account for the lack of international diversification by domestic and foreign investors, despite significant risk-return benefits. Therefore, this phenomenon is known as the home-bias puzzle.

Home bias usually refers to a preference by investors to hold domestic assets. Here we refer to more than proportional investments of Dutch pension funds in the euro area, as the data do not present greater detail. International diversification provides substantial risk-return benefits and hence home bias indicates a certain degree of shortsightedness that suggests less sophistication. Table 8.7 shows that, on average, large pension funds invest 34% of their assets within the euro area, while investments of small pension funds in the euro zone average 53% of assets.[14] The home preference for assets from the euro area is at 47% stronger in less sophisticated pension funds (which round to 5%) than in sophisticated

Table 8.7 Home bias of equity investments[a] (1999:Q1–2006:Q4)

Size classes pension funds [b]		Investments within the euro area (in %)		
		All	*Funds using 5% multiples*	*Funds not using 5% multiples*
0–100	(small)	53	59	42
100–1,000	(medium-sized)	42	40	44
>1,000	(large)	34	39	32
All funds		*43*	*47*	*39*

Note: All percentages are simple averages.

[a] Including exposure from derivatives; [b] Based on total investments (in € millions).

ones (39%). This finding is consistent with a study by Karlsson and Norden (2007), who report a higher likelihood of home bias for less sophisticated investors with lower education levels and no previous experience with investments in risky assets. Remarkably though, the home bias is stronger for sophisticated small and medium-sized funds compared to unsophisticated funds of these size classes (which is unexpected), whereas it is much smaller for sophisticated large funds compared to unsophisticated large funds, in line with 'theory'. On average, home bias fell from 50% to 42% during 1999–2001 (a similar fall is observed in all size classes), with a slight upward bound in 2006.

We also observe home bias in total investments of pension funds, where small and medium-sized funds hold around 85% of their investments in assets located in the euro area against 63% for large funds. This total-investment euro-area bias confirms the equity euro-area bias of Table 8.7. Incidentally, pension funds tend to hedge their currency risk with derivatives, reducing their net non-euro exposure to only 4% for small funds and 8% for large funds. Note that currency risk insurance does not wipe out the euro-area bias above, as the lack of international diversification remains.

8.3.4. An overall index of sophistication

Following Calvet *et al.* (2009b) we investigate the relationship of each of the three sophistication measures with a number of pension fund characteristics in order to explain which features of pension funds determine the developed measures. The relationship we use is:

$$y^k_{i,t} = \sum_j \beta^k_j x_{i,j,t} + e^k_{i,t} \tag{8.1}$$

where y refers to the three measures of sophistication ($k = 1, 2, 3$), x to the j considered pension fund characteristics listed in Table 8.8, β to the respective coefficients, e to the error terms, i to the pension funds and t to time. The first three columns of Table 8.8 present the estimation results.

Each of the three measures correlates significantly with size, expressed as the logarithm of total assets, and the signs of the estimated coefficients are in line with expectations that larger size is associated with higher sophistication. This is what we also observed earlier and it is in line with the idea that size and risk management go hand in hand. Note that gross rounding and home bias point to less sophistication, whereas diversification into alternative assets indicates more sophistication; see the first row of Table 8.8. Pension funds with larger investments per participant tend to round less and diversify more in alternative assets. Apparently, funds paying higher individual pension benefits are more sophisticated. Funds offering defined-contribution plans are also more sophisticated, possibly related to the fact that most of these funds in the Netherlands were established more recently and at that time introduced the current state of knowledge. The measures vary across pension fund type: particularly the industry-wide funds have less rounding and more diversification, indicating more sophistication, which is as expected. The low R-squares point to the fact that these pension fund characteristics only explain

Table 8.8 Measures of sophistication and pension fund characteristics (1999:Q1–2006:Q4)

Correlation with sophistication	Gross rounding		Diversification in alternative assets		Home bias		Overall index	
	−		+		−		−	
Size (logarithm of total assets)	−0.043	***	0.013	***	−0.045	***	−0.044	***
Investments per participant	−0.210	***	0.002		−0.005		−0.196	***
Percentage pensioners	0.014		−0.005		0.084	*	0.024	***
Funding ratio	−0.019	*	0.012	***	0.109	***	−0.017	**
Industry funds	−0.243	***	0.073	***	0.100	***	−0.241	***
Professional group funds	−0.063	**	0.015	*	−0.091	***	−0.068	***
Defined-contribution plan	−0.174	***	0.012		0.110	***	−0.154	***
Gross-rounding intercept	−0.043	***	−		−		1.167	***
Asset-diversification intercept	−		0.013	***	−		−0.113	***
Home-bias intercept	−		−		0.013	***	0.697	***
Gamma2	−		−		−		−0.281	***
Gamma3	−		−		−		0.437	***
Number of observations	16,937		16,937		2,092		35,966	
F-statistics	267		253		57		−	
R-squared, adjusted	8.6		9.8		14.0		62.9	

Note: ***, ** and * denote significance at the 1%, 5% and 10% levels, respectively.

a minor part of the variation in the measures: sophistication varies widely across pension funds, even within size classes, et cetera.

Further following Calvet *et al.* (2009b), we construct an overall index of sophistication by regressing the vector of measures of sophistication on (vectors of) pension fund characteristics:

$$
\begin{bmatrix} y_{i,t}^1 \\ y_{i,t}^2 \\ y_{i,t}^3 \end{bmatrix} = \begin{bmatrix} \sum_j \beta_j x_{i,j,t} \\ \gamma_2 \sum_j \beta_j x_{i,j,t} \\ \gamma_3 \sum_j \beta_j x_{i,j,t} \end{bmatrix} + \begin{bmatrix} e_{i,t}^1 \\ e_{i,t}^2 \\ e_{i,t}^3 \end{bmatrix} \tag{8.2}
$$

Equation (8.2) combines the three Equations (8.1) – for $k = 1, 2, 3$ – into one vector, and imposes a set of restrictions $\beta_j^1 = \gamma_2 \beta_j^2 = \gamma_3 \beta_j^3 (= \beta_j$ by definition) for each j. These restrictions force the impact of the pension funds characteristics on the three measures of sophistication to be identical, apart from scaling factors γ_2 *and* γ_3. This construction of an overall index is based on the assumption that the three measures have a common component, interpreted as (lack of) sophistication. This common component, $\Sigma_j \beta_j x_{i,j,t}$, is the overall index. The last column of Table 8.8 presents the estimates of Equation (8.2). The values of the two gammas lower than 1 (in absolute terms) reflect that the first measure, 'gross rounding', is more strongly correlated with this underlying common factor than the other two measures. The negative sign of γ_2 indicates that 'diversification into alternative assets' is correlated positively with sophistication while the other two are correlated with *lack of* sophistication, hence negatively. Table 8.9 shows the mutual correlations between the measures.

The correlations reflect the fact that gross rounding, home bias, the overall index and total investments are negatively associated with sophistication, while diversification is positively correlated. The correlations are quite low, indicating that the measures reflect various dimensions of sophistication. The overall index reflects gross rounding and home bias more closely than diversification. This index is highly (but inversely) correlated with pension fund size. In part, this is due to the construction of the index: it reflects the model $\Sigma_j \beta_j x_{i,j,t}$, including size, which covers the sophistication measures only poorly, and ignores their residuals. The next section will show that the measures explain the risk appetite of pension funds, even when controlling for size.

8.4. Investor sophistication and risk-taking

We investigate a possible relationship between the measures of investor sophistication and risk-taking. We hypothesize that pension funds with less investment expertise are generally more risk averse. Assuming that they are less knowledgeable about how to invest assets optimally, less sophisticated funds may deliberately choose a lower risk profile for their asset allocation. This strategy makes sense intuitively, as small funds with limited sophistication and expertise are likely to feel less comfortable with these risks. Conversely, sophisticated pension funds are more likely to have significant in-house expertise and to use sophisticated modelling techniques, which may make them less averse to risk-taking. Sophisticated funds may also suffer from overconfidence because they put too much trust in the theories and models they have developed (Griffin and Tversky, 1992). As the recent credit crisis shows, risk-taking is not always a rewarding strategy

Table 8.9 Mutual correlations between measures of sophistication and pension fund size (1999:Q1–2006:Q4)

	Gross rounding	Diversification	Home bias	Overall index	Total investments
Gross rounding	1.00				
Diversification	−0.14	1.00			
Home bias	0.15	0.24	1.00		
Overall index	0.29	−0.17	0.22	1.00	
Total investments	−0.29	0.08	−0.30	−0.86	1.00

since over the last decade, investments in bonds have yielded higher rewards than equities in most countries.

Fig. 8.2 presents the average strategic equity and bond allocations over time for pension funds in different size categories. On average, large pension funds invest a greater share of their assets in equities and less in bonds, as also observed in Table 8.5. The graphs show that this finding is persistent across the sample period.

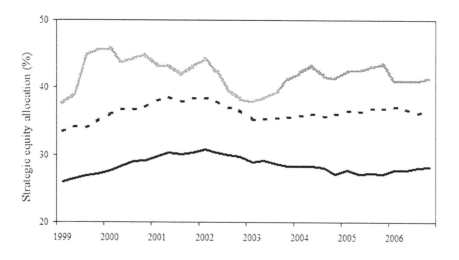

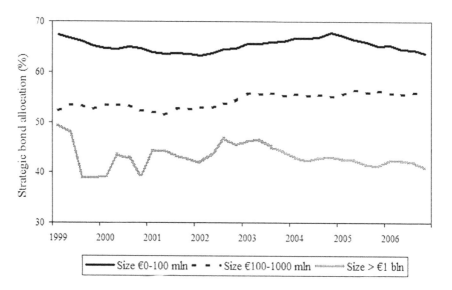

Figure 8.2 Strategic equity and bond allocations by pension fund size over time (1999:Q1–2006:Q4)

Investing more in bonds, as small funds do, reduces the mismatch between the duration of assets and liabilities, and reduces the exposure to volatile equity markets.[15] Hence, the graphs indicate that small and less sophisticated funds tend to choose a lower risk exposure. Fig. 8.2 further shows that strategic asset allocations vary significantly over time, reflecting the dynamic nature of investment policies. Over time, large pension funds have most volatile strategic asset allocation. This suggests that they update their investment policy more frequently but may also reflect the fact that the average of large funds is based on a lower number of pension funds (see Table 8.1).

To examine the impact of investor sophistication, or the lack of it, on risk-taking, we estimate the following equation:

$$
\begin{aligned}
Bond°allocation_{i,t} = {} & \alpha + \beta\,Heaping_{i,t} + \gamma\,Diversification_{i,t} \\
& + \delta\,Home°bias_{i,t-1} + \varepsilon\,Size_{i,t-1} \\
& + \zeta\,Risk°preferences_{i,t-1} + \eta\,Governance_{i} \\
& + \theta\,Pension°plan_{i} + e_{i,t}
\end{aligned}
\tag{8.3}
$$

The dependent variable $Bond°allocation_{i,t}$ is the strategic bond allocation of pension fund i ($i = 1, \ldots, N$) at quarter t ($t = 1, \ldots, T$). The explanatory variables $Heaping$ and $Diversification$ are variables indicating sophistication in asset allocation. $Heaping$ equals one if the strategic equity and bond allocation are multiples of 5% and zero otherwise. $Diversification$ stands for sophisticated diversification and is defined as 'the strategic allocation to alternative complex assets' minus 'the strategic investment in alternative simple assets', each presented as a percentage of total assets. $Home°bias$ is the percentage of investments in the European Monetary Union (EMU). Positive estimates for β and δ, and a negative estimate for γ would indicate that pension funds with less developed strategies choose a lower risk profile for their portfolio by investing a higher share of their wealth in bonds.

The other explanatory variables are standard elements in bond (or equity) allocation models for pension funds (Alestalo and Puttonen, 2006; Gerber and Weber, 2007; Lucas and Zeldes, 2006, 2009). The variable $Size$, measured as the log of total investments, is included to estimate the impact of scale on the risk profile of pension funds. This variable is included with a lag to avoid possible endogeneity problems, even though such problems are unlikely. Bond price shocks may lead to an increase in *both the actual bond allocation and* total investments during the same period, but equity price shocks would have opposite effects on *actual bond allocation and* total investments. More importantly, we explain the strategic and not the actual allocation. But the strategic allocation may gradually over time be influenced by asset price shocks (Bikker *et al.*, 2010).[16] A negative estimate for ε would indicate that the investments of larger pension funds tend to be riskier. Scale advantages should enable large pension funds to apply a more highly developed allocation policy and, therefore, this variable may also pick up some of the variation that is not explained by the first two variables (*Heaping* and *Diversification*), which are used as indicators for the level of sophistication of asset allocation.

Risk°preferences is a vector of three variables that control for risk preferences of participants and sponsors. The variable 'assets per participant' is included to control for the impact of higher average pension assets on risk preferences. A negative coefficient would indicate that participants with higher pension fund investments are less risk averse. The age variable 'percentage of pensioners' is included to control for the duration of liabilities (Lucas and Zeldes, 2009).[17] A positive coefficient for this variable would indicate that pension funds where relatively many participants have a short investment horizon will choose a lower risk profile (see Chapter 7). The variable 'funding ratio', calculated as total investments divided by discounted pension liabilities, is included because, from a risk-management perspective, a bigger buffer provides room to invest more in risky assets.[18] A negative coefficient could also indicate decreasing relative risk aversion in line with *e.g.* Cohn *et al.* (1975). This variable is included with a one-quarter time lag because it may take some time for changes in a fund's funding ratio to affect its strategic bond allocation.

Governance is a vector of three dummy variables that control for differences in the governance of pension funds. The variable 'industry-wide pension funds' equals one if the pension fund provides pension plans for employees in an industry and zero otherwise, whereas the variable 'professional group pension funds' equals one if the pension fund provides a pension scheme to a specific professional group (*e.g.* medical profession, public notaries) and zero otherwise. Note that 'company pension funds' is the reference group. Finally, the variable 'defined-contribution plan' equals one if a defined-contribution pension scheme is offered, as opposed to a defined-benefit plan (zero).

Columns 1, 3 and 4 of Table 8.10 report estimation results for Equation (8.3), though excluding the home-bias variable, both for all pension funds and for company and industry funds separately.[19] Inclusion of 'home bias' would reduce the number of observations from 13,517 to 2,007.[20] All key variables enter with the expected signs and are significant at the 1% significance level in all three specifications, except the DC dummy for industry funds, which is significant at the 10% confidence level only. The results provide strong evidence that small pension funds with less than optimal allocation policies are more likely to choose low-risk asset allocation strategies. Specifically, the heaping variable's coefficient has a significant positive sign, showing that pension funds with less advanced asset allocation policies invest more in bonds. The coefficient indicates that pension funds using multiples of 5% for their asset allocation invest, on average, 3.2 percentage points more in bonds (first column). The coefficient is even higher for *Diversification*, indicating that pension funds investing 10% of total assets more in alternative complex assets or less in alternative simple assets, invest 2.9% of total assets less in bonds. Note that in this multiple-regression model (which includes size as explanatory variable) the coefficients of the two sophistication variables reflect the sophistication effect corrected for the size effect. Finally, the size variable enters with a negative sign, indicating that large pension funds raise their risk profiles by investing relatively less in bonds. An alternative size measure, that is, number of participants instead of total assets, leads to virtually identical estimation results.[21]

Table 8.10 The strategic bond ratio and indicators of sophistication for various pension fund types (1999:Q1–2006:Q4)

Column	All pension funds		Company pension funds	Industry-wide pension funds
	1	*2*	*3*	*4*
Heaping (gross rounding)	0.031 ***	–	0.021 ***	0.079 ***
Diversification in alternative assets	−0.212 ***	–	−0.153 ***	−0.554 ***
Overall index	–	0.465 ***	–	–
Pension fund size (t-1)	−0.025 ***	–	−0.027 ***	−0.016 ***
Investments per participant (t-1)	−0.039 ***	–	−0.044 ***	−0.820 ***
Percentage pensioners	−0.044 ***	–	−0.043 ***	0.088 ***
Funding ratio (t-1)	−0.048 ***	–	−0.048 ***	−0.026 ***
Industry pension funds	−0.040 ***	–	–	–
Professional group pension funds	0.054 ***	–	–	–
Defined-contribution plan	−0.064 ***	–	−0.048 ***	−0.026 *
Intercept	0.962 ***	0.871 ***	−0.080 ***	−0.099 ***
Number of observations	16,260	16,937	13,484	2,436
F-statistics	377	2,499	226	220
R-squared, adjusted	19.9	13.8	13.9	42.7

Note: One and three asterisks denote significance at the 10% and 1% levels, respectively.

Two of the three included risk preference variables carry their expected sign for all three samples: a higher funding ratio and more investments per participant each imply relatively lower allocation to bonds, in line with Chapter 7. A higher percentage of pensioners should result in a lower risk profile with relatively more bonds, but this is observed for industry-wide funds only. Studies which use average age (not available in our dataset) instead of percentage of pensioners found a similar negative impact of age (Alestalo and Puttonen, 2006; Gerber and Weber, 2007). Compared to company pension funds, industry funds hold relatively less in bonds, while the reverse is true for professional group funds. The latter is explained in Bikker, Broeders and de Dreu (2010). Defined-contribution plans, which have no nominal pension benefit target, tend to hold lower investments in bonds. The goodness of fit (R^2) in Table 8.10 for 'all pension funds' is, at 19.9, rather low, indicating that many other determinants of the bond ratio are not captured by Equation (8.3). This indicates a heavy impact of non-observed preferences, risk aversion and human judgement on strategic allocation. Note that the model fits much better for the – generally larger – industry pension funds; see adjusted R^2 of 42.7 versus 19.9 for all funds.

Column 2 of Table 8.10 presents the coefficient of the 'overall index of (lack of) sophistication', estimated in Section 8.3.4. This index is defined as $\Sigma_j \beta_j x_{i,j,t}$ with $x_{i,j,t}$ the variables already occurring in Equation (8.3) and β_j the corresponding coefficients, estimated under restrictions. Inclusion of both this index and the indicators as explanatory variables would by definition cause (full) multicollinearity,[22] so that we estimate the coefficient of this index only. As expected, the *t*-value of this coefficient is higher than each of the *t*-values of the two separate measures of sophistication, which are now combined in the index. This outcome confirms that the overall index is a useful proxy for the underlying measures of (lack of) sophistication and that less sophisticated pension funds invest more in bonds.

8.5. An update for 2007–2010 as a robustness check

In 2007, a new regulatory regime for pension funds in the Netherlands came into force. At the same time, the prudential supervisor updated the reporting system for pension funds and adjusted the definition of asset classes. One essential change was that hedge fund investments must henceforth be reported as a separate category, apart from equity. Another change was that mixed funds were split into their constituting components and merged with bonds, equities, et cetera. These changes have a significant impact on our diversification measure 'alternative assets' and on the dependent variable 'bonds' in our risk-taking model of Equation (8.3). This is why we cannot append the 2007 and later data to our basic sample period 1999–2006 and apply our approach for the entire period at once.

Our dataset extends from 2007:I to 2010:IV, so that we have another 16 quarters of observations available. We use this second dataset to check whether the financial sophistication characteristics of pension funds that we find over 1999–2006 also hold for the successive years. Note that this period is short, compared to the 32 quarters of our sample period 1999–2006, and that we use different definitions of asset classes in accordance with the new reporting standards. We duplicate all calculations of this chapter for 2007–2010 and briefly discuss the results (available on request). Typical trends in the summary statistics of this later period (as in Table 8.1) are a reduction in the number of smaller pension funds from, on average, 368 to 126, and, consequently, larger (remaining) pension funds. Average total assets increased as a result of both consolidation and overall growth. The updated frequency distribution of strategic equity and bond allocations (as in Fig. 8.1) looks similar, with the same remarkable spikes at multiples of 5%. The share of bonds is lower now and zero allocations for equity are no longer reported. Rounding to multiples of 5% declined during 2007–2010 from 62% to 43%, the reduction being stronger in both relative and absolute terms for medium-sized and larger funds (compare Tables 8.2 and 8.3). The reduction in heaping appears suddenly in early 2007, which is probably related to the new reporting system, adding force to the argument that the two considered periods cannot be analyzed jointly. Therefore, we do not interpret the decrease in heaping as an increase in sophistication. The use of complex investments has increased somewhat in all size classes, but remains the highest by far for larger pension funds. The use of simple assets is now low in all pension fund size classes. Over time, the proportions of equities and bonds for larger pension funds have come to differ less from those for smaller funds, due in part to the lower number of smaller funds (compare Tables 8.4 and 8.5). Differences in home bias across size classes remain unchanged (compare Table 8.7). The general picture is that the difference between large and small pension funds increases for one indicator (diversification) and decreases for the two others (heaping and home bias).

In explaining the strategic allocation to bonds over 2007–2010, the coefficient of the measure 'diversification in alternative assets' is larger and more significant than before, due to the improved definition of alternative assets (compare Table 8.10). While heaping was the most statistically significant measure during 1999–2006, it is less prominent in later years and, in fact, not significantly different from zero for the industry-wide pension funds, probably due to its lower frequency. The estimated overall index of (lack of) sophistication, defined by Equation (8.2), is also a highly significant explanatory variable in explaining the strategic allocation to bonds: less sophistication goes hand in hand with lower bond investments.

We conclude that the measures of sophistication continue to work well during 2007–2010, but with less emphasis on heaping and a more prominent role for diversification into alternative assets. Furthermore we find that two out of three measures point to increasing sophistication over time.

8.6. Conclusions

We examine the impact of investor sophistication on risk-taking. We focus on pension funds since their size and other characteristics vary widely and comprehensive data is available. To measure investor sophistication, we construct three measures of the sophistication of pension funds' investment policies. The first indicator gauges the use of attractive, but imprecise, numbers for the strategic allocation of assets to both equities and bonds. Most pension funds in the Netherlands apply such rule of thumb, using particularly multiples of 5%. This supports the observation that in current practice, asset allocation does not follow directly from optimization of ALM models. Rather, it is determined by human judgement, given results from ALM studies. The second indicator is the use of alternative, complex investments other than equities and bonds, as an instrument to diversify the investment portfolio. We observe that many pension funds invest little in alternative, more complex asset classes, suggesting suboptimal portfolio diversification. The third indicator is home bias in the equity investment portfolio. We show large differences in terms of relative investments in the euro area, suggesting suboptimal international diversification in many pension funds. We find that these three measures correlate with pension fund size indicating that smaller pension funds tend to be less sophisticated than larger ones. Nevertheless, investment sophistication contributes independently to the explanation of risk aversion, showing that investment expertise also varies among pension funds in the same size class. These results suggest that the asset allocation policies of many pension funds, particularly small ones, are suboptimal.

A notable finding is the huge variation in asset allocation practices across pension funds, in a broader context also referred to as the asset allocation puzzle. Part of this variation can be explained by the pension fund's size, its type of pension plan, its preference indicators, such as assets per participant, participant age distribution and the funding ratio and, finally, its governance type. In addition, we find that all our indicators of investor sophistication are highly statistically significant.

Even when controlling for size, sophistication and other fund-specific variables, pension funds make significantly diverging portfolio choices. We believe that this reflects widely varying views regarding the optimal investment mix. It seems likely that differences in risk-return assumptions for the various asset classes, in the level of expertise of pension fund investment managers and in personal preferences of pension boards, also play an important role. The analysis of this latter phenomenon is outside the scope of this chapter, but is suggested as an interesting topic for future research.

Our findings suggest that further consolidation of the Dutch pension sector, by mergers or increased cooperation (*e.g.* in so-called general pension institutions, which can administer pensions plans for several companies or industries) may contribute to improve the sophistication of pension funds' investment policies. Such benefits of consolidation are in line with previous studies, in which we find a negative correlation between the size of pension funds and the administrative and investment costs per participant (Bikker and de Dreu, 2009; Bikker, Steenbeek, and Torracchi, 2012 Chapter 3; Alserda *et al.*, 2017).

Notes

1 An alternative is estimating using instrumental variables. Since the variable total assets is highly correlated with number of participants (0.87), the latter may be considered as a relevant and valid instrumental variable for the former. Estimation results hardly differ.

2 Update of: J. de Dreu and J.A. Bikker, 2012, Investor sophistication and risk taking, *Journal of Banking & Finance* 36, 2145–2156.

3 Whilst the use of the $1/n$ rule points to lower sophistication, it is disputed whether this 'naive' strategy also leads to lower returns. DeMiguel *et al.* (2007) show that investment strategies following 14 different models derived from modern portfolio theory generate inferior out-of-sample results relative to the use of the $1/n$ strategy. They conclude that the gain from optimal diversification for mean-variance models is more than offset by estimation error.

4 Alternative refers to all assets except bonds and equities.

5 We also compare the results for a balanced sample comprising 381 pension funds that report at least seven years of data. The results are similar to the tables that are presented, suggesting that survivorship bias is not a significant issue.

6 Two thousand and eighty-two (10.2%) of the observations have been deleted: zero or negative number of participants (37 observations), strategic allocation not adding up to 100% (10), observations of pension funds with total investments below € 100,000 which are assumed to be not representative (332), too large fluctuation in values of bonds or equity (73), too large difference between actual and strategic allocation (803) and lacking strategic bond or equity allocation (827).

7 Company funds provide pension plans to the employees of their sponsor company. They are separate legal entities, but are run jointly by the sponsor company and employee representatives. Industry funds provide pension plans for employees working in an industry. Such pension plans are based on a collective labour agreement between an

industry's companies and the labour unions, representing the employees in that industry. Finally, professional group funds offer pension schemes to groups such as general practitioners and public notaries.

8 Here, we disregard other asset categories, which represent relative small shares in total assets. For a number of (smaller) pension funds these shares are even zero; see Table 8.3. Section 8.3.2 investigates this further.

9 This is also clear from the histograms of actual equity and bond ratios, not shown here. These figures show smooth distributions (actual allocations are influenced by market movement and hence not rounded), but with the same wide dispersion.

10 As well as the combination of both 2% and 5%, not shown in Table 8.2. The test is based on the assumption that pension funds round their asset allocation to integers.

11 Note that if the equality of means between (i) small and medium-sized funds and (ii) medium-sized and large funds has been rejected, the rejection of the equality of means between small and large funds follows automatically. An alternative is the binomial probability test. This test gives virtually the same results.

12 These test results may have been influenced by the fact that large pension funds tend to invest more in alternative assets. Though rounding plays an important role for other assets too, investment allocations with percentages below the rounding multiple would reduce the probability of rounding for equity and bond allocations. This would affect the last test, but not the rest of the analysis.

13 Mixed mutual funds are investment funds that combine investments in both debt and equity instruments. Money market instruments are short-term debt investments such as certificates of deposits and commercial paper. Our data do not include information regarding underlying investments in these funds. Note that investment assets do not include liquidity for *e.g.* ongoing payments.

14 The current share of EMU assets in the worldwide total is just below 28% (IMF Global Financial Stability report, April 2009).

15 Nominal defined-benefit pension liabilities are best resembled by nominal government bonds. Instead, defined-benefit pension liabilities that are fully indexed to prices are best resembled by inflation linked bonds. In many Dutch defined-benefit pension deals, indexation is contingent on the funding ratio of the pension fund. The market value of this contingent indexation can be derived using option pricing theory. In this case it might be optimal to have considerable equity exposure; see *e.g.* Broeders (2010).

16 Nevertheless, we also estimate this equation with 2SLS or replace total assets by number of participants.

17 Our dataset for 1999–2006 does not contain the average age of participants, as used in Alestalo and Puttonen (2006) and Gerber and Weber (2007).

18 This is also according to the Dutch regulatory regime, which requires that the probability of a funding ratio falling below 100% within one year must be less than 2.5% (Broeders and Pröpper, 2010) and pension funds must always hold a minimum buffer of 5%. For risky portfolios a higher buffer is required. The Netherlands does not have a pension benefit guarantee fund.

19 We estimate with pooled OLS and correct the standard errors for heteroskedasticity, using the Huber-White sandwich estimators.

20 We estimate also Equation (8.3) including 'home bias'. This variable enters significantly and with the expected sign (more home bias implies higher investments in bonds). The other two measures of (a lack of) sophistication show up with the expected sign when they are significant, that is, for diversification (all variants) and heaping (industry funds). The results are available upon request from the authors, but have not been not reported, since the number of observations for 'home bias' is relatively low.

21 The results are available upon request from the authors. We also estimate Equation (8.3) with two-stage least squares (2SLS) where the instrument for total assets is number of participants (all in logs). The results are virtually identical.

22 Full multicollinearity if we had the same lags in Equation (8.1) and (8.3). Hence, near multicollinearity, as Equation (8.1) does not include lags.

References

ABP, 2017. *Annual Report 2016*, http://jaarverslag.abp.nl/docs/ABP_JV_2016/index. php?nr=16&r_code=ABP_JV_2016 (accessed May 23, 2017).

Agnew, J., P. Balduzzi, A. Sundén, 2003, Portfolio choice and trading in a large 401(*k*) plan, *American Economic Review* 93, 193–215.

A'Hearn, B., J. Baten, D. Crayen, 2009, Quantifying quantitative literacy: age heaping and the history of human capital, *Journal of Economic History* 69, 783–808.

Alestalo, N., V. Puttonen, 2006, Asset allocation in Finnish pension funds, *Journal of Pension Economics and Finance* 5, 27–44.

Alserda, G., J.A. Bikker, S.G. van der Lecq, 2017, *X-efficiency and economies of scale in pension fund administration and investment*, DNB Working Paper No. 547, De Nederlandsche Bank, Amsterdam.

Bachi, R., 1951, The tendency to round off age returns: measurement and correction, *Bulletin of the International Statistical Institute* 33, 195–221.

Banerjee, A.V., 1992, A simple model of herd behavior, *Quarterly Journal of Economics* 107, 797–817.

Benartzi, S., T. Thaler, 2001, Naïve diversification strategies in defined contribution saving plans, *American Economic Review* 91, 79–98.

Bikker, J.A., D.W.G.A. Broeders, J. de Dreu, 2010, Stock market performance and pension fund investment policy: rebalancing, free float, or market timing? *International Journal of Central Banking* 6, 53–79.

Bikker, J.A., J. de Dreu, 2009, Operating costs of pension funds: the impact of scale, governance, and plan design, *Journal of Pension Economics and Finance* 8, 63–89.

Broeders, D.W.G.A., 2010, Valuation of contingent pension liabilities and guarantees under sponsor default risk, *Journal of Risk and Insurance* 77, 911–934.

Broeders, D.W.G.A., Pröpper, M.H., 2010, Risk-based supervision of pension funds in the Netherlands, in: M. Micocci, G.N. Gregoriou, G.B. Masala, (eds.), *Pension Fund Risk Management: Financial and Actuarial Modelling*, Chapman and Hall, Boca Raton.

Budd, J.W., T. Guinnane, 1991, Intentional age misreporting, age heaping and 1908 old age pensions act in Ireland, *Population Studies* 45, 497–518.

Calvet, L.E., J.Y. Campbell, P. Sodini, 2007, Down or out: assessing the welfare costs of household investment mistakes, *Journal of Political Economy* 115, 707–747.

Calvet, L.E., J.Y. Campbell, P. Sodini, 2009a, Fight or flight? Portfolio rebalancing by individual investors, *Quarterly Journal of Economics* 124, 309–348.

Calvet, L.E., J.Y. Campbell, P. Sodini, 2009b, Measuring the financial sophistication of households, *American Economic Review* 99, 393–398.

Campbell, J.Y., 2006, Household finance, *Journal of Finance* 61, 1553–1604.

Canner, N.N., G. Mankiw, D.N. Weil, 1997, An asset allocation puzzle, *American Economic Review* 87, 181–191.

Cohn, R.A., R.C. Lease, W.G. Lewellen, G.G. Schlarbaum, 1975, Individual investor risk aversion and investment portfolio composition, *Journal of Finance* 30, 605–620.

DeLong, J.B., Shleifer, A., Summers, L.H., Waldmann, R.J., 1990. Noise trader risk in financial markets. *Journal of Political Economy* 98, 703–738.

DeMiguel, V., L. Garlappi, R. Uppal, 2007, Optimal versus naive diversification: how inefficient is the 1/N portfolio strategy? *Review of Financial Studies* 22, 1915–1953.

Dhar, R., N. Zhu, 2006, Up close and personal: investor sophistication and the disposition effect, *Management Science* 52, 726–740.

French, K.R., J.M. Poterba, 1991, Investor diversification and international equity markets, *American Economic Review* 81, 222–226.

Gerber, D.S., R. Weber, 2007, Demography and investment behaviour of pension funds: evidence for Switzerland, *Journal of Pension Economics and Finance* 6, 313–337.

Goetzmann, W.N., A. Kumar, 2008, Equity portfolio diversification, *Review of Finance* 12, 433–463.

Grable, J.E., 2000, Financial risk tolerance and additional factors that affect risk taking in everyday money matters, *Journal of Business and Psychology* 14, 625–630.

Griffin, D., A. Tversky, 1992, The weighing of evidence and the determinants of confidence, *Cognitive Psychology* 24, 411–435.

Hirshleifer, D., A. Subrahmanyam, S. Titman, 1994, Security analysis and trading patterns when some investors receive information before others, *Journal of Finance* 49, 1665–1698.

Huberman, G., W. Jiang, 2006, Offering versus choice in 401(k) plans: equity exposure and number of funds, *Journal of Finance* 61, 763–801.

Kang, J.K., R.M. Stulz, 1997, Why is there a home bias? An analysis of foreign portfolio equity ownership in Japan, *Journal of Financial Economics* 46, 3–28.

Karlsson, A., L.L. Norden, 2007, Home sweet home: home bias and international diversification among individual investors, *Journal of Banking and Finance* 31, 317–333.

Lucas, D.J., S.P. Zeldes, 2006, Valuing and hedging defined benefit pensions obligations: the role of stocks revisited, Working Paper, Columbia University.

Lucas, D.J., S.P. Zeldes, 2009, How should public pension plans invest? *American Economic Review: Papers and Proceedings* 99, 527–532.

Markowitz, H., 1952, Portfolio selection, *Journal of Finance* 6, 77–91.

Myers, R.J., 1976, An instance of reverse heaping of ages, *Demography* 13, 577–580.

OECD, 2011, *Pension Markets in Focus*, Issue 8, OECD, Paris.

OECD, 2016, *Pension Markets in Focus 2016*, OECD, Paris, www.oecd.org/finance/private-pensions/globalpensionstatistics.htm (accessed May 16, 2017).

Sharpe, W.F., 1964, Capital asset prices: a theory of market equilibrium under conditions of risk, *Journal of Finance* 19, 425–442.

Shleifer, A., L.H. Summers, 1990, The noise trader approach to finance, *Journal of Economic Perspectives* 4, 19–33.

Tobin, J., 1958, Liquidity preference as behaviour towards risk, *Review of Economic Studies* 25, 65–85.

9 Investment risk-taking by institutional investors[1]

Janko Gorter and Jacob A. Bikker

9.1. Introduction

Investment behaviour of pension funds and insurance firms, particularly their risk-return preferences, is of great importance. While more investment risk typically results in higher expected returns, it also tends to increase their asset-liability mismatch, thereby endangering future pension and insurance benefits. Recent crises in the financial markets have made the potential adverse consequences of institutional investment risk-taking crystal clear. Indeed, the financial positions of defined-benefit (DB) pension funds all over the world have been eroded. Buffers of insurance firms have also been affected, yet less materially so. While it is widely known that in practice DB pension funds tend to run a larger mismatch risk than insurance firms (see, *e.g.* Broeders *et al.*, 2011), empirical research into the root cause of this stylized fact is, to the best of our knowledge, yet absent. We aim to fill part of this void in the literature by comparing investment risk-taking of DB pension funds, life insurers and non-life insurers in the Netherlands.

Theory offers two main hypotheses on investors' risk appetite. According to the risk-management hypothesis, financially constrained investors have an incentive to invest prudently because of bankruptcy costs (Smith and Stulz, 1985) and the potential inability to accept profitable future investment projects (Mayers and Smith, 1987). Sommer (1996) and Cummins and Danzon (1997) present empirical evidence that insurance firms face financial distress costs which limits their risk-taking. Specifically these authors show that insurance is priced as risky debt, and that insurance prices are inversely related to insurer default probabilities. Hence, taking more investment risk comes at a cost of lower insurance policy profit margins. Additional risk-management incentives are provided for by insurance regulation. Indeed, when capital falls below the regulatory minimum, the prudential supervisor, De Nederlandsche Bank (DNB), assumes control over the respective insurer. As a result policyholders are protected against extensive losses and owners and management have an incentive to stay away from the regulatory minimum.

Risk-management incentives are also expected to be relevant for pension funds. Occupational pension funds are principally funded by employers that are likely to have risk-management incentives. In fact, Rauh (2009) concludes for US DB pension plans that risk-management incentives dominate investment behaviour. That being so, in comparison to insurers, we expect the risk-management incentives of pension funds to be more subdued, as pension funds do not face financial distress costs. Pension funds are trusts and when assets fall below liabilities, a fund does not go bankrupt, employees are not laid off and non-marketable assets are not lost.

The other leading hypothesis about investor risk-taking is the *risk-shifting hypothesis*, which states that investors have an incentive to invest in risky securities, especially when in financial distress (Jensen and Meckling, 1976). The incentive for risk shifting originates from an asymmetry of payoffs; stakeholders in institutional investors that benefit from the upside of more investment risk and face limited downside may have an incentive to increase portfolio risk. Because of limited liability, stock owners have such asymmetric payoffs. Accordingly, the *ownership-structure hypothesis* predicts that stock-owned insurers have stronger risk-taking incentives than their mutual peers (Lee *et al.*, 1997). The underlying logic is that stock owners are able to increase the value of their claims by increasing portfolio risk while mutual owners typically are not, as mutual owners are by definition also policyholders. Consequently, in case of mutual insurers, the benefits from risk shifting are low and more diffuse (Esty, 1997).

As the organizational form of pension funds appears more comparable to that of mutual insurers than to that of stock insurers, one may expect that risk-shifting incentives are relatively less important in the pension domain. However, occupational pension funds have company sponsors that could engage in risk-shifting behaviour vis-à-vis their pension plan participants. Risk-shifting incentives may be especially relevant when sponsors are not fully liable for shortfalls in the pension fund, which happens to be the case in the Netherlands. But even when a sponsoring company is fully liable, limited liability restricts the downside risk for its owners. This then creates an incentive for the sponsor to favour a risky investment strategy when financial conditions deteriorate (Sharpe, 1976; Treynor, 1977).

This chapter assesses the relevance of risk-management and risk-shifting incentives for Dutch institutional investors over the 15-year period 1995–2009. Our dataset covers defined-benefit pension funds, life insurers and non-life insurers that collectively manage over € 1 trillion in assets (2009 figure), which is almost twice the Dutch gross domestic product (GDP). The chapter is related to the empirical literature on the investment policies of pension funds (*e.g.* Lucas and Zeldes, 2009; Rauh, 2009; Bikker *et al.*, 2010, Chapter 7) and insurance firms (*e.g.* Cummins and Sommer, 1996; Baranoff and Sager, 2002, 2003). Note that the Dutch setting is particularly suitable to examine investment behaviour, since institutional investors in the Netherlands are, in principle, free to choose their desired risk-return trade-off, and allocate their assets accordingly. In many other countries, on the contrary, investors face quantitative restrictions to limit risk-taking.[2]

A natural and often-used measure for investment risk-taking is the equity allocation, *i.e.* the percentage of equities in the investment portfolio (see, for instance, Lee *et al.*, 1997; Rauh, 2009). Indeed, equity investments expose investors to considerable income and balance sheet volatility. A potentially important drawback of the equity allocation as a risk proxy is that it ignores interest-rate risk. As Dutch investors with a large interest-rate-risk exposure also tend to have a large equity-risk exposure, and vice versa, this drawback does not appear to be

particularly important in the context of this research. We examine equity allocations both across investors and over time. In the cross-sectional analysis we focus
on differences in the level of risk-taking across institutional investors. In the time-
series analysis we examine how trading behaviour responds to past returns, that
is, we examine feedback trading. While there is a sizeable literature on feedback
trading,[3] the microprudential risk implications of such behaviour have typically
been passed over. It can easily be shown, however, that if equity prices follow
a random walk, buying equities when equities are down (*i.e.* negative-feedback
trading, or rebalancing) is risky – where risk is defined as the probability of losing
the entire capital buffer. Under the same definition, positive-feedback trading can
also be risky, that is, in upward markets.

The setup of this chapter is as follows. The next section presents further background to risk-taking behaviour of institutional investors and introduces testable
hypotheses. Section 9.3 explains the used methodologies, describes the dataset
and provides summary statistics and information about developments over time.
Section 9.4 shows empirical results, both for the comparison of risk-taking across
types of institutional investors and for the comparison of investment risk-taking
over time. The last section concludes.

9.2. Hypotheses

9.2.1. Risk-bearing capacity

As mentioned in the introduction, theory provides two competing hypotheses
about the relationship between risk-bearing capacity and risk-taking: the risk-
management hypothesis and the risk-shifting hypothesis. Given that Dutch insurers generally hold capital levels well in excess of the regulatory requirements (De
Haan and Kakes, 2010), and given Rauh's (2009) finding that risk-management
incentives dominate risk-shifting incentives for US DB pension plans, we expect,
on average, a positive relationship between risk-bearing capacity and investment
risk-taking.

H_1:   *Investors with more risk-bearing capacity take more investment risk, and
        vice versa.*

This chapter uses several empirical measures of investors' risk-bearing capacity. The first is the capital ratio, which provides a direct insight into risk-bearing
capacity.[4] With more capital, an institution can shoulder riskier asset portfolios
and/or provide safer returns to its stakeholders (Gatzert and Schmeiser, 2008).
There are, however, costs involved in holding capital (Merton and Perold, 1998).
This means that, in practice, a relatively large capital buffer is likely to be either
paid out or to be used to take on additional risk. Consequently, we expect institutional investors with more capital to take more investment risk, and vice versa.

H_1a: *Institutional investors with more capital take more investment risk, and
        vice versa.*

Another risk factor is size. Larger firms generally have more diversification bene-fits, both on the asset- and the liability-side of their balance sheets. As diversifica-tion reduces an investor's overall risk profile, larger investors are expected to have more risk-bearing capacity. Accordingly, we expect a positive relationship be-tween investment risk-taking and size. Larger firms also benefit from scale econo-mies, in being able to set up a more sophisticated risk-management organization. Paradoxically, more intensive risk management often leads to more risk-taking, as it allows financial institutions to measure their risks more accurately and de-ploy their scarce capital in the supposedly most efficient way. Large firms may also suffer from overconfidence when they put too much trust in (self-developed) theories and models. Hence, we expect larger firms to take more investment risk, though it is not entirely clear whether this is due to greater risk-bearing capacity or due to less risk aversion.

H_1b: Larger institutional investors take more investment risk, and vice versa.

The insurance industry consists of various lines of business with diverging risk profiles. We anticipate that in more volatile lines of business, insurers are less eager to take investment risk. An interesting finding from the *5th Quantitative Impact Study (QIS5) of Solvency II* is that underwriting risk is typically larger for non-life than for life insurers (EIOPA, 2011). Consequently, life insurers can allocate relatively more capital to market risk. In that context, it is important to differentiate between traditional life insurance, where the insurer bears the in-vestment risk, and unit-linked life insurance, where the investment risk is borne by the policyholders. This difference is recognized by Dutch insurance regula-tion, which puts a lower capital charge on unit-linked reserves (De Haan and Kakes, 2010).

Within non-life insurance, five lines of business are distinguished: (i) ac-cident and health, (ii) motor, (iii) marine, transport and aviation, (iv) fire and other property risk and (v) miscellaneous insurance. Some of these lines are more volatile than others. An often-used measure to capture non-life under-writing risk is the standard deviation of the loss ratio (*e.g.* Lamm-Tenant and Starks, 1993; Guo and Winter, 1997). The loss ratio is the ratio of losses in-curred to premiums earned and is an often-used measure for underwriting prof-itability. Table 9.1 shows percentiles of the distribution of this risk measure for Dutch non-life insurers, both on the line-of-business and the firm level (based on our dataset, described in Section 9.3.2). The figures show that motor insur-ance tends to be a relatively stable line of business in the non-life insurance industry.

For insurers, reinsurance and group affiliation are also potential determinants of investment behaviour. Insurers that cede more business to reinsurers have less underwriting risk and can thus allocate more capital to investment risk. If group control is imperfect, *i.e.* there is considerable independence on the part of af-filiated firms, as Bikker and Gorter (2011) suggest, then affiliated firms have an incentive to take more risk.

Table 9.1 Standard deviation of the loss ratio (non-life insurers, 1995–2009)

	N	*Percentiles*		
		P_{75}	P_{50}	P_{25}
Line of business level				
Accident and health	*107*	0.21	0.12	0.07
Motor	*62*	0.16	0.08	0.05
Marine, transport and aviation	*54*	0.49	0.18	0.13
Fire and other property risk	*126*	0.26	0.15	0.09
Miscellaneous insurance	*89*	0.19	0.11	0.06
Firm level	*199*	0.19	0.12	0.07

Note: Standard deviations have been calculated for non-life insurers with eight or more consecutive years of data.

H_1c: *Insurers with more underwriting risk take less investment risk, and vice versa.*

For pension funds, we hypothesize the share of active participants positively influences the degree of risk-taking. There are three main reasons for this. First, Sundaresan and Zapatero (1997) and Lucas and Zeldes (2009) argue that equity investing (our measure of risk-taking) may hedge against increases in pension benefits. Pension benefits of active participants are determined by real wage developments, which are positively correlated with equity returns. Second, the share of active participants largely determines the effectiveness of raising contributions to stave off underfunding of the pension fund. Third, active participants can accommodate investment losses by working more and/or longer (Chapter 7).

H_1d: *Pension funds with more active participants take more investment risk, and vice versa.*

Another pension-fund-specific variable we consider is total pension wealth per plan participant. At the end of the day, pension funds invest for private persons, who, on average, invest more in equities the larger their savings are (Cohn *et al.*, 1975).

H_1e: *Pension funds with wealthier plan participants take more investment risk, and vice versa.*

9.2.2. Pension funds versus insurers

Pension funds are trusts that do not go bankrupt and do not face financial distress costs. When assets fall below liabilities, plan participants cannot walk away, as they are obliged to take part in the pertaining pension scheme. By contrast, insurers are likely to lose policyholders when solvency capital runs low. In fact, empirical evidence shows that insurers do indeed face financial distress costs (Sommer, 1996; Cummins and Danzon, 1997). Another, related reason why pension funds are expected to take more investment risk concerns regulation. When an insurer's capital ratio falls below the regulatory minimum, DNB – the prudential supervisor – assumes control over the insurer. Regulation is different for pension funds. When a pension fund falls below the minimal capital ratio of 5%, it is normally given three years to recover, which may be extended by the Dutch government in exceptional circumstances. Consequently, we expect pension funds to take more investment risk than insurance firms.

H_2: *Pension funds take more investment risk than insurers.*
H_3: *The relationship between capital and investment risk-taking is more pronounced for insurers than for pension funds.*

We anticipate H_2 and H_3 to hold true, despite the relative risk insensitivity of the current insurance solvency requirements. Though underwriting risk is to some extent reflected in the solvency requirements, investment risk is not (De Haan and Kakes, 2010).[5] By contrast, pension funds regulation in the Netherlands has been risk based since 2007, when the Financial Assessment Framework (in Dutch: Financieel Toetsingskader, FTK) became effective (Bikker and Vlaar, 2007). According to this risk-based regulatory framework, pension funds are required to hold a higher risk margin for risky investments such as equities. In principle available capital should be sufficient to maintain a less than 2.5% probability of insolvency over a one-year horizon. For an average pension fund, this implies a target capital ratio of around 30%. Since pension funds do not have to de-risk when buffers run low, we do not expect them to be more risk sensitive in their investment behaviour than insurers.

9.2.3. Stock versus mutual insurers

The stock and mutual organizational form are present in insurance markets around the world (Swiss Re, 1999). This chapter focuses on the risk implications of both types of organizational form. Lamm-Tenant and Starks (1993) investigate this issue for the US insurance market, yet they look at underwriting rather than investment risk. They find that stock insurers bear significantly more underwriting risk than mutual insurers. Lee *et al.* (1997) examine investment risk-taking across stock and mutual insurers. They propose the ownership-structure hypothesis, which predicts that stock-owned firms have stronger risk-taking incentives than mutual insurers. Limited liability enables stock owners to increase the value of their claims by increasing portfolio risk. For mutual owners, risk-shifting incentives are low or non-existent (Esty, 1997). Mutual ownership claims are held by policyholders and are principally inalienable. Stock insurers' ownership claims, on the other hand, are held by specialized residual claimants whose claims are alienable. This alienability facilitates stock owners to offer management pay-for-performance compensation packages, including equity holdings and equity options, therewith encouraging them as well to take asset risk (Mayers and Smith, 1992).

H_4: *Stock insurers generally take more investment risk than mutual insurers.*

9.2.4. Types of pension funds

In the Netherlands, there are three types of pension funds: company pension funds, industry-wide pension funds and professional group pension funds. While company pension funds are most common, industry-wide pension funds govern more assets. Professional group pension funds manage the pension assets of professionals such as doctors and notaries. A key difference between these pension fund types is that in professional group pension funds, the participants are typically self-employed, while in the other funds the participants are employees of the employer. Hence, while there are potentially risk-shifting incentives in company and industry-wide pension funds, such incentives are absent in professional group pension funds. On this basis, we expect less risk-taking by professional group pension funds compared to other types of pension funds.

H_5: *Professional group pension funds take less investment risk than company and industry-wide pension funds.*

9.3. Methodology and data

9.3.1. Methodology

This chapter investigates investment risk-taking from two angles. We start by investigating equity allocations across investors and disregard market developments over time by including year dummies. Subsequently, we turn our focus to market developments and analyze how the various investor types react to these developments over time. Since prudent investors are more likely to survive than aggressive investors, especially during our sample period with turmoil years, one could argue that survivorship bias is likely to drive our results. As our dataset includes institutional investors that have ceased operations, we can compare balanced and unbalanced estimation results to gauge the survivorship bias.

9.3.1.1. Equity allocations across investors

Equity investments typically expose investors to considerable income and balance sheet volatility and have therefore been frequently used to measure risk-taking. Lee *et al.* (1997), Cummins and Nini (2002) and De Haan and Kakes (2010) use this measure for insurers, while Lucas and Zeldes (2009) and Bikker *et al.* in Chapter 7 use this measure in a study of, respectively, US and Dutch pension funds. Unfortunately, the equity allocation does not take interest-rate risk into account, which is an important risk for (life) insurers and pension funds. Ideally we would therefore also use an interest-rate-risk proxy, such as the duration gap or a regulatory capital requirement for interest-rate risk. Unfortunately such proxies are unavailable over the studied time frame. We expect our results are robust, though, as data over 2009 show a positive correlation between interest-rate risk and equity risk, both for insurers and pension funds.[6]

Our empirical specification reads as follows:

$$
\begin{aligned}
W_{i,t} = {} & \alpha_0 + \alpha_1 CR_{i,t\text{-}1} + \alpha_2 \ln SIZE_{i,t\text{-}1} \\
& + D_i^I \left[\begin{array}{l} \alpha_3 + \alpha_4 CR_{i,t\text{-}1} + \alpha_5 \ln SIZE_{i,t\text{-}1} + \alpha_6 STOCK_i \\ + \sum \alpha_{7+q} LOB_{i,q,t} + \alpha_{13} G_{i,t} + \alpha_{14} RR_{i,t\text{-}1} \end{array} \right] \\
& + D_i^{PF} \left[\alpha_{15} SA_{i,t} + \alpha_{16} \ln WP_{i,t\text{-}1} + \alpha_{17} IF_i + \alpha_{18} PG_i \right] \\
& + \sum \alpha_{19+t} YD_t + \varepsilon_{i,t},
\end{aligned}
\tag{9.1}
$$

where $W_{i,t}$ is the equity allocation of investor i in year t, written as a linear function f of coefficient vector α and a set of explanatory variables. Dummy variables D_i^I (1 for insurers) and D_i^{PF} (1 for pension funds) allow for differences in the coefficients between insurers and pension funds. $CR_{i,t-1}$ and $\ln SIZE_{i,t-1}$ stand for, respectively, lagged capital ratio and lagged investor size (measured by total investment portfolio size) in logarithms, and are available for both insurance firms and pension funds. We take lags to avoid simultaneity bias. Nonetheless, even lagged the capital ratio is potentially endogenous. All else equal, more equity in the investment portfolio requires an investor to hold more capital to attain the same level of risk, where risk is the probability of insolvency for insurers and the probability of underfunding for pension funds. We address this potential endogeneity problem in our estimation procedure.

$STOCK_i$ is a dummy variable that takes the value 1 for stock insurers and 0 otherwise, and captures equity-allocation differences between stock and mutual insurers. $LOB_{i,q,t}$ for $q = 0$ to $q = 5$, are insurance line-of-business dummies for six of the seven lines, which take the value 1 if a firm is predominantly active in the respective line.[7] The relatively stable non-life insurance line of business motor insurance acts as the reference group. Dummy variable $G_{i,t}$ (1 for firms affiliated to a group) is included to control for group affiliation. $RR_{i,t-1}$ is the reinsurance ratio lagged, *i.e.* last year's premiums ceded as a percentage of last year's total premiums. This reinsurance proxy is used by, among others, Cummins and Nini (2002) and De Haan and Kakes (2010). $SA_{i,t}$ and $\ln WP_{i,t-1}$ are pension-fund-specific variables, which measure, respectively, the share of active participants and lagged total assets per participant (in logarithms). IF_i and PG_i are dummy variables that are 1 for industry-wide and professional group pension funds, respectively, and 0 otherwise. The reference group is the omitted pension fund type 'company pension funds'. Year dummies YD_t are included to account for equity-market developments over the sample period. Finally, the error term is represented by $\varepsilon_{i,t}$.

9.3.1.2. Equity allocations over time

The second part of our analysis, on equity allocations over time, touches upon the issue of feedback trading. There is a sizeable empirical literature on feedback trading by institutional investors. This literature distinguishes between positive and negative-feedback trading. Positive-feedback traders buy equities when their prices rise, and sell equities when their prices fall. Negative-feedback traders do exactly the opposite: they sell equities when equities are up, and buy equities when they are down. While available studies find that past equity returns significantly influence today's trading behaviour, evidence on the sign of such feedback trading is mixed. Grinblatt *et al.* (1995) find evidence of positive-feedback trading for US institutional investors, yet Lakonishok *et al.* (1992) and Gompers and Metrick (2001) do not observe significant positive-feedback trading. The question then rises, why some institutional investors engage in positive-feedback trading and others do not. We argue that risk-bearing capacity probably plays an important role.

Existing studies on Dutch pension funds and insurance firms report negative-feedback trading (Kakes, 2008; Bikker *et al.*, 2010; De Haan and Kakes, 2011). Negative-feedback trading, or rebalancing, is often motivated by mean reversion in equity prices. Under mean reversion, an institution can achieve higher returns by buying equities when markets are down and selling equities when markets are up. However, since the equity cycle can be long and volatile (Balvers *et al.*, 2000; Spierdijk *et al.*, 2012) and the degree of mean reversion is likely to be small and uncertain (Pástor and Stambaugh, 2012), rebalancing can be a particularly risky trading strategy. When equity prices fall, risk-bearing capacity of equity investors also falls. Buying equities when risk-bearing capacity is down is risky business and only possible for unconstrained or loosely constrained investors. Constrained investors, on the other hand, can be forced to liquidate their equity holdings just when the majority of investors are trying to shed risk, a phenomenon known as fire sales (Shleifer and Vishny, 1992). The reverse happens in upturns. Rising equity markets increase investors' willingness and ability to take risk (Black, 1988).

To investigate the relationship between equity trading and equity price changes, we decompose the equity allocation of investor i in year t, $W_{i,t}$, into three factors:

$$W_{i,t} = \frac{E_{i,t}^{REV}}{\mathrm{TI}_{i,t}} + \frac{E_{i,t}^{NCF}}{\mathrm{TI}_{i,t}} + W_{i,t-1}\frac{\mathrm{TI}_{i,t-1}}{\mathrm{TI}_{i,t}}, \tag{9.2}$$

where $E_{i,t}^{REV}$ is the euro amount of equity gains or losses. $E_{i,t}^{NCF}$ is the euro amount of net purchases or sales and $\mathrm{TI}_{i,t-1}/\mathrm{TI}_{i,t}$ is the inverse of portfolio growth. When non-equity assets grow and the value of equity holdings remains constant, the equity allocation drops as a result of positive portfolio growth.

Equation (9.2) is an identity where the three factors on the right-hand side of the equation all have a one-to-one effect on the equity allocation. What we are interested in, however, is whether price changes and equity trading are generally reinforcing (evidence of positive-feedback trading) or counterbalancing (evidence of negative-feedback trading). To investigate this, we introduce the following empirical model:

$$W_{i,t} - W_{i,t-1} \frac{TI_{i,t-1}}{TI_{i,t}} = \frac{\Delta E_{i,t}}{TI_{i,t}} = \beta_0 + \beta_1 \frac{E_{i,t}^{REV}}{TI_{i,t}} + \upsilon_{i,t}, \tag{9.3}$$

with $\Delta E_{i,t}$ representing equity portfolio growth (in euros) of investor i in year t. Comparing Equations (9.2) and (9.3), notice we have dropped trading factor $E_{i,t}^{NCF} / TI_{i,t}$, yet added parameters β_0 and β_1, and disturbance term $\upsilon_{i,t}$. Estimating Equation (9.3) by OLS gives for parameter β_1 an estimate

$$b_1 = \frac{\hat{Cov}(E_{i,t}^{REV}/TI_{i,t}, \Delta E_{i,t}/TI_{i,t})}{\hat{Var}(E_{i,t}^{REV}/TI_{i,t})} = 1 + \frac{\hat{Cov}(E_{i,t}^{REV}/TI_{i,t}, E_{i,t}^{NCF}/TI_{i,t})}{\hat{Var}(E_{i,t}^{REV}/TI_{i,t})},$$

where we have used the identity $\Delta E_{i,t} = E_{i,t}^{REV} + E_{i,t}^{NCF}$. Hence, when $b_1 > 1$ ($b_1 < 1$), the sample correlation between equity returns and equity net purchases is positive (negative), suggesting positive (negative) feedback trading. Note that feedback trading implies exogenous equity returns, which seems likely as equity returns are mainly determined by the market rather than by individual investors.

In order to allow for asymmetric feedback trading, that is different trading behaviour in bear and bull markets, we generalize Equation (9.3) to

$$\frac{\Delta E_{i,t}}{TI_{i,t}} = \beta_0 + D_{i,t}^{POS} \beta_1^{POS} \frac{E_{i,t}^{REV}}{TI_{i,t}} + D_{i,t}^{NEG} \beta_1^{NEG} \frac{E_{i,t}^{REV}}{TI_{i,t}} + \upsilon_{i,t}, \tag{9.4}$$

where $D_{i,t}^{POS}$ and $D_{i,t}^{NEG}$ are investor-specific dummy variables that take the value 1 if equity returns in year t are positive and negative, respectively, and 0 otherwise.

9.3.2. Data

This chapter draws on a comprehensive regulatory dataset from DNB. The data have an annual frequency and cover all regulated pension funds and insurance firms (life and non-life) in the Netherlands over the 1995–2009 period.[8] Note that for life insurers, we only include investments for their own account, so that unit-linked investments are excluded from the equity allocations used in estimations of Equation (9.1). After sanitization, the dataset contains 12,799 institution-year observations.[9] For pension funds, transaction and revaluation data are only available from 2000 and onwards. In our analysis, the focus is on individual entities regulated by the Dutch supervisory authorities, because, in contrast to banking supervision, insurance supervision is non-consolidated.

Table 9.2 summarizes the data. While life insurers are larger, on average, than pension funds, in terms of balance sheet size, the latter invest relatively more in equities. On average, pension funds invest even more in equities than their surplus or buffer. This is generally not the case for life insurers and certainly not for

Table 9.2 Full sample summary statistics, monetary values in 2009 prices (1995–2009)

	Pension funds		Life insurers		Non-life insurers	
	mean	median	mean	median	mean	median
Equity holdings (in € millions)	372	15	365	12	28	1
Total investments (in € millions)	956	60	2204	286	145	15
Equity allocation (%)	28	28	14	8	16	9
Capital ratio (%)	10	12	15	9	47	47
Investments per participant (x 1,000 €)	119	54				
Number of participants (x 1,000)	26	1				
Share of active participants (%)	42	42				
Type of pension funds						
Company	0.85	1				
Industry	0.14	0				
Professional group	0.01	0				
Reinsurance ratio (%)			6	1	24	15
Organization form (1=mutual insurer)			0.11	0	0.45	0
Group (1=group affiliation)			0.73	1	0.65	1
Line-of-business dummies						
Traditional life			0.76	1		
Unit-linked			0.24	0		
Accident and health					0.29	0
Motor					0.08	0
Fire and other property risk					0.34	0
Marine, transport and aviation					0.05	0
Miscellaneous insurance					0.08	0
Institution-year observations	8,234		1,218		3,347	

non-life insurers. Non-life insurers have relatively large capital buffers, which apparently are not used to take on additional investment risk. As mentioned in the previous section, underwriting risk is their dominant risk category. The average wealth per defined-benefit pension plan participant is about € 120,000, which is more than twice the median value. Boards of directors tend to have their own pension schemes and such schemes tilt up considerably the average pension fund wealth. Notice that non-life insurers are relatively small investors compared to life insurers and pension funds. This is a direct result of the short-term nature of non-life insurance policies. The organizational form dummy shows that mutual insurers are most prevalent in the non-life industry. The number of non-life insurers is almost three times that of life insurers, while about 45% of the non-life insurers is mutual-owned.

9.4. Empirical results

9.4.1. Equity allocations across investors

Because of the potential endogeneity of capital, we estimate Equation (9.1) using the two-stage-least-squares estimator (2SLS). The idea of 2SLS is to use a proxy for the (potentially) endogenous variable – here capital – that is uncorrelated with the disturbance term in the regression equation. This proxy is generated in the first stage of the 2SLS procedure, using instrumental variables. To obtain reliable results, the instrumental variables need to be both relevant (*i.e.* sufficiently correlated with the endogenous variable) and valid (*i.e.* uncorrelated with the disturbance term in the original equation). As instruments we use two lags of portfolio size, two lags of an insurance firms' profitability measure (*i.e.* profits after tax divided by total assets) and three lags of a pension funds' liability measure (*i.e.* the difference between contributions and payouts divided by total assets). Table 9.3 gives the 2SLS estimation results, where the last three rows indicate the instruments used are both relevant and valid.

Column I of Table 9.3 shows full sample results, while Column II presents outcomes for the shorter sample period 1995–2005. The shorter sample period is more stable in terms of regulatory and accounting regimes. In 2006 the former national health insurance funds were privatized (Bikker, 2017) and in 2007 risk-based regulation of pension funds was introduced. Column III provides balanced-panel results for the 1995–2005 period. Differences between the balanced and unbalanced panel results may give an indication of the magnitude of survivorship bias. Of course, the varying set of observations may also have an effect on the parameter estimates.

Surprisingly, the capital ratio is insignificant for pension funds (α_1). This suggests that for pension funds as a group, neither risk-shifting nor risk-management incentives seem to dominate. This finding contrasts with research on US pension plans, where risk-management incentives have been found to dominate investment behaviour (Rauh, 2009). What could explain this difference? An important dissimilarity between the US and the Netherlands concerns the position of the sponsor in relation to the pension plan. While in the US, the sponsoring company fully bears the investment risk of its DB pension plan (until bankruptcy, of course), in the Netherlands the investment risk is typically shared between the plan sponsor and the plan participants (Ponds and Van Riel, 2009). Because of this difference in risk bearing, Dutch sponsors may well be relatively less worried about the risk of pension shortfalls, which could (partly) explain the insignificance of the capital ratio.

By contrast, for insurers the capital ratio is highly significant ($\alpha_1 + \alpha_4 > 0$), where the positive sign indicates risk-management incentives dominate. A positive relationship between capital and asset risk is also reported by Cummins and Sommer (1996) and Baranoff and Sager (2002) for property-liability and life insurers in the US, respectively. So, while we reject that investors with larger capital buffers take more equity risks in general (H_1a), we find support for H_3 as the results show that insurers choose their asset allocations in a more risk-sensitive manner than pension funds.

Table 9.3 2SLS estimation results of the equity-allocation model

	Coefficient	1995–2009 unbalanced	1995–2005 unbalanced	1995–2005 balanced
		I	II	III
Constant	α_0	**28.72	**31.28	**32.78
Capital ratio (lagged)	α_1	4.41	−0.77	−13.46
Portfolio size (logarithm, lagged)	α_2	**2.47	**2.93	**2.60
D^I	α_3	**−13.69	**−13.55	**−11.43
D^I•Capital ratio (lagged)	α_4	**46.06	**48.73	**54.96
D^I•Portfolio size (logarithm, lagged)	α_5	**−1.44	**−1.60	**−1.87
D^I•STOCK	α_6	**5.20	**5.37	**5.43
D^I•LOB$_{health}$	α_7	**−4.22	*−3.78	−3.10
D^I•LOB$_{transport}$	α_8	**−9.70	**−7.05	−0.23
D^I•LOB$_{fire}$	α_9	**−9.57	**−8.72	**−7.53
D^I•LOB$_{miscellaneous}$	α_{10}	**−7.02	**−7.20	**−7.23
D^I•LOB$_{traditional\ life}$	α_{11}	1.12	0.32	−0.28
D^I•LOB$_{unit\text{-}linked\ life}$	α_{12}	**11.62	*10.03	*7.10
D^I•Group affiliation	α_{13}	0.11	0.09	−1.44
D^I•Reinsurance ratio (lagged)	α_{14}	0.33	*0.51	0.72
D^{PF}•Share active participants	α_{15}	**3.63	2.53	0.59
D^{PF}•Assets per participant (logarithm, lagged)	α_{16}	**1.48	**1.55	**2.03
D^{PF}•Industry fund	α_{17}	0.82	1.09	2.33
D^{PF}•Professional group fund	α_{18}	**−6.31	**−9.12	**−10.63
Number of observations		7,811	5,550	3,400
R^2, adjusted		22	25	31
First-stage F-test for Capital ratio (lagged)		38.43	19.80	15.89
First-stage F-test for D^I•Capital ratio (lagged)		56.68	49.40	25.03
Hansen test (p-value)		0.06	0.60	0.68

Notes: * and ** denote significance at, respectively, the 5% and 1% level, calculated using Huber-White robust standard errors. The dependent in these regressions is the equity allocation in percentages. The capital ratio variables have been instrumented, using two lags of portfolio size, two lags of insurance firms' profitability and three lags of a pension fund liability measure. The first-stage F-tests test the joint significance of these instruments for the two capital ratio variables. The Hansen test tests the joint null that the chosen instruments are valid. D^I is a dummy, which is 1 for insurers and 0 for pension funds. *LOB.* are the different lines of business dummies, which take the value 1 for insurers that are predominantly active in the respective line, and 0 otherwise. Organizational form dummy *STOCK* is 1 for stock insurers and 0 otherwise. D^{PF} is a dummy, which is 1 for pension funds and 0 for insurers. Year dummy estimates are not shown. The year dummies are jointly significant (test results available on request). For expositional purposes, all non-dummy variables are in deviation from their sample means.

Portfolio size is found to have a significant and positive effect on the investment risk-taking of pension funds: when total investments increase by 1%, the equity allocation rises with 2 to 3 basis points (α_2). This result is in line with earlier estimates for pension funds (Bikker *et al.*, 2010, Chapter 7). For insurers, the relationship between portfolio size and risk-taking is weaker (α_5 is significantly negative). Nonetheless, the results are overall in line with hypothesis H_1b. An explanation for the weaker relationship for insurers is that there is less room for overconfidence in the insurance industry, as the financial constraints are binding. In line with H_2 we find that pension funds take significantly more investment risk than insurers, even after correcting for capital and size. The (weighted) sum of the insurer dummy coefficient (α_3) and the interaction coefficients α_6-α_{13} are significantly negative,[10] which means that insurers have significantly lower equity allocations than pension funds.

We now turn to the hypothesis about underwriting risk and investment risk-taking by insurers (H_1c). The estimates of α_1-α_{10} show that health, transport, fire and miscellaneous insurers tend to take significantly less investment risk than motor insurers (reference group). Since motor insurers typically have more stable underwriting results (see Table 9.1), this finding supports H_1c. Equity investments of unit-linked life insurers (to be sure: on their own account) are significantly larger than those of motor insurers (α_{12}). Apparently, where unit-linked investment does not imply risk for insurers, they 'compensate' that by investing more in equities on their own account (supporting H_1c). Note that the sign of the reinsurance ratio coefficient (α_{14}) also supports H_1c, yet this result is only significant for the shorter period unbalanced sample (Column II).

Hypotheses H_1d and H_1e concern pension funds. The estimates of α_{15} indicate that the share of active participants has a significantly positive effect for the 1995–2009 sample, but not for the 1995–2005 samples. One argument is that active participants largely determine the effectiveness of raising premiums to stave off underfunding. A second reason is that the life-cycle theory states that active (and younger) participants can take more risk – and, hence, should invest more in equities – than retired ones (Chapter 7). Once more, risk-bearing capacity is the main explanation: active participants can compensate negative returns on investment by extending working hours or delaying retirement. Higher wealth per participant implies a significantly higher equity ratio (α_{16}), in line with H_1e.

Our last two hypotheses are about differences in risk-taking between types of insurers and pension funds. The results in Table 9.3 show that stock insurers indeed take significantly more investment risk than mutual insurers (α_5). Corrected for the relevant risk factors, stock insurers have an average equity allocation that is more than 5 percentage points higher than that of mutual insurers, confirming H_4. Hypothesis H_5 states that professional group funds take less investment risk than company funds and industry-wide funds, and this is supported by the significant estimates of α_{18}.

9.4.2. *Equity allocations over time*

Table 9.4 provides OLS and Weighted Least Squares (WLS) estimation results of Equations (9.3) and (9.4). The WLS estimations weight the changes in equity ratios with real equity holdings, thereby providing insight into possible behavioural differences between small and large equity investors. The first four columns present the results for pension funds, while the last four columns present the results for insurers.

Table 9.4 Estimation results of equity-trading model (2000–2009)

Column	Pension funds				Insurers			
	OLS		WLS		OLS		WLS	
	I	*II*	*III*	*IV*	*V*	*VI*	*VII*	*VIII*
Equity returns	**0.58	–	*0.75	–	**0.81	–	0.97	–
	(0.04)	–	(0.11)	–	(0.07)	–	(0.06)	–
Positive returns	–	**0.55	–	0.71	–	**0.54	–	0.96
	–	(0.11)	–	(0.15)	–	(0.16)	–	(0.09)
Negative returns	–	**0.60	–	0.76	–	0.95	–	0.98
	–	(0.05)	–	(0.21)	–	(0.07)	–	(0.12)
R^2, adjusted (in %)	33	33	57	57	20	20	36	36
No. of observations	4,451	4,451	4,451	4,451	2,151	2,151	2,151	2,151

Notes: * and ** denote significantly different from 1 at, respectively, the 5% and 1% level, calculated using Huber-White robust standard errors. The dependent variable in these regressions is the change in total equity holdings divided by year-end total investments. Only investors holding equities in their portfolio, either at the beginning or the end of the book year, are included in these regression analyses. The WLS estimation uses real equity holdings (in 2009 prices) as weighting factor.

Several findings stand out. First, Column *I* and *II* show that pension funds rebalance, on average, 40% of market price movements (in line with Bikker *et al.*, 2010) and that rebalancing is more or less symmetric in terms of positive versus negative returns. The coefficients 0.55 and 0.60 in Column *II* represent free-floating behaviour of around 60%, which is the complement of rebalancing. Second, insurers tend to rebalance about 50% of market price movements in bull markets, yet let their equity allocation fall in bear markets (Column *VI*). Since negative-feedback trading (or rebalancing) increases an investor's risk profile compared to a free-float strategy, these trading results provide further support to hypotheses H_2 (insurers take less investment risk) and H_3 (insurers are more risk sensitive in their investment behaviour). Apparently, insurers moderate their risk-taking when returns are negative and their risk-bearing capacity is down, which is trading behaviour along the lines of an investment strategy known as contingent immunization (Leibowitz and Weinberger, 1982). Contingent immunization is a kind of portfolio insurance strategy that aims to benefit from the upside of a risky investment position, yet limit the corresponding downside. Third, the WLS results in Columns *III* and *IV* indicate that large pension funds generally rebalance less than their smaller peers. This finding over 2000–2009 contrasts with what has been found in earlier research on the investment behaviour of Dutch pension funds by Bikker *et al.* (2010) over the 1999–2006 period. We can replicate the results of this earlier study by taking approximately the same sample period (*i.e.* 2000–2006). A possible explanation for the different behaviour over our sample period is that large pension funds were unable to rebalance their sizcable equity losses of 2008 to the extent that they had done that before. Our new finding is interesting from a macro perspective, since pension funds are typically perceived as providers of risk-bearing capital when it is most needed, yet did not perform this role at the height of the global financial crisis. Notice that the adjusted R^2 statistics of the WLS regressions are much larger than those of the OLS regressions, indicating that market returns are a better predictor of equity portfolio changes of large funds than those of small funds. The fourth and final finding from Table 9.4 is that large insurers pursue a completely free-float investment strategy, whether markets are up or down, where smaller insurers rebalance under favourable market conditions. Columns *VII* and *VIII* show that the estimated slope coefficients are not significantly different from 1, indicating that, on average, equity price movements feed roughly one-to-one into the equity allocation.

9.5. Conclusion

According to theory, institutional investors face both risk-management and risk-shifting incentives. When risk-management incentives are leading, lower risk-bearing capacity is accompanied by less investment risk-taking. Conversely, if risk-shifting incentives are more prominent, worse financial conditions lead to more investment risk-taking. This chapter assesses the relevance of these conflicting incentives for Dutch pension funds and insurance firms over the period 1995–2009. Two measures of investment risk-taking are used. The first measure is the allocation of equities in the total investment portfolio, which is intuitive and widely used. Our second measure concerns equity feedback trading. While there is a sizeable literature on feedback trading, the microprudential risk implications of such behaviour have typically been passed over. Buying equities when equities are down (*i.e.* negative-feedback trading) is a risky strategy, however, since the exposure to equities is raised when risk-bearing capacity is down. In upward markets, positive-feedback trading is relatively risky, that is compared to negative-feedback trading or no feedback trading.

Using annual investments data, we find risk-management incentives seem to dominate risk-shifting incentives in the Dutch insurance industry. Insurance firms with more risk-bearing capacity invest a larger share of their portfolio in equities, and vice versa. This result agrees with prior studies on US life and property-liability insurers. For Dutch pension funds, on the other hand, we do not find a significant relationship between the funding ratio and the asset allocation. Hence, neither risk-shifting nor risk-management incentives seem dominant. Also over time, pension funds are more risk tolerant. Pension funds rebalance, on average, about 40% of market price movements, in both bull and bear markets. Insurance firms also rebalance in bull markets but generally do not buy equities in bear markets to restore their equity allocation. This finding confirms that, in bear markets when risk-bearing capacity of insurers has been eroded, they are more risk averse. Insurance firms face direct and indirect costs of financial distress, while pension funds do not face bankruptcy risk under detrimental market conditions. Even so, unfavourable investment results do hit pension fund participants, just as they benefit from favourable outcomes. It is the responsibility of pension funds to adequately inform their participants about the consequences of investment risk-taking on the safety of pension benefits.

Though risk-management incentives appear dominant among Dutch insurance firms, we also find evidence of risk-shifting behaviour. In line with the ownership-structure hypothesis by Lee *et al.* (1997), stock insurers have more risky investments than their mutual peers. Interestingly, we find that professional group pension funds take significantly less investment risk than other types of pension funds. This result is in line with expectations, as the participants in professional group pension funds are typically self-employed, which excludes the possibility of risk shifting by the employer.

Notes

1 Update of: J.K. Gorter and J.A. Bikker, 2013, Investment risk-taking of institutional investors, *Applied Economics* 45, 4629–4640.
2 In a study of the regulation of institutional investors in the major OECD countries, Davis (2002) reports that only the United Kingdom and the Netherlands do not impose quantitative restrictions on equity holdings for life insurers.
3 See Badrinath and Wahal (2002) for a literature overview.
4 In this chapter, the capital ratio is an important proxy of an investor's risk-bearing capacity. The capital ratio is defined as net asset value (*i.e.* assets minus liabilities) to total assets. While common in banking, the capital ratio is not the typical solvency indicator in the insurance and pensions industry. In the insurance industry, solvency conditions are usually presented in terms of the solvency ratio. The solvency ratio equals the actual solvency margin divided by the required solvency margin. In the context of pension funds, solvency conditions are typically presented in terms of the funding ratio, which is the ratio of total assets to total liabilities. For ease of comparison, however, we use capital ratios for both insurers and pension funds.
5 This has changed in 2016 when in the European Union a new, risk-based regulatory approach for insurance companies, called Solvency II, came into effect.
6 For life insurers, we use data from the Solvency II QIS5 study to establish a sample correlation of 0.5 between interest-rate risk and equity risk, where both risks are approximated by the respective solvency capital requirements scaled by total investments. For pension funds, we use comparable data, but then from the Dutch financial assessment framework data, to establish a sample correlation of 0.4 between interest-rate risk and equity risk.
7 Note that non-life insurers are not permitted to write life insurance policies, and, vice versa, life insurers are not permitted to write non-life insurance policies. That being so, insurance holding companies are allowed to have both life and non-life subsidiaries. A non-life insurer is predominantly active in a specific non-life insurance line of business when more than 50% of its premium income comes from this line. When a specific non-life insurer has multiple lines of business and is not predominantly active in any line of business, the line-of-business dummies are all 0 for this insurer. For life insurers, our dataset discerns two lines of business: traditional life insurance and unit-linked life insurance. Given the long-term nature of life insurance, we distinguish between both types of life insurers by reserves rather than by premium income. A life insurer is predominantly active in traditional life when more than 50% of its reserves are traditional life reserves.
8 The dataset does not include funeral insurers and tiny mutual non-life insurers exempted from supervision.
9 The raw dataset contains 18,416 institution-year observations. We have excluded defined-contribution (DC) pension funds (573 observations), as they would confound our analysis. In DC funds, the investment risk is typically borne by the pension-fund participants and not by the pension fund itself. We have also excluded observations that have zero or negative total assets, negative equity allocation, equity allocation > 100%, capital ratio > 1 or capital ratio < -0.3. Note that our data source does not distinct between zeroes and missing values.
10 The average equity-allocation difference between pension funds and insurance firms is picked up by the insurance dummy. Since the insurance dummy is interacted with other dummy variables (*i.e.* STOCK, LOB and G), the equity-allocation difference between insurers and pension funds is a weighted sum of the estimated coefficients of α_3 and

coefficients α_6-α_{13}. Note that coefficients α_4, α_5 and α_{14} do not play a role in this respect, since the corresponding variables are in deviation from their respective sample means.

References

Badrinath, S.G., S. Wahal, 2002, Momentum trading by institutions, *Journal of Finance* 57, 2449–2478.

Balvers, R., Y. Wu, E. Gilliland, 2000, Mean reversion across national stock markets and parametric contrarian investment strategies, *Journal of Finance* 55, 745–772.

Baranoff, E.G., T.W. Sager, 2002, The relations among asset risk, product risk, and capital in the life insurance industry, *Journal of Banking and Finance* 26, 1181–1197.

Baranoff, E.G., T.W. Sager, 2003, The relations among organizational and distributional forms and capital and asset risk structures in the life insurance industry, *Journal of Risk and Insurance* 70, 375–400.

Bikker, J.A., 2017, Competition and scale economy effects of the Dutch 2006 health care insurance reform, *Geneva Papers on Risk and Insurance – Issues and Practice* 42, 53–78.

Bikker, J.A., D.W.G.A. Broeders, J. de Dreu, 2010, Stock market performance and pension fund investment policy: rebalancing, free float, or market timing? *International Journal of Central Banking* 6, 53–79.

Bikker, J.A., J. Gorter, 2011, Restructuring of the Dutch non-life insurance industry: consolidation, organizational form and focus, *Journal of Risk and Insurance* 78, 163–184.

Bikker, J.A., P.J.G. Vlaar, 2007, Conditional indexation of defined benefit pension plans, *Geneva Papers on Risk and Insurance – Issues and Practice* 32, 494–515.

Black, F., 1988, An equilibrium model of the crash, NBER Chapters, *NBER Macroeconomics Annual* 3, 269–276.

Broeders, D.W.G.A., A. Chen, B. Koos, 2011, An institutional evaluation of pension funds and life insurance companies, *Insurance: Mathematics and Economics* 49, 1–10.

Cohn, R.A., W.G. Lewellen, R.C. Lease, G.G. Schlarbaum, 1975, Individual investor risk aversion and investment portfolio composition, *Journal of Finance* 30, 605–620.

Cummins, J.D., P.M. Danzon, 1997, Price, financial quality and capital flows in insurance markets, *Journal of Financial Intermediation* 6, 3–38.

Cummins, J.D., G.P. Nini, 2002, Optimal capital utilization by financial firms: evidence from the property-liability insurance industry, *Journal of Financial Services Research* 21, 15–53.

Cummins, J.D., D.W. Sommer, 1996, Capital and risk in property-liability insurance markets, *Journal of Banking and Finance* 20, 1069–1092.

Davis, E.P., 2002, Prudent person rules or quantitative restrictions? The regulation of long term institutional investors' portfolios, *Journal of Pensions Economics and Finance* 1, 157–191.

De Haan, L., J. Kakes, 2010, Are non-risk based capital requirements for insurance companies binding? *Journal of Banking and Finance* 34, 1618–1627.

De Haan, L., J. Kakes, 2011, Momentum or contrarian investment strategies: evidence from Dutch institutional investors, *Journal of Banking and Finance* 35, 2245–2251.

Esty, B.C., 1997, Organizational form and risk taking in the savings and loan industry, *Journal of Financial Economics* 44, 25–55.

European Insurance and Occupational Pensions Authority (EIOPA), 2011, *EIOPA Report on the Fifth Quantitative Impact Study (QIS5) for Solvency II*, https://eiopa.europa.eu/fileadmin/tx_dam/files/publications/reports/QIS5_Report_Final.pdf (accessed May 18, 2017).

Gatzert, N., H. Schmeiser, 2008, Combining fair pricing and capital requirements for non-life insurance companies, *Journal of Banking and Finance* 32, 2589–2596.

Gompers, P. A., A. Metrick, 2001, Institutional investors and equity prices, *Quarterly Journal of Economics* 116, 229–259.

Grinblatt, M., S. Titman, R. Wermers, 1995, Momentum investment strategies, portfolio performance, and herding: a study of mutual fund behavior, *American Economic Review* 85, 1088–1105.

Guo, D., R. A. Winter, 1997, The capital structure of insurers: theory and evidence, *Working Paper*, Sauder School of Business.

Jensen, M. C., W. H. Meckling, 1976, Theory of the firm: managerial behavior, agency costs and ownership structure, *Journal of Financial Economics* 3, 305–360.

Kakes, J., 2008, Pensions in a perfect storm: financial behaviour of Dutch pension funds (2002–2005), *Applied Financial Economics Letters* 4, 29–33.

Lakonishok, J., A. Schleifer, R. W. Vishny, 1992, The impact of institutional trading on stock-prices, *Journal of Financial Economics* 32, 23–43.

Lamm-Tenant, J., L. T. Starks, 1993, Stock versus mutual ownership structures: the risk implications, *Journal of Business* 66, 29–46.

Lee, S. J., D. Mayers, C. W. Smith Jr., 1997, Guarantee funds and risk taking: evidence from the insurance industry, *Journal of Financial Economics* 44, 3–24.

Leibowitz, M., A. Weinberger, 1982, Contingent immunization: part 1: risk control procedures, *Financial Analysts Journal* 38, 17–31.

Lucas, D. J., S. P. Zeldes, 2009, How should public pension plans invest? *American Economic Review: Papers and Proceedings* 99, 527–532.

Mayers, D., C. W. Smith Jr., 1987, Corporate insurance and the underinvestment problem, *Journal of Risk and Insurance* 54, 45–54.

Mayers, D., C. W. Smith Jr., 1992, Executive compensation in the life insurance industry, *Journal of Business* 65, 51–74.

Merton, R. C., A. F. Perold, 1998, Theory of risk capital in financial firms, in: J. M. Stern, D. H. Chew, Jr. (eds.), *The Revolution in Corporate Finance*, Blackwell Business, Malden, MA, 266–282.

Pástor, L., R. F. Stambaugh, 2012, Are stocks really less volatile in the long run? *Journal of Finance* 67, 431–478.

Ponds, E.H.M., B. Van Riel, 2009, Sharing risk: the Netherlands' new approach to pensions, *Journal of Pension Economics and Finance* 8, 91–105.

Rauh, J., 2009, Risk shifting versus risk management: investment policy in corporate pension plans, *Review of Financial Studies* 22, 2687–2733.

Sharpe, W. F., 1976, Corporate pension funding policy, *Journal of Financial Economics* 3, 183–193.

Shleifer, A., R. Vishny, 1992, Liquidation values and debt capacity: a market equilibrium approach, *Journal of Finance* 47, 1343–1366.

Smith, C., R. Stulz, 1985, The determinants of firms' hedging policies, *Journal of Financial and Quantitative Analysis* 20, 391–405.

Sommer, D. W., 1996, The impact of firm risk on property-liability insurance prices, *Journal of Risk and Insurance* 63, 501–514.

Spierdijk, L., J. A. Bikker, P. Van der Hoek, 2012, Mean reversion in international stock markets: an empirical analysis of the 20th century, *Journal of International Money and Finance* 31, 228–249.

Sundaresan, S., F. Zapatero, 1997, Valuation, optimal asset allocation and retirement incentives of pension plans, *Review of Financial Studies* 10, 631–660.

Swiss Re, 1999, Are mutual insurers an endangered species? *Sigma*, 4.

Treynor, J., 1977, The principles of corporate pension finance, *Journal of Finance* 32, 627–638.

Part III
Risk-taking and regulation

10 Measuring and explaining implicit risk sharing in defined-benefit pension funds[1]

Jacob A. Bikker, Thijs Knaap and Ward E. Romp

10.1. Introduction

Ageing and the corresponding rising old-age dependency ratios render pay-as-you-go pension systems unsustainable. More and more countries are moving to funded systems in which participants save via pension funds for their retirement (EU, 2011). Depending on the type of pension arrangement, pension funds face uncertainties with respect to their assets and liabilities, stemming from the rate of return on their assets, the mortality rate of their participants, the inflation rate, wage growth and the discount rate. The surplus of assets over liabilities forms the buffer of the pension fund. If this buffer is too little, pension fund boards can use different instruments to restore the buffer. The board can add a surcharge to the pension premium, suspend indexation to wage or price inflation, adjust the asset mix to limit further downside risks, or ask the associated company, if any, for extra financial support. A more radical measure is to cut accrued benefits, which is legally limited to emergency conditions. When a pension fund's buffer becomes luscious, the fund can provide indexation, raise benefits or lower pension premiums, or the sponsor may receive part of the excess return as a reverse financial support.

Despite the growing popularity of funded pension systems, relatively little is known about the use pension funds make of these risk-sharing instruments. The key question in this chapter is whether the fund uses its reserves to absorb solvency shocks or lets the participants absorb the shock. A second research question is whether a systematic relationship exists between known properties of the pension fund (such as its age structure, its size, and the presence of an external sponsor) and the way it handles solvency problems.

To assess how the solvency governance of a pension fund is conducted in practice, we use a unique dataset made available by the Dutch central bank (DNB) which supervises pension funds in the Netherlands. Every pension fund has to submit yearly and quarterly reports to DNB, in which it outlines its financial position. The more detailed yearly reports constitute our dataset, together with balance sheets of all registered pension funds in the Netherlands for the 1993 to 2007 period, 15 years in total. They do not, however, specify the actual use of such risk-sharing instruments as are listed above. We can only recover part of this risk-sharing behaviour for the period 1993 to 2005, but not for 2006 and 2007, due to a change in solvency regulation in 2006, the replacement of the fixed-discount rate by the market rate. Until 2006 the fixed-discount rate allowed us to calculate future liabilities without knowing their durations. This is why we only use the subsample 1993–2005 in our regressions. We do use 2007 data, not available from earlier years, to determine the demographic characteristics of the pension funds.

Our approach is relevant for all countries with a pension system which have (strong) defined-benefit (DB) characteristics and which use fixed interest rates to calculate liabilities, or rates which are fixed for some period and which may differ per pension fund. Chen and Beetsma (2015, Table 9.4) explain that pension systems in Chile, The Netherlands, Switzerland, the UK and the US have strong or substantial DB features, while those in Australia, Denmark and Iceland have certain elements of DB. More countries have a DB system, particularly Canada. OECD (2011) sums up that fixed rates are common in Germany, Ireland, Norway, Portugal, Spain, Switzerland, while the same is true for state pension funds in the US. In the UK, pension funds are allowed to use expected returns, set fixed over a certain period.

The dataset was used earlier by Bikker, Broeders, Hollanders and Ponds in Chapter 7 on the asset allocation of pension funds. These authors show that the type of assets held is correlated significantly with the age of the fund's active participants. Bikker *et al.* (2010) and de Dreu and Bikker in Chapter 8 use a quarterly version of this dataset to argue that the asset management of large pension funds is markedly different from that of small pension funds, which may apply less sophisticated risk management.

We use the reported financial and miscellaneous data to investigate both the assets and the liabilities of pension funds. An interesting feature of the Dutch supervisory framework, a fixed-discount rate, allows us to estimate whether changes in a fund's funding ratio are absorbed by its buffers or by its participants' pension rights. We condition these pension insurance actions on time and on the pension fund's characteristics. As expected, we find a positive relation between the funding ratio and the generosity of the pension fund. However, our main finding concerns the existence of two types of strong non-linear pension fund responses to funding ratio changes. When the funding ratio falls below 105%, pension fund participants (active workers, inactive participants and retirees) see their rights promptly impaired by 4 percentage points. When the funding ratio reaches 130%, the rights promptly increase by 2 percentage points. Second, we observe that the average age and number of retirees correlate positively with the generosity of their fund. Lack of data prevents us from determining whether this is due to pressure from the older participants through labour unions to increase benefits or to avoid reductions in indexation, or to other reasons. We also find that larger funds have larger transfers in comparable situations – possibly the benefit of returns to scale (Chapters 2 and 3). Finally, company pension funds are observed to be – on average – more generous to current participants compared to industry-wide funds, ascribed to the sponsor relations of the former (Broeders and Chen, 2013).

The rest of this chapter is organized as follows: Section 10.2 introduces the dataset and Section 10.3 presents our method for recovering pension insurance policy from the available data. Section 10.4 specifies the models used to describe the impact of the pension funds' solvability and their pension insurance responses, and presents estimation results. Section 10.5 concludes.

10.2. Data and trends

The Dutch pension sector is large with 514 registered pension funds (at end-2011; 279 at end 2015), controlling an invested wealth of more than € 830 billion, that is, 138% of the Dutch GDP. In 2015, these numbers are € 1,210 billion and 178% of GDP (OECD, 2016), ranking the Dutch pension system in terms of the asset-to-GDP ratio as the largest in the world, after Denmark. Approximately 94% of all employees participate in one or more pension funds. The population of pension funds is very heterogeneous in terms of size. The largest fund, ABP, has in 2010 about 2.8 million participants and controls 208 billion euro (ABP, 2010)[2] whereas a number of small pension funds have fewer than ten participants. Most of these pension funds operate a defined-benefit (DB) plan. The benefit entitlement is determined by years of service and a reference wage, which may be final pay (as during most years of our sample) or the average wage over the years of service, as is nowadays most common.

More than 85% of all pension funds are of the *company pension fund* type. Of the remaining 15%, most are industry-wide pension funds. Participation in industry-wide pension funds is (under certain conditions) mandatory for all employers in a particular sector. The circa 95 industry-wide pension funds are the dominant players, both in terms of active participants (market share above 85%) and in assets under management (over 70%). In 2007, almost 600 company pension funds encompassed over a quarter of the assets, serving 12% of plan participants. A small number of generally small *professional group* pension funds form the third type of pension funds, organized for a specific group of professionals such as physicians or notaries.

Each year, a pension fund must report an extensive, prescribed set of variables to DNB, which exercises supervision on the sector. The number of pension funds declined during the period under our observation. The solid line in Fig. 10.1 shows the decline from over 1,100 funds in 1993 via 700 in 2007 to 290 in 2016. The main cause of this decline is a process of mergers and liquidations, possibly driven by increasing regulatory demands on pension funds and unused scale economies (see Bikker and de Dreu 2009; Chapter 3).

This chapter uses a subset of the available data, comprising pension funds with at least 150 participants. We exclude smaller funds because many of them are tax vehicles for *e.g.* company owner-managers, and their small size severely limits their capacity to pursue solvency policies. Excluding smaller funds eliminates almost half the sample in 1993. As Fig. 10.1 shows, consolidation and liquidation reduced the number of excluded funds over time. The number of funds included in our analysis rose initially and in the final year of our sample, close to 80% of the registered funds met our selection criterion.

After our selection, the sample still includes pension funds of very different sizes as shown in Table 10.1. The number of small funds (150–500 participants) declined over time, whereas the number of large funds (10k–100k and 100k+) increased, at least until 2007. The smaller funds either merged into a bigger fund or

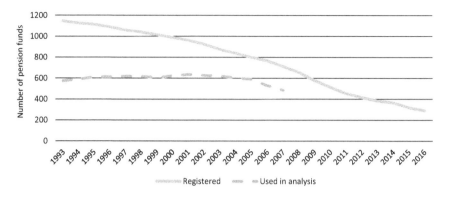

Figure 10.1 The number of pension funds in the dataset and the number of funds actually used in the analysis per year

transferred their liabilities to an insurance company, and hence disappeared from our dataset. After a merger we discard the receiving fund in the year immediately after the merger. Most other changes concern funds that were too small to be included and as such do not affect our estimates.

Each year, pension funds must report on the following items, all in current euro or number of people:

1   *Technical reserve (TR,)*. This is the actuarial value (using standard life tables) of the liabilities the fund has incurred. Up to 2005, liabilities were discounted by a fixed 4% interest rate; from 2006, liabilities have been discounted using market-based interest rates.

2   *Assets (A,)*, at market value, split into five categories: fixed income, real estate, stocks, bonds and other. Dividing total assets by the technical reserve gives the *funding ratio*, the main indicator of financial health.

3   *Benefits (B,)* paid out in the current year, split into straight pension benefits, survivor pension benefits and disability pension benefits.

4   *Premiums (P,)* received in the current year, split into premiums paid by employers and by employees.

5   *Participants* divided into three categories; active participants, retirees and deferred participants ('sleepers'). The latter are former active participants who no longer contribute premiums but have not yet reached the age of retirement. They may have quit the labour force, moved to a different pension fund or suffered a decrease in wage income that puts them below the level of eligibility.

We know little about the participants of pension funds, except for their classification as active (working), retired or sleeper. Only for the last year in our dataset, 2007, we also have the number of active participants, retirees and sleepers split into 5-year cohorts. This data gives us an idea of the demographic structure of each fund. Fig. 10.2 shows the distribution of the average age of

Table 10.1 Pension funds classified by number of participants over time

Year	150–500	500–1k	1k – 10k	10k – 100k	100k+	Total
	Pension funds after the selection					
1993	163	103	220	74	16	576
1994	173	105	219	76	15	588
1995	186	114	222	74	17	613
1996	172	117	234	74	17	614
1997	171	115	240	74	18	618
1998	178	109	242	72	17	618
1999	167	102	248	71	17	605
2000	165	98	271	70	18	622
2001	158	102	285	71	21	637
2002	151	93	285	77	21	627
2003	145	96	275	83	22	621
2004	129	94	272	88	21	604
2005	119	86	274	89	22	590
2006	93	79	253	86	20	531
2007	76	75	232	86	18	487
	Pension funds with more than 150 participants (no selection applied)					
2007	84	84	260	91	22	541
2008	64	78	233	91	22	488
2009	48	65	219	91	22	445
2010	37	55	212	83	21	408
2011	26	47	197	79	21	370
2012	16	46	182	76	21	341
2013	14	43	165	74	21	317
2014	11	31	142	75	20	279
2015	9	22	128	73	21	253

participants for each member type per pension fund. For instance, 230 pension funds have active participants with an average age of between 40 and 45, see first panel. Table 10.2 shows the average and median ages across types of funds and types of participants, where the average and median ages are quite similar. Retirees are, of course, much older than the other participants but, on average, deferred participants are only slightly older than the active participants. If anything, the 80 industry-wide pension funds have, on average, a slightly younger active population than the 399 company pension funds and the eight other funds.

Fig. 10.3 shows the ratio of retired participants over active participants for the sector as a whole and for the three different types of pension funds. The ageing process is clearly visible as the ratio for the Netherlands rises from 35% in 1993 to 47% in 2007. Until the mid-1990s early retirement was made very attractive in the Netherlands, lowering the number of active participants and, if the pension fund offered an early retirement scheme, increasing the number of retired. In the late 1990s the government made early retirement less attractive, which resulted in a drop in the retired/active ratio. The ratio for the 'other' (mostly professional) pension funds follows a volatile path mainly because this group is

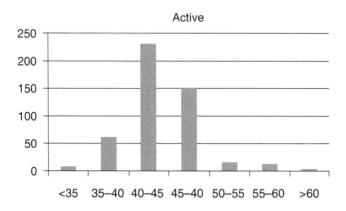

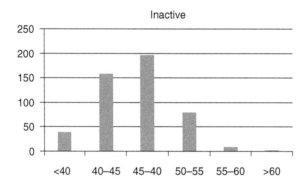

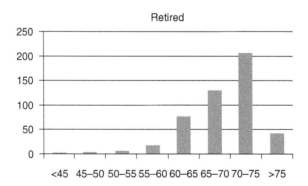

Figure 10.2 Distributions of average ages per pension fund (in absolute numbers) of different member classes

Table 10.2 Average and median ages across types of pension funds and types of participants

	All	*Industry*	*Company*	*Others*
# of funds	487	80	399	8
Active average (median)	44.3 (43.8)	44.2 (42.8)	44.3 (44.1)	45.3 (42.6)
Sleeper average (median)	46.3 (46.1)	46.8 (47.0)	46.1 (46.0)	49.1 (47.3)
Retired average (median)	68.7 (70.1)	69.4 (70.7)	68.5 (69.9)	71.3 (71.1)

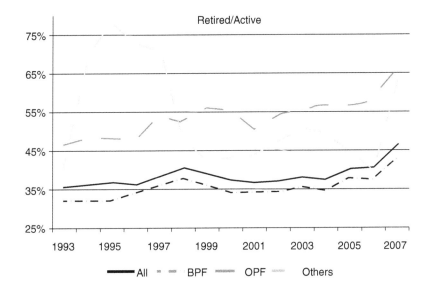

Figure 10.3 Retired participants as percentage of active participants of the fund, for different fund types

small and because mergers with and cessations to industry-wide pension funds have a big impact.

10.3. Recovering behaviour

The dataset consists mostly of balance sheet items per fund and per year, but does not reveal such pension fund policy parameters as premium rates or degrees of indexation. The latter is an instrument that can be used to influence the level of benefits immediately. In Dutch DB plans, the benefits are specified and guaranteed in nominal rather than real terms. These nominal rights are used to determine a fund's technical reserves. Each year, the pension fund board decides whether to increase benefits and rights in line with the pension plan's stated indexation ambition, that is, adjustment to the general price level or to the contract wages in the sector. This discretionary room for manoeuvre affords the board some limited leeway on the obligation side. Outright nominal devaluation of existing rights would be a major breach of the contract, and is considered only when all other measures fall short. As uniform information on changes in the provided pension insurance is lacking, we will use the financial information that is available to develop an indicator of a pension fund's pension insurance stance.

We aim to unearth facts about pension funds' insurance policies by observing unexpected changes in individual funds' liabilities. Until 2005, pension funds used a fixed 4% discount rate to discount their future liabilities. We use this feature in our method of recovering pension behaviour. Note that the technical reserves are equal to

$$TR_t = \sum_{\tau=t+1}^{\infty} \frac{B_{t,\tau}}{(1+r)^{\tau-t}} \tag{10.1}$$

with $B_{t,\tau}$ the benefits the fund expects it has to pay to its retired in year τ, given the information and accumulated rights in year t.

Equation (10.2) shows that the technical reserves by the end of period t+1, TR_{t+1}, can be decomposed into the technical reserves from the previous period minus the expected payout in period t+1 plus the present value of the change in expected future payouts.

$$\begin{aligned} TR_t &= \sum_{\tau=t+1}^{\infty} \frac{B_{t,\tau}}{(1+r)^{\tau-t}} \\ &= (1+r)\left\{ \sum_{\tau=t+2}^{\infty} \frac{B_{t+1,\tau} - B_{t,\tau}}{(1+r)^{\tau-t}} + \sum_{\tau=t+1}^{\infty} \frac{B_{t,\tau}}{(1+r)^{\tau-t}} - \frac{B_{t,t+1}}{1+r} \right\} \\ &= (1+r)TR_t + (1+r) \sum_{\tau=t+2}^{\infty} \frac{B_{t+1,\tau} - B_{t,\tau}}{(1+r)^{\tau-t}} - B_{t,t+1} \end{aligned} \tag{10.2}$$

The value of the change in expected payouts consists of (i) a term to reflect that old liabilities are now discounted less (1+r), (ii) changes in the expected future benefits ($B_{t+1,\tau} - B_{t,\tau}$) and (iii) the removal of benefits paid out this year ($B_{t,t+1}$). The change in expected benefits comes from the addition of new rights, but also from changes stemming from indexation, revaluations due to updated mortality tables, transfers, mergers and acquisitions. Note that the actual payout in period t+1, B_{t+1} may differ from the expected payout, for the same reasons.

Observation of the pension-related cash flows, that is, the premium income and the actual pension payout, and the current development in the technical reserves, allows us to define a policy action indicator Γ as

$$\Gamma_t \equiv TR_{t+1} - \left[(1+r)TR_t + P_{t+1} - B_{t+1} \right]. \tag{10.3}$$

Substitution of Equation (10.2) gives

$$\Gamma_t \equiv \left\{ (1+r) \sum_{\tau=t+2}^{\infty} \frac{B_{t+1,\tau} - B_{t,\tau}}{(1+r)^{\tau-t}} - P_{t+1} \right\} + \left\{ B_{t+1} - B_{t,t+1} \right\}. \tag{10.4}$$

This links the policy action indicator Γ to unexpected changes in future payouts during the current period due to policy choices. The first term in parentheses shows the difference between the present value of the change in future benefits and this year's premium payments. Regulation requires that for the fund as a whole, on average, total premium payments to the fund should be equal to the expected present value of the new entitlements, the so-called self-funding premium. The second term in parentheses shows the difference between expected pension payouts at the beginning of the year and actual payouts.

This Γ is an indicator of net transfers between the fund and its participants. If pension contributions exceed the present value of the change in expected payouts and/or actual payouts are lower than expected, then there is a net transfer from the participants to the fund, indicated by a negative Γ. If the Γ-indicator is positive, there is a net transfer from the fund to its participants. Positive transfers lower the financial position of the fund and are paid for by excess return on the fund's assets or by actually lowering buffers. Negative transfers are used to improve the financial position of the fund. These transfers can take many different forms:

- The fund increases the accumulated nominal pension rights (indexation or backservice).[3]
- Contributions do not match the actuarial value of new rights, for instance due to a recovery premium mark-up designed to increase the funding ratio, or to pension holidays.
- The present value of accumulated pension rights changes, due to changes in the expected mortality rate. If mortality decreases, and pensioners receive a life annuity, their claim on the fund increases in value.
- Mergers or individual transfers of participants.
- Deviation of the actual mortality of the fund's participants from the average mortality rate occur.

Note that changes in the value of the liabilities (due to changes in mortality), when taken on board by the pension fund, can be seen as a transfer regardless of whether money changed hands in the current year. Changes in liabilities due to external factors show that the fund is the owner of the respective risk, and serve to insure its participants. Such changes therefore imply policy actions. In this sense, only the last two items do not point directly to a transfer between the fund and its participants. The assumption we make in the subsequent analysis is that these shocks are orthogonal to the funds' financial position.

The policy action indicator Γ depends on the size of the fund. To make it comparable between funds, we scale it with the level of the technical reserves:

$$\gamma_t \equiv \frac{\Gamma_t}{TR_t} = \frac{TR_{t+1} - P_{t+1} + B_{t+1}}{TR_t} - (1+r). \tag{10.5}$$

This method of measuring insurance policy action does not allow us to see who the beneficiaries or victims of the pension rights transfers are. More specifically, we cannot distinguish whether a transfer affects the active or the retired participants of the fund.

Since 2006, pension funds have been required to use the market swap rate to calculate their technical reserves, instead of the fixed interest rate of 4%. To take the maturity of the liabilities into account, pension funds use the demographic composition of the pension fund's participants and their individual pension rights. In our approach presented above we could reproduce the technical reserve without knowing the demographic composition of the pension fund's participants and their individual pension rights, thanks to the fixed interest rate. Because we do not have information on the duration of the pension fund liabilities and as the term structure showed non-parallel movements, we cannot construct our indicator for 2006 and later years. This leaves us with the sample 1993–2005.

10.4. Estimating pension insurance policy reactions

To determine the impact of a fund's solvability on its pension insurance policy, we estimate the relationship between the fund's net transfer to its participants (γ) and the funding ratio $FR_{i,t} = A_{i,t} / TR_{i,t}$. This funding ratio is the key financial soundness indicator used in the pension funds' supervisory framework.[4] Transfers between the fund and its participants are conditional on the financial state of the fund; in fact, levying extra premiums or moderating rights indexation in times of reduced solvency, and vice versa, are widely used policy measures. If we can recover this relationship, this would confirm that γ_t is a useful indicator of transfers. The characteristics of this relationship may tell us more about the reaction of funds' pension insurance policies to their funding ratios. Is the marginal effect of a change in the funding ratio constant as in a linear relationship, or non-linear, *e.g.* do regime breaks exist?

10.4.1. The impact of the funding ratio

In its simplest form, the relation we estimate is:

$$\gamma_{i,t} = \alpha_i + \beta FR_{i,t-1} + \epsilon_{i,t}. \tag{10.6}$$

We use the panel dataset at our disposal to estimate a pension-fund-specific effect α_i that accounts for the fact that different pension funds may take different approaches to plan sponsorship, leading to different average rates of pension transfers.

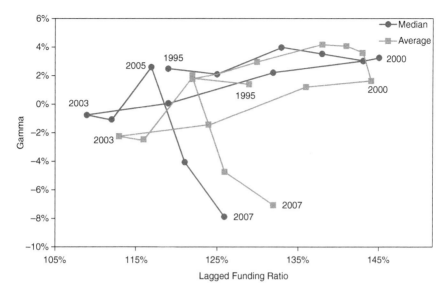

Figure 10.4 The lagged funding ratio versus the γ (not necessarily of the same fund)

Fig. 10.4 shows the relation between the median γ and the median one-year lagged funding ratio over time; these observations need not apply to the same fund. As this figure shows, there is a positive relation between these two variables from the first observation in 1994 until 2005. If we replace medians by averages, the respective graph in Fig. 10.4 presents a similar positive relation. As mentioned above, a change in solvency regulation in 2006 causes a clear break. From 2006 onwards, pension funds must use the market swap rate to discount their future liabilities, instead of the fixed 4% discount rate. The discount rates in 2006 and 2007 were well above 4% for all maturities, resulting in the lower technical reserves, which explains the low γ's in these years. *Because of this change in the calculation of the technical reserves, we exclude the years 2006 and 2007 from our estimations.*

In preliminary estimations we experimented with the lag structure of equation (10.6). Using the current funding ratio to explain γ is not realistic as pension funds take pension insurance policy actions only after new information on their solvency is released, that is not until the next year.[5] Using the lagged value of the funding ratio (*FR*) takes care of this, but there is no reason to include it as the only explanatory variable. In principle, the value of *FR* two (or more) years lagged can be included and may provide extra information on the impact of the funding ratio. In all specifications used, however, we find that adding extra lags of *FR* does not contribute to the explanatory power of the model.

Apart from the funding ratio we have indicators of the demographic composition of the pension fund, its size and its type. However, those variables show little or no variation beyond a simple time trend. This means that we can only estimate panel regressions with the funding ratio as single explanatory variable. We start with this strategy, and later continue to explore models with more explanatory variables but without a panel structure.

Regulation in the Netherlands as in force since 2006 assigns special meaning to funding ratios of 105% (minimum requirement) and (around) 127% (long-term requirement, necessary for *e.g.* full indexation).[6] These thresholds reflect existing common sense: a pension fund needs a funding ratio well above 100% to remain solvent, while a larger buffer is needed for in the long run. They are also the result of a long negotiation process between the supervisor, the government and representatives of employers and employees. Note that the new regulatory plan has been designed in the late '90s, and have been discussed with the sector since around 2000. It is not unlikely that, long before 2006, pension funds may have adjusted their responses to solvency shocks, being aware of upcoming supervisory standards, if not already behaving in such a responsible manner on their own.

The threshold regression methods for non-dynamic panels with individual specific fixed effects of Hansen (1999, 2000) allows for such changes in policy regimes. The threshold and slopes are estimated using traditional fixed effect least square estimators. The computation of the least squares estimate of the threshold involves searching for a threshold that minimizes the sum of squared errors and a bootstrapping method to determine the significance of this threshold.

For a one-threshold specification with varying intercept and coefficient, the estimated equation changes to

$$
\gamma_{i,t} = \begin{cases} \alpha_i^0 + \beta^0 FR_{i,t-1} + \epsilon_{i,t}, & FR_{i,t-1} \leq T \\ \alpha_i^1 + \beta^1 FR_{i,t-1} + \epsilon_{i,t}, & FR_{i,t-1} > T \end{cases} , \tag{10.7}
$$

where the level of the threshold T is estimated simultaneously with the other parameters.

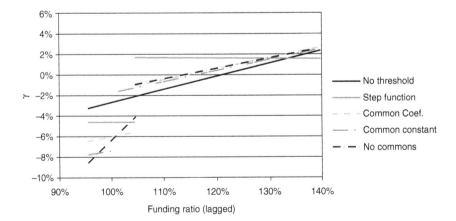

Figure 10.5 Estimated relationship between γ and the lagged funding ratio with one break

and 6 percentage points in all specifications, with an average of 4.8 percentage points in the one-break specifications and 4.9 percentage points in the two-break specifications. The second jump is estimated at a funding ratio between 124% and 132%, depending on the specification. The jump is smaller than the first one, but still ranges from 1 to 4 percentage points with an average of 2.5 percentage points.

These estimation results show that the relationship between a pension fund's transfer to its participants and its funding ratio is non-linear. When the funding ratio falls below 105%, the transfer rate γ drops about 4 percentage points. Less robust, but still significant, is the non-linearity around a funding ratio of 130%, where the transfer rate makes another jump of around half that size. Between the two jumps, there exists a weak, positive relation between the pension transfer indicator γ and the funding ratio.

The form of the relationship between the funding ratio and the transfer indicator γ shows the existence of distinct pension insurance policy regimes on either side of the thresholds. Below the 105% threshold, funds transfer significantly less to their participants. In this situation there is most likely a net transfer to the fund. This changes dramatically when funds cross the threshold and the situation is seen as quite safe. At that point, there is only a weak impact of funding on transfers. A second behavioural change occurs at high funding levels, where transfers to participants are increased but with a lesser (but statistically significant) jump.

The location of the first break can be explained by a desire to stay solvent. Although participation in the pension plan is (and was) mandatory and participants could not claim entitlements immediately, pension funds aim to possess sufficient assets to cover their liabilities. The second break coincides with the solvency requirement where under new regulation pension funds are also allowed to provide full indexation to prices or wages.

Part of the size of the first jump may be explained by the transition from final wage to average wage schemes when after the end of the dot-com bubble the funding ratio fell below the lower threshold. Under a final wage scheme pension entitlements increase with the wages of the active participants (the so-called backservice). Under an average wage scheme, there is no backservice, so no automatic increase of the technical reserves due to wage growth. This limits the increase in pension entitlements, hence contributing to a lower gamma. During the transition there was no jump in the technical reserves and as such no jump in the funding ratio either, because the pension funds did not change already existing pension entitlements. This combination, a low but non-jumping funding ratio and a lower γ due to the switch from a final wage scheme to an average wage scheme may show up in the data as a break.[7]

Role of demographics, type and size of the pension fund

In the previous section we regressed γ on the lagged funding ratio, allowing for a fund-specific intercept. This variable intercept indicates that different pension funds have systematically larger or smaller transfers. In this section we explain these differences between funds from observables such as the average age of the fund's participants, the shares of the various participant categories, the type of pension fund and the pension fund size. These characteristics are either roughly constant over time – the type of fund does not change, and member shares only add a (very flat) time trend – or we only have observations for the last year in our sample. This means that we cannot run fixed effect panel regressions, as the coefficient on the observables would not be identified. Instead we resort to pooled regressions, where we estimate an 'average transfer rate' for each individual pension fund. Because there is no time variation in the additional variables, these variables pick up systematic differences between pension funds, that is, the fund-specific intercepts.

Table 10.5 shows the impact of the average age of participants, the number of participants and the type of pension fund on the lagged transfer indicator γ. First note that the inclusion of these additional explanatory variables have no significant effect on the relationship between the lagged funding ratio and γ: the size of

Table 10.5 Effect of the participants' ages, size of the fund and type of fund on transfers (γ)

	No break	*Common coefficient*	*No commons*
Age active	−0.0019	−0.0019	−0.0019
	[−3.0]	[−3.0]	[−3.0]
Age deferred	0.0016	0.0015	0.0013
	[2.1]	[1.9]	[1.7]
Age retirees	0.0017	0.0017	0.0017
	[3.2]	[3.1]	[3.2]
Log(participants)	0.0072	0.0076	0.0076
	[4.2]	[4.4]	[4.5]
Industry-wide fund	−0.079	−0.073	−0.076
	[−5.3]	[−5.0]	[−5.2]
Company fund	0.005	0.005	0.002
	[0.5]	[0.5]	[0.2]
Constant	−0.233	−0.208	−0.245
	[−6.6]	[−5.5]	[−1.1]
Funding ratio	0.067	0.015	0.060
	[6.7]	[1.0]	[0.3]
Threshold (T_1)	–	102%	102%
Constant ($\geq T_1$)	–	0.039	−0.040
	–	[4.1]	[−0.2]
Funding ratio ($\geq T_1$)	–	–	0.064
	–	–	[0.3]
Threshold (T_2)	–	125%	125%
Constant ($\geq T_2$)	–	0.024	0.164
	–	[3.3]	[2.6]
Funding ratio ($\geq T_2$)	–	–	−0.120
	–	–	[−2.2]
obs	1168	1168	1168
obs < T_1	–	81	81
$T_1 \leq$ obs < T_2	–	571	571
obs $\geq T_2$	–	516	516
R^2	13.4%	15.4%	15.7%

the coefficients, the location of the breaks and the size of the jump are all similar to the results found in the previous section.

For 2007 we have the number of participants per category – active, deferred and retired – in five-year age cohorts. From these cohort sizes we can proxy the average age of each group; Fig. 10.2 already provided a crude overview of these age distributions.

Table 10.5 shows the relationship between the average ages and γ for various specifications of the link between γ and the lagged funding ratio. Note that by using the 2007 age structure in regressions about earlier years, we assume a tendency of constancy in demography. That is, we use the fact that demographic measures tend to move slowly over time and assume that the average age in 2007 contains some information on the (relative) average age in earlier years. This table shows that if the average age of the retired increases ten years, the transfer indicator γ of a fund over the whole sample is, on average, 1.7 percentage points higher per year. These results are significant at the 99% level in all specifications.

Table 10.5 also shows the effect of the logarithm of the total number of participants as a measure of size alongside the lagged funding ratio. The results show that larger funds have a higher γ; the coefficient for our sample varies from 0.72% to 0.76%. This implies that the rate of transfer from a pension fund with one million participants is 1.1 percentage points higher than that of a fund with 10,000 participants. The effect of the size is significant at the 99% level in all specifications. A possible explanation for this positive impact on γ is the existence of economies of scale these bigger funds have (see Bikker and de Dreu, 2009; Chapter 2). Lower costs imply that a larger part of the paid premiums can be used to create new pension rights, either permitting lower premiums or increasing the next year's technical reserves, *e.g.* indexation.

Finally, the table shows the differences between the various pension fund types. We classify each fund into one of three types: industry-wide pension funds, company pension funds and 'others'. This third category consists of professional group funds (including non-academic occupational groups) and three special funds created for legal reasons. Since every fund has a type and funds typically do not change type, we cannot include dummy variables for all three types in the regression model. We take the 'others' as baseline.

The parameters γ of industry-wide pension funds are, on average, percentage points to 7.9 percentage points lower than those of other funds, while company pension funds have slightly higher γ values. One potential explanation for the relative generosity of company pension funds is that they have the support of a sponsor which may help to absorb negative shocks.

Another indicator of the demographics of a pension fund is given by the relative shares of active participants, inactive participants and retirees.

Table 10.6 shows the same regressions, but with the shares of the active and retirees as indicators of the fund's age. This table again shows that older funds – with a larger share of retirees – have a positive effect on γ. The shares of the active, sleepers and retirees add up to 1, forcing us to drop one variable; we select the share of the sleepers as the benchmark variable. The share of active participants does not have a significant effect on γ in any specification. The share of the

Table 10.6 Effect of group share, size of the fund and type of fund on transfers (γ)

	No break	Common coefficient	No commons
Share active	0.012	0.018	0.016
	[0.7]	[1.1]	[1.0]
Share retirees	0.099	0.103	0.099
	[4.4]	[4.6]	[4.4]
Log(participants)	0.0089	0.0091	0.0090
	[5.0]	[5.2]	[5.1]
Sectoral fund	−0.081	−0.074	−0.076
	[−5.4]	[−5.0]	[−5.1]
Company fund	−0.001	0.002	−0.001
	[−0.1]	[0.1]	[−0.0]
Constant	−0.137	−0.140	0.037
	[−5.1]	[−4.6]	[0.1]
Funding ratio	0.045	−0.003	−0.178
	[4.3]	[−0.2]	[−0.6]
Threshold (T_1)	–	102%	102%
Constant ($\geq T_1$)	–	0.052	−0.244
	–	[5.2]	[−0.9]
Funding ratio ($\geq T_1$)	–	–	0.285
	–	–	[1.0]
Threshold (T_2)	–	125%	137%
Constant ($\geq T_2$)	–	0.019	0.151
	–	[2.4]	[2.9]
Funding ratio ($\geq T_2$)	–	–	−0.116
	–	–	[−2.9]
obs	1610	1610	1610
obs < T_1	–	111	111
$T_1 \leq$ obs < T_2	–	783	1038
obs $\geq T_2$	–	716	461
R^2	8.3%	10.1%	10.3%

retirees does; its coefficient is significant at the 99% level in all specifications. A 10 percentage points bigger share of the retired increases γ by an average of 1.0 percentage points. All other coefficients and breaks are fairly the same as before.

Both indicators of the 'age' of a pension fund's participants point in the same direction: grey funds have higher transfer rates to participants. From our data we cannot infer which group stands to benefit from this transfer. It could be due to lower pension premiums or higher indexation. Note that it is not the level of the payout that creates this higher γ (grey funds always have large outflows simply because they are in the payout phase), but the ratio of benefits over technical reserves. Note also that retirees do not generally have a formal vote in pension fund boards. A possible explanation is that the employee representatives (*e.g.* labour unions) take the interests of retirees into account in order to obtain higher indexation.

10.5. Conclusions

This chapter investigates how pension rights are adjusted in response to developments in the pension funds' funding rate. Changes in pension rights are not recorded systematically, but we use a sample of more than 1,000 Dutch pension funds from 1993–2007 to proxy changes in pension rights per pension fund and per year. We exclude funds with fewer than 150 participants, as they generally have different objectives, and we drop observations from the years 2006–2007 because a new pension regime introduced in 2006 causes a change in our methodology. Using a panel data approach, the first finding is that pension rights increase with the funding rate, in line with expectations. On average, an increase of the funding ratio by 10 percentage points adds 1.0 percentage point to the participants' pension rights. The second finding is that this relationship between newly assigned pension rights and the funding ratio includes two highly significant breaks. When the funding ratio falls below 105%, the transfer of pension rights drops by 4 percentage points. When the funding ratio reaches 130%, the transfer rate increases by 2 percentage points. These breakpoints exhibit a remarkable coincidence with essential funding levels in the new regulatory regime, which was established after the sample period: the funding ratio of 105% is a minimum requirement whereas a ratio of around 125–130% is the required level, needed for full indexation. This chapter only describes the behaviour of the pension funds; we do not compare this with the optimal or desirable use of the control mechanisms. It seems, however, unlikely that jumps in the response function are optimal.

If we expand our model with additional explanatory variables such as the age distribution of participants, the type of participants and the type of pension fund, we lose the panel structure as these additional explanatory variables have limited variation over time. Using pooled regression we find that indicators of the average age of a pension fund's participants have a positive impact on the funds' generosity. With respect to types of participants, the share of retirees is an especially important determinant. A possible explanation is that participants of higher age cohorts have more influence, because they are overrepresented in labour unions. We also find that larger funds are more generous to current participants, possibly reflecting better scale efficiency. Finally, company pension funds are more generous than industry-wide funds, possibly because the first type has the benefit of a de facto risk-absorbing sponsor company. All these extensions of our model confirm our earlier results of increasing pension rights when funding rates are higher and with the existence of two highly significant breaks at plausible funding rate levels and with substantial jumps.

Our findings seem to be relevant also with the introduction of the new regulatory framework in 2006. The crisis of 2008 and beyond resulted in funding rates below 105% and these funds were forced to recover to 105% within 5 years. For the first time in history, funds were even forced to lower accumulated entitlements. Those funds, whose funding rates have recovered already announced indexation plans. New datasets, including duration of liabilities are needed for a more formal test.

Notes

1 Update of: J.A. Bikker, T. Knaap, W. Romp, 2014, Measuring and explaining implicit risk sharing in defined-benefit pension funds, *Applied Economics* 46, 1996–2009.
2 End 2016 ABP controls 420 billion euro (ABP, 2017).
3 Backservice is the change of the pension rights due to a change in the actual wage of the participants in a final wage scheme.
4 Investment portfolios with relatively safe AAA-bonds are safer than equity portfolios, but for our financial soundness indicator we consider only the funding ratios. Investment risk has not been considered in our analyses.
5 The current funding ratio is also problematic from an econometric point of view as this choice would result in a spurious regression. Indeed, unexpected changes in the level of fund obligations (through *e.g.* demographic realizations or decisions about indexation) would show up in both the funding ratio and the transfer rate.
6 The required funding ratio of around 127% is determined so that the probability of underfunding within one year is limited to 2.5%.
7 This jump can be significant. Suppose that for a pension fund 40% of the technical reserves are due to the pension rights of active participants, whereas the rest are provisions for the currently retired and deferred. Assume that individual wages grow with 5%. This implies that the technical reserves of this fund under a final wage scheme increase by 2%, just because of the backservice. Switching to an average wage scheme would eliminate both the backservice and the increase, and would result in a 1γ that is 2 percentage points lower. Once the fund has implemented an average wage scheme, it has much more control over its technical reserves as all indexation is, within limits, at the discretion of the board.

References

ABP, 2010, *Annual Report 2010*, Heerlen. Available at http://abp.turnpages.nl/DS2/public/slot072/pdf/compleet.pdf (accessed 17 February 2014)..

ABP, 2017, *Annual Report 2016*, http://jaarverslag.abp.nl/docs/ABP_JV_2016/index.php?nr=16&r_code=ABP_JV_2016 (accessed May 23, 2017).

Bikker, J.A., D.W.G.A. Broeders, J. de Dreu, 2010, Stock market performance and pension fund investment policy: rebalancing, free float, or market timing, *International Journal of Central Banking* 6, 53–79.

Bikker, J.A., J. de Dreu, 2009, Operating costs of pension funds: the impact of scale, governance, and plan design, *Journal of Pension Economics and Finance* 8, 63–89.

Bovenberg, A.L., R. Koijen, T. Nijman, C.N. Teulings, 2007, Saving and investing over the life cycle and the role of collective pension funds, *De Economist*, 347–415.

Broeders, D.W., A. Chen, 2013, Pension benefit security: a comparison of solvency requirements, a pension guarantee scheme and sponsor support, *Journal of Risk and Insurance* 80, 239–272.

Chen, D.H.J., R.M.W.J. Beetsma, 2015, Mandatory participation in occupational pension schemes in the Netherlands and other countries: an update, *Netspar Discussion Paper* No. 10/2015–032.

EU, 2011, *Pension Systems in the EU – Contingent Liabilities and Assets in the Public and Private Sector*, European Union, European Parliament's Committee on Economic and Monetary Affairs, IP/A/ECON/ST/2010–2026, Brussels, www.europarl.europa.eu/activities/committees/studies.do?language=EN.

Hansen, B.E., 1999, Threshold effects in non-dynamic panels: estimation, testing and inference, *Econometrica* 93, 345–368.

Hansen, B.E., 2000, Sample splitting and threshold estimation, *Econometrica* 68, 575–603.

OECD, 2011, *Competition and Financial Stability*, OECD, Paris.

OECD, 2016, *Pension Markets in Focus 2016*, OECD, Paris, www.oecd.org/finance/private-pensions/globalpensionstatistics.htm (accessed May 16, 2017).

Appendix 10.1
Estimated equations

We estimate the following one-break specifications

$$\gamma_{i,t} = \begin{cases} \alpha_i^0 + \epsilon_{i,t}, \ FR_{i,t-1} \le T \\ \alpha_i^1 + \epsilon_{i,t}, \ FR_{i,t-1} > T \end{cases} \qquad \text{(Step function)}$$

$$\gamma_{i,t} = \begin{cases} \alpha_i + \beta^0 FR_{i,t-1} + \epsilon_{i,t}, \ FR_{i,t-1} \le T \\ \alpha_i + \beta^1 FR_{i,t-1} + \epsilon_{i,t}, \ FR_{i,t-1} > T \end{cases} \qquad \text{(Common constant)}$$

$$\gamma_{i,t} = \begin{cases} \alpha_i^0 + \beta FR_{i,t-1} + \epsilon_{i,t}, \ FR_{i,t-1} \le T \\ \alpha_i^1 + \beta FR_{i,t-1} + \epsilon_{i,t}, \ FR_{i,t-1} > T \end{cases} \qquad \text{(Common coefficient)}$$

$$\gamma_{i,t} = \begin{cases} \alpha_i^0 + \beta^0 FR_{i,t-1} + \epsilon_{i,t}, \ FR_{i,t-1} \le T \\ \alpha_i^1 + \beta^1 FR_{i,t-1} + \epsilon_{i,t}, \ FR_{i,t-1} > T \end{cases} \qquad \text{(No commons)}$$

For the two-break specifications we estimate

$$\gamma_{i,t} = \begin{cases} \alpha_i^0 + \epsilon_{i,t}, \ FR_{i,t-1} \le T_1 \\ \alpha_i^1 + \epsilon_{i,t}, \ T_1 < FR_{i,t-1} \le T_2 \\ \alpha_i^2 + \epsilon_{i,t}, \ FR_{i,t-1} > T_2 \end{cases} \qquad \text{(Step function)}$$

$$\gamma_{i,t} = \begin{cases} \alpha_i + \beta^0 FR_{i,t-1} + \epsilon_{i,t}, \ FR_{i,t-1} \le T_1 \\ \alpha_i + \beta^1 FR_{i,t-1} + \epsilon_{i,t}, \ T_1 < FR_{i,t-1} \le T_2 \\ \alpha_i + \beta^2 FR_{i,t-1} + \epsilon_{i,t}, \ FR_{i,t-1} > T_2 \end{cases} \quad \text{(Common constant)}$$

$$\gamma_{i,t} = \begin{cases} \alpha_i^0 + \beta FR_{i,t-1} + \epsilon_{i,t}, \ FR_{i,t-1} \le T_1 \\ \alpha_i^1 + \beta FR_{i,t-1} + \epsilon_{i,t}, \ T_1 < FR_{i,t-1} \le T_2 \\ \alpha_i^2 + \beta FR_{i,t-1} + \epsilon_{i,t}, \ FR_{i,t-1} > T_2 \end{cases} \quad \text{(Common coefficient)}$$

$$\gamma_{i,t} = \begin{cases} \alpha_i^0 + \beta^0 FR_{i,t-1} + \epsilon_{i,t}, & FR_{i,t-1} \le T_1 \\ \alpha_i^1 + \beta^1 FR_{i,t-1} + \epsilon_{i,t}, & T_1 < FR_{i,t-1} \le T_2 \quad (\text{No commons}) \\ \alpha_i^2 + \beta^2 FR_{i,t-1} + \epsilon_{i,t}, & FR_{i,t-1} > T_2 \end{cases}$$

11 Utility-equivalence of pension security mechanisms

*D.W.G.A. Broeders, An Chen, and
Birgit Schnorrenberg*

11.1. Introduction

Many defined benefit pension funds around the globe suffer from funding deficits caused by a combination of volatile equity returns, declining market interest rates and unanticipated improvements in longevity expectations. Protection of pension benefits is the subject of investigation in this chapter. We consider solvency requirements, a pension guarantee fund, and sponsor support as possible pension security mechanisms. The key contribution of this chapter is to consider under which pension contract specifications these security mechanisms offer equivalent utility to the beneficiary.

The analysis of pension funds is challenging for two reasons. *First*, the institutional framework is extraordinary. Unlike a commercial insurance enterprise, a pension fund has no external shareholders who bear the residual risk. As a consequence all funding risks are ultimately borne by the pension fund's beneficiaries, the sponsor[1] or a pension guarantee fund. As such pension funds need to be analyzed differently from other financial institutions. *Second*, defined benefit pension plans typically face an investment dilemma. On the one hand, pension funds invest in risky assets trying to earn a risk premium. On the other hand, the primary concern is to secure the pension benefits. From this point of view, a pension fund may choose to closely match assets and liabilities, for example by hedging interest rate risks by investing in high grade bonds and fixed income derivatives that replicate the stream of liability payments. Also insurance can be used to safeguard pension benefits, e.g., using longevity risk hedges. A pension fund may however find it difficult to fully implement such a hedging strategy. Due to liquidity constraints, it is usually impossible to invest in assets that exactly replicate the size and nature of its liabilities. This is especially true for defined benefit plans.[2] For defined contribution plans the liabilities by definition replicate the assets.

Adequate funding of occupational pension plans is key to benefit security. In addition, different methods of securing funding exist in occupational plans. Based on Merton and Bodie (1992), CEIOPS (2008) and Kortleve *et al.* (2011), we identify the following security mechanisms for defined benefit pension plans:

- solvency requirements
- a pension guarantee fund
- sponsor support

Solvency requirements are the additional assets that a pension fund should at least own in excess of the present value of liabilities as a means of a 'buffer'. The European Pension Directive, e.g., states that if the pension fund rather than the sponsor bears the risk, or, if the pension fund guarantees a specific level of benefits, then it should hold additional assets above the value of the liabilities.

A pension guarantee fund insures pension benefits, typically, in case the pension fund's sponsor defaults. In return for this protection the pension guarantee fund receives a fee. Many industrialized countries have such a pension guarantee scheme (e.g., United States, UK, Germany and Japan). For a description of pension guarantee funds see, e.g., Bodie and Merton (1993), Chen (2011) and Broeders and Chen (2013). Sponsor support is defined as the commitment and ability of the sponsor to support its pension fund. That is to continue to pay sufficient contributions to ensure that benefits are paid. CEIOPS (2008) states that sponsor support can also take the form of a claim on the sponsor.

The key goal of this chapter is to investigate the welfare implications to the beneficiary for these three different pension security mechanisms. For that we compare certainty equivalents assuming a power utility function. Specifically, we are interested under which conditions the pension security schemes offer equivalent utility. This research is useful for comparing different regulatory regimes. The European Commission (EC, 2011), e.g., has issued a Call for Advice to explore the possibilities for harmonization across different regulatory regimes. One of the assumptions underlying this Call for Advice is that "Irrespective of the security mechanisms used, the level of protection of the scheme members and beneficiaries should be similar" (page 6). Following this call for advice, EIOPA has developed the concept of a 'holistic balance sheet approach' as the way to achieve as much harmonization as possible (EIOPA, 2012). This is also being referred to as the common framework's balance sheet (EIOPA, 2016)

The holistic balance sheet approach can be used to capture different pension security mechanisms into a single balance sheet by putting a market consistent value to all available security mechanisms. In the holistic approach not only the available pension fund's assets can be used to provide adequate funding. Other mechanisms providing security may also be placed on the pension fund's holistic balance sheet. The holistic balance sheet approach than assesses whether the pension fund is compliant with overall requirements. Although theoretically sound, the approach also offers some challenges before it can be made readily available. It is technically difficult to implement. This is discussed, e.g., in Broeders, Kortleve et al. (2012), De Haan et al. (2012) and Fransen et al. (2013).

The utility-equivalence approach presented in this chapter could serve to strengthen to the holistic balance sheet or the common framework's balance sheet approach. It can be used to assess whether different regulatory regimes offer similar utility to beneficiaries of pension plans. The utility-equivalence approach is potentially less complicated from a modeling perspective and is more closely related to standard asset-liability management tools being used by pension funds.

This chapter is organized as follows. Section 11.2 describes the model setup and 11.3 introduces the three pension security mechanisms in more detail. In Section 11.4 we define the assumptions for a fair contract analysis which we need for the utility-based comparison. In Section 11.5 we numerically derive so called fair participation rates. Section 11.6 focuses on the utility comparison between the three different mechanisms. Section 11.7 concludes the chapter.

11.2. Model setup

This chapter analyzes the welfare implications for pension beneficiaries under three different pension security mechanisms. In this section, we outline the model setup and introduce the following security mechanisms: solvency requirements, a guarantee fund (PGF) and sponsor support. The chapter extends the analysis of Broeders and Chen (2013). In order to ease a utility-based comparison, we make some adjustments to the model assumptions.

Solvency requirements are typically implemented for pension funds that have no external guarantor. The additional assets ensure that the pension fund will be able to meet its liabilities with a high degree of certainty. The amount of additional assets is often defined such that the probability of a funding ratio dropping below threshold $K\%$ is less than $\varepsilon\%$ over a certain time frame T.[3] Providing full insurance through a pension guarantee fund (PGF) implies that the aggregate pension assets will always be worth at least as much as the guaranteed liabilities.[4] A sponsor can also act as an external guarantor. However, unlike the PGF-case, there is a chance that the beneficiaries may not obtain the full guarantee due to insolvency of the sponsor. A sponsor guarantee is usually considered less creditworthy compared to a PGF. External guarantees may provide better downward protection to the beneficiaries. However, this certainty comes at a cost, as a fee must be paid for acquiring external insurance.

11.2.1. Contract specification

We consider a hybrid pension plan in the form of a conditionally indexed defined benefit pension, for a homogeneous group of employees that has to work for another T years.[5] Such a benefit combines a minimum pension income with an extra return if the pension fund's assets perform well.[6] It is a hybrid form between a defined benefit and defined contribution plan, see Broeders *et al.* (2013). The homogeneous group can also be regarded as a representative beneficiary. The assumption of considering a representative beneficiary is justified by the observation in practice that pension funds often take the average beneficiary as a benchmark in contribution and asset allocation decisions.

Let us assume that at time $t_0 = 0$ the hybrid pension scheme is issued to a representative beneficiary who provides an upfront contribution equal to L. The pension fund also receives an initial contribution S_0 from the sponsor at time $t_0 = 0$. In return, the sponsor receives a claim on the pension fund's surplus as a compensation for underwriting the pension fund's downside risk. Consequently, the initial asset value X_0 of the pension fund is given by the sum of the contributions from both the beneficiary and the sponsor

$$X_0 = L + S_0. \tag{1}$$

From now on, we shall denote $L = \alpha X_0$ with $\alpha \in [0, 1]$. We will call α the wealth distribution parameter. It specifies which part of the initial pension fund's wealth is paid for by the beneficiary. We now describe two possible situations. The payment to the beneficiary at maturity and the payment in case of early termination of the pension contract.

11.2.1.1. Payment at maturity

We assume that the pension benefits are paid as a lump sum at maturity. The defined benefit can be represented as the initial contributions of the beneficiary accumulated with a (nominal) guaranteed rate of return δ

$$L_T = Le^{\,\delta T}. \tag{2}$$

The beneficiary in our hybrid plan is exposed to risk in the following way. If the assets perform well, the beneficiary is entitled to sharing in the pension fund's surplus. This "bonus" is described by Ballotta *et al.* (2006) and Kling *et al.* (2007a, 2007b). However, in case of a funding shortfall at maturity the benefit is reduced accordingly. Without external support, the pension fund cannot pay out more than its available assets. Combing all three elements, at maturity, the payment to the beneficiary is given by

$$\psi_L(X_T) := L_T + \beta\alpha\left[X_T - \frac{L_T}{\alpha}\right]^+ - [L_T - X_T]^+ \tag{3}$$

where β is the rate with which the beneficiary participates in the pension fund's surplus. In Section 11.4 we will specify how the participation rate is chosen. The payoff given in (3) is the payoff if there is no premature liquidation of the pension fund. It is a combination of a fixed payment L_T, a call option on the pension fund's assets to reflect the bonus payment and a short put option on the assets to reflect the potential reduction in the benefit.

11.2.1.2. Payment at early contract termination

We allow for the possibility that the pension fund is liquidated before maturity. For instance because the pension fund is severely underfunded. The trigger for the premature liquidation of the pension fund may also be a default of the sponsor. Upon premature liquidation time τ a rebate payment is paid to the beneficiary and is denoted by $\Theta_L(\tau)$. For time consistency reasons we assume that this rebate payment accrues at the risk-free rate r over the remaining time to maturity. This way it is as if the rebate payment is also due at maturity. To sum up, the beneficiary's contract payoff consists of two parts: the terminal payment and a rebate payment in case of early termination

$$\tilde{V}_L := \psi_L(X_T)1_{\{\tau > T\}} + \Theta_L(\tau)e^{r(T-\tau)}1_{\{\tau \leq T\}}. \tag{4}$$

This ends the definition of the liabilities in the pension contract.

11.2.2. *Asset processes*

We now turn to the definition of assets. We need to distinguish between the pension fund's assets and the sponsor's assets. We assume that the pension fund has two investment opportunities: a diversified risky asset (the market portfolio) and a risk-free asset. The traded risky asset A satisfies

$$dA_t = \mu A_t dt + \sigma A_t dW_t^1,$$

where W^1 is a standard Brownian motion under the physical probability measure P. The risky asset follows Black-Scholes dynamics with an instantaneous rate of return $\mu > 0$ and a constant volatility $\sigma > 0$. Also assume the existence of a risk-free asset B which satisfies

$$dB_t = rB_t dt$$

for a deterministic risk-free rate r. The pension fund can only trade in these two assets in a self-financing way starting with initial wealth x_0, which is assumed to be larger than the initial contribution level L. The pension fund's wealth process is given by the following stochastic differential equation (SDE)

$$dX_t = X_t(r + \theta(\mu - r))dt + \theta\sigma X_t dW_t^1, X_0 = x_0. \tag{5}$$

Here θ denotes the fraction of wealth invested in the risky asset A, while the remainder fraction $(1 - \theta)$ is invested in the risk-free asset B. We assume continuous rebalancing. Pension funds typically follow a rebalancing strategy in which the actual asset allocation fluctuates closely around a given strategic asset allocation, see Bikker, Broeders and de Dreu (2010).

We assume the sponsor's assets C_t also follow Black-Scholes dynamics according to

$$dC_t = \mu_c C_t dt + \sigma_c C_t(\rho dW_t^1 + \sqrt{1 - \rho^2}\,dW_t^2), \tag{6}$$

with instantaneous rate of return $\mu_c > 0$ and volatility $\sigma_c > 0$. W_t^2 is a Brownian motion independent of W_t^1 under the probability measure P. The sponsor's asset return correlates with the risky asset's return with a correlation coefficient ρ.

This ends the definition of the assets.

11.2.3. *Triggers for early contract termination*

We now consider two triggers for early contract termination: either underfunding of the pension fund or a default of the pension fund's sponsor. In order to proceed our analysis we need to define the, so-called, first-hitting time in both cases. When the default event is triggered by the underfunding of the pension fund, the default time is the first time the pension fund's assets X_t breach the following regulatory threshold $\eta L e^{\delta t}$. We use

$$\tau_p := \inf\{t | X_t \leq \eta L e^{\delta t}\}. \tag{7}$$

to denote the first hitting-time, where $\eta < 1$ is a regulatory parameter. By choosing the height of this parameter the regulator can control the strictness of regulation. Furthermore, it is assumed that initially the pension fund is compliant with regulation ($X_0 > \eta L$), as otherwise the pension fund already terminates at inception.

On the other hand, when early contract termination is triggered by the default of the sponsor we use

$$\tau_c := \inf\{t | C_t \leq \phi C_0 e^{gt}\} \tag{8}$$

to denote this first-hitting time. The threshold level for the sponsor to default is its debt level ϕC_0, $\phi \in (0, 1)$. Note that ϕ needs to be smaller than 1, as otherwise the sponsor defaults at inception. ϕC_0 can be considered the initial debt level and for simplicity reasons, we assume ϕ is a constant. However, we also allow for the possibility that the debt level increases over time with a constant growth rate g.

This ends the definition of the triggers for early contract termination.

11.3. Description of security mechanisms

We consider three different security mechanisms: solvency requirements, a pension guarantee fund and sponsor support. We give a brief description of the technicalities of these security mechanisms below.

11.3.1. Solvency requirements

Under solvency requirements, the early default trigger is a severe level of underfunding of the pension fund. The intervention time at which the pension fund is liquidated is τ_p. We assume continuous monitoring and prompt corrective action by the regulator.[7] At the default time, the pension fund pays what remains in the pension fund to the beneficiary. The rebate payment to the beneficiary at default time τ_p by definition equals η times the guaranteed amount

$$\Theta_L(\tau_p) = X_{\tau_p} = \eta L e^{\delta \tau_p}. \tag{9}$$

11.3.2. Pension guarantee fund

We assume that in this case the pension fund closes a contract with a pension guarantee fund (PGF). The PGF receives an upfront premium from the pension fund and will take over its assets and liabilities should the sponsor default.[8] If the pension fund has a deficit at that point in time, the pension guarantee fund will be liable for this. In line with practice in most countries, we assume the intervention trigger is the sponsor's default. If the sponsor defaults at τ_c, the PGF intervenes and makes any necessary payments to the pension fund.

To correctly model the insurance provided by the pension guarantee fund we need to distinguish between two cases: no premature default of the sponsor ($\tau_c > T$) and a premature default of the sponsor ($\tau_c \leq T$). In the former case, the

PGF needs to cover the deficit of the pension fund, if any. Hence, the payoff of the pension insurance at maturity is simply

$$G_T = \max(Le^{\delta T} - X_T, 0).$$

This is the amount the PGF would have to pay to cover the deficit in the pension fund, if there is a deficit at maturity. In the latter case, the PGF intervenes immediately at the sponsor default's time (τ_c). It takes over the pension fund's assets and liabilities and the operation of the pension fund is terminated. We assume that the PGF needs to cover the deficit immediately at τ_c. The premature payoff of the pension insurance is

$$G_{\tau_c} = \max(Le^{\delta \tau_c} - X_{\tau_c}, 0).$$

This is the amount the PGF would have to pay to cover the pension fund's deficit, if there is a deficit any time before maturity. A deficit occurs if the pension fund's assets are insufficient to pay the target guarantee $Le^{\delta \tau_c}$. Given this payout structure we can determine the cost G of the pension insurance paid by the pension fund to the PGF. It is given by

$$\begin{aligned} G &= G_T 1_{\{\tau_c > T\}} + G_{\tau_c} 1_{\{\tau_c \leq T\}} \\ &= \max(Le^{\delta T} - X_T, 0) 1_{\{\tau_c > T\}} + \max(Le^{\delta \tau_c} - X_{\tau_c}, 0) 1_{\{\tau_c \leq T\}}. \end{aligned}$$

The cost of insurance can be decomposed into two parts: a rainbow down-and-out put option and a rainbow down-and-in put option. Rainbow barrier options are a well-known form of barrier options where the option is written on one underlying asset while the knock-in or knock-out condition is triggered by a second asset.[9] In the case of a pension guarantee fund, the underlying asset is formed by the pension fund's assets while the knock-out is triggered by the plan sponsor's assets. Upon default of the sponsor, the pension fund is taken over by the PGF. We have a rainbow down-and-out put option if there is no premature termination of the pension fund, and a rainbow down-and-in put option if there is premature termination at τ_c. The premium for the PGF insurance can be considered as the market value of these rainbow options

$$\begin{aligned} G_0 &= E^*[e^{-rT} G_T 1_{\{\tau_c > T\}}] + E^*[e^{-r\tau_c} G_{\tau_c} 1_{\{\tau_c \leq T\}}] \\ &= E^*[e^{-rT}[Le^{\delta T} - X_T]^+ 1_{\{\tau_c > T\}}] + E^*[e^{-r\tau_c}[Le^{\delta \tau_c} - X_{\tau_c}]^+ 1_{\{\tau_c \leq T\}}], \end{aligned} \tag{10}$$

where E^* denotes the expected value under the risk-neutral measure P^*. We are able to obtain a closed-form solution for this premium. We refer the reader to Broeders and Chen (2013) for a detailed derivation.

11.3.3. Sponsor support

We now turn to the case where the sponsor offers protection against the premature default of the pension fund. As in the case of solvency requirements, the trigger is underfunding of the pension fund. Again, the intervention time, τ_p, is the first time the pension fund's assets breach the regulatory threshold. We assume continuous monitoring by the regulator. If the pension fund defaults at τ_p, it holds assets worth $X_{\tau_p} = \eta L_{\tau_p} \le L_{\tau_p}$. Or alternatively, the deficit at that point in time equals $Le^{\delta\tau_p} - X_{\tau_p}$. We make the following two assumption on the actions of the sponsor to cover the deficit

- covering the pension fund's deficit does not lead to a default of the sponsor,
- if the sponsor is not insolvent but unable to cover the entire pension fund's deficit, it pays what it has left after paying back its own corporate debt in full.[10]

We again consider two different default times. A premature default of the pension fund ($\tau_p \le T$) and a default at maturity ($\tau_p > T$). According to these descriptions, the financial support that the sponsor needs to provide at time $\tau_p \le T$ is described by

$$
\Phi_c(\tau_p) = (Le^{\delta\tau_p} - X_{\tau_p})1_{\{C_{\tau_p} > \phi C_0 e^{g\tau_p} + (Le^{\delta\tau_p} - X_{\tau_p})\}}
$$
$$
+ (C_{\tau_p} - \phi C_0 e^{g\tau_p})1_{\{\phi C_0 e^{g\tau_p} < C_{\tau_p} \le \phi C_0 e^{g\tau_p} + (Le^{\delta\tau_p} - X_{\tau_p})\}}. \tag{11}
$$

The first term on the right-hand side corresponds to the situation in which the sponsor is able to cover its own outstanding debt and all the pension fund's deficit. The second term represents its inability to do so: after repaying its own creditors, the sponsor can only pay the remainder to the pension fund.

If default occurs at maturity, it means that the pension fund's assets X_t have not hit the regulatory threshold ηL_t and outperformed it during the entire period [0, T], and particularly it holds $X_T > \eta Le^{\delta T} = \eta L_T$. If, furthermore, $X_T \ge L_T$, the pension fund's assets are sufficient to provide the promised pension payment. Hence, the sponsor does not have to provide the guaranteed amount in this case. On the other hand, if $\eta L_T < X_T \le L_T$, i.e. the pension assets at T exceed the regulatory threshold, but are still lower than the promised pension payments, the sponsor must cover the following deficit

$$
\Phi_c(T) = (L_T - X_T)1_{\{C_T > \phi C_0 e^{gT} + (L_T - X_T)\}}1_{\{\eta L_T < X_T \le L_T\}}
$$
$$
+ (C_T - \phi C_0 e^{gT})1_{\{\phi C_0 e^{gT} < C_T \le \phi C_0 e^{gT} + (L_T - X_T)\}}1_{\{\eta L_T < X_T \le L_T\}}. \tag{12}
$$

Unlike in the case of a premature default, we do not know the terminal value of the pension fund's assets (X_T). Again, here the sponsor provides either a full or a partial guarantee, depending on its ability to redeem its own debt.

Similar to the case of a pension guarantee fund, we assume that the sponsor gets a fair reward for underwriting the pension fund's shortfall risk. However, in this case the reward is paid implicitly. The fair "pseudo-premium" S_{C_0} the sponsor would have obtained for providing support is the market value of the sum of the support in case of early termination in (11) and support at maturity in (12). More specifically, we can express this premium as

$$S_{c_o} = E * \left[e^{-r\tau_p} \Phi_c(\tau_p) 1_{\{\tau_p \leq T\}} \right] + E * \left[e^{-rT} \Phi_c(T) 1_{\{\tau_p > T\}} \right],$$ (13)

under the risk-neutral probability measure P^*. The value is calculated explicitly in Broeders and Chen (2013).

11.4. Fair contract analysis

After the model specification and the description of the security mechanisms, we now need to prepare for the utility analysis. In order to ease a utility-based comparison between the three different security mechanisms, we will make two assumptions about the initial investment and about the fairness of the pension contract. Assumption one is that the initial investment of the beneficiary is the same in all cases. Assumption two is that we adjust the participation rate (β) to comply with the fair contract principle. We will first elaborate on these assumptions below. Thereafter we show how to calculate the fair participation rate in the three situations we distinguish.

According to our model description, the *real* initial investment of the beneficiary is not automatically identical under the different security mechanisms. The reason is that the beneficiary needs to pay an insurance premium to either the pension guarantee fund (G_0) or to the sponsor (Sc_0). The *real* initial investment of the beneficiary under solvency requirements, PGF support and sponsor support is respectively: L, $L + G_0$ and $L + Sc_0$. For a fair utility-bases comparison we need to correct for this. We scale the underlying factors such that the total investment is the same in all three cases. Therefore we introduce assumption 4.1.

Assumption 4.1. *The real initial investment of the beneficiary is the same under all the three security mechanisms and this amount is denoted by L.*

Assumption 4.1 implies the following: (i) Under solvency requirements, amount L can be used in full for investing, supplement with the initial contribution of the sponsor, i.e., $X_0 = L + S_0$. (ii) In case of PGF-support, amount G_0 is used to pay the insurance premium for the PGF support and $L - G_0$ can be used for investing. Supplemented with the initial contribution of the sponsor, the initial asset value of the pension fund is $L - G_0 + S_0$. In what follows below, we will provide an elaborate analysis about how to determine this adjusted initial asset value. (iii) In case of sponsor-support the initial asset value of the pension fund equals the beneficiaries' contribution minus the pseudo premium plus the sponsor's contribution $L - Sc_0 + S_0$.

There is another issue to address before we can do utility comparisons. Under the PGF and sponsor support, more parameters are involved compared to the solvency requirements. Specifically the dynamics of the sponsor plays a role. To correct for this and to be able to compare the security mechanisms, we will fix all the parameters except the participation rate β. We make the following assumption.

Assumption 4.2. *Under all pension security mechanisms, the participation rate is endogenously determined according to the fair contract principle.*

Assumption 4.2 states that the participation rate is determined so that the market value of the amount received by the beneficiary coincides with his upfront contribution. We will call this the fair participation rate β^*. The fair contract principle implies that the market value of the amount received by the beneficiary corresponds to the expected discounted payoff under the risk neutral measure P^*, see Grosen and Jørgensen (2002).

11.4.1. Fair participation rates

In this section, we will show how to determine the fair participation rate β for the three pension security mechanisms, following Assumptions 4.1 and 4.2.

Under solvency requirements, we do not need to adjust the initial investment L. Assumption 4.2 requires

$$E^*\left[e^{-rT}\left(Le^{\delta T} + \beta^*\alpha\left[X_T - \frac{Le^{\delta T}}{\alpha}\right]^+ - [Le^{\delta T} - X_T]^+\right)1_{\{\tau_p > T\}}\right]$$
$$+ E^* e^{-r\tau_p}\eta Le^{\delta\tau_p}1_{\{\tau_p \leq T\}}] = L \tag{14}$$

The left-hand side of the equation gives the market value of the benefits paid to the beneficiary. Equating this to the initial investment L of the beneficiary allows to determine the fair participation rate β^* implicitly.

Under the guarantee provided by the PGF, Assumption 4.1 induces an adjustment of the initial value L. This also leads to a change in the initial asset value X_0 of the pension fund. We use $\widetilde{X}_0$ to denote the adjusted initial asset value

$$\tilde{X}_0 = \underbrace{L - G(\tilde{X}_0)}_{\text{adjusted initial beneficiaries' contribution}} + S_0. \tag{15}$$

Solving (15) is not straightforward. The adjusted initial asset value $\tilde{X}_0$ is not explicitly given but defined implicitly by satisfying (15), because the insurance premium G_0 paid to the PGF in itself depends on $\tilde{x}_0$. The change in L and in x_0 requires a different value for the wealth distribution factor α because α is defined as L/X_0. We use $\tilde{\alpha}$ to denote the adjusted wealth distribution factor which is defined as

$$\tilde{\alpha} = \frac{L - G(\tilde{X}_0)}{X_0 - G(\tilde{X}_0)} = \frac{L - G(\tilde{X}_0)}{\tilde{X}_0}.$$

Since the insurance premium $G(\tilde{X}_0)$ is positive, the new fraction $\tilde{\alpha}$ is smaller than the original wealth distribution factor α. Based on the adjusted parameters, we can now write the fair contract principle for the PGF case as follows

$$E^*\left[e^{-rT}\left(Le^{\delta T} + \tilde{\beta}^*\tilde{\alpha}\left[\tilde{X}_T - \frac{Le^{\delta T}}{\tilde{\alpha}}\right]^+\right)1_{\{\tau_C > T\}}\right] + E^*[e^{-r\tau_C}Le^{\delta\tau_C}1_{\{\tau_C \leq T\}}] = L. \tag{16}$$

Hereby we have used $\tilde{X}_T$ to denote the terminal asset value of the pension fund starting with the initial wealth $\tilde{X}_0$. Accordingly, $\tilde{\beta}^*$ is the fair participation rate resulting under the PGF-support mechanism. Note that $\tilde{X}$ is independent of $\tilde{\beta}$ because the premium of the guarantee $G(\tilde{X}_0)$ does not depend on $\tilde{\beta}$. Therefore, using equation (10), we obtain $\tilde{X}$ implicitly and consequently also $\tilde{\alpha}$. Then all these parameters are used to determine the fair participation rate $\tilde{\beta}\,*$.

Under sponsor support, we can make similar adjustments to the parameters. The adjusted initial asset value $\widehat{X}_0$ of the pension fund is now implicitly determined by solving

$$\tilde{X}_0 = \underbrace{\frac{L - Sc_0(\hat{X}_0)}{}}_{\text{adjusted initial beneficiaries' contribution}} + S_0.$$

As a result, the adjusted wealth redistribution factor $\widehat{\alpha}$ is given by

$$\widehat{\alpha} = \frac{L - Sc_0(\widehat{X}_0)}{X_0 - Sc_0(\widehat{X}_0)} = \frac{L - Sc_0(\widehat{X}_0)}{\widehat{X}_0}.$$

Finally, the fair participation rate $\widehat{\beta}^*$ under sponsor support results from satisfying the fair contract principle

$$E*\left[e^{-rT}\left(Le^{\delta T} + \widehat{\beta}*\widehat{\alpha}\left[\widehat{X}_T - \frac{Le^{\delta T}}{\widehat{\alpha}}\right]^+ - \left[Le^{\delta T} - \widehat{X}_T\right]^+ + \Phi_c(T,\widehat{X}_T)\right)1_{\{\tau_p > T\}}\right] \tag{17}$$
$$+ E*\left[e^{-r\tau_p}\left(\eta Le^{\delta T} + \Phi_c\left(\tau_p, \widehat{X}_{\tau_p}\right)\right)1_{\{\tau_p \le T\}}\right] = L$$

where $\widehat{X}_T$ is the terminal asset value of the pension fund starting with the initial wealth $\widehat{X}_0$. Similar to the calculation in the PGF case, $\widehat{X}_0$, $\widehat{\alpha}$ and $\widehat{\beta}$ can be determined sequentially. We use (13) to determine $\widehat{X}$ and $\widehat{\alpha}$. Again a fair-contract principle leads to $\beta*$.

11.5. Numerical derivation of fair participation rates

After making these additional assumptions we are now ready for some numerical analysis. As a first step to the utility analysis in the next section, we start by calculating fair participation rates. We calibrate the parameters as follows. The risk-free rate r is 5%, the guaranteed rate of return in the pension contract δ is 4.6%, the volatility of equity returns σ is 20%, the volatility of the return on the sponsor's assets σ_c is 33.3%, the time to maturity T is 15 years, the initial beneficiaries' contribution L equals 90, the initial sponsor's contribution S_0 equals 10, the regulatory threshold η is 90% and the sponsor's debt ratio ϕ is 50%. Table 11.1 shows the fair participation rate $\beta*$ as a function of the pension fund's equity allocation θ and the correlation coefficient ρ between the return on the pension fund's and the sponsor's assets. We consider equity allocations ranging from 50 to 90% to test the efficiency of the security mechanisms. Assuming a (very) low equity allocation would not be very insightful as the security mechanisms would only be rarely deployed. We have several observations from this specific set of parameters. The results cannot be generalized.

Table 11.1 Fair participation rates. Parameters: $\delta = 4.6\%$, $\sigma = 0.20$, $\sigma_c = 0.333$, $T = 15$, $L = 90$, $S_0 = 10$, $r = 0.05$, $\eta = 0.9$, $\Phi = 0.5$. ρ is the correlation between the pension fund's and the sponsor's assets. β^*, $\widetilde{\beta}^*$ and $\widehat{\beta}^*$ are the fair participation rates under solvency requirements (SR), a pension guarantee fund (PGF) and sponsor support (SS) respectively.

		$\rho = 0.25$		$\rho = 0$		$\rho = -0.25$	
	SR	PGF	SS	PGF	SS	PGF	SS
θ	β^*	$\widetilde{\beta}^*$	$\widehat{\beta}^*$	$\widetilde{\beta}^*$	$\widehat{\beta}^*$	$\widetilde{\beta}^*$	$\widehat{\beta}^*$
0.5	62.9%	58.4%	39.6%	71.0%	37.1%	94.2%	34.7%
0.6	61.2%	56.4%	32.8%	66.3%	31.1%	86.8%	29.1%
0.7	59.9%	55.7%	27.6%	62.9%	26.4%	80.9%	24.9%
0.8	58.9%	56.1%	23.6%	60.5%	22.8%	76.2%	21.6%
0.9	58.1%	57.3%	20.5%	58.6%	20.0%	72.3%	19.1%

First, under solvency requirements, the fair participation rate β^* does not depend on the correlation between the pension fund and the sponsor. This is obvious as the role of the sponsor in the default process is absent in this case.

Second, under solvency requirements, the fair participation rate β^* decreases for higher equity allocations. This results from the following complex underlying processes. The market value of the beneficiary's benefits under solvency requirements consists of two components: the market value of the benefits upon natural termination and the market value of the benefits upon premature termination, see (14). The former component can be split into three parts: a) the down-and-out value of the fixed payment, b) the down-and-out surplus call option and c) the short down-and-out put option. Part a) decreases for higher equity allocations, Part b) increases for higher equity allocations and Part c) does not change monotonically for higher equity allocations due to the non-monotonic effect on the value of the short position in the down-and-out put. The latter component increases in the equity allocation, because a premature default becomes more likely to occur for higher risk exposures. Hence, the total market value might increase or decrease in the equity allocation, depending on which part dominates. For *the given parameters*, the part in charge of the premature termination seems to dominate, i.e., the market value increases in the equity allocation. Therefore, a lower participation rate is required to make the contract fair.

Third, under a PGF, the fair participation rate β^* decreases for higher equity allocations. According to the fair contract principle in (16), the correlation only influences the surplus call option. A higher correlation implies that it is more likely that the pension fund is underfunded when the sponsor defaults. As a consequence, the PGF needs to balance more deficits of the pension fund. Therefore, a higher premium G_0 and consequently a lower initial real investment for the beneficiary results. On the other hand, a higher correlation coefficient implies that it is more likely that the pension fund performs well too, when the sponsor's assets do well. It consequently raises the probability that the surplus option is in-the-money and not yet knocked out at the same time. The first effect would lead to a lower surplus option value while the second effect would cause a higher option value. Altogether, the effect on the surplus option value is ambiguous. For the chosen parameters, the surplus option increases for higher correlations. Therefore, a lower fair participation rate results for a higher correlation coefficient. Only for a positive correlation between pension fund and sponsor ($\rho = 0.25$) and for a very high equity allocation we observe a slight non-monotonic effect of the equity allocation on the fair participation rate in case of PGF-support.

Fourth, under sponsor support, again we observe the same effect. The fair participation rate β^* decreases for higher equity allocations. In case of sponsor support, all components of the market value of the beneficiary's benefits are affected by a change in the correlation coefficient (c.f. (17)). A higher correlation makes a double default scenario, in which both the pension fund and the sponsor default simultaneously, more likely. When the pension fund defaults, it is more probable that the sponsor is also underfunded and is unable to provide support. As a result, the sponsor pseudo premium decreases for higher correlations. Consequently, a higher initial investment $\widehat{X}_0$ results, which by definition lowers the pension fund's default probability. The benefit can be decomposed into two parts. (i) The same payments as under solvency requirements but based on the adjusted values for the wealth distribution parameters $(\widehat{\alpha})$ and the initial investment $(\widehat{X})$. For this part, we adopt the same decomposition we used for the analysis of the effect of the equity allocation under solvency requirements. For default at maturity, the down-and-out value of the fixed payment (part a) is increasing in the correlation. Through the lower default probability and the higher initial investment $(\widehat{X}_0)$ and wealth distribution parameter ($\widehat{\alpha}$, part b) is increasing in the correlation as well. The down-and-out put option behaves not monotonically. For premature defaults, the market value of the remaining part is decreasing in the correlation due to the lower default probability. (ii) The additional payment through the sponsor in case of default. The market value of the second part is just the additional premium transferred to the sponsor, which decreases in the correlation (see above). Overall, the effect of the correlation coefficient is ambiguous. Here, the market value decreases, which is connected with a higher fair participation rate.

11.6. Utility-based comparisons

We now have completed all the necessary steps to compare welfare implications for the beneficiary. To start, we concentrate on calculating certainty equivalents. Furthermore, we are interested in discovering under what contract specifications the security mechanisms are equivalent in the perspective of protecting the beneficiary. We assume that the representative beneficiary is risk averse and has the following power utility function

$$U(x) = \frac{x^{1-\gamma}}{1-\gamma} \text{ with } \gamma \neq 1,$$

Where γ is the coefficient of relative risk aversion and x is the terminal wealth of the beneficiary. A higher value of γ corresponds to a more risk-averse beneficiary $\gamma = 0$ gives the special case that the beneficiary is risk-neutral. For ease of comparison, we will derive the certainty equivalents from

$$E[U(x)] = U(\text{CEQ}).$$

In what follows, simulation paths. all the results are obtained through simulation. We use 10,000 simulation paths.

11.6.1. Certainty equivalents

Table 11.2 compares the certainty equivalents obtained under the three pension security mechanisms for the parameters used in the numerical analysis above. In addition, we assume a return μ of 8% on the risky assets and the expected return on the sponsor's assets μ_c is 10%. We confine our analysis to a correlation coefficient of 0.25 as it reasonable to assume that a company's equity is positively correlated to the market portfolio. The equity allocation again ranges from 50 to 90% and we consider three levels of relative risk aversion. We observe the following.

First, for all the cases, a more risk-averse beneficiary has a lower utility for the same parameter combinations. This follows from the general fact that the certainty equivalent of a risky payoff x is equal to $E[x]$ for a risk-neutral individual and lower than $E[x]$ for a risk-averse individual. The rationale behind this argument is Jensen's inequality. *Second*, solvency requirements always deliver the highest utility for a risk neutral beneficiary. This can be explained as follows. In case of solvency requirements, neither the sponsor nor a PGF balances the pension fund's deficit. The payoff to the beneficiary is in comparison more risky and therefore delivers the highest expected payment. As a risk-neutral agent benefits from a higher mean but is indifferent about the risk, the certainty equivalent is greatest under solvency requirements. *Third*, for a moderate allocation to equities (θ= 0.5), insurance through a PGF or the sponsor causes relatively high insurance

Table 11.2 Certainty equivalents given different security mechanisms: solvency requirements, a pension guarantee fund (PGF) and sponsor support. Parameters: $\mu = 0.08$, $\sigma = 0.20$, $\sigma_c = 0.333$, $\mu_c = 0.1$, $T = 15$, $L = 90$, $S_0 = 10$, $r = 0.05$, $\delta = 0.046$, $\eta = 0.9$, $\phi = 0.5$, $\rho = 0.25$. θ represents the equity allocation and γ the coefficient of relative risk aversion.

	Solvency			PGF			Sponsor		
θ/γ	0	3	5	0	3	5	0	3	5
0.5	215.4	199.8	193.5	203.7	197.6	195.2	203.0	198.3	196.2
0.6	217.0	197.4	190.7	204.3	197.2	194.7	201.8	197.3	195.4
0.7	219.9	195.3	188.3	204.7	196.7	194.1	200.5	196.2	194.4
0.8	223.4	193.9	186.7	206.7	196.7	193.8	199.3	195.3	193.7
0.9	226.5	192.3	185.2	206.7	195.6	192.8	199.7	195.3	193.8

costs. A low/medium risk-averse beneficiary minds the insurance cost and does not benefit much from the insurance for moderate equity allocations as extreme down turn scenarios are less likely to occur. Therefore, the beneficiary does not benefit much from the insurance. As a consequence, solvency requirements provide the highest utility. *Fourth*, for higher equity allocations, insurance provided by the PGF offers the highest utility to the beneficiary. For instance, for θ= 0.7 and γ =3, the insurance through PGF outperforms solvency requirements and sponsor support. Note however that for extremely high equity allocation sponsor support outperforms the other two mechanisms.

11.6.2. Utility-equivalence approach

The analysis in Table 11.2 can only be used for illustrative purposes. It cannot be used to show that one security mechanism is dominant over the others. Obviously, for different parameters the ranking might be very different. However, our model can be used to show under which assumptions the different security mechanisms offer equivalent utility. For that we allow the pension contract specification to be adjusted. Effectively, it is now possible to make the beneficiary indifferent between the three pension security schemes by, e.g., varying the guaranteed interest rate in the pension contract (δ). This change in δ results in a new participation rate β to make the adjusted contract remain fair.

Table 11.3 shows the resulting fair combinations for a risk-neutral beneficiary ($\gamma = 0$).[11] The calibration is similar to Table 11.2. For instance, for an equity allocation of 60%, a guaranteed interest rate of 4.6% and a participation rate of 61.2% under solvency requirements lead to the same utility as a guaranteed rate of 4% and a participation rate of 94.6% under a PGF as well as a 3.2% guaranteed interest rate and a 71.7% participation rate under sponsor support.

For our specific example we observe the following. For solvency requirements to be equivalent with the offer security mechanisms, the pension fund must offer a high guaranteed interest rate while the surplus participation rate can be lower. In case of a pension guarantee fund, the guaranteed interest rate can be moderate

Table 11.3 Fair combinations of participation rate β and guaranteed return δ, which lead to the same CEQ's for a risk neutral beneficiary (γ= 0). Parameters: μ= 0.08, σ= 0.20, c = 0.333, μ_c = 0.1, T = 15, L = 90, S_0 = 10, r = 0.05, η = 0.9, ϕ = 0.5, ρ = 0.25. θ represents the equity allocation, δ the guaranteed return, β *, $\widetilde{\beta}$* and $\widehat{\beta}$* are the fair participation rates under solvency requirements, a pension guarantee fund and sponsor support respectively

	Solvency		PGF		Sponsor	
θ	δ	β*	δ	$\widetilde{\beta}$*	δ	$\widehat{\beta}$*
0.5	4.6%	62.9%	4.0%	98.3%	3.5%	74.0%
0.6	4.6%	61.2%	4.0%	94.6%	3.2%	71.7%
0.7	4.6%	59.9%	4.0%	92.5%	2.7%	70.9%
0.8	4.6%	58.9%	4.0%	91.4%	2.2%	70.4%
0.9	4.6%	58.1%	4.0%	91.3%	1.7%	69.6%

but the surplus participation rate must be relatively high. Finally, in the case of sponsor support, the guaranteed interest rate must be relatively low while the surplus participation rate may be moderate to be equivalent to the other security mechanisms.

Furthermore we observe that the guaranteed interest rate of 4% under a PGF is independent of the investment policy. At the same time, under PGF support, a very high participation rate results. In contrast, the sponsor support requires a lower guaranteed interest rate and a lower participation rate. The guaranteed interest rate and the participation rate are two pension contract parameters which are revealed to the beneficiary directly. Based on our example, a "naive" beneficiary would probably prefer the PGF scheme over sponsor support because the PGF is able to offer a higher interest rate guarantee combined with a high surplus participation rate. However, there is something hidden behind these two promising parameters. Since PGF provides a full insurance guarantee for underfunding, the premium charge could be relatively high. Hence, the pension fund's real initial investment $\widetilde{X}_0$ becomes comparably lower. The high guaranteed rate of return and the high participation rate compensate this effect.

11.7. Conclusion

Adequate funding of occupational pension plans is key to benefit security. The present chapter addresses a utility-based comparison between three methods of securing funding that exist in occupational plans – solvency requirements, a pension guarantee fund and sponsor support. These mechanisms are modeled and compared for a general class of hybrid pension schemes. We analyze the welfare implications for pension beneficiaries under these different security mechanisms using a stylized utility function.

To allow for a fair utility based comparison we make two important assumptions. First, the initial contribution of the beneficiary must be the same under all pension security mechanisms. Second, under all three security mechanisms, the surplus participation rate is endogenously determined according to the fair contract principle. In addition the key determinants of the overall utility level are the coefficient of relative risk aversion, the pension fund's investment policy, the pension contract's guaranteed interest rate and the correlation between the pension fund's and sponsor's assets.

Our model can be used to make the three security mechanisms equivalent by choosing the pension contract specifications. For solvency requirements to be equivalent with the offer security mechanisms, a pension fund must offer a high guaranteed interest rate while the surplus participation rate can be lower. In case of sponsor support the guaranteed interest rate can be relatively low while the surplus participation rate may be moderate to be equivalent to the other security mechanisms. Mostly interestingly, a pension guarantee fund scheme requires a relatively high guaranteed interest rate and at the same time a high surplus participation rate. However, in this case the insurance premium will be high, thereby lowering the pension fund's real initial investment.

The utility-equivalence presented in this chapter could serve to strengthen the holistic balance sheet approach. It can be used to assess whether different regulatory regimes offer similar utility to beneficiaries of pension plans. The utility approach is potentially less complicated from a modeling perspective and is more closely related to standard asset-liability management tools currently being used by pension funds.

Notes

1 We define sponsor as the corporation which helps to finance pension accrual of its employees by paying contributions or making occasional lump-sum payments.
2 Hedging longevity risk is particularly difficult. A recent Joint Forum report estimates that the total global amount of annuity and pension-related longevity risk exposure ranges from USD 15 to 25 trillion. Annually no more than one thousandth is transferred to (re) insurers, or, through longevity swaps, to the broader capital market. See BIS (2013).
3 This effectively equals the well-known Value-at-Risk (VaR) risk measure on a T year horizon and a confidence level of $\varepsilon\%$.
4 In reality, the PGF's insurance payment is often capped. The PBGC insurance program in the US, e.g., pays pension benefits up to the maximum guaranteed benefit set by law to participants who retire at age 65.Currently the maximum monthly guarantee is USD 4,500 for a 65 year old person. See www.pbgc.gov. We assume that the benefits in our analysis do not exceed this limit.
5 This way we disregard any intergenerational transfers between different age cohorts.
6 This additional return is typically labeled as indexation. It is a periodic adjustment of pension benefits to reflect changes in costs and standards of living.
7 Allowing for a certain waiting time before action is taken would exponentially complicate the analysis.
8 In reality, periodic premiums are charged by the pension guarantee fund. Here a single premium is assumed for simplicity and for consistency with the single liability for the representative beneficiary.
9 These options were firstly analyzed in Heynen and Kat (1994), Zhang (1995) and Carr (1996).
10 In our model we assume that pension assets and liabilities are held in a separate legal entity. Therefore it is reasonable to assume that a pension fund's deficit is less senior compared to regular corporate debt. In a recent decision on Nortel Companies and Lehman Brothers Companies, the UK Supreme Court judged that pension liabilities rank equally with a company's unsecured creditors (Trinity Term [2013] UKSC 52).
11 For $\gamma = 3$ or 5 the results are highly comparable and therefore not shown here.

References

Ballotta, L., S. Haberman, N. Wang, 2006, Guarantees in with-profit and unitized with-profit life insurance contracts: fair valuation problem in presence of the default option, *The Journal of Risk and Insurance* 73(1), 97–121.

Bikker, J.A., D.W.G.A. Broeders, J. de Dreu, 2010, Stock market performance and pension fund investment policy: rebalancing, free oat, or market timing? *International Journal of Central Banking* 6(2), 53–79.

BIS, 2013, Longevity risk transfer markets: market structure, growth drivers and impediments, and potential risks, *Basel Committee on Banking Supervision*, Joint Forum, www.bis.org.

Bodie, Z., R.C. Merton, 1993, Pension benefit guarantees in the United States: a functional analysis, in: R. Schmitt (ed.), *The Future of Pensions in the United States*, University of Pennsylvania Press for the Pension Research Council, Philadelphia.

Broeders, D.W.G.A., A. Chen, 2013, Pension benefit security: a comparison of solvency requirements, a pension guarantee fund and sponsor support, *Journal of Risk and Insurance* 80(2), 239–272.

Broeders, D.W.G.A., A. Chen, D.R. Rijsbergen, 2013, Valuation of liabilities in hybrid pension liabilities, *Applied Financial Economics* 23(15), 1215–1229.

Broeders, D.W.G.A., N. Kortleve, A. Pelsser, J.W. Wijckmans, 2012, The design of European supervision of pension funds, *Netspar Design Paper* No. 6, www.netspar.nl.

Carr, P., 1996, Two extensions to barrier option valuation, *Applied Mathematical Finance* 2(3), 173–209.

CEIOPS, 2008, *Survey on Fully Funded, Technical Provisions and Security Mechanisms in the European Occupational Pension Sector*, www.ceiops.org.

Chen, A., 2011, A risk-based model for the valuation of pension insurance, *Insurance: Mathematics and Economics* 49(3), 401–409.

De Haan, J., K. Janssen, E. Ponds, 2012, The holistic balance sheet as the new framework for European pension supervision, *Evaluation From a Dutch perspective*, www.ssrn.com.

EC, 2011, *Call for Advice From the European Insurance and Occupational Pensions Authority (EIOPA) for the Review of Directive 2003/41/EC (IORP II)*, March 30, European Commission.

EIOPA, 2012, *Response to Call for Advice on the Review of Directive 2003/41/EC: Second Consultation*, https://eiopa.europa.eu/.

EIOPA, 2016, *Opinion to EU Institutions on a Common Framework for Risk Assessment and Transparency for IORPs*, https://eiopa.europa.eu/.

Fransen, E., N. Kortleve, H. Schumacher, H. Staring, J.W. Wijckmans, 2013, The holistic balance sheet as a building block in pension fund supervision, *Netspar Design Paper* No. 18.

Grosen, A., P.L. Jorgensen, 2002, Life insurance liabilities at market value: an analysis of insolvency risk, bonus policy, and regulatory intervention rules in a barrier option framework, *The Journal of Risk and Insurance*, 69(1), 63–91.

Heynen, R.C., H.M. Kat, 1994, Crossing barriers, *Risk*, 7(6), 46–49.

Kling, A., A. Richter, J. Ru, 2007a, The impact of surplus distribution on the risk exposure of with profit life insurance policies including interest rate guarantees, *The Journal of Risk and Insurance* 74(3), 571–589.

Kling, A., A. Richter, J. Ru, 2007b, The interaction of guarantees, surplus distribution, and asset allocation in with-profit life insurance policies, *Insurance: Mathematics and Economics* 40(1), 164–178.

Kortleve, N., W. Mulder, A. Pelsser, 2011, European supervision of pension funds: purpose, scope and design, *Netspar Design Paper* No. 4.

Merton, R.C., Z. Bodie, 1992, On the management of nancial guarantees, *Financial Management*, 21(4), 87–109.

Zhang, P.G., 1995, A unified formula for outside barrier options, *Journal of Financial Engineering*, 4(4), 335–349.

Index

For Product Safety Concerns and Information please contact our EU
representative GPSR@taylorandfrancis.com
Taylor & Francis Verlag GmbH, Kaufingerstraße 24, 80331 München, Germany